⤳ I am so excited to immerse
scholar; she has been walkin.
learning, healing, teaching and expanding.w I know this book will
change lives in a myriad of ways. For anyone looking to understand
their lives, their spirit and the greater connections to the universe
and beyond, this is the book you have been waiting for.

— Candice Watanabe ⤳

⤳ Lia has an intellectual and intuitive way of combining spirituality,
science, metaphysics and healing through her experiences in life
and found a way to share them with us.

— Billy Beehler ⤳

⤳ I found Connecting the Dots *to be an excellent resource for every-*
one interested in the hidden arts of healing. Lia skillfully weaves
together ancient wisdom and modern science.

— Donna Coane ⤳

⤳ Lia is a natural storyteller.

— Lucas Van Enger ⤳

⤳   ⤳   ⤳   ⤳   ⤳

Connecting the Dots is a complete transformation manual that can be used
to create a life of greater ease and more support than many of us dreamed
possible. Practicing the techniques in this book will improve your relationships (including with yourself). You will begin to understand how you
are manifesting unconsciously and therefore not creating the life you desire. You will learn how to identify the "sound" of your intuition's voice
and develop a relationship with this vital part of yourself, make heart-cen-
tered decisions (where you will never experience vacillations) and know
for certain if you are in the right place at the right time. You will experi-
e nce less anxiety as well as fewer dis-eases that result from long-term
e. xposure to anxiety. Learning how to open yourself to nature and recog-
ni. ze connections there will sustain you in consistent, powerful ways. Doing so allows you to turn away from empty calorie (non-nutritive) addictions, purchases, and other destructive behaviors that result from being
connection starved.

Connecting the Dots

Ancient Wisdom, Modern Science

Lia Russ

Connecting The Dots

Ancient Wisdom, Modern Science

MASKED PATH PUBLISHING

For additional material related to this book, see
www.connectingthedots.guru

This book contains many references to web sites, which were current as of October 2021, but may change in the future.

This book discusses some practices that people have found useful in improving their health. However, the author is not a medical doctor. Readers who are dealing with medical issues should always consult a qualified medical professional.

Cover illustration by Rob Bockholdt (Wyndagger).

Typeset in Linux Libertine, an excellent open-source font family by Philipp H. Poll, available at https://sourceforge.net/projects/linuxlibertine/.

Book design and typesetting by David J. Perry.

Perfect bound edition   ISBN 978-1-7361957-0-3
Coil bound edition   ISBN 978-1-7361957-2-7
Hardbound edition   ISBN 978-1-7361957-3-4
E-book edition   ISBN 978-1-7361957-1-0

Contents

Part V: PSYCHOSPIRITUAL

Introduction

The Earth Is Flat

Hi. I'm here to tell you the world is flat. Oops — wrong paradigm! Paradigms are accepted ways of looking at and understanding our world. Put another way, paradigms form frameworks of accepted thought that govern a society's view of *anything*, from physics to geography, even the concepts of good and bad. I find paradigms fascinating because they reveal so much about where a culture stands.

People can be comforted by paradigms because they give the illusion that the corners of our world are tacked down, safe, predictable. They can also give us a sense of belonging; if we believe in the same paradigm, we seem connected. Maybe you even feel safe to me, or like you are a good person, just because you believe the same things I do. Conversely, people with beliefs outside our paradigm can seem foreign, even scary.

The problem with belief systems is that we often stop "seeing" things which exist outside those systems, even if they are right in front of our faces. They can also lead to complacency, especially if they encourage people *not to think for themselves*, exactly what our current paradigm teaches. The information in this book is my life's work, and writing it has transformed my life. I used to have trouble trusting many of the things that I sensed or knew until I began researching the connections between the topics in this book that I refer to as "dots."

Discoveries

I did not ask to write this book; I did not deliberately plan it. I was in the editing stages of my first book *Winging It*, a memoire of my journey to the Orient, when I was asked to give a lecture at the American Society of Dowsers in Vermont on a theory I had come up with in my early twenties about vibrational frequency and crystal awareness. Because a lot of science has changed since I first developed my theory, I needed to research recent findings to see if it still held water. I put *Winging It* on hold to do that research and to create my presentation.

There has always been information that made my brain tingle, that gave me energy, that excited me. These tingly pieces of information, when I think about them in a certain way, spread out in space above me, glowing softly like stars in the night sky. When I learn something new that relates to any of these pieces of information, it is almost as if they glow more brightly and reveal the links between them.

The information that I discovered in 2014 formed some of these very brightly glowing dots which connected to form patterns like constellations. When I stepped back, I could see connections between many dots, causing a cascade of visions that culminated in the need to write this book.

I imagine that I, much like astronomers of old, saw inherent connections between groups of dots in the night sky that for them became the Archer, the Big Dipper, and the other zodiac signs. Only mine were not in the sky, but within our human experience.

I have never been someone who has existed inside the box, so naturally the way I connect the dots will be unorthodox. I believe that unorthodox thinking has merit individually, socially and culturally.

But unorthodox thinking can be disturbing for some. I have my theories as to why that is, but the reason remains unimportant in the face of how essential it is for each of us to pass the things I discovered into our consciousness and allow the light of our awareness to bathe them.

Each of us is created unique. This means that each of our "lenses" — the perspective through which we behold — causes us to see things differently. This is not a mistake nor is it a coincidence. What it does mean, whether through God's plan or the process of evolution, is that humanity is designed to benefit from the unique perspective that we each possess.

I believe there is great value in studying how things exist naturally. The laws that govern everything have much to teach us. No matter how powerful and convincing the constructs of human minds are — no matter how much we have deluded ourselves that we are not a part of this natural order — the fact remains that everything is connected, including us.

The Basic Structure of the Universe

If you look at the basic structure of the universe (molecular structure and bonding, the rules of physics, and biology both plant and animal), it becomes apparent that there are deep truths that affect us all cellularly, mentally and emotionally. Once you become aware of these cellular and molecular patterns, it changes your sense of connection to yourself and to the natural world, drawing the circle larger, embracing both. Yet our attention (through our educational systems as well as social media) is not brought to these interconnections.

What's astounding is if you investigate the lore of our ancient relatives, you will find awareness and understandings of these complex, subtle patterns. Our ancestors understood deep truths about our existence that modern-day science, with its very sensitive equipment, has only recently been able to identify.

How ironic that a young science itself (along with closed theological systems) drew the first small circles around humanity and began cutting us off from ourselves, our instrument (our miraculous bodies), our neighbors, and the planet, on whom we are deeply dependent and to whom we are just as deeply connected.

We need to re-learn how to draw the bigger circle. This book is meant to bridge the inner human with the outer human, older cultures and information with new scientific findings, and so connect us back to ourselves and the natural world, of which we are an inseparable part.

The Bottom Line

As I stated before, my unique vision is not what is important in this book. My primary goal is to lay out information in front of you; my guess is some of it will be new to you. Furthermore, I will be dealing with a wide variety of topics that may seem unconnected at first. After laying them out, I will show you the dots I have connected that form these individual constellations. I want you to have this information so that you can truly begin to make your own decisions ... about *everything*.

Structure of This Book

The book is divided into five parts.

- The first part, PHYSICAL, deals with scientific facts about our bodies and our world that many of us have not looked at.
- The second part, PSYCHOSOCIAL, addresses issues of how humans behave due to psychological factors.
- The third part, INTELLECTUAL, looks at our mind's role in the way we experience and even create our lives.
- The fourth part, ENERGETIC, illustrates many ways that our bodies are hardwired to be aware of and utilize energy. It gives

us concrete ways to experience and work with energy, both from the perspective of information gleaned from our ancestors and from modern science, showing us many ways to facilitate healing and prosperity in our lives.

- The fifth part, PSYCHOSPIRITUAL, looks at the natural relationship between psychology and spirituality, and at the power struggles that have arisen when some humans have tried to develop a monopoly around controlling either. It also explores the devastating effects these power plays have had on our cultures. Often unrecognized, these lies created to control others are still a part of our unconscious decision making.

The book does build on itself; if the concepts presented here are new to you, a more complete understanding will be gained from reading the chapters in order. If you have some understanding of these subjects, you can simply read about things that you are not familiar with.

If you look at the diagram below (Figure 1, page xii), you will see one possible view of how ideas and energies come into us from the outside. When we are presented with something in our physical world, it enters our thoughts. Our thoughts affect our feelings, and our feelings bleed into the imaginal realm (see Chapters 19, "Imagination" and 20 "Imaginal Realms" for more information), where they begin to affect our core self. Interestingly the opposite is also true. Our core self, or spirit, affects the imaginal realms, which affects our emotions, which changes our thoughts, which alters our reality.

So this is a cycle, one we can consciously address to change our lives. What affects this process comes to us from the eight outer ovals you see: concepts from our families, cultures, religions, school systems, peers, workplaces, epigenetic inheritance and ancestors or history. There is perhaps what will seem like repetition in the various chapters as I address different aspects of the challenges we face in each of those areas. The challenges can be similar.

Because each of us in in a different place in life, I did not want to assume that everyone would be aware of how the dynamics of trauma and healing have played out historically, or how they are continuing to play out now, in each of these areas. And, believe me, we have all been bombarded by repetition in our wounding (the process by which we have been removed from trusting ourselves, our bodies and what I see as our true relationship with God). So even if you recognize similar concepts being restated in different chapters, there are slight differences, which may be very important for some people to read. Repetition will also be useful for those who are reading chapters that speak to them rather than the entire book in order.

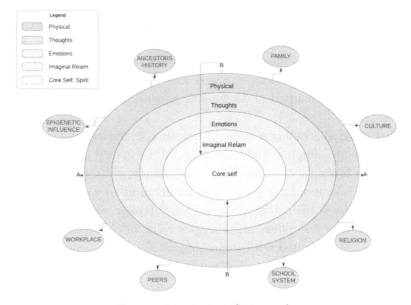

Figure 1. Learning/manifesting cycle.

Additional Information

You can find more material related to this book at the following website: *www.connectingthedots.guru.*

After reading the book, you will probably be able to identify all the items in the cover illustration. If you are unsure about any, see the Key to Cover Illustration on page 420.

Acknowledgments

First and foremost, I would like to thank David Perry who has been a complete godsend to me in the process of bringing this book to light. His years as a Latin teacher in the Rye City School District made him the perfect editor for me because of his knowledge of history, linguistics, and many of the other areas this book delves into. His experience teaching also provided me with an education that I missed in school because of my dyslexia and how much my mom and I moved. We did not always see eye to eye on my subject matter, but he stuck with me and did his best to try to understand what I was attempting to say and then how best to express it. David has become a mentor and helped me in so many ways that I will be humbly, eternally grateful for.

I would like to thank DeeDee Johnson Hughes for her help making sense of and giving shape to the blob of information that this book started out as. The idea for the five sections and organization of the different subjects were hers; she also wrote the back cover blurb.

Dee O'Brien, my English teacher from junior high school, showed me the magical world of writing (despite my being dyslexic).

Additional thanks go to all the people who believed in me as I struggled to write this book over the last eight years: J. Angus Munro, Joel Leitner, Christian Randhahn, Candice Watanabe, Adhi Two Owls, Deborah Meyerriecks, Lailani Flor Celestial, Liam Juanis, Daniel Pratt, Casey Brophy and many others.

I am grateful to all my teachers along the way, those seen and unseen, who have guided and supported me in my fumbling, stumbling way.

I am very grateful to Brian Knight for putting up with the hours, days, weeks and months that have slipped past as I was buried in the work that bringing this work to light has required. You were always willing to make sure I was fed, or got out of the house for a walk or to dance, and often talked with me late into the night about Lakota history or the intricacies of the spirit realm or energy work. Your tireless work in befriending not only me, but my parrots Professor Goose and Meggie, my two dogs Skeeter Bump and Harley, as well as the bobcat mix Turbo and crazy Luna Bean — and let's not forget all my house plants — has touched my heart deeply. I could not ask for a better friend or partner.

My intention is that this book aid in the awakening, growth towards the light and healing of all beings for their highest good. Aho!*

---

*Lakota term used in this instance as an affirmation.

Part I

PHYSICAL

1. Healing a Horse

My path has not been a typical one. It could not have been for me to arrive at many of the conclusions that I have. In the following chapters I will share these discoveries with you, but first I would like to tell you a little about myself and how I came to be able to write such a book.

I have been on a quest for over four decades. My quest was born without my conscious volition one summer in my ninth year. My mom was newly remarried, and perhaps so that she could have alone time with her new husband, I was sent to horseback riding camp for two weeks. This might have upset some children, but since I adored anything horse (even the smell), I was in absolute heaven! I didn't get to be around horses at all in my everyday life, but I dreamed about riding. I had learned to ride almost before I could walk because I had been born way up high in the Rockies. Unfortunately, we left that area when I was four and I hadn't gotten to ride (or see my dad) since.

At camp I got to work with and ride horses, all day, every day. My horse's name was Hombre, a buckskin quarter horse gelding, and I fell immediately in love with him. He played this silly game with me where he would stick his tongue out of his mouth and I would gently grab it, and he would retract it and then do it again. I was responsible for his care while I was there: grooming, feeding, saddling, bridling, bathing, cooling him down after a ride, basically everything.

At the end of my third day in heaven, one very large counselor took out the smallest horse in the stable, named, oddly enough, Gigolo. I say oddly because it was the strangest sounding name for a horse that I had ever heard; I had no idea that "Gigolo" meant anything. I thought it quite a bizarre name for a young solid horse, because it made him sound jiggly, like Jell-O, which he was not. Anyway, on this particular evening, the tall, overweight counselor saddled Gigolo, hopped on and started whipping him viciously. They took off towards the trails at a gallop.

At the time I didn't know that a horse could be too small for a human — they were such large animals, after all, and so strong. But something didn't feel right to me as he did that. To this day I can still see that scene in my mind, the counselor whipping Gigolo with the reins ... and I can still feel the wrongness of it.

The next day Gigolo was lame on three of his legs. A week later, when he still showed no signs of improving, there was talk of his being sent to a dog food canning factory in a neighboring town. He was too expensive to feed if he wasn't rideable.

I was devastated. I was all too familiar with feeling hurt and abandoned. Even back then I felt closer to animals than I did people.

Back home, I was being bullied in school, shunned by my new stepfather's three kids as well as by my stepfather, who wouldn't let me call him "Dad." I was also struggling in vain with the problems I was having in school. I was an undiagnosed dyslexic, and teachers who heard my advanced vocabulary assumed the only reason for my poor spelling and punctuation was laziness and disrespect. There could not have been anything further from the truth! But that's how they labeled, and therefore treated, me. I withdrew from my fellow humans and integrated myself into the natural world as much as possible.

So there I was, seeing a horse who was guiltless and suffering, about to lose his life. I cannot explain to you why I did what I did next. I just know that I burned with the desire to help that horse. That evening, while my bunkmates were seated in the mess hall at dinner, I excused myself to go to the girls' room. Once there, I opened the window and climbed out. (I have never before or since exited a dwelling in this manner!) I took off for the stables, sticking to any cover available. I made it, some minutes later, and in the twilight I found the injured horse. I touched one leg after the other, running my hands down them, tears streaming down my face, asking God to heal him. I pleaded my case aloud, stating how unfair it was that he was to be killed because of something a human had done to him.

I had only gotten to three of his legs (my dyslexia made it impossible to remember which ones were injured so I had decided to do all four) when I was stopped by an authoritative male voice saying "Hey you! ... What are you doing there?"

I dove for the fence, scrambled under it and into the woods. I evaded the stable attendant who had spotted me and headed back towards the mess hall, meeting my group as it was returning to our bungalow for the night. I told no one what I had done. Strangely, no one asked me where I had been. I went to bed that night, not understanding anything but the burning desire I had to help that horse.

The next day after breakfast, as we walked towards the stables, there was murmuring from the girls next to me. Rumor was the injured horse had spontaneously healed overnight! I kind of froze inside ... could it be true?

I wasn't sure what I was feeling. When we got to the stables, I went with some other girls to look at Gigolo, and there he was striding around the paddock with no limp, no trace of the injury that had left him lame on three legs for over a week.

What had happened? My knees got weak and I felt queasy. Could what I did have actually cured him? I wanted to believe that it had. I needed so badly to be able to connect this inner world where I felt things to the outer world of reality — but I didn't know how. I didn't have any way to connect those dots concretely. Nothing in my young life had given me any context to put this in. I felt alternately proud, elated, incredulous and stupid. Stupid because I wanted to believe so badly, but I had no "proof." And so, like a word that is spelled similarly, "poof," up went the whole experience in a cloud. I shared this with no one for several decades.

I didn't come from a religious family. At least my mom wasn't, stating for decades that she was an atheist, and insisting that my dad had been as well. I was not exposed to the concept of "laying on of hands" at that point. Whatever experiences or beliefs my dad had he took to the grave with him when I was way too young to have begun to question these things. My mom and I moved around so much that I didn't have any close friends. These experiences made me feel alienated from my peers. The result was that I tried very hard not to be me, but to be more like those around me.

However much I wanted to shut out my awareness and be more like the other kids, I just couldn't. Deep inside, what happened that day ignited a need in me to understand what might have transpired.

Ever since then I have been on a quest, but there were no answers that presented a solid enough framework for me to stand comfortably upon. So I began collecting and connecting dots.

2. Trust Your Gut?

What does it mean when someone tells you to "Trust your gut"?

What kind of wisdom could reside there, nestled in the folds of slightly more than 29 feet of digestive tract? How would a type of discernment be available through a part of our body with no eyes to see and no ears to hear? Can there be any science behind a "gut reaction"?

We have something referred to as our enteric nervous system (ENS) embedded in the length of our gut. Did you know that you have more neurons in your ENS than you do in both your spinal column and your peripheral nervous system combined? According to an article in *New Scientist* "It comprises an estimated 500 million neurons."[1] Just think for a moment about how many things your spinal cord enables you to do: walk, run, dance, reach out, grasp and embrace. To put this in perspective, the human spinal column has 100 million neurons. What does your gut do that it would need to have more neurons than your spine?

500 million is a lot of neurons! Let's look at what neurons do. One of their functions is to receive sensory input from the world around us. How exactly do all those neurons buried deep in your gut receive information? How could they then use that information to enable you make a balanced analysis of anything? That is a lot of transmitting, computing, and reacting power for a part of the body with no ability to move us around, nor with any sensory organs (that we have yet identified).

When people say, "Trust your gut," they are saying to trust the information from this source above that of your head. Could all those neurons have something to do with this sixth or seventh sense? To gain insights, let's look at some qualities unique to gut.

Have you ever had the feeling of "butterflies in your stomach?" It's a very common experience. During my travels to the Far East in 1982, I

---

[1] Emma Young, "Gut instincts: The secrets of your second brain." https://www.newscientist.com/article/mg21628951.900-gut-instincts-the-secrets-of-your-second-brain/ (accessed May 25th 2014).

wrote in my journal a description of how I felt on my first excursion into the Japanese wilderness by myself, saying, "I feel fine, except for the all the frogs trying to catch the butterflies in my stomach."

In an article from *Scientific American*, Adam Hadhazy says of Olympians competing for gold in Vancouver, "even the steeliest are likely to experience that familiar feeling of butterflies in the stomach."[2] He goes on:

> Underlying this sensation is an often-overlooked network of neurons lining our guts that is so extensive some scientists have nicknamed it our second brain ... The little brain in our innards, in connection with the big one in our skulls, partly determines our mental states ...

So scientists are starting to call our guts a second brain. That's interesting, but some are seeing it in a more radical way. In his book *The Second Brain: A Groundbreaking New Understanding of Nervous Disorders of The Stomach and Intestine,* Michael Gershon says of the gut:

> It is the biggest endocrine organ in our body. It is the biggest portion of our immune system. It is the main storage site for serotonin. It has its own so called intricate nervous system, which, as you know, has been called the second brain, even though really it is the first brain.[3]

The gut might be our first brain? ... Wow; in one decade we have gone from believing that the gut is just a dumb organ, to recognizing it as a second brain, to considering it as possibly the first brain! If nothing else this should convince us that we cannot presume anything based on our previous understandings. We must re-evaluate *everything*, a theme that will appear frequently throughout this book; a radical shift in our paradigm is necessary.

Other studies have found that the ENS can trigger large emotional shifts: "For decades researchers and doctors thought that anxiety and depression contributed to [IBS, constipation, bloating, pain and stomach upset]. But our studies and others show that it may also be the other way around."[4]

---

[2] Adam Hadhazy "Think Twice: How the Gut's 'Second Brain' Influences Mood and Well-Being." https://www.scientificamerican.com/article/gut-second-brain/ (accessed 5/29/14).

[3] Michael Gershon, *The Second Brain: A Groundbreaking New Understanding of Nervous Disorders of the Stomach and Intestine.* New York, NY: Harper Perennial, 1999.

[4] "The Brain-Gut Connection." https://www.hopkinsmedicine.org/health/wellness-and-prevention/the-brain-gut-connection (accessed 5/30/14).

What got me thinking about all this was a book I read about fifteen years ago called *The Tao of Equus* by Linda Kohanov.[5] There she proposes a theory for how horses, as well as other herbivore prey animals, can sense the "mood" of predators, including us. Working with horses, Linda was struck over and over again how they were able to sense when humans were acting differently than they were feeling. Horses are not comfortable when a human is acting inconsistently in this way. She also discovered that some horses could help people recognize this and work with being present to transform past traumas and more. She now works with horses as therapeutic gauges for human states of consciousness. It was through her book that I first learned about ganglia, clusters of neurons in our gut that resemble little brains.

Ganglia have support cells that are like the astroglia of the brain, star-shaped cells involved in the structuring of the brain. What are similar cells doing in our gut? Another similarity to the brain is that these ganglia have a diffusion barrier around them that is similar to the blood-brain barrier of cerebral blood vessels.[6]

Obviously, there is a lot more going on in our gut than most of us were aware of, so let's keep exploring. The ENS operates both with and independently of the brain and spinal cord. Studies show that, if cut off from the brain (by severing the vagus nerve), the ENS can still perform things like coordinating reflexes and that it still affects the central nervous system (CNS). "The ganglia in the ENS are able to communicate to the CNS directly."[7] More studies have revealed that the gut can affect our sense of wellbeing directly: "The gut can actually slow the rate of our hearts." [8]

So our guts have a lot more influence in our bodies than was originally understood. What I am interested in exploring is how our guts take in information, other than by ingesting something. We have all heard of reading tea leaves to predict the future, but I don't think my gut gets information about the relative correctness of a situation I am about to walk into from minute particles of tea leaves present in my morning Earl Grey!

---

[5] Linda Kohanov, *The Tao of Equus: A Woman's Journey of Healing and Transformation through the Way of the Horse*; New World Library, 2007.

[6] Dee Unglaub Silverthorn, *Human Physiology: An Integrated Approach*, Pearson, 7th edition 2016.

[7] Pathway Medicine. "Autonomic GI Neural Control." Pathwaymedicine.org. http://www.pathwaymedicine.org/Autonomic-GI-Neural-Control (accessed 7/05/15).

[8] UC Davis Health. "Heart Rate." health.ucdavis.edu. https://health.ucdavis.edu/sports-medicine/resources/heart_rate_description.html (accessed 7/05/15).

We talked about the feeling of butterflies as it relates to a "gut reaction," but what about if someone stands right in front of you and yells loudly? Where in your body do you feel it? Most people feel it along their gut somewhere (from the throat tightening to a sensation in the bowels). If it comes from someone important (a parent, a boss, a partner), it's often felt in the solar plexus. Why might that be? According to the Google Dictionary the solar plexus is "a complex of ganglia and radiating nerves of the sympathetic system at the pit of the stomach."[9]

The pit of the stomach (solar plexus) is often a place where we can become aware of a sense of impending doom, described by some as *a sinking feeling in the pit of their stomach.* Not only is this plexus at the bottom of the stomach, but it is close to the largest mass of gut material we have in our bodies. According to the Merriam-Webster Dictionary the solar plexus is "a nerve plexus in the abdomen that is situated behind the stomach ... and contains several ganglia distributing nerve fibers to the viscera."[10] Viscera, by the way, are guts, so although the solar plexus ganglia are not in the actual gut, they distribute nerve fibers into it, linking themselves to it, kind of like a computer to an array.

When we look at a diagram of this area, we can see that there is a cluster of three ganglia there. The only other place in our bodies (that I know of) where we have such a cluster of ganglia is the basil ganglia in the brain. Why would a cluster occur here, in the gut?

I like to look at ancient people's beliefs to help me find new meaning in scientific findings. The chakra system, well known to the Hindus, places the "seat of our will" here. So I wonder if those three ganglia come into play when we are exerting our will. I will explore this further with you in the chakra section of the book.

Getting back to our anatomy, here is an interesting question: why is the largest nerve plexus we have in our bodies, coupled with the majority of our gut, sitting just under the skin, completely unprotected by bone? That just doesn't make any sense at all ... or does it?

All of this sits behind a taught skin stretched over a frame, much like a drum. Interesting random layout, right? Perhaps not. A bone here would dramatically alter vibrational frequencies coming into this area. So this vulnerable part of our body is wide open to any and all vibrational frequencies coming at it. Look at Figure 2 below.

---

[9] Google Dictionary, "Solar Plexus."

[10] "Solar Plexus," *Mirriam-Webster.com* 2019. https://www.merriam-webster.com/dictionary/solar%20plexus, 1. (accessed 2/15/19).

See the open hollow that the makes up the solar plexus? It looks more drum-like than any other part of our body and, although you don't see it here, it's got lots of gut coiled up in this space. You can see how vibration would be able to resonate here and be transmitted directly to the neurons embedded in the gut.

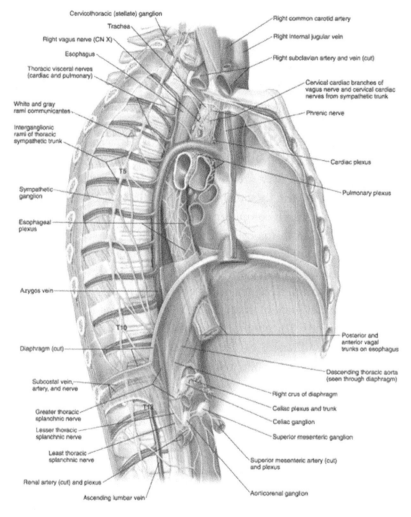

Figure 2. Solar plexus and associated regions of the body. [11]

Speaking of instruments, do you know that gut has been used to create and carry vibrational frequency in stringed instruments for thousands of

[11] Diagram: http://wiki.ahuman.org/index.php/HumanNervesSpinalThoracic. Used by permission.

years? You might have heard of "cat gut" in terms of materials used for strings. Relax cat lovers! No cats were harmed in the making of stringed instruments ... well, perhaps cat ears were abused in hearing humans learn to play these instruments but ... it was actually sheep gut that was primarily used for strings.[12] The use of gut to produce strings for musical instruments can be traced back to the Old Kingdom in Egypt. Gut was also used in snare drums to produce their distinctive sound.[13] Why gut? Well, apparently gut material carries vibration exceedingly well, almost as if it were designed to do so.

What would be the evolutionary reason for gut material to carry vibrations or to resonate with them? And what are all those neurons doing while the gut is transmitting vibrational frequencies through its length?

What if all of those neurons in our gut are needed to translate those vibrations? To make sense of them? To digest them? According to Jay Patsricha, M.D., Director of the Johns Hopkins Center for Neurogastroenterology, "The enteric nervous system doesn't seem capable of thought as we know it [note 'as we know it'] but it communicates back and forth with our big brain with profound results."[14]

It is important to look at current findings in sciences like plant and animal biology, because so much new information shows clearly how the "as we know it's" have been radically changing. People refer to a gut reaction as being a palpable sense or disturbance felt in their guts. People judge all kinds of scenarios based on their gut, without having any clue as to the science behind it, but they know it works.

Michael Gershon's book *The Second Brain*[15] "has made physicians, scientists, and the lay public aware of the significance of the unique ability of the ENS to regulate GI (gastro intestinal) activity in the absence of input from the brain and spinal cord."[16] Gershon says Patsricha is not alone in thinking that the complexity of the second brain could not be explained by digestive processes alone.

---

[12] Wikipedia Foundation. "Catgut." Wikipedia.org. https://en.wikipedia.org/wiki/Catgut (accessed 9/19/16).

[13] Daniel Larson, "Making Gut Strings," https://www.gamutmusic.com/new-page (accessed May 2, 2018).

[14] Jay Patsricha, quoted in "The Brain Gut Connection." *Health,* https://www.hopkins-medicine.org/health/wellness-and-prevention/the-brain-gut-connection.

[15] Michael D. Gershon, M.D. *The Second Brain*, (New York, N.Y.: Harper Collins, 1998), pp. 1-312.1.

[16] Gershon, Michael D. "Gut Instincts: The Secrets of Your Second Brain," https://www.newscientist.com/article/mg21628951-900-gut-instincts-the-secrets-of-your-second-brain.

According to Emeran Mayer, professor of physiology, psychiatry, and behavioral sciences at the David Geffen School of Medicine at the University of California, Los Angeles, "The system is way too complicated to have evolved only to make sure things move out of your colon."[17] So, if the complex evolution of our guts was not necessary simply for digestion and elimination, then why did it evolve the way it has?

But before we go on, remember, it's hard to find something you are not looking for. It's also difficult for most folks to see beyond the box that they were indoctrinated in. Nobel prize winning biologist Albert Szent-Györgyi stated in 1972 that "Discovery consists of seeing what everybody has seen, and thinking what nobody has thought."[18] So if we are to make a new discovery, we must open our minds and connect some new dots here. Kaitlin Luna says:

> This is all in the early stages. But, some intriguing findings have emerged. People with GI disorders have higher than average rates of bipolar disorders and depression. People with schizophrenia often have blood markers that suggest GI inflammation, and people on the autism spectrum have higher rates of GI problems.[19]

Obviously there is a lot more going on in the gut than we believed. Scientists are beginning to ask new questions of the gut's role in our lives beyond digesting food and disseminating nutrients. But there are questions they are still not asking, like "What's a gut reaction?" Let us review what we have discovered thus far: the gut has all these neurons, and the material that encases those neurons is especially well suited to conducting vibrational frequencies. There is one more piece of evidence that should allow us to connect even more: our very sensitive gut instrumentation is able to function without the brain. That the gut can operate independently from the brain means that we might do well to look outside the roles, processes and functioning of thought in the brain for the answers to the question of how there is such a thing as a gut reaction.

---

[17] Emeran Mayer, "Understanding the constant dialogue that goes on between our gut and our brain." https://newsroom.ucla.edu/stories/understanding-the-constant-dialogue-that-goes-on-between-our-gut-and-our-brain (accessed 5/11/20).

[18] Albert Szent-Györgyi Quotes, https://www.brainyquote.com/quotes/albert_szentgyorgyi_390767.

[19] Kaitlin Luna, *Speaking of Psychology: The Mind-Gut Connection*, The American Psychological Association, https://www.apa.org/research/action/speaking-of-psychology/mind-gut-connection (accessed 5/5/20).

If you looked at the vibrational receptivity and transmission ability of the gut itself, coupled with all that neuro-power, and you asked why, the answer would appear to be to interpret vibrational states around us. I believe this to be what a "gut reaction" is.

Isn't that amazing? Whether you believe in God, a higher power, or evolution, the bottom line is that things are not the way they are in the natural world for no reason. Our bodies are very complex, with systems in place that we are just beginning to recognize, even if we have yet to understand them. Our gut has a complex system to read vibrational frequencies around us.

How could being in touch with, and practiced in, this form of discernment help us? Animals can sense when an earthquake or tsunami is building. It makes sense that they accomplish this by discerning the building vibrational frequencies of these events. I can think of no other way that they could know.

Prey animals have spent thousands of years learning to tune into and translate the vibrations of the world around them, through their much larger gut. Ever see an African nature show on TV where there is a pride of lions lying in a field, and not too far away you can see zebras and gazelles grazing? This co-habitation of a small space between predator and prey seems insane on the prey's part, and it can go on for an extended period of time. If the camera catches it, you can watch as nothing outwardly changes, but all of a sudden, the herbivores spring into action. Almost as one, the prey flees the area. Seconds later the pride visibly begins to organize itself for a hunt.

When thoughts change from unfocused and relaxed to focused, the vibrational frequencies change, the parts of the brain being used change, and prey animals can sense this through their guts. Perhaps this is why we know when someone is watching us. You feel someone looking at you, glance up quickly and discover that you are right. That's your gut giving you information.

Many prey animals have more gut and more ganglia than we do. It is no secret that horses, who have much more of both, are quite adept at reading humans.

Can you test this ability within yourself? Yes; begin by paying attention to how you feel as you enter a new situation or encounter people. When you become aware of your body picking something up, or you have a bodily sensation that you can't explain, pay attention. Try to ascertain if this feeling is originating within you, or if it feels like it's originating outside yourself. Be open, converse with your senses, see what you can discern. Initially, using these senses can feel like trying to move an atrophied limb. It takes patience to exercise these fledgling sensory "muscles."

It is by such explorations that I came to understand the difference between a gut reaction, which I now refer to as discernment, and intuition, which is information gleaned through the third eye. The gut receives vibrational frequency and sends these readings to the nervous system and the brain. How much digesting and interpreting of this information is done in the gut before it is transmitted is unclear. This information would be sensory, not visual. The third eye is more of a doorway that a part of our awareness can step through to retrieve information and bring it back to the brain. Information from the third eye is visual in nature (which is why this center is referred to as an eye). There are not any sensing organs here. All of this can be experienced and learned just by observing.

Give it time and remember this is a practice that will be facilitated by repetition. When you begin to feel something that you are not certain originates within you, look around you for correlations. There may be similarities in events that are going on in your environment when you feel certain things. You can use these similarities over time to begin to teach yourself about your very own instrument. For instance, you may discover that you have similar sensations in different situations, where the common denominator is that you would be better off if you walked away. Unfortunately you only learn these things using hindsight. You must be willing to pay attention, self-evaluate, and analyze not just the situations, but the outcomes. No one can figure out your instrument except you. Become a master of your own world by developing awareness of your abilities.

If we were not trained to ignore this type of information that we receive daily, I imagine that we would be more comfortable in our own skin. Years of learning how to discern the meaning of different vibrational "signatures" would alert us to all kinds of information that we would have the ability to interpret and use. We would not be caught off guard by anyone's mood — we would feel it coming several feet, or even blocks, away.

If our bodies, independently of our minds, are picking up the "vibes" of things around us and translating them, understanding them, and communicating these findings to our brains, but our brains have been conditioned to ignore this input, what effect does that have on our bodies? What happens to intelligent creatures who are chronically suppressed? Not respected? Not acknowledged? Not heard? Typically, they withdraw, become depressed, and begin to exhibit all manner of stress responses. Emotional, mental and physical imbalances occur when biological systems are in a state of constant suppression. Imagine the stress this causes our bodies, compounded over decades. Such stress could easily raise levels of anxiety, insomnia, eating disorders, emotional disorders, the need to self-medicate or receive medication from a doctor, and dis-ease (disease).

Our bodies are doing their jobs, making information available to us, but due to cultural training and desensitizing, our conscious minds are not following through; we do not allow ourselves to respond. We are taught from the moment we are born to begin to un-friend our bodies. Where does that leave us?

What would happen if our culture taught us to honor and embrace this bodily knowledge? Many of our ancestors in the not too distant past did. Many native cultures still teach the use of this type of discernment.

What happened? Why would we have developed cultural imperatives to ignore this discernment? Interestingly, being cut off from ourselves in this manner benefits a host of institutions, such as big pharmaceutical companies and organized religions. We will continue exploring this in the following chapters.

3. Our Brains

Have you ever attempted to learn to drive a stick shift vehicle? I remember how difficult it was, especially because of my dyslexia! Brake, clutch, gas … yikes! Which foot? Which pedal? The location of all the different gears! I never thought I could remember all those variables!

Then one day as I was driving along, I was forced to down shift suddenly and I realized the only thing I had been thinking about while I did it was wishing the guy in front of me had learned how to use a signal blinker! I had performed multiple processes without thinking, only reacting to the need to slow down quickly. How did that happen? It felt like magic.

It is possible because when we repeat a process consciously, enough times, something happens. I am not a neuroscientist, so I cannot explain the dynamics to you. But as an observer, I can tell you what I have witnessed.

Have you ever heard the axiom "It takes two weeks to create a habit"? Why would that be? From a layman's perspective I would say that a connection between neurons forms, and this path (for lack of a better word) between neurons facilitates an ease of "discourse" between those synapses. Once this type of path has been created and followed for some time, there exists the possibility that we will no longer need to actively direct the connection between these particular synapses. We then find we can perform tasks without conscious thought, and voilà! A habit has been created. Philippa Lally conducted a study of 96 people and found that it took them "18 to 245 days"[20] to form a habit, with the average being about 66 days.

If you think about this, it is very exciting. It may take some folks two weeks to create a habit, and others longer, but the point is that nothing is out of your reach! So what if you have to commit a year to achieving the kind of life you want (healthy lifestyle, dream job, loving relationship,

---

[20] Philippa Lally, "How Long Does it Take to Form a Habit?" *UCL News*, 4 August 2009, https://www.ucl.ac.uk/news/2009/aug/how-long-does-it-take-form-habit (accessed January 12 2016).

etc.)? It doesn't seem like a bad investment. After all, if you do nothing, you will still be your old self in a year, living the same life you do now. Why not start creating the habits you need to succeed and change your life? Maxwell Maltz, M.D., F.I.C.S. wrote a fascinating book called *Psycho-Cybernetics* where he goes into detail about the life-changing possibilities within our psyche. Among other things, he says "Happiness is a habit."[21]

Dr. Pascale Michelon has a Ph.D. in cognitive psychology and has worked as a research scientist at Washington University in Saint Louis. Her research has revealed some interesting things such as "when you become an expert in a specific domain, the areas in your brain that deal with this type of skill will grow."[22] For example, "those who are bilingual have a larger left inferior parietal cortex than monolinguals." The ability of the brain to reorganize itself, either from new information being learned or after a brain injury, is called plasticity, specifically neuroplasticity. It is this neuroplasticity that allows us to keep learning even as we age.

In an article published in the *Journal of Neuroscience,* Christian Gaser and Gottfried Schlaug report that their studies found "musicians have more grey matter (cortex volume) than non-musicians."[23]

This is exciting information because it proves not only can we change our habits through directed use of our brains, but by doing so we affect the strength and size of the parts involved, and therefore our capabilities in these areas. How empowering for us that we can consciously guide the formation of these connections between neurons and this brain growth. It takes work and practice, but there are very real benefits. It brings a new meaning to the phrase "Practice makes perfect."

It makes sense to me that the formation of these often-used pathways is what allows an electrical thought impulse to travel without conscious guidance, once the neural pathway is established. It is a kind of magic, if you think about it. For example, such well-worn neural pathways can enable us to drive home from work (or anywhere) without paying attention to landmarks. Have you ever been driving on a familiar route and suddenly found yourself looking around, unable to recognize any landmarks for a

---

[21] Maxwell Maltz, *Psycho-Cybernetics,* Pocket Books, New York, London, Toronto, Sydney 1960.

[22] Dr. Pascale Michelon, "Brain Plasticity: How Learning Shapes your Brain." *Sharp Brains*, Feb. 26, 2008.

[23] Christian Gaser, Gottfried Schlaug, "Brain Structures Differ Between Musicains and Non-Musicians" *Journal of Neuroscience* 8 October 2003, 23 (27) 9240-9245; DOI: https://doi.org/10.1523/JNEUROSCI.23-27-09240.2003, https://www.jneurosci.org/content/33/36/14629.

mile or more? As a dyslexic that is very unnerving for me. But if I relax (meaning do not turn around, believing that I missed my turn), eventually I recognize a very familiar landmark further down. This is the type of thing I am talking about. Our brains can perform complex tasks without conscious thought, without conscious awareness, due to established neural connections.

These connections don't go away, even if we stop doing an activity for years or even decades. Take for example bike riding. Remember how hard it was to coordinate balance, while pushing down with force on each opposing pedal? Trying to keep that incredibly sensitive steering device straight, and the whole contraption upright? But even if it's been twenty years since you last rode, you get on a bike and unless you've damaged that part of your brain, the connected neurons are there, waiting for you to use again.

Like many things in our lives, though, these established connections within our brain can be a curse as well as a gift. What do I mean by "curse"? I believe that *anything* that diminishes our ability to be aware of what is happening in the present moment robs us of a lot. First, our ability to respond appropriately is removed. Think about the times your consciousness wanders but you keep doing things. The result? The goldfish end up being fed the cat's food ... or something similar. I remember one morning in high school, getting my eggs ready to cook. I got the bowl out to crack my eggs into. I cracked one egg, then the second, threw the shells away, picked up my fork to scramble them and ... the bowl was empty! There was an ash tray next to the bowl and there were the two yolks and whites siting nestled amongst ashes and butts. Disgusting.

Seriously, being able to function without complete awareness is not really such a great thing. Not only can it get us into trouble, but it also encourages us, or at least enables us, to ignore an awful lot.

If we want to be the masters of our instruments that we have the potential to be, we need to consciously strive to stay aware of the world around us. Awareness equals mastery: it's a simple equation to embrace.

I set myself a goal a couple of years ago to respond to the actual input I was getting in each moment. Perhaps that sounds odd. But as a highly task-oriented Taurus, I can easily plow past "deviations" from what I'm expecting. Plowing past a "deviation" can result in things like pushing a piece of equipment to the point of being irreparable as opposed to responding to abnormal noises and stopping. Exploring what is happening rewards me with being able to get the problem fixed easily.

I chose to focus on this due to several incidents where my tendency to plow ahead had a side effect, which produced some less than desirable outcomes, all because I ignored sensory information.

I have benefited greatly from this conscious pursuit of increasing my respond-ability. For example, I'm getting out of my truck and hear a noise as I close the door. Instead of just ploughing ahead on my prescribed course, I stop and ... Oh look, my phone slid out of my pocket as I was exiting the vehicle and it's now lying on the ground just under my truck. What a gift! Locating it at that moment, as opposed to finding it missing the next time I go to use it, is very helpful!

The well-used connections between neurons aren't the only function of our brain that reduces our need for awareness. As humans evolved and our world became more complex and technical, our ability to survive depended on a different part of our brain than when we were hunter gatherers (which we were for a long time in comparison). Meet the frontal lobe. Did you know that the frontal lobe is a drug user? Our frontal lobe, which allows us (among other things) to sit still and focus for long hours on a single task, uses dopamine-sensitive neurons to do its job. In fact, it has more dopamine sensors than any other part of the cerebral cortex.

The problem here is that dopamine sets limits to, and even selects, what type of sensory information it allows to reach the brain.[24] This means that by virtue of relying heavily upon this part of our brains, a lot of data gets shut out. This type of processing relies less on direct sensory experience and more on a narrow band of awareness, like a small slice of the pie in front of you, rather than the whole. That may work well in an office, but on the open plains, you would be easy prey for a hungry predator. Our ancestors had to be able to put up a tent, collect firewood, and at the same time be hyper-vigilant regarding the sounds in the woods around them.

Creating a world where we depend so heavily on frontal lobe functionality to navigate, as opposed to our, gut, intuition, and discernment, has had the side effect of pushing us more and more in the direction of being "stuck in our heads." You might say that dopamine distances us from the nuances of the present moment. This leaves us disconnected from the world around us and, consequently, closer to the possibility of developing addictions.

This is just the type of thinking our overcrowded school systems require. Long before we leave elementary school, most of us have probably

---

[24] Psychologist World, Biological Psychology, "Dopamine Neurotransmitter." https://www.psychologistworld.com/biological/neurotransmitters/dopamine.

given up thinking for ourselves. We learned that we are not rewarded for asking our own questions. We are rewarded when we follow rules, absorb information presented to us, and regurgitate it back on demand.

And just like with riding a bike, this way of learning, of winning approval, becomes habit. Thanks to the well-traveled neural connections in our brains and our dopamine-hungry frontal lobe, we don't listen to the rich stream of information coming to us from our bodies' awareness.

We no longer listen to what we are told with an open mind, one capable of connecting its own dots. We don't point out flaws in the theories that we hear. We often don't consider the inconsistencies in stories we hear. We take what we are told at face value. We do what we are told.

We are allowing our children to be raised as perfect unthinking cogs. This is exactly what supports a corporate, institutional ruling system.

The good news is that you have the choice to start asking questions, to revive your curiosity and sense of wonder. It might take some work, but you will regain the benefit of having an open mind.

Here's another interesting fact about our brains. The temporal lobe is the part of our brain that gives us our ability to understand all the nuances of spoken words. It also gives us selective listening (versus selective hearing). When we hear stories, our temporal lobe takes it all in and then sends it to other areas of the brain. Scientists have found that when we hear a story about eating, for example, the parts of the brain responsible for jaw movement activate, as do the parts associated with taste and swallowing. You may have experienced someone describing a food or recipe to you and found your mouth watering. That is a perfect example of this process at work. What's even more interesting is that they have found that our brains synchronize somewhat with the brain of the person who's telling the story. Narratologists refer to this as "transportation." [25]

According to Paul J. Zak, when we hear a story that leads us into transportation, our oxytocin levels increase. Oxytocin is the neurochemical responsible for empathy and narrative transportation. Our ancestors' tradition of sharing stories around the fire as a method of entertainment, education, and cultural preservation worked exceedingly well for creating group cohesion, collective consciousness, and instilling communal values.

---

[25] Paul J. Zak, "How Stories Change the Brain." *Greater Good Magazine* December 17, 2013, https://greatergood.berkeley.edu/article/item/how_stories_change_brain (accessed 5/11/19).

Do our TV and movie producers create their programs with an eye to group consciousness? Given this new information, perhaps they should.

It seems like our ancestors were smarter than we! The old ways of teaching were completely opposite to what happens in the typical modern classroom, where we are forced to use our dopamine-infused frontal lobe, which isolates us not only from our internal somatic selves and much of our external awareness, but from each other and the natural world as well. What a lonely reality we are passing down to our children.

The good news is that many people are becoming aware of the dis-functionality of our current world paradigm. Remember that one defini-tion of insanity is "To keep repeating the same thing and expecting differ-ent results." So, if we are aware of dysfunction, and we begin to ask ques-tions and look for our own answers, then we can change, thanks to neuro-plasticity (among other things). Listen: God, or the universe, or evolution, did not create us all different for us to conform! Anything that can help us to remain open, to question, to make decisions, is good. Having a clearer picture of exactly why something is not working brings us as much as 75% closer to change and a possible solution!

It is easier to think of a solution when the problem is laid out clearly in front of you. An interesting study was done in Japan that showed that exposure to cedar phytoncides, chemicals released from cedar trees (often included in the scent of the particular tree), resulted in decreased activity in the prefrontal lobe, as well as lower blood pressure. So, walking in the woods where cedar trees grow can help you not just be healthier, but open yourself to connect and to change.

I had learned years ago (while studying with Lakota elders) that cedar was used primarily to change the energy of something or someone. Imag-ine the dots that got connected for me when I saw this current research! It is a perfect example of the discernments available through your body's "array" that modern science is only just beginning to have instrumentation sensitive enough to corroborate. The question is not whether we have these abilities, but rather why have we been taught to deny them?

4. White Mouse

Did you know that "ancestral experience can influence future genera-tions"?[26] And I'm not talking about just being influenced by what our grandparents ate, hearing their stories or even being influenced by their learned behaviors (although all of those do play a role in our makeup). No, what I'm talking about is being genetically altered by our ancestors experiences! The study of this phenomenon is called epigenetics. Epigenetics generally refers to the effect the environment can have on gene expression – not if a gene is present in someone's DNA, but whether it's turned on or off. Brian Dias of Yerkes National Primate Research Center says: "transgenerational inheritance of trauma are paradigms wherein an ances-tral generation is subjected to perturbations that can then be followed across generations."[27]

There have been many studies done on this subject, from groups of humans whose parents were exposed to massive trauma, to mice, to earth-worms. In one such experiment[28] Dr. Dias took a male mouse, put it in an environment where he could control all scents present, and shocked its foot every time a certain smell was introduced. It didn't take the poor mouse much time to exhibit severe anxiety any time it encountered that smell. Dias then sent sperm from that mouse to a different lab and impreg-nated a female mouse with it. The experiment was repeated many times; the results were always the same. Offspring from the conditioned male mouse all exhibited anxiety when exposed to this smell. So the trauma was inherited, but beyond that the mice were altered physiologically. The

---

[26] B.G. Dias, K.J. Ressler "Influencing behavior and neuroanatomy in the mammalian nervous system via ancestral experiences." *Neuroscience*, November 12, 2013 (accessed May 9, 2014).

[27] Ibid.

[28] Brian Diaz, Kerry J. Ressler, "Parental olfactory experience influences behaviour and neural structure in subsequent generations," *Nature*, 1 December 2013, https://www.nature.com/articles/nn.3594/ (accessed 11-19-20), or https://www.ncbi.nlm.nih.gov/pmc/articles/PMC3923835/.

scent receptors in the offsprings' noses were larger. So not only had they inherited fear of this smell, but they were able to smell it from farther away! The trauma was inherited, not just in the form of emotional stressors, but as genetic enhancements or mutations to the physical body as well. Further studies have revealed that "RNA in sperm can be altered by direct exposure to trauma even in early life, and it can stay altered throughout life."[29] It has also been determined that these same types of changes can be passed through the mother's reproductive cycle just as reliably.

The heritability of trauma opens whole new dimensions in psychology as well as in caring for and understanding each other. I want to explore that further, but for now let me stick to physiology.

The physical/chemical reason for this process is present in human genetics as well. Did you know that in every tiny nucleus in our cells, there is a six-and-a-half-foot DNA strand? These strands contain all the information needed to create each and every cell that makes up you. What allows a heart cell to form, rather than a hand cell, is how the DNA is "marked." Marking occurs through epigenetics. An example of this is methyl markers binding with the DNA sequence. They block our bodies' ability to read certain parts of the strand. The only part of the DNA "recipe" that can be followed is what can be read.

Here's a new thought for most of us in the Western world: our ancestors not only affected our material inheritance; their experiences affected our emotional and physical inheritance as well!

Now that we have established that epigenetic inheritance exists, let's look at how that could that be affecting us. It's easy to infer that these messages from our ancestors written into our DNA are perceivable as subtle (and perhaps sometimes not so subtle) feelings, as preferences, as comfort levels, as likes and dislikes. Instincts could be attributed to them as well. Not taking the time, not having guidance, we make no effort to tune into these DNA "voices," which no doubt causes anxiety within the organism (us).

For the last two centuries (at least), instincts have been portrayed as baser cellular information, compared to intellect, and relegated to "dumb" animals. So any information that comes from the body has been viewed as untrustworthy or inferior. Attributing wisdom to the body is an old

---

[29] Dana G. Smith, "Scientists Are Discovering How Trauma Can Be Inherited," https://elemental.medium.com/scientists-are-discovering-how-trauma-can-be-inherited-f6bde9430675.

concept that is beginning to resurface in our consciousness. But it is not something our paradigm supports comfortably.

Our modern mechanized world asks us to ignore our bodies' wisdom daily, if not hourly. So we are not in the habit of listening to the subtle whisperings, but perhaps it's time we started.

Here is another question: how has inherited fear, shaped by conquerors, affected our ability to be whole? Iva B. Zovkic and J. David Sweatt found that:

> Epigenetic molecular mechanisms underlie the formation and stabilization of context- and cue-triggered fear conditioning based in the hippocampus and amygdala, a conclusion reached in a wide variety of studies using laboratory animals. Given the relevance of cued and contextual fear conditioning to post-traumatic stress, by extension we propose that these mechanisms may contribute to post-traumatic stress disorder (PTSD) in humans.[30]

This is interesting because fear may play an important part in our reaction to oppression. This is especially true in any nature-based culture, where people have been tortured and murdered for connecting with their innate sensitivities, as well as other beings, in a spiritual, mystical way.

Let's say you had a great-great-grandmother who was Celtic, and she saw friends and family burned at the stake for their beliefs, labeled "witchcraft." Then she experienced weeks, months, or even years being terrified that someone would see her practicing her sacred rites. This fear of being "seen" connecting with the spirits of nature around her could well be passed down through her DNA markers as fear of the "spiritual world." Such fear comes not from any intrinsic dangers, but rather from persecution from the Church. In this case, our current paradigm of fearing the spirit world may come from our ancestor's persecution and oppression.

This is true of any and all genocide survivors from any culture or religion. Can you tell how much of the anxiety that bubbles up inside you has a definite, direct cause in each moment? Some of it for sure, at least at times, but I bet some of what triggers you is epigenetic inheritance.

Inherited fear may be part of the reason that most of us have to fight an innate insecurity about stepping fully into ourselves and "shining."

---

[30] Iva B. Zovkic, J. David Sweatt, "Epigenetic mechanisms in learned fear: implications for PTSD," *Neuropsychopharmacology* 2013 Jan; 38(1):77-93. doi: 10.1038/npp.2012.79. Epub 2012 Jun 13. PMID: 22692566; PMCID: PMC3521992. https://pubmed.ncbi.nlm.nih.gov/22692566/.

There could well be genetic markers cautioning us not to attract too much attention to ourselves because of ancestral persecution and oppression.

It's an interesting perspective to view things from. I know there are times when I feel uneasy, and I consciously look around me for possible reasons; sometimes I find reasons, while other times I don't. In the times when I don't, I used to assume I was picking up on someone else's anxiety. In light of new findings such as epigenetics, there may be more than just what is going on around us, or even within us; our ancestors may be speaking to us through our DNA. Could this be part of why so many cultures feel it's important to connect with ancestors? Perhaps there is something to be gained. Is it possible to help heal the past generations, and thereby help heal ourselves by doing so?

These are things we are just beginning to become aware of. How much more is out there? If you are interested in learning more, check out two articles by Brian Dias et al. and by Hannah Critchlow.[31]

---

[31] Brian Diaz, Stephanie Maddox, Torsten Klengel, Kerry J Ressler. "Epigenetic mechanisms underlying learning and the inheritance of learned behaviors." Author manuscript available in PMC 2016 Feb 1. Published in final edited form as *Trends Neurosci.* 2015 Feb; 38(2): 96–107. Published online 2014 Dec 24. doi: 10.1016/j.tins.2014.12.003 PMCID: PMC4323865 https://www.ncbi.nlm.nih.gov/pmc/articles/PMC4323865/.
Hannah Critchlow, "The Conversation: How much do our genes restrict free will?" https://medicalxpress.com/news/2020-10-genes-restrict-free.html, Oct. 14, 2020.

5. Cellular Mandates

I have coined a term "cellular mandates" to refer to the transmission of information that we receive (with varying amounts of consciousness) from our cells and from one generation to another. Information transmitted in this way strongly influences how living creatures both behave and feel.

What are some of our cellular mandates?

- To plant seeds, to nurture them and the soil they are in.
- To be in harmony with the phases of the moon and the seasons for planting and harvesting as well as hunting and the tides for fishing.
- To sleep during the darkness of night and be awake during the daylight.
- To feel the weather on our faces and dirt under our nails.
- To slow down in the winter and work shorter hours.

We all have information streaming to us from our cellular memories. Our modern day lives and practices do not honor these cellular directives. Far from it — we not only do not honor what our cells tell us, we don't even acknowledge that it happens.

How does ignoring these cellular mandates affect our psyche? How much of the anxiety, depression, mood swings, and other disorders, both physical and emotional, that plague people today could be healed, or at least eased, by consciously fulfilling some of these directives?

We force ourselves to get up when it's dark in the winter, when every cell in our body is telling us to sleep in, stay under the warm blankets, rest, conserve energy, rejuvenate.

Today, people who cannot ignore their cellular mandates to slow down in winter are labeled as having "seasonal mood disorder." Ha! And instead of encouraging such people to tune into their bodies, science has discovered if you increase a certain frequency of light on them per day, you fool their cells into believing it is not winter and trick them into being more productive.

In the old days inclement weather would affect activities. There were no lights, beside those created by fire, our fabulous ally. You cannot do that much by candlelight. Winter, a time of less light, was put to good use, sitting by the fire, mending the nets, darning the socks, telling stories, and making babies. It was a time for being close to home and to our families and communities.

Our modern-day inventions of lights and artificial environments don't necessitate slowing down any longer ... but guess what? Our cellular mandates crave it.

All of nature hibernates to some extent. Brightly colored birds, like the goldfinch, become drab for the winter. The trees shed their spring finery, becoming bare and focusing on their roots. It is a natural time for slowing down and reconnecting ... living off what you have stored up.

Can you recognize any such calls within you? What would they feel like? How would they express themselves? And perhaps most importantly, what effect would ignoring them have on you? Our ancestors were hunter gatherers. Their survival depended on their ability to tune into the natural world. How has ignoring these cellular drives been affecting our anxiety levels? Currently things like stress, anxiety, PTSD, insomnia, and depression have reached extremely high levels.

I would say there is an as yet unrecognized correlation between our current state of mental health, individually and collectively, and unmet ancestral cellular mandates. Our cellular wisdom whispers to us that there is something we should be doing ... but most of us are so far removed from being directly involved in working with growing and caring for our own food that we are clueless about the cause of these promptings. This lack of awareness, of clear communication between the inner and outer human being, causes anxiety in our bodies.

There's a good chance, if you are experiencing any of these symptoms, that you would benefit from tending plants and getting your hands in soil — even if with only a pot of herbs on a window sill or a potted tomato on your front stoop. Plant seeds, tend them, even if you have to give them to someone else when they reach 4″ high. Honoring the dictates of your epigenetic, somatic inheritance makes you calmer.

Pay attention to the seasons, to the full moons, noticing if there are correlations between what is going on in the natural world and how you feel. Keep a journal and make note of any changes in your internal climate. Such correlations are important. We are not as separated from nature as we have come to believe.

Not only do we demand of ourselves that we live out of accordance with our cellular mandates, we are forcing animals to do the same thing, especially the animals we consume. If it is unhealthy for us, who have some knowledge of why we are doing without, how much more disturbing, and therefore unhealthy, is it for these creatures?

It's interesting that many people today have negative images of hunters or feel that getting meat that grew itself naturally is somehow dirty. Nothing could be farther from the truth.

Take cows for instance. They are nomadic; they would never stay in the same area for long. They would move on when the grasses were eaten down to a certain point. They would never linger, much less eat, where they had relieved themselves. It goes against their cellular mandates. Our current mass farming practices force them to live on ground contaminated by thousands of other cows relieving themselves for decades. They lack the ability to get away, even though their noses and cells are screaming at them to move on.

Forced to dwell in filthy mud, created from urine and feces …. . At best this would produce an anxious animal, at worst a miserable and unhealthy one. And this is the meat we consume? Do you think we can't feel that? That our own bodies at a cellular level don't absorb some of that depression, futility, and dis-ease?

An animal that can run when it is frightened will burn off its anxiety, its tension. Captive animals have no ability to do this. Their fears and tensions are conditions they are forced to live with. Unfortunately, such anxious feelings are stored in their bodies, and therefore probably in the meats we eat. Think about that for a minute.

In contrast, an animal allowed to live "wild" in harmony with the mandates of its cellular memory is a far happier, healthier being. Its body is free from the toxic residue of a miserable life, of being forced to live against its cellular mandates, which, unlike us, it "hears" loud and clear.

I honor hunters who seek out their own food. I also honor those who raise the animals that they will eat or trade with other people — as long as they have been raised in a manner that honors the creature's cellular mandates. Not tending to the flocks or herds we depend on for survival creates a deficit in our lives as well. Eating meat that is as far removed from warm, furry and breathing as it could possibly be, wrapped in sterile cellophane, is an illusion, a lie. It does not change the fact that a creature has given its life for us to consume.

What it does do is change our ability to be grateful, to acknowledge the sacrifice. Does it make you uncomfortable to feel connected to the creature you eat and its gift of life? Being aware of this sacrifice imbues our eating experience. If we are grateful and conscious that we are being gifted by ingesting the life force of another being, it changes our experience. But we are estranged from this reciprocal exchange of life force and the gratitude it should engender, at least in most of the USA.

Our comfort with seeing sterile meat at the supermarket is a bit obscene if you think about it. It is another step on the road away from our true nature and fuels the illusion of being separate from nature. Because we do not see that we are eating an animal, we do not have to feel like we are predatory animals ourselves, or that what we are eating has died for us, no matter who has killed it. The truth is everything we eat is alive, everything. From a Native American perspective, a plant you eat is no less alive than an animal. Modern science is now supporting the concept of plant intelligence and awareness that we had long dismissed because of our short-sightedness. Even when you breathe you kill microbes. We cannot live without ending life. The question is, do you honor that sacrifice?

6. The Earth and Us

I lived in very rural areas until I was about six. During that time my only playmates were the living beings who dwelled in the woods, fields and streams near me. I was able to feel their energies (although I had not realized that then), which meant that I could always find them wherever they were hiding. I could also feel the earth and drew sustenance from that connection. We never lived so rurally again after my sixth birthday, but I discovered that no matter where we went — city, suburb, countryside — there she was under my feet and I could still connect with her denizens.

I would rescue other girls from cicadas, dragonflies or spiders by catching them in my hands. Wasps and bees I would catch in a cup or similar container and always release them. I've caught my fair share of birds in various situations where they weren't welcome, sometimes in a net, but often in my bare hands, feeling their strong fast hearts beat in my palms as I carried them outdoors. In the winters it was harder, but then I would feel for nature under her snowy robes with my mind/heart, because I needed her in order to survive. Despite all we have done to her, nature still welcomes us.

There are countless stories amongst indigenous peoples describing not only intelligence in nature, but a willingness therein to help us. To the Quechua people of South America, we are considered "walking trees." In fact, physiologically humans and trees are intricately linked. For example, the breathing cycles of trees and humans are symbiotically connected. Trees produce oxygen during the day, which we utilize. Then at night trees inhale the carbon dioxide that we exhale. We are inexorably connected. Could there be more to this connection? Can trees affect us in other ways?

In Japan there have been scientific studies done on the effects of immersing yourself in nature, specifically in a forest. The practice, called Shinrin-Yoku (forest bathing), is a traditional Japanese practice of immersing oneself in nature by mindfully using all five senses. From 65 studies conclusive evidence was found to support that forest bathing has therapeutic effects on: (1) the immune system function (increase in natural killer cells/cancer prevention); (2) cardiovascular system (hypertension/coronary artery disease); (3) the respiratory system (allergies and respiratory disease); (4) depression and anxiety (mood disorders and stress); (5) mental relaxation (Attention Deficit/Hyperactivity Disorder) and; (6) human feelings of "awe" (increase in gratitude and selflessness). [32]

Forest bathing is not limited to Japan; many oriental cultures recognize the benefits of this practice. In Mandarin it is called "Senlinyu" and in Korean "Sanlimyok." Forest bathing has been proven to boost immune system function, increase the body's NK (natural killer) cells, and reduce blood pressure. These effects are thought to be the result of phytoncides (anti-microbial compounds) emitted by the trees. Different kinds of trees release different phytoncides, which produce different physiological and psychological changes in humans.[33] These positive effects can be seen with as little exposure as one hour a day and can last for up to two weeks. In another study the effect was proven to "last for seven days."[34]

What drug have we created of which a single dose can similarly affect you for up to two weeks? None! The only other thing I can think of that can affect you like that is being in love. Our ancestors realized the benefits of being in a natural environment from their own experience. More and more we are seeing evidence in science that much of what our ancestors perceived about the nature of the universe was accurate.

What could have caused us to shun this form of discernment? A big reason why we turned away from nature for our cures was early science, that believed in itself too much. Science and religion both had much to gain from controlling people's beliefs around our separation from, and superiority to, nature. We were encouraged to believe that natural cures are dirty and inferior to human products. For example, in Africa the Nestlé corporation decided to push its baby formula. Nestlé paid for a huge

---

[32] Margaret M. Hansen, Reo Jones, and Kirsten Tocchini, "Shinrin-Yoku (Forest Bathing) and Nature Therapy: A State-of-the-Art Review" *International Journal of Environmental Research and Public Health* 2017 Aug; 14(8): 851. Published online 2017 July 28. doi: 10.3390/ijerph14080851, or https://pubmed.ncbi.nlm.nih.gov/28788101 (accessed 5/23/18).

[33] NYS Department of Environmental Conservation, *Immerse Yourself in a Forest for Better Health,* https://www.dec.ny.gov/lands/90720.html.

[34] Quin Li, "Effect of Forrest Bathing Trips on Human Immune Function," *Environ Health Prev. Med.* 2010 Jan; 15(1): 9–17, https://pubmed.ncbi.nlm.nih.gov/19568839/.

campaign to convince African women that their own breast milk was not just inferior to formula, but actually bad for their babies!

What mother would not want the best for her baby? So even though these women had a poverty level existence, they took the plunge. How was this possible? Nestlé offered a free sample of dried milk product.

There are several things that are horrifying to me here.

1. Women living in these countries most often didn't have access to clean drinking water, nor resources to purify what water was available — and water is necessary to make the powdered baby formulas into a drinkable liquid. So these poor infants went from having few to no pathogens passed to them in their mothers' breast milk to having their fledgling immune systems hammered with powerful bacteria, parasites and diseases from the untreated water.

2. These babies also lost the benefit of their mother's immune system, because God, or evolution, created a beautiful symbiotic relationship between a mom and her infant. As the mother kisses her baby and breaths in her baby's breath, her incredible immune system analyses what her baby is being exposed to and creates the proper immune responses to these challenges in her breast milk! It's magical really.

But here we go with technologically advanced societies, telling "us" (the little people) that what came naturally to us is inferior, compared to what "they" can produce. It makes us afraid to trust our bodies and more.

3. This campaign offered poor women a month's supply of formula for free. What is horrifying about this? A mother's milk dries up if she stops breastfeeding for a week or so. This marketing locks a woman into using formula because her own breast milk would dry up during that one-month free trial. The babies became completely dependent on this formula, produced by companies that had no concern for anything but their profit.

It was common for those who distributed these free packets for corporations like Dumex in Singapore, Bristol Meyers in Jamaica and Nestlé in Africa to employ women who dressed like nurses to pass out the packets. That confused the new mothers, who thought that these women in nurse outfits were actually nurses. The mothers were more likely to believe that these women knew what they were talking about when they claimed this product was better for babies than breast milk.

This is a perfect example of corporate practices that consciously hurt us and, if you think about it, almost enslave us. These marketing practices started decades ago and they continue today. According to the article I mentioned above, the companies producing baby formula have now focused on hospitals as their targets. Abbot Laboratories even offers a "free architectural service to hospitals which are building or renovating facilities for newborn care. Abbot Laboratories helps design 200 maternity departments a year in the US alone."[35]

Interestingly, the layout of these wards "makes breast-feeding difficult because newborns are separated from their mothers." The article goes on to say for a nurse to bring the baby to the mom, "babies have to be carried long distances to their mothers for feeding, a task that the nurses resent." The layout of these wards encourages nurses to just feed the newborns the free formula supplied by Abbot Labs. It's not a bad deal for Abbott "when one considers that for every 100 infants discharged on a particular formula brand, approximately 93 infants remain on that brand."

If you think that the only area in our lives in which corporate media attempts to lead us astray is baby formula, you need to think again. The "Babies Mean Business" article states that we need to "organize and educate people to protect themselves against the global marketing onslaught." Have you ever thought about that?

4. Now here's the final insult: "In the *Times*, United States Agency for International Development official, Dr. Stephen Joseph, blamed reliance on baby formula for a million infant deaths every year through malnutrition and diarrheal diseases."[36]

We need to renew our connection to nature and our beautifully powerful, magical instruments (our bodies)! Speaking of which, did you ever have a crazy (hopefully lovable) older person in your life tell you that "Eating a little dirt is good for you!"? I remember hearing that from my grandmother, and at the time I thought "What the heck? ... dirt is ... dirty! You're crazy, grandma." What if I told you that grandma was right?

Science has recently identified microbes in soil that are anti-inflammatory in our systems, as well as being antidepressants. How we evolved naturally was good for us! In *Discover Magazine* 7, Christopher Lowry shares his discovery that the soil bacterium *Mycobacterium vaccae* "activated a set of serotonin-releasing neurons in the brain — the same nerves targeted by Prozac."[37] Lowry determined that injections of *M.*

---

[35] Edward Baer, "Babies Mean Business," *New Internationalist*, April 1, 1982, https://newint.org/features/1982/04/01/babies.

[36] Jill Krasny, "Every Parent Should Know The Scandalous History Of Infant Formula" *Business Insider,* June 25, 2012, https://www.businessinsider.com/personal-finance/nestles-infant-formula-scandal-2012-6.

[37] Christopher Lowry, "Is Dirt the New Prozac?", http://discovermagazine.com/2007/jul/raw-data-is-dirt-the-new-prozac.

vaccae "had the exact same effect as antidepressant drugs." Can you wrap your brain around that for a minute? The planet, through her body (earth) has an anti-inflammatory, antidepressant effect on us humans.

Lowry's article states: "Microorganisms and microbiota with which we coevolved are essential for the induction of immuno-regulation." Working with the earth herself builds our immune system, and getting "dirty" (as in covered with soil) is really good for a person.

When did it become "bad" for children to get "soiled"? All I can say is that if this is a philosophy that you espouse, you are hurting your children or grandchildren. Lowry also states: "Depletion of these organisms [in soil] by modern life is leading to increased chronic inflammatory disorders." Inflammatory diseases include but are not limited to asthma, chronic pain, tuberculosis, rheumatoid arthritis, periodontia, ulcerative colitis, Crohn's disease, sinusitis, and active hepatitis.

The bottom line is that children spending less time outside playing is contributing to a weakened immune system. Lowry goes on to state "Depression is strongly associated with inflammation and with chronic inflammatory disorders." There are many diseases connected to inflammation, but I had not realized that depression was one of them. Who would have thought that getting into contact with the earth, whom indigenous people refer to as our Mother, would end up being a physiological antidote!

According to the studies presented thus far, you can boost your serotonin levels, immune system and mood just by spending time in nature. Go for a walk in the woods.

By digging in the garden, you will inhale enough *M. vaccae* to affect your wellbeing. Lowry says "You can also ingest mycobacteria either through water sources or through eating plants — lettuce that you pick from the garden, or carrots."

Dirt is not "dirty" in and of itself. Dirt can become contaminated by waste from many things (animals, humans, machines, chemicals) but the earth herself is clean, nurturing and beautiful! Go out and roll in the dirt today!

7. Plants

It is only human arrogance, and the fact that the lives of plants unfold in what amounts to a much slower dimension of time, that keep us from appreciating their intelligence and consequent success.[38]

Ever since I can remember, I knew that plants felt things. They were alive after all! Why would they not have feelings? Plus, I know this might seem weird to some of you, but I could feel them feeling. Try convincing others who aren't in touch with these kinds of sensations that they might actually exist! My path has not been an easy one.

Did you know that Charles Darwin's grandfather Erasmus Darwin (1731–1802) was a naturalist?[39] I had not. He wrote quite a bit on the subject and "argued that plants are animate, living beings, attributing to them sensation, movement, and a degree of mental activity."[40] He saw many similarities between humans and plants. It has taken 200 years for science to begin to identify and consider these things. If I had been familiar with the elder Darwin's work, I would not have felt so alone in my awarenesses.

Even though I had no scientific proof, I could not shake my conviction that plants were conscious. It was obvious to me through observations that plants had preferences. They breathed, well, transpired (consuming oxygen) and they moved to follow the sun. The concept that they did not feel or that they were not aware of their surroundings did not make any sense to me. I persisted in believing this despite teachers and scientists scoffing at these ideas for most of my life. This hurt me, but even though it would have been easier to pretend to think the way the majority of my peers did,

---

[38] Michael Pollan, "The Intelligent Plant: Scientists debate a new way of understanding flora," *The New Yorker*, December 15 2013 (accessed 12-9-20).

[39] Erasmus Darwin, *Zoonomia or Laws of Organic Life*, 3rd ed. 4 vols., London, 1801.

[40] Gagliano, Monica & Ryan, John & Vieira, Patricia. "The Language of Plants: Science, Philosophy, Literature," 2017, https://www.researchgate.net/publication/317427606_The_Language_of_Plants_Science_Philosophy_Literature.

I could not deny the awareness that I had of plants, nor my connection to them. I can feel a plant that is thirsty. If I walk into a room where there is a plant that needs help, I notice it immediately. Because of this dichotomy between my awareness and the paradigm I was born into, I had no choice but to pull away from my fellow humans. I could not shut off or deny my awareness and that fact caused me to withdraw from mainstream anything, that is, until recently.

It used to be that scientists thought a seed "mechanically" sprouted, due to something they labeled "instinct." It was nothing more than a program that the plant followed "blindly." This instinctual behavior was ascribed to animals and plants as the "dumb" reason they did what they do to survive.

Scientists and religious sects (generally folks seeking control) felt a need to claim that humans had no instincts. Both science and the church were and are heavily invested in separating us from nature and our instincts, which may be, in part, the epigenetic whisperings of our ancestors in our cellular ears.

This attempt to separate humans from their instincts is intriguing to me because what I would call "instinct" is an ability to read the subtle energies inside you as well as those around you. This is possible through a variety of methods, such as intuition and discernment, or being in tune with epigenetic information.

In order for such information to be helpful, we need to be able to respond quickly, synthesizing multiple streams of information each instant. Does that sound complicated? We are fully capable of this. Each of us. Yet, for strange reasons, we are not taught how to do it. More than not being taught how to gain mastery of this very natural part of us, we are actually encouraged to deny the existence of these awarenesses.

We have been systematically stripped of our ability to put faith in these intrinsic methods of knowing, operating and being in the world. Intrinsic to every cell of our bodies! Intrinsic to every being on this planet as well!

To what end has this stripping taken us? It has curtailed our ability to trust ourselves. It has furthered the illusion of separateness from the natural world, the world that gave birth to us and sustains us, that we are connected to in very real ways. How can that be good? Is it good to poison our water, air, and soil? What about our bodies? Some of the ways we have been separated to our detriment are obvious; others were not able to be empirically evidenced until very recently.

Anthony Trewavas, Professor of Plant Cellular Biology at the University of Edinburgh, has published 250 scientific papers and three books on the subject of plants and their abilities. In 2002 he wrote an article titled "Plant Intelligence: Mindless Mastery." In it he writes:

> Plants continuously screen at least 15 different environmental variables with remarkable sensitivity — a footprint on the soil or a local stone, for example, are perceived and acted upon ... Quite how individual plant cells accommodate this prodigious amount of information is not understood. But even anatomically uniform cells exhibit enormously different responses to a single signal. A huge reservoir of individual cell behaviors can be coordinated to produce many varieties of organism behavior ... Plants decide what kind of appendages to grow depending on soil nutrient, light and the proximity of neighbors ... Roots track three-dimensional humidity and mineral gradients in soil with explosive growth responses when resource-rich patches are encountered, but deliberate evasive action is taken when competitors' roots approach.[41]

I want you to pay particular attention to this sentence, "Quite how individual plant cells accommodate this prodigious amount of information is not understood." Humans realizing that we do not know everything is a significant change! Here is a quote from Albert Szent-Györgyi in 1965:

> The more we know about it [muscle] the less we understand, and it looks as if we would soon know everything and understand nothing. The situation is similar in most other biological processes and pathological conditions ... This suggests that some very basic information is missing.[42]

How can we find this new information, which of necessity will require new paradigms? How did people originally discover truths? By entering into a relationship with the natural world with a sense of wonder ... .

Open your senses. You will constantly have to remind yourself not to prejudge these relationships. Sit with plants or a plant. Open your mind, your heart and your imagination. Think about this new perspective, that there is more to plants' intelligence and functioning that we are currently

---

[41] Anthony Trewavas, "Plant intelligence: Mindless Mastery," *Nature, International Journal of Science.* Vol. 415, 21 February 2002, https://www.nature.com/articles/415841a (accessed 7/21/18).

[42] Albert Szent-Györgyi, "Bioenergetics." *Science*, 2 November 1965, Number 3227. https:// www.jstor.org/stable/1751153?seq=1.

privy to. What comes to you? We are talking about a new type of experience here, one that cannot rely on what you've been taught, because that picture was not whole, not complete, and in some cases what we had been taught was even downright wrong.

Dr. Toshyuki Nakagaki of Hokkaido University in Japan studied slime molds and found that they could solve mazes with incredible accuracy. In a *New York Times* article from 2010 he states: "We've found an unexpectedly high ability of information processing in this organism."[43]

Let's think about that for a minute. These are single-celled entities we're talking about here, with no brains as we would recognize them. How could they possibly process information without the characteristic grey matter that we call brains? It must mean that there are other types of intelligence available in biology than just wrinkled grey matter.

This is a major finding, and it should turn our belief systems, our ways of judging intelligence, and our understanding of other beings (at least plants) on its ear. But who is talking about it?

Information like this is a gift for those with open hearts and minds. It can validate our experiences and encourage the formation of new ideas for connecting to the rest of nature. If the perception/presumption of our being so different from the rest of creation (that we are alone in our possession of intelligence on this planet) has been false, then we need to look at everything with new eyes.

How might it change your life to view all living beings as intelligent or sentient? What if you included the possibility for communication with these other beings? What kind of support might you be able to receive on a daily basis from these sources? Let me tell you, enough to keep you alive, even when your heart has been ripped out by other humans or by our cold, mechanistic modern world. Trust me — I *know* this to be a fact! And I will share many examples throughout the following chapters.

If nothing else, it certainly illustrates that there are other ways to discern things than science previously believed. This information can open many different doors within us! Keep this in mind as you read this book and as you move through your life.

In her book *Thus Spoke the Plant*, biologist Monica Gagliano says:

Still, we humans walk through nature not seeing plants as highly evolved creatures, but rather as inanimate, passive, and inferior

---

[43] Henry Fountain, "Slime Mold Proves to Be a Brainy Blob," *New York Times*, Jan. 25 2010, https://www.nature.com/articles/35035159 (accessed 6-19-18).

species. We have constructed a simple vision of plants as lacking in intelligence, agency, or sentience. We have relegated them to the lowest rung of hierarchy that is headed by humans.[44]

In one of my favorite lectures, titled "Intelligence in Nature," Jeremy Narby, Ph.D., said "We now know that plants can see you when you are standing next to them. They can tell what color shirt you are wearing. Plants don't have eyes, but they have the same photoreceptor proteins as we have in the back of our retina, all over their bodies."[45] They don't have brains, but they translate information into electro-chemical signals in their cells, identical to the ones used by our own neurons.

In other words, their whole bodies act like brains. Narby also points out that the word neuron comes from the Greek word for vegetable fibers, because neurons look like a cross section from inside a plant.

Plants are so sensitive to touch that if they are on a path taken by mammals, they react by letting their branches that are being brushed die off, thereby "moving away" from the creatures touching them.

Sending roots branching out into the soil is not done "thoughtlessly" either. It involves a plant being able to react to, in seconds, and interpret many types of data, such as nutrient content of soil layers, moisture, competitive roots, friendly roots, stones, etc.

We had trouble recognizing this because we were only looking for "intelligence" in beings who functioned similarly to us. How arrogant, and small minded really, but we had to start somewhere I suppose.

In my research for this chapter, I found many references to plants having intentions. There is even a plant that has developed a form of walking. The Amazonian stilt palm grows on prop roots that come out of its trunk like spider legs. As the plant encounters competitive plants or an increase or decrease in optimal sunlight, moisture levels or nutrients, it sends out new root "legs" in the chosen direction and allows the roots on the opposite side to die back and release their hold in the earth. We do not witness this movement because we don't sit still in one place for years, but over time these plants completely change their locations.

Peter Wohlleben, a German forester in the Eiffel Mountains of western Germany, says "Trees are far more alert, social, sophisticated — and even

[44] Monica Gagliano, *Thus Spoke the Plant*, North Atlantic Books, Berkeley, Cal., 2018.

[45] Jeremy Narby, "Intelligence In Nature," Bioneers Convention 2005. National Bioneers Conference is part of the *Ecological Design*, Vol. 1 and *Nature, Culture and Spirit*, Vol. 1 Collections. https://www.youtube.com/watch?v=uGMV6IJy1Oc.

intelligent — than we thought."[46] He describes the complex relationships between trees and their parents (well, mothers, because there is not a paternal lineage amongst plants) and other elders. Young trees under their mothers' shadowing bulk are forced to delay growth, sometimes for hundreds of years. What's interesting is that this forced delay benefits the young tree in many ways, increasing the strength and flexibility of the wood.

Wohlleben says that in order to reach "enormousness" giant trees depend on each other and a complicated web of "kinship alliances." He uses the term "wood wide web" to illustrate this networking. He says that all trees, in every forest that is not too damaged (meaning that has elders, amongst other things) are connected to each other using underground fungal networks. These are called mycorrhizal networks, which the trees use to share nutrients and water as well as to communicate things like drought, pestilence, disease etc. The trees receiving these messages make changes in their chemistry to help them cope with these stressors.

Large ancient "mother" trees feed their saplings with sugar utilizing these mycorrhizal networks in stressful times, helping them survive. Wohlleben describes this phenomenon saying that "Mother trees suckle their young," and that is a powerful analogy. By the way, a stressful time for a young tree can be its entire "childhood." With their mothers, aunts and uncles looming above them, they are deprived of the sunlight they need to photosynthesize (the process that trees use to produce their food) because they are too short to reach the sunlight. Without being suckled, they would die.

It is the elders who warn neighboring trees of approaching danger. They also know what it takes to survive in intense conditions, something the youngsters do not. Young trees take risks. They are quick (in tree time, which is slow motion for us humans) to jump on optimal conditions like drinking too much water in periods of heavy rain, chasing light and becoming too tall too quickly, or shedding leaves early. All of these things can cost them their lives. Grant describes "Crown Princes" as patiently waiting "for the old monarchs to fall, so they can take their place in the full glory of the sunlight."

Plants have been around much longer than mammals on this planet!

In order to have the success rate that they have achieved, plants have to be resourceful and adaptive. Plants dominate every ter-

---

[46] Peter Wohlleben, *The Hidden Life of Trees*, David Suzuki Institute, Greystone Books, Vancouver/Berkeley 2016.

restrial environment, composing ninety-nine per cent of the bio-mass on earth. By comparison, humans and all the other animals are, in the words of one plant neurobiologist, "just traces."[47]

There's a good chance that plants have information passed to them through epigenetic inheritance just like mice, worms, and us. Not only that, but think of the depths that their learning and awareness could travel to within their lifespans (100–800 years). If our human elders can glean appreciable wisdom in 50 to 100 years (and build upon what is passed down to them), imagine the accumulated wisdom of a 300-year or older tree. Now add to that what it would glean from living in an ancient community ... it gives me shivers just thinking about it.

Having connected these dots, it becomes obvious that our current practice of forestry management, which has us culling only old large trees (leaving young, inexperienced trees to try to raise themselves), is actually harmful to a forest. According to Richard Grant:

> There is now a substantial body of scientific evidence that refutes that idea [of taking out larger trees to promote a healthy forest]. It shows instead that trees of the same species are communal, and will often form alliances with trees of other species. Forest trees have evolved to live in cooperative, interdependent relationships, maintained by communication and a collective intelligence similar to an insect colony. These soaring columns of living wood draw the eye upward to their outspreading crowns, but the real action is taking place underground, just a few inches below our feet.[48]

The mycorrhizal networks that allow trees to connect and communicate over miles are around "four hundred and fifty million years old!"[49] Can you imagine what information might be contained in that network? We are a young, arrogant, species!

In his article Grant describes Wohlleben coming across a beech stump four or five feet in diameter, the remains of a tree that had been cut down four to five hundred years ago. He was amazed when he cut into the wood

---

[47] Michael Pollan, "The Intelligent Plant: Scientists debate a new way of understanding flora," *The New Yorker*, December 15 2013 (accessed 12-9-20).

[48] Richard Grant, "Do Trees Talk to Each Other?," *Ask Smithsonian,* mailbox://C:/Laptop_Data/Thunderbird_profile_1/Mail/Local Folders/ https://www.smithsonianmag.com/science-nature/the-whispering-trees-180968084/.

[49] Bob Macfarlane, "The Secrets of the Wood Wide Web," *The New Yorker*, August 7 2016, https://www.newyorker.com/tech/annals-of-technology/the-secrets-of-the-wood-wide-web.

because it was still green! He explained that the surrounding trees must be feeding this stump. Without leaves it could not be producing chlorophyll on its own. Wohlleben said that "When beeches do this, they remind me of elephants, they are reluctant to abandon their dead, especially when it's a big, old, revered matriarch."

Wohlleben attributes the surrounding trees keeping the stump of this elder alive to "sentimental reasons." But if, as we have learned, there is communication underground and this tree is kept alive through underground connections to surrounding trees, then perhaps this matriarch is still communicating and sharing her wisdom with the trees she is connected to! Why else would they keep sharing their resources and feeding her if she wasn't actually still alive and able to communicate? It's an amazing possibility!

Life is amazing! We barely understand half of it. Use all your senses! It is what we were given them for (or why we evolved them)!

Edward Farmer, a Professor at the University of Lausanne in Switzerland, has been studying one of the three ways trees communicate, electrical pulses (the other two being chemical and hormonal). He has identified a signaling system based on voltage that "appears strikingly similar to animal nervous systems." [50]

If our guts' neural power helps us identify frequency, then there is no reason that we should not be able to communicate with trees ... or at least understand them. Perhaps we are communicating with them all the time, only we don't realize it. Could this be another reason why forest bathing is so beneficial for humans?

At the University of Western Australia, Monica Gagliano has found evidence that some plants emit and detect sounds. Her research points to "crackling" noises emitted at a frequency of 220 hertz.[51] Wohlleben describes how trees scream in extreme drought. He says that at this time scientists are attributing this elevated noise to a physical reaction of the wood itself as it dries out. However, given our history of denying interspecies communication and intelligence, I would caution against outright dismissal.

---

[50] Edward Farmer et al., "Identification of cell populations necessary for leaf-to-leaf electrical signaling in a wounded plant." PNAS, October 2 2018, https://www.pnas.org/content/115/40/10178.

[51] Monica Gagliano, "The Language of Plants," https://www.researchgate.net/publication/317427606_The_Language_of_Plants_Science_Philosophy_Literature.

We have drawn the circle smaller for hundreds of years now, and we are clearly being shown evidence that we were wrong. Perhaps we should start allowing the possibility of sentience where we least expect it. Wohlleben describes the physical process of how humans make noise in our vocal cords and he illustrates how trees' speech is not that different.

Trees can detect scents through their leaves, which could qualify as a sense of smell. This explains how easily trees communicate above ground, not just with each other but with other creatures as well, through pheromones. A tree in distress from a caterpillar infestation will emit a pheromone that attracts parasitic wasps, the wasps lay their eggs inside the caterpillars, and the offspring of these wasps slowly kill the caterpillars, by feeding off them as they grow.

In the article "Do Trees Talk To Each Other?" (footnote 48), Richard Grant quotes a recent study from the German Center for Integrative Biodiversity based at the University of Leipzig. Researchers at the Center have found that "when a deer is biting a branch, the tree sends defending chemicals to the area to make the leaves taste bad." What's interesting is that a tree will respond very differently when a branch is randomly broken. When "a human breaks a branch with their hands, the tree knows the difference" and instead of becoming defensive, the tree "brings in substances to heal the wound." In *The Hidden Life of Trees*, Wohlleben says that the trees are able to identify or "taste the saliva of what is biting them." This proves that trees are not only cognizant of what is eating them, but able to bring specific defenses to combat the offending creature.

Another example of Wohlleben's cited by Grant occurs in Africa, between giraffes and the wide-crowned umbrella thorn acacia. A giraffe chewing on one of these trees will cause the tree to emit a form of ethylene gas. Neighboring acacias "reading" this signal begin pumping their leaves full of tannins. Large enough amounts of this compound can easily sicken or kill a sizable herbivore.

Recent discoveries of how trees communicate are a perfect example of it being hard to find something that you are not looking for. It's also a great plug for independent thinking, a thinking that is not afraid to challenge conventional paradigms. It also involves a type of thinking that does not originate in our heads, reasoning not limited to drawing inside the lines or staying in the "box." *You* can feel these things (and so can plants)!

Beginning in April 2018 Ikea did an experiment in which they took two identical plants and supplied them with the same amount and quality of light and nutrients. "One of the plants was fed compliments and words of encouragement, the other was verbally bullied with hateful words."[52] The result 30 days later? Looking at the two plants, the difference between them breaks my heart. The bullied plant is stunted and scraggly. I certainly hope someone nurtured the poor plant after that experiment!

Remember that to the Quechua people, we two-leggeds are considered "walking trees." Interestingly, they are not alone in seeing a connection. The ancient Norse had a myth that describes the creation of the first humans, saying "the man and woman were created from two trees," the male Ask [Ash] and the female Embla [Elm?], "and from Ask and Embla have sprung the races of man that live in Midgard."[53]

Our cultural evolution has been short-sighted, perhaps understandable and therefore forgivable, for a species so young to science. We couldn't see far enough under the skin to recognize the similarities within the differences, unable to attribute sentience to other beings. But now we can, and with that comes a new responsibility — and a new, exciting freedom to make our own connections in the universe!

---

[52] Ikea bullying experiment, https://globalnews.ca/news/4217594/bully-a-plant-ikea/.

[53] D.L. Ashliman, "The Norse Creation Myth ,"abstracted from *The Prose Edda of Snorri Sturluson* https://www.pitt.edu/~dash/creation.html (accessed May 2016).
or Daniel McCoy, "Ask and Embla," *Norse Mythology for Smart People.* https://norse-mythology.org/gods-and-creatures/others/ask-and-embla/.

8. Our Fellow Inhabitants

Recent studies of cognitive behavior in both animals and insects have surprised the Western world with the abilities of these creatures. Martin Giurfa[54] of the National Center for Scientific Research in Toulouse, France has been studying bees. What he found indicates that bees have minds of their own, as shown by the fact that they are able to extract the logical structure of the world. Here again we are being asked to look beyond our preconceived notions about grey matter and size. Bee brains are about the size of a pinhead, yet bees can handle abstract concepts.[55] According to the findings of Wen Wu and his colleagues:

> Honeybees (*Apis mellifera*) have remarkable visual learning and discrimination abilities that extend beyond learning simple colours, shapes or patterns. They can discriminate landscape scenes, types of flowers, and even human faces. This suggests that in spite of their small brain, honeybees have a highly developed capacity for processing complex visual information, comparable in many respects to vertebrates … Honeybees learned to simultaneously discriminate between five different Monet and Picasso paintings, and that they do not rely on luminance, colour, or spatial frequency information for discrimination. When presented with novel paintings of the same style, the bees even demonstrated some ability to generalize. This suggests that honeybees are able to discriminate Monet paintings from Picasso ones by extracting and learning the characteristic visual information inherent in each

[54] Martin Giurfa, "Honeybees Foraging for Numbers," *Journal of Comparative Psychology*, 205, 439–450 (2019). https://doi.org/10.1007/s00359-019-01344-2 or https://link.springer.com/article/10.1007/s00359-019-01344-2.

[55] Aurore Avargues-Weber, Adrian G. Dyer, Maud Combe, Martin Giurfa, *PNAS* May 8, 2012 109 (19) 7481-7486; https://www.pnas.org/search/Aurore%252BAvargues-Weber%252C%252BAdrian%252BG.%252BDyer%252C%252BMaud%252BCombe%252C%252B2BMartin%252BGiurfa%252C%252B%20content_type%3Ajournal.

painting style. Our study further suggests that discrimination of artistic styles is not a higher cognitive function that is unique to humans, but simply due to the capacity of animals — from insects to humans — to extract and categorize the visual characteristics of complex images.

The upshot: bees are sentient, minded beings.

Further studies by different scientists revealed:

- Ants cultivate mushroom gardens
- Pigeons have better memory for paintings than college students
- Parrots can say what they actually mean
- Crows can build standardized tools
- Dolphins can recognize themselves in mirrors
- Brainless plants make correct decisions
- Proteins can transcribe and edit DNA molecules
- Plants can communicate using chemical substances
- Octopi have brains at the end of each tentacle [56]

These findings take many of the presuppositions that came out of the systems we have developed to measure intelligence and capacity and throw them out the window — concepts such as you need eyes to "see," or that a "brain" is required to think, or that the size of that brain indicates intellectual capacity. None of those concepts is now relevant. Our supposition that other beings need skin and hearts to feel, or possess other attributes that resemble us or the way we function, in order to be considered sentient is scientifically incorrect. We will not get into the question of morality at this point, but many things need to be rethought!

We simply cannot look at the natural world the way we have been taught. Speaking of looking at the world, in his studies Martin Giurfa found "Free-flying honeybees learn to associate different visual cues with a sucrose reward and may deploy sophisticated cognitive strategies to this end."[57]

It is becoming increasingly clear that we cannot judge things by their lack of similarity to us. We do happen to be a form of life with opposable

---

[56] Wen Wu, Antonio M. Moreno, Jason M. Tangen, Judith Reinhard, "Honeybees can discriminate between Monet and Picasso paintings," *Journal of Comparative Physiology*, 18 October 2012. https://link.springer.com/article/10.1007/s00359-012-0767-5.

[57] Nino Mancini, Martin Giurfa, Jean-Christophe Sandoz, Aurore Avarguès-Weber. "Aminergic Neuromodulation of Associative Visual Learning in Harnessed Honey Bees," *Neurobiology of Learning and Memory, https://www.researchgate.net/publication/325290076_Aminergic_neuromodulation_of_associative_visual_learning_in_harnessed_honey_bees.*

thumbs, and thus the ability to change our environments drastically, but not necessarily for the better.

We were more challenged than most soft-bodied species, possessing neither terribly impressive fangs nor claws, the proverbial naked ape. We had to rely on our ingenuity to survive ... and our ingenuity is impressive (but so is our short sightedness).

Perhaps because of this flawed frame of reference, it is understandable that we formed such a perspective of our superiority and our place in the world. This belief system is so myopic that we can't stop at just stripping other species of their claim to "humanity." No, we seem to have a need to keep drawing smaller and smaller circles ... shutting out more and more ... drawing lines not just in nature, but within the family of man as well, ascribing "less than a human" rating to other humans.

Remember that old adage "Divide and conquer"? It is a strategy that has been used throughout time to subjugate people. Division within ourselves makes us weaker. This applies whether we are dealing with the micro or the macro, as universal truths often do. So, if I divide you by removing your comfort with parts of yourself, I have gained a measure of power over you, or at the very least I have weakened you. Do that on a larger scale, with nature and our fellow humans, and you will find that not only are we weakened individually, but that our communities are weakened and more vulnerable because of that isolation.

Now we have been clearly shown that the view of our current paradigm, of isolationism and separatism, only serves to disconnect us. It disconnects us from ourselves, nature, and fulfillment. What this process serves is two-fold. First, it weakens us and our communities, as well as encouraging us to destroy the ecosystem, because we feel so unrealistically removed from it. Second, the dis-eases that arise from this separation give institutions the opportunity to profit from us. If we cannot be "fed" by our tenuous connections to the "real" world (the natural world), institutions are able to offer us our only consolation (whether it be medicinally, spiritually or through general consumerism). It increases our dependency on outside sources.

The separation that weakens us is an illusion and it is also real (because we have believed it so long). What can we do to alter our perceptions? To re-member ourselves not just in relation to our intrinsic human abilities, but to the natural world as well?

According to ancient shamanic teachings, we share a kinship with all life, something science is just discovering; molecular biology is finding that we have identical genetic sequences to those found in bananas and even in bacteria.

Many older cultures evolved to include animistic ways of understanding the world, believing that animals, natural objects, phenomena and even the universe itself are, if not equal beings, then certainly forces to be reckoned with — ones that we are able to have meaningful relationships and even communicate with.

In 1984, Jeremy Narby, an anthropologist, was sent to the Peruvian Amazon to work with, and help protect, the Ashaninka people living there. In attempting to do this he came face to face with his inability to let go of the cultural paradigms he was raised with. Even though it was his job to bridge these two worlds in an effort to preserve theirs, when confronted with cultural beliefs that were so radically different from his, he found it virtually impossible. He describes struggling with this for years.

These were a people who believed that plants and animals are intelligent beings and that these beings of the natural world have intentions and personalities. The Ashaninka believe that we share a deep kinship with these other beings and that communication is not just possible, but something that is practiced on a daily basis.

Narby describes himself at the time as a "humanist," a "materialist" and "agnostic." He "viewed plants as passive automatons that were not capable of communication." He describes struggling with knee-jerk reactions that caused him to be "ethnocentric and anthropocentric" and that he kept "running into my own disbelief." This struggle was very real for him, and he didn't actually believe that his perspective could change. It took years for the shamans of the Ashaninka, who are able to communicate with plants and other natural beings, to show him another reality. His talk "Intelligence in Nature"[58] describes his struggles and subsequent findings which he explores in greater depth in his book *Intelligence in Nature: An Inquiry into Knowledge.*[59]

He is not alone in this; many scientists have great difficulty seeing outside the box of the reality in which they have been indoctrinated. The very word "nature" is defined as "everything that is not human." That is very telling!

---

[58] Jeremy Narby, "Intelligence In Nature," Bioneers Convention 2005. National Bioneers Conference is part of the *Ecological Design*, Vol. 1 and *Nature, Culture and Spirit*, Vol. 1 Collections. https://www.youtube.com/watch?v=uGMV6IJy1Oc.

[59] Jeremy Narby, *Intelligence in Nature: An Inquiry into Knowledge.* New York: Tarcher/Penguin, 2006.

We have not ascribed "intelligence" to anything in nature previously. According to an article in the journal *Nature*, "What most people know about intelligence is, at best, distorted and, at worst, just wrong."[60] That's a profound statement.

When I heard Narby's talk "Intelligence in Nature" and how he kept running into his own disbelief, I understood completely. I had done this myself for decades. Eventually both of us felt that we needed to do research outside our own fields into areas that we experienced but science (at the time) claimed could not exist. Let me tell you that is not a very comfortable place to be. I wrote a poem about my relationship with this conflict in the early 1980s titled "Forever." The first two lines say it all:

Forever I have run to these shores,
Forever I have run from these shores ...

The poem goes on, but these lines sum up my relationship with the world that I could "touch" without my hands and "see" without my eyes. Like a moth to the proverbial flame, no matter how hard I tried to ignore or avoid these shores, I was inexorably drawn back.

It was torturous for me in many ways. I did not feel as though the things I was aware of were valuable, and on top of that, sometimes the things I was aware of scared me.

I wanted to be more like everyone else. I tried so hard, but no matter how much I swore off working with energy, connecting and communicating with plants, animals and nature in general, I simply could not maintain it for long.

Any time I was feeling hurt or lonely (which was often), I found myself drawn to water — a stream, a pond, the Long Island Sound or the ocean. A stream among the trees was exquisite. I would not just find solace in these places, but they provided me with what I described as a food of sorts. I could feel energy I was receiving very strongly on the tops of my forearms, an inch or two below the elbow. Back then I knew nothing of chakras, so feeling this sense of being energized through that part of my arm made no sense to me at all. I talked to friends, but no one else that I knew experienced this. As I got older and learned about the seven chakras, I still got absolutely no help, because these are located along our trunk, not our extremities. So you see, even what I was able to learn from more exotic sources left me in the dark, believing that my senses were lying to me. How

---

[60] *Nature*, May 22 2017. https://www.nature.com/news/intelligence-research-should-not-be-held-back-by-its-past-1.22021.

ironic that in my research for this book, I learned that the seven most widely recognized chakras are not all of the chakras; in fact, there are many all over the body! How exciting to realize that I was aware of something real.

To know and understand things in a deep place inside me that I could not defend (much less explain) to other people was incredibly isolating. It took me decades to come to terms with both being isolated and being so radically different. On top of being dyslexic, I grew up feeling very out of sync with most of what humans did and valued.

I have had many experiences in my life, starting from about four years old, that might be considered "supernatural." Because I had no teachers and no cultural or spiritual context to put these in, I often found myself vacillating between denial, despair and sometimes terror. Not that there were not beautiful things that occurred (like healing the horse), but not having guidance or a context to put things in caused so much angst! The only thing I could do to try and keep functioning at all normally was to file each incident away as being an odd experience, not to be dwelled upon.

In an attempt to find peace with this mysterious world I was privy to, but had no understanding of, I took psychic awareness development classes in my early 20s with Craig Junjulas[61] (amongst others). I did well at them in general but was really successful at psychometry (the reading of objects or photos). But even this was not enough for me to fully believe or stop my vacillations.

Still, because I was unsuccessful at blocking these awarenesses and experiences, I was forced to keep studying and learning, collecting dots. I studied with several South American shamans. Here again I had some profound experiences, dreams and visions that were very powerful, without the use of any plant medicine/teachers.

Studying Reiki increased my experience in working with energy, as well as in seeing the unseen, and by the time I became a Reiki Master and Instructor in 2008, I had learned to accept, and even value, the things I "saw" during a Reiki session. However, it wasn't until I started studying modern Shamanism that I had a deeper context to put these experiences in. I truly began to understand myself and my place in the world. I began to find true peace.

By 1994 Jeremy Narby had a radical shift in his thinking. He had succeeded in stepping beyond his ethnocentric beginnings and was now

---

[61] Craig Junjulas, "Higher Self Discovery," http://higherselfdiscovery.com/ (accessed 12-28-20).

convinced that plants and animals could communicate. But he still had internal work to do since he was not able at that point to go beyond his anthropocentric perspective. During this time, he wrote a book called *The Cosmic Serpent.* Here is the first quote you see when you open the book: "Those who love wisdom must investigate many things" (Heraclitus).[62] After completing that book, he began in earnest to search for scientifically provable signs of intelligence in nature (the title of his second book). He pored through scientific literature in biology, zoology, and botany (not unlike what I have done). He said, "It seemed that the more deeply science looked into the intricacies of how nature works, the more intelligence it found."[63] Nothing that an open heart could not tell us.

Go out in nature, be open. Wander. The art of wandering can be a profound experience. Let yourself be pulled by the beauty of a tree or a rock; walk in that direction. Let a bird's song or its direction of flight carry you. Become entranced by a beam of sunlight on the dark forest floor, or a far-off glistening of sunlight on water. Allow the sound of water or the calls of spring peepers to wash through your body and heal you. Pretend for a moment that these things are all secret messages for you (just for you), leading you on a magical journey. Be open. Look at the immediate environment that envelops you ... what has led or called you.

All that we have been taught encourages us away from these experiences. Sit for a moment and savor the feeling of each thing that catches your attention. Study these things, take them into your heart. Taste them with your senses. Breathe them in.

In studying something we can open ourselves to "knowing" it on other levels. With each breath, feel the magic of life oscillating around you. Breathe with it. How does that feel to you? Do parts of you feel nourished? Energized? Are you more relaxed? Develop a relationship with these experiences. Move on when you feel called to.

We don't understand everything. We don't need to. We are a part of an intricately interconnected web of life. Let it fill you. Don't judge inner promptings as silly or nonsensical. Just follow them in a childlike manner, with joy and wonder. The more you can incorporate or embody this childlike wonder, this belief that nature is communicating with you, the more open you will become to experiencing this biofeedback loop between

---

[62] Jeremy Narby, *The Cosmic Serpent: DNA and the Origins of Knowledge,* Jeremy P. Tarcher/Putnam, 1999.

[63] Jeremy Narby, *Intelligence in Nature: An Inquiry into Knowledge.* New York: Jeremy P. Tarcher/Penguin, 2006.

yourself and nature. This connection nourished humanity for thousands of years. It kept me alive through a childhood packed with isolation, self-doubt, and pain. It can and will nourish and heal you as well.

9. Somatic Experience

Where do emotional memories live? And why would that even matter?

If trauma is stored only in the mind, as psychologists thought for a long time, then treating it with drugs and talk therapy should stop a person from reliving the traumatic moment, as in a post-traumatic (PTSD) flashback. However, these practices have been only moderately effective.

Sit for a moment, close your eyes, take a couple of deep, slow breaths and remember a time you experienced a strong emotion. It can be a positive memory or a negative one. Sit with it. Remember as many details from this moment as you can. After a minute or two of this, tell me where in your body does the feeling of this experience reside?

Do you experience a sense of tension or tightness somewhere? A sense of folding in on yourself? Some people are aware of a pressure or a weight in a part of their bodies. If it's a positive experience, you might feel a tingling, a sense of release or expansiveness, or perhaps a feeling of unwinding. Where does it seem to generate from? Do you feel it in your mind? Or do you feel it somewhere in your body?

There are no right or wrong answers. This is an exercise for you to explore yourself, at whatever level of self-awareness you are at. Remember, knowledge is power. Self-knowledge leads to mastery, and when you have mastered yourself, all things are possible! You are your own best friend … or your own worst enemy; most of us are a combination of the two. The point is we have choices, different ones than we were probably taught about.

As I said earlier, in the field of psychology they used to believe trauma was stored in the mind, as some kind of chemical imprint in the brain. Recently a new paradigm has evolved, one that recognizes trauma as being stored in the cells of our body as well. Psychologists refer to this as a somatic experience.

Having a somatic experience triggered is like suddenly finding yourself in a snow globe. Trapped in an encapsulated environment, you experience in detail every sensation that occurred at the exact moment the experience got stored here. The entirety of the traumatic moment, the sounds, smells, sights and physical sensations, is all encapsulated.

Experiencing a traumatic somatic memory, like a PTSD flashback, is like suddenly finding ourselves flung from our beds, or car, or office chair into in a snow globe that's being shaken — we are tossed around, engulfed in the turmoil, the blinding swirling snow and the howling freezing winds, instantaneously. It can be completely overwhelming and totally compelling.

From a sensory perspective, if you are someone that dissociates, I believe that you may actually be entering a protective, sensory-deadening somatic snow globe.

The dissociated snow globe gets created when a being is so afraid, and/or in so much physical pain, that it feels completely powerless to change its situation; it feels trapped and in great danger. The response to this much stress seems to be to create a snow globe in which most sensory information is deadened. It can feel like it's filled with a soft packing material, or as though the air inside is denser than that outside this globe. It can be experienced as pressing against you, deadening outside sounds and other stimuli. Time operates differently within these globes; it is distorted. You feel your body, but things around you are distanced; you are once or twice removed from the world around you. Sometimes it is hard to speak when you are inside this type of snow globe. It is a protective bubble, but like any coping mechanism, the bubble can outlive its usefulness. Entering a dissociative bubble may have helped you survive an abusive parent when you were young and powerless, but make it easier for an abuser to have power over you when you are older, because you cannot access your power to make changes from here. This is strictly a place where you run to help you endure things you cannot change.

Because these moments are stored within us, they can seem closer to us, and in some ways more real, than the external world or "reality." We have a unique relationship with them because they "live" inside us. We live the same moment over and over, which brings about great familiarity. This intimate relationship with our traumatic somatic memories, over time, can cause us to feel a little lost. Our ability to feel connected to the outer world, where loved ones, friends, and family dwell, can become blocked or even feel severed, because these things are less compelling; they are outside us, while our somatic traumatic memories are inside us.

Being transported from the present moment into our somatic snow globes, without consciously willing it, distances us from people around us, who can't usually understand what we experience, nor can they visit with us there. Somatic memories are isolating because they are so personal.

Great breakthroughs in helping people with things like PTSD have evolved because of this new somatic understanding. However, there seems to be little to no study of where positive memories are stored, while psychiatrists and psychologists have put lots of time into studying where negative emotions are kept.

It makes sense because these professionals are rarely asked to help people deal with positive experiences. For example, most people don't experience being crippled by positive memories. Also, there is not much profit in big business discovering the location of positive memories — quite the opposite, actually. And that is why it's important for you to identify where your positive somatic memories are within you, as well as to practice accessing them. Dr. Maxwell Maltz states, "Experimental and clinical psychologists have proved beyond a shadow of a doubt that the human nervous system cannot tell the difference between an 'actual' experience and an experience imagined vividly and in detail."[64]

From the perspective of self-healing, which is what much of this book is about, it is important for us to understand that all the feelings that we have ever experienced are stored in their entirety in the cells of our bodies. This includes pleasant snow globes as well as unpleasant ones.

Within this profound concept is the possibility of having more choice and more power than we currently realize in terms of where we "dwell" internally. Remember earlier when I stated that new experiences create new somatic memories? This is important because, if we have the ability to change which somatic memory we are in, perhaps we do not need to stay in a traumatic one; we can consciously switch to a positive one. Remember that the positive ones we usually reach by choice, whereas the traumatic ones are often thrust upon us. Actors for example are taught to enter different somatic memories, both good and bad, to fulfill their roles.

To switch a snow globe to a beach globe takes strength. It can feel exactly like wrestling with a powerful opponent who outweighs you and has you pinned! Extracting yourself from this position takes practice. The practice creates an inner agility. Here is where we can utilize those pathways between neurons to our advantage. If practicing something allows us to travel particular pathways with greater ease and speed, then practicing on a daily basis visiting your positive snow globes is powerful. In a

---

[64] Maxwell Maltz, *Psycho-Cybernetics*, New York: Pocket Books, 1969.

time of need, you will be able to muscle your way out of a traumatic one into the one with the beach. Intimate familiarity with the positive ones, and the transition, is required to accomplish this.

Imagine a world of people being able to access positive snow globes at will. These folks would undoubtedly need less therapy, fewer drugs, and fewer outside distractions (like food, sex, or shopping). They might also be more relaxed, happier, less stressed, more creative, more deeply connected to and more aware of themselves. They would also be farther down the path of self-acceptance and more able to love themselves.

Because we have grown up in a culture that does not honor the power of a wholistic being, or wholistic awareness, somatic experiences are only honored in their unbalanced, negative manifestations, the treatment of which has become a profitable business.

This view, like many others embraced by modern western thinking, dismembers us. "United we stand, divided we fall." This truism exists in the microcosm and the macrocosm.

If you are someone who is subject to experiencing dramatic, unpleasant somatic memories without your conscious volition, it is easy to feel overwhelmed, stressed, violated, and terribly isolated.

According to all the great mystics, we come into this world alone, and that is how we leave. So somatic experiences isolating us is not necessarily a bad thing. Cocooning ourselves deeply in our own positive snow globe can be very natural, soothing, and beneficial.

It can have another interesting benefit for the skilled practitioner. With practice, any energy that you ever connected to is available for you to access any time you want. All you have to do is step into the somatic globe connected to that energy. The vibrational signature of any energy you have experienced is recorded by your body, just the way your mind records visual information. Think about that. You have the ability to recall that signature at any time and by doing so immerse yourself in that vibration. This is one of the very real reasons that you don't need to "possess" things, or places, or people. The energy imprint within your body is yours to experience any time you wish.

There have been recent studies showing how water catches the energetic imprint of everything ever placed in it. We are some 90-odd percent water ... think about that.

This is something Dr. Bach discovered and he used this principle to develop the Bach flower remedies. His remedies, called Bach Flower Essences, are literally the energy imprint of specific flowers in water. This might sound utterly odd, but his discoveries work. His formula called Rescue Remedy is the number one selling stress aid in the world. Here is a quote from his book *Heal Thyself* that you can download from the Bach Center: "Disease is in essence the result of conflict between Soul and Mind ... No effort directed to the body alone can do more than superficially repair damage." [65]

More recently, in an effort to demonstrate the effect of vibrational frequencies produced by our thoughts and spoken words on cellular structure, Dr. Masaru Emoto[66] subjected water specimens to specific thoughts and feelings. He then froze those specimens and photographed the effects of projected energies on the shape of the frozen water crystals. The results are quite dramatic; you can read about the experiments and the results in his book *The Hidden Messages in Water* or locate videos on line.

If you are uncomfortable in your life, you need to move. Do something different. Alcoholics Anonymous has a great maxim "Move a muscle, change a thought," and it is a powerful tool. I am a highly emotional person; I feel things very deeply. When I am upset, if I am lucky enough be with someone that I can express my feelings to (and I feel heard), I still often need to change my physical location to actually feel better. If I don't feel heard, then I won't feel better with that person, and moving physically is still important to my finding my own peace. Taking a brisk walk in nature is my preferred coping tool. It allows me to transition. Physically staying in the same place tends to keep me in a similar emotional space. If a walk is not possible, then even changing rooms can help free up the energy enough for me to successfully shift it. It ties back into to the definition of insanity, "Doing the same thing and expecting different results." If you are uncomfortable in your skin, do something different.

---

[65] Edward Bach. *Heal Thyself, An explanation of the real cause and cure of disease,* 1931. The Dr Edward Bach Centre, Mount Vernon, Bakers Lane, Brightwell-cum-Sotwell Oxon OX10 0PZ, United Kingdom, www.bachcentre.com, https://www.bachcentre.com/wp-content/uploads/2019/10/heal_thy.pdf.

[66] Masaru Emoto, *The Hidden Messages in Water.* Atria Books, Sept. 20, 2005.

10. Feelings

Why do I include feelings in the section called Physical? I do so because feelings are vibrational frequencies and very much a part of our physical makeup, while still being energetic in nature.

Let's start by exploring the concept that there are no bad feelings! Some aren't pleasant to experience, but we were created to feel the whole gamut of human feelings, the ones currently labeled "bad" and the ones labeled "good." Everything within us has a good purpose; what has gone wrong is our education. For instance, we are not taught to communicate anger constructively. Instead we have been taught that the realm of emotions is like a competition. To "win" at being angry, you need to be the loudest person in the room, or the one throwing the biggest tantrum. Then you "win" because you overpower your partner/opponent. But what does that behavior win us over time? Not the love and support we each crave.

It's not rocket science. We all want to be heard, accepted and loved. We all have the very same emotions. How is it that we have evolved the ability to create an airplane to sail through the sky but we can't sail through our own emotional tides, surfing with our loved ones and coworkers with finesse, confidence and deep-seated joy?

The expression of all of your true feelings need not hurt or damage anyone! Did you know that that was possible?

Owning how you feel is an important step. You are not owning what you feel when you say "You made me feel ... (angry, hurt, etc.)." This is an inflammatory statement; it will probably elicit more of the same. However, saying "When you said ..., I felt .... " is owning the feeling that you felt. What transpired, and your resultant feelings, were simply where that experience took you. Or, if you are more comfortable with this phraseology, you could say "When ... happened, I felt ... ."

Don Miguel Ruiz says[67] that we should not take what others say about us personally. He teaches that what others say about you is not about you, it is about them. This may feel hard to integrate into your thinking initially, especially if you have been taught by a parent, sibling, or spouse about being a victim. Being a victim is unempowering. Your only power there is to demonstrate how much you have been hurt. The effectiveness of that stance is limited by your audience. Do they care? Are they supportive? Neither of these is a given. If you are being a victim, and your audience is not responding in a way that feeds you, that supports you, what are your choices? One common choice is to escalate your stance of being hurt. We do this by focusing ourselves and our audience on our being wounded, which is not really a powerful place to be. But if you understand why you did what you did, as well as what about the situation made you feel as you did, it gives you power in those situations. From this perspective, you can endeavor to either not place yourself in a situation like that again or communicate your position on the subject next time. You could also choose not to be around that particular audience again.

I am not referring here to how we should respond to criminal activities, but to the stances we take in our everyday lives with our peers, family and coworkers.

Shining the light of your awareness on the situation when you felt unempowered or victimized and exploring what you find with a curiosity that originates in a desire to grow, to get your needs met, to feel stronger, is beneficial to you. To steep yourself in self-awareness is the first step. Doing so makes perfect sense, and the fact that we are taught to ignore our internal workings is ludicrous. You need to learn how to communicate your internal processes without the unhealthy ways we see around us every day; blaming, bullying, and whining all are forms of misdirecting and manipulation, which essentially amount to powerlessness because they do not allow us to find ourselves, connect to others in meaningful ways or set ourselves free.

When people practice this type of honest self-awareness and communication, curiosity develops. Communication changes from a threatening thing to one of exploration that brings people closer together, not drives them apart.

If you or your partner is not versed in constructive communication, sit down and discuss guidelines that you will both attempt to adhere to. The

---

[67] Don Miguel Ruiz, *The Four Agreements*, Amber-Allen Publishing, Inc. July 10, 2018.

first rule should be that when the person who is hurting shares, the listener repeats what he or she believes the hurt person said. This often helps the hurt person examine what is going on in a different way. He or she will typically say "Well yes, that's exactly how it was for me!" or "No, it was more like this .... " Together you can arrive at an understanding of what the hurt person was feeling. It may take several rounds for the hurt person to feel fully heard. It would be helpful if you do not take what is said personally, again adopting a curious attitude, one that focuses on improving the relationship.

If you have ever felt hurt by an interaction and had the person you experienced this with respond supportively, it is an amazing feeling. It is a rare gift in our modern world. It is also a very healing experience, one that brings people closer together.

Once the first speaker (the person who was hurting) feels heard, then he or she needs to switch from being the communicator to being the one who is listening. At that point it is time for the person who was listening initially to share any feelings that came up. The former hurt person now repeats back what he or she understood the new communicator to say, always being conscious to own what he or she is expressing. It is not about having the floor and trying to exact as much damage as you can. Keep your eye on the bigger goal of growing closer and creating a relationship where there is trust. This encourages a deep respect and compassion that grows, thereby creating a lovely relationship.

This is just an example of what educated, constructive communication looks like. It is not rocket science, but it is foreign to our current paradigm. So, if you are not getting relief or not feeling closer to others when you try to express your feelings, perhaps you need to look at how you communicate, rather than labeling the feeling, or yourself, as bad. It also may indicate that you need to cultivate new relationships and let go of others.

I have practiced these techniques for decades. I studied them in a program called Receptive Listening in the early 1980s where we learned about putting our own feelings/reactions aside while the speaker expressed him- or herself. The instructors used the analogy of "tucking your feelings under your arm" while receptively listening to the speaker. Here's one of the tricky parts. The first person to bring up feelings is always the speaker until he or she feels heard. But this person must endeavor to own all his or her feelings. It is not a forum for beating up the listener. It takes practice.

Carl Rodgers developed a therapeutic model known as person-centered therapy. It also involves the listener (therapist) restating the speaker's (client's) position, to the satisfaction of the speaker.

How many of you have experienced trying to tell someone how you feel, hoping for relief, and find that the mere act of expressing yourself causes the other person to react strongly and you end up in an argument? Did you feel any better afterwards? Having your feelings acknowledged rather than being dismissed or argued with is priceless. It allows you to move beyond needing to defend yourself to a place where you can actually open up more. This causes you to experience feeling safe and cared about by the other person, which allows you to relax and let your guard down. The process helps individuals establish their own integrity within themselves and within the relationship.

I studied Receptive Listening for two years. I have continued practicing the receptive listening techniques since and would like to think I have gotten good at it. I also recently became certified in Creative Arts Therapy, developed by Natalie Rodgers, Carl Rodgers's daughter, which helped me deepen my awareness, techniques and practice of receptive listening.

I often find myself in the position of practicing what I have learned, even though partners, friends, or business associates do not reciprocate. My training asks me to stick to the high road, putting my feelings aside in order to help others find their truths and a state of balance. I will listen quietly to them, tucking my own reactions under my arm. Then I feed back to them what I think I have heard them say. What I am getting at here is that even if you become adept at this skill, honoring and reflecting back to the speaker what you heard, there is no guarantee that, when it's your time to share your truth, your partner will return the favor.

Trust me: there is a value in practicing these skills even if you are doing it in a vacuum, so to speak. There is *no* way to heal rifts in relationships using our current techniques. There are some great books and workshops available. I can't find a reference to Receptive Listening as a program anymore, but Marshall Rosenberg created Non-Violent Communication (NVC), which utilizes many of the same principles. Before his death he trained some others and one of them, Pan Vera, is continuing his teachings.[68] As I mentioned earlier *Talking Together* is a book we used for Receptive Listening. There is a site called "14 Conflict Resolution Skills" that will help you get a better understanding of the importance of these skills.

---

[68] Pan Vera, "LifeServing Communication," https://lifeserving.com/lifeserving-communication/.

With the new understanding in psychology that feelings are stored in our cells comes the very real fact that what you have felt in your life is always yours, and not just the bad stuff! You may not fully grasp this yet, but ultimately you get to choose which emotional snow globe you spend your time in. Like a muscle that is atrophied, with diligence we can remember, or figure out, how to flex it, practice our successes and gain more control.

So how can you do this? Here are some practices to give you the greatest ability to respond to whatever snow globe you've popped into and to transition out.

Our consciousness is our first tool. Creating appropriate paths or connections in our brains which facilitate moving our consciousness to a different place in our bodies is a great start.

Knowing the general location of feelings (like trauma, depression and hopelessness) in our bodies that distract us from being present and sap our energy is helpful — just as is being aware of where in your body joy, bliss or happiness is stored.

To locate the latter, sit or lie quietly in a comfortable place. Close your eyes and breathe slowly and deeply. Remember a time when you were really happy or felt love washing over or through you. You could also look for a moment of joy, bliss or safety. Take all the time you like visiting this place. Maxwell Maltz says in *Psycho-Cybernetics*:

> Experimental and clinical psychologists have proved beyond the shadow of a doubt that the human nervous system cannot tell the difference between an 'actual' experience and an experience imagined vividly and in detail. . . . You can acquire information from reading a book. But to 'experience' you must creatively respond to information. Acquiring information itself is passive. Experiencing is active. When you 'experience,' something happens inside your nervous system and your midbrain. New 'engrams' and 'neural' patterns are recorded in the grey matter of your brain. [69]

The more detailed you make these immersions in positive somatic feelings, the more benefits you gain. Recall any sounds associated with this experience. Perhaps there was a smell, like flowers, or the ocean or the rich loam of the forest floor. It could be the smell of your mother's apple pie, cookies, anything really. Was there a color or a quality to the light in this moment? Spend time here and become intimately aware of each nuance.

---

[69] Maxwell Maltz, *Psycho-Cybernetics*, New York: Pocket Books, 1969.

Next notice if there is a place in your body that resonates with this feeling. If not, don't worry about it; just come back to this practice often. Try to do it at least once a day using each of the positive feelings mentioned above. Each positive feeling may be located in a different place in your body, or not. If they are different, make note of the locations. Once you have located a positive somatic memory, stay with it. Dwell there; notice the sights, sounds, smells and sensations. Breathe into them. Imagine the feeling to be a beautiful spark of colored light, see it pulsating, and each time it pulsates it grows wider. Breathe into this light, this feeling, and see it expanding with each breath. Experience the feeling becoming stronger. Sit with this sensory experience/visualization for at least a minute. The longer you stay there, the more effect it will have on you.

If you practice this exercise at least once a day, perhaps as you are getting ready to fall asleep at night or upon first awakening, you will not only grow positive feelings within your body, you will facilitate your ability to access such feelings. Remember, what we focus on grows.

This is very important when you are combating an emotional experience that you are not enjoying, like PTSD. When you pop into a tumultuous snow globe, if you have exercised the pathways to positive feelings (and created the new connections in your brain), the positive experiences will be easier to get to and quite possibly more powerful when you need them. If you turn to them only when you are in the middle of a traumatic episode, it will be harder (but never impossible) to change your location somatically within yourself. What do I mean by that? Think of these snow globes and beach globes as constellations within your body or as destinations. You have to know someplace, including its relative location, to get to it reliably. Because these are often sensory memories, how we can find them is by their feel. The more you get to know the details of a positive snow globe, the easier it is to get there. As Dr. Maltz points out in *Psycho-Cybernetics*, the human nervous system can't tell the difference between a vividly imagined experience and a "real" one.

If you experience traumatic flashbacks, the understanding that these are encapsulated emotional memories stored within your body can help change your relationship with them.

Here is a truism. Positive feelings don't generally knock you off your feet. But negative ones can feel as if they smack you across the face, knock you down and sit on your chest. This is why developing your awareness and learning to focus it are so important. What we focus on grows. If you can learn to choose and direct your focus, you can be more comfortable in your life. A very helpful tool set in shifting where we come from internally is the Bach Flower Remedies I spoke of earlier in the chapter. These have the ability to lift us out of somatic experiences where we no longer choose to dwell. They are inexpensive and very effective.

11. Acupuncture

What is your immediate response to the words "energy" and "healing" in the same sentence? Does it strike you as mumbo-jumbo? Make you feel incredulous, suspicious ...? I get that. For decades, no matter how often I was exposed to powerful, unconventional experiences involving either of them, I would typically start to doubt those experiences within hours or days. I couldn't find a way past the perspectives of my culture, which said that either these experiences were dangerous or they were not real. The cycle of experiencing something outside the box, and then either being afraid or doubting it, was exhausting. I needed teachers that I could trust to help guide me, but they were not present in my life. It was hard enough being a young person trying to navigate my way towards adulthood; navigating the supernatural all by myself in addition was almost too much.

Everyday experience tells us you can only fit a single cup of water in a one-cup measuring cup — you cannot put more. Is there a valid reason to push past our familiar, familial perspectives? To go from being a cup to become a quart or gallon container? According to Albert Szent-Györgyi and Dr. Maxwell Maltz, to name a few, there is. Maltz points out that:

> Any breakthrough in science is likely to come from outside the system. 'Experts' are the most thoroughly familiar with the developed knowledge inside the proscribed boundaries of a given science. Any new knowledge must usually come from the outside — not from 'experts,' but from what someone has defined as an 'inpert.'[70]

So it is vitally important for all of us to really look at things and, from the information that we find, draw our own conclusions. Maltz points out examples such as the fact that the men who developed the first airplanes were bicycle mechanics, not aeronautical engineers. Einstein was a mathematician, not a physicist. Madame Curie was a physicist yet made

---

[70] Maxwell Maltz, *Psycho-Cybernetics*, Pocket Books, New York, 1969.

important findings in medicine. If these examples are not enough to illustrate the importance of being open to ideas outside popular thinking, then let's look at some historical facts.

What if I told you that five thousand years ago there was a culture so aware of energy that its members were able to accurately map minute energy flows through the body? Their awareness of this energy flow enabled a body of knowledge to emerge in which the practitioners were able to demonstrate a connection between specific ailments when the energy in different pathways became sluggish. They also determined that other diseases would manifest when these pathways became blocked, as well as which pathways could be stimulated to heal many ailments. Who were these folks? The Chinese!

They called these energy pathways meridians. The early practitioners of acupuncture couldn't actually see these pathways. There was no technology available to allow them to do so, outside their own intuition, discernment and external observation. As a matter of fact, it has only been in the last 60 years that science has been able to "discover" (see) them. In the early 1960s Dr. Bong-Han Kim,[71] a Korean scientist, was the first person to work with a technology that allowed these meridians to actually be seen by a human. Dr. Kim's findings were called the Bong-Han Theory.[72]

Scientists are also finding parallels between the ancient concepts and modern anatomy. Many of the 365 acupuncture points correspond to nerve bundles or muscle trigger points. Several meridians track major arteries and nerves. "If people have a heart attack, the pain will radiate up across the chest and down the left arm. That's where the heart meridian goes," says Peter Dorsher, a specialist in pain management and rehabilitation at the Mayo Clinic in Jacksonville, Fla. "Gallbladder pain will radiate to the right upper shoulder, just where the gallbladder meridian goes."[73]

---

[71] Vitaly Vodyanoy, Oleg Pustovyy, Ludmila Globa, and Iryna Sorokulova, "Primo-Vascular System as Presented by Bong-Han Kim." *Evidence-Based Complementary and Alternative Medicine*, Volume 2015, Article ID 361974. https://www.hindawi.com/journals/ecam/2015/361974/.

[72] Kwang-Sup Soh, Kyung A. Kang, and Yeon Hee Ryu, "50 Years of Bong-Han Theory and 10 Years of Primo Vascular System," *Evidence-Based Complementary and Alternative Medicine*, Volume 2013, Article ID 587827. https://www.hindawi.com/journals/ecam/2013/587827/.

[73] Melinda Beck, "Decoding an Ancient Therapy: High-tech Tools Show How Acupuncture Works in Treating Arthritis, Back Pain, Other Ills," *The Wall Street Journal*, March 22, 2010, https://www.wsj.com/articles/SB10001424052748704841304575137872667749264.

There are striking differences in the anatomical structure of acupuncture points versus non-acupuncture points. Dr. Kim published five papers on his findings between 1962 and 1965, after which he suddenly vanished. His work was not explored further until recently. The renewed interest was spurred by Dr. Kwang-Sup Soh and a group of researchers on his team, put together specifically to study Dr. Kim's work. They realized that the failure of other scientists to repeat Dr. Kim's work was partly due to the need for the researchers to be adept surgeons, because of the extremely small nature of the vascular systems involved. Dr. Soh's team was able to confirm many of Kim's findings. They renamed what Kim had called the Bong-Han theory as the primo vascular system.

Further research on the primo vascular system has shown that stem cells, which play an important part in healing, are present in these channels. According to the U.S. National Library of Medicine:

> Stem cells are cells with the potential to develop into many different types of cells in the body. They serve as a repair system for the body. There are two main types of stem cells: embryonic stem cells and adult stem cells.
>
> Stem cells are different from other cells in the body in three ways:
> - They can divide and renew themselves over a long time
> - They are unspecialized, so they cannot do specific functions in the body
> - They have the potential to become specialized cells, such as muscle cells, blood cells, and brain cells[74]

Acupuncture does have real effects on the human body, which scientists are documenting using high-tech tools. Neuroimaging studies show that acupuncture seems to calm areas of the brain that register pain and activate those involved in rest and recuperation. Doppler ultrasound shows that acupuncture increases blood flow in treated areas. Thermal imaging shows that it can make inflammation subside.

In 1991 Russian researchers at the Institute for Clinical and Experimental Medicine in Novosibirsk, USSR, discovered that these meridians not only carry light, but that they do so even if they are bent or twisted! Under the leadership of Professor Kaznachejew, a light beam was directed at a right angle onto several different parts of people's skin to measure the

---

[74] "Stem Cells," Courtesy of MedlinePlus from the National Library of Medicine or Source: MedlinePlus, National Library of Medicine. https://medlineplus.gov/stem-cells.html.

reaction of the skin to visible light. A simple laboratory lamp was used with the addition of

> several different filters in front of the beam of light between the skin and the lamp. Suddenly the experimenters registered a light signal, a small speck of light on a place that was not lit up (about 10 cm. away from the lit area). One can imagine how astounded the researchers were when they found this light on a place other than the lit area which proves that the light has traveled beneath the skin."[75]

The method used was a photometric unit magnified by a photoluminescence microscope with a photomultiplier. Of particular interest is the finding that "The light conducting ability of the human body exists only along the meridians, and can enter and exit only along the acupuncture points."

Professor Fritz Albert Popp is a distinguished German physicist and researcher in cell biology. He is considered the father of biophotons, a type of light that has a high degree of order, which he describes as a "biological 'laser'" with a very stable field strength. "Because of their stable field strength, its waves can superpose, and by virtue of this, constructive and destructive interference effects become possible that do not occur in ordinary light." [76]

Popp has found that these particles of light, which have no mass, transmit information within and between cells. His work reveals that "DNA in a living cell stores and releases photons creating 'biophotonic emissions' that may hold the key to illness and health." There are other interesting aspects of DNA that we will get into later in this chapter, but for now can you guess where these biophotons travel? Only in the tubes described by the Chinese as acupuncture meridians!

Dr. Morry Silberstein of Curtin University has developed a new theory about the cutaneous intrinsic visceral afferent nervous system, which he refers to as "C fibers" that run along the acupuncture meridians. He says "We have known for some time that acupuncture points have a much lower electrical resistance than nearby areas of skin." [77] This means that not only

---

[75] Dr. Sergei Pankratov, *Meridians Conduct Light,* Published by Raum and Zeit, Germany, 1991, Translated from the German by Wolfgang Mitschrich. https://photonicthera-pyinstitute.com/meridians-conduct-light.

[76] Fritz Albert Popp, https://biontologyarizona.com/dr-fritz-albert-popp.

[77] Morry Silberstein, M.D., "Curtin researchers unlock the secrets of acupuncture." Media Release, Monday 5 October 2009. https://news.curtin.edu.au/media-releases/curtin-re-searchers-unlock-the-secrets-of-acupuncture/ (accessed 6/13/19).

do these channels carry light within the body, but they carry and respond to electromagnetic frequency more easily than the rest of our bodies.

Scientists have located twelve primary meridians (all of which were identified by the ancient Chinese). Three pairs flow up the body (considered yin by the Chinese), and three pairs flow down the body (considered yang). Each meridian was found to have a time of day when it was most active, as well as being influenced (weakened or strengthened) by a season and/or element. These correlations can be found in the Five Element Theory in Chinese medicine. This theory illustrates, beyond a doubt, that at a cellular level we are interconnected to the natural world, and that it is absolutely possible to discern deep truths about the functioning of our universe and our bodies without scientific equipment.

Ancient Chinese energy workers used the abilities that our human bodies evolved naturally to figure all this out. They were not alone. The Japanese developed a form of massage, called Shiatsu, that works directly with these meridians. It moves blocked energy (referred to by the Chinese as Chi) in these meridians, as do acupressure and forms of exercise such as Tai Chi and Qigong. These techniques can be employed to move and even increase energy in the meridians. The development of yoga in India some 2000 years ago was based on the awareness of 72,000 "nadis" (centers and pathways of energy). The Thai refer to them as "sen." Thai massage was developed using a combination of techniques, similar to Shiatsu, to move energy. Pain or disease can be relieved when energy that is stagnant or blocked is moved.

I can tell you personally that it works. In my search for dots to connect, at the tender age of nineteen I found myself in the Orient. That journey lasted for almost three years. During my travels, I picked up amoebas and some other intruders. The doctors over there put me on incredibly high doses of antibiotics. The result, between the the amoebas and the antibiotics to kill them, was that for several years I could barely eat because of pain in my gut. I lost way too much weight.

When I got home, my mom cried when she hugged me, saying that I looked and felt in her embrace like I had just come from a concentration camp. To say that my digestive system had not recovered even a year after returning home was putting it mildly. I had developed colitis, and there was not much that science or western medicine was doing for me. I was not eager to try acupuncture because I have never loved needles. Honestly, I just got to the point where I was willing to try anything. After my first treatment, the constant pain I had for over a year was 90 percent gone!

I was able to eat more food at dinner that night than I had in a whole day going back for months. I was ecstatic!

Since that day I have used acupuncture for many issues. I also personally witnessed amazing transformations in other patients whom I got to know in the waiting rooms of my acupuncturists.

DNA

I have shared some recent findings regarding DNA in several of the chapters we have covered, but I just ran across something new that I want to pass on to you. It comes from an article titled "DNA — the phantom effect, quantum hologram and etheric body" by Linda Gadbois. She opens by stating that modern science used to see DNA as something that was written in stone (so to speak), that what you saw was what you got. In other words, since DNA was first discovered folks felt that we were at the mercy of our genes. Gadbois says that only about two percent of our DNA is used to construct proteins from our parents' encoded genetic material. The other ninety-eight percent is referred to as "junk DNA," meaning that scientists don't know what it's used for.

This is a typical response from our current culture, to ignore what we don't understand or to label what we don't understand as valueless. Think of all the interesting, powerful things we could be missing because of this tendency. Dr. Gadbois states that we know now that instead of being static, "DNA is actually composed of a liquid crystalline substance that acts like an antenna, receiver, and transmitter of holographic information." DNA continually reads the vibrational signature of what is around it, both in the physical world and the unseen world she refers to as ether. Apparently DNA interprets information from "signs, archetypes and imagery" that are around it, whose vibrational frequency is within its range, translating it into holograms!

> It acts as a receiver for various forms of information within that same frequency that comes in as an acoustic wave that serves to form an electromagnetic field (EMF) as a holographic shape that's composed initially of subtle energy, which provides the blueprint or spatial mapping for constructing an exact replica as its material equivalent.[78]

---

[78] Linda Gadbois, "DNA — the phantom effect, quantum hologram and etheric body." *Scribd.com*, Vol. 7 Issue 1 2018, https://www.scribd.com/document/416285235/Phantom-DNA-and-etheric-body (accessed September 7 2019).

12. Crystalline Structures

In ancient Norse mythology there is a creation myth that has surprising relevance in our lives today. The Norse perceived a pre-world that existed before ours, consisting of two elements. When these two elements, Niflheim (northern land of cold, mists and fog) and Muspelheim (southern land of fire and smoke), interjected the essence of themselves (elemental sex?) into Ginnungagap (chaos/the dark void/nothingness), this exchange of opposite energies caused the crystallization of the visible universe.[79]

The fact that the Norse were accurate in their assessment of the universe being crystalline in nature blows me away! And this assessment was made without the aid of microscopes!

How is that possible? We will be looking at possible answers to that later in the book. For now I want to establish what recent findings are saying about the nature of the universe. In a study done in 2012 the Australian researchers say that the "Big Bang should be modeled as a phase change: the moment when an amorphous, formless universe analogous to liquid water cooled and suddenly crystallized to form four-dimensional space-time, analogous to ice."[80] But we are only just figuring this out.

Let's look at what we (science) know now. In the last sixty or seventy years science has discovered crystals in amazing places, from minerals, to metals, to organic creatures (like us). Did you know we have crystals in our bodies?

There are calcium carbonate crystals (similar to pearl) in our ears that allow us to find balance. They float in a viscous liquid in our inner ear, and when we shift our head position, they tip and press on nerves that send signals to our brain. Our calcium carbonate crystals act much like the

---

[79] D.L. Ashliman, "The Norse Creation Myth," abstracted from *The Prose Edda* of Snorri Sturluson, https://www.pitt.edu/~dash/creation.html (accessed May 2016).

[80] Natalie Wolchover, "Big Bang Was Actually a Phase Change, New Theory Says," *Space.com*, https://www.space.com/17217-big-bang-phase-change-theory.html (accessed 12-16-20).

needle in a compass does. Anyone who's experienced vertigo knows how important the proper functioning of these crystals in our ears is! Fish, who need to track themselves in a three-dimensional water world, have aragonite crystals in liquid in their heads to keep them oriented.

Our bones are calcium phosphate crystals in a lattice with hydroxyapatite crystals (which make up 65% of an adult's bone mass). We have a coating of apatite crystals covering the exposed surface of our teeth, making them hard enough to eat with. Our connective tissue, collagen and even the proteins that make us up are crystalline structures. Biological membranes, cell membranes and spider silk are all liquid crystal.[81]

What constitutes something being crystalline in nature? Its molecular structure. Crystals are highly organized structures, where the constituent molecules create a unit that is repeated three dimensionally in a lattice.

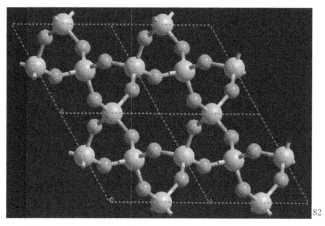

Figure 3. Crystal structure of an inorganic material: quartz.

This is important because highly organized molecular structures have some very interesting properties that will change the way you think about crystals. We will get into that further in a moment. Let's look at some examples of organic crystals within our bodies first.

Here is an example of the organic crystalline structure of a protein.

[81] "Cristales, Crystals of Your Body," (https://cristales.fundaciondescu-bre.es/?page_id=2151http://www.xtal.iqfr.csic.es/Cristalografia/parte_01-en.html.
[82] Martín Martínez Ripoll, Félix Hernández Cano, "Cristales - the Structure of Crystals," http://www.xtal.iqfr.csic.es/Cristalografia/parte_01-en.html.

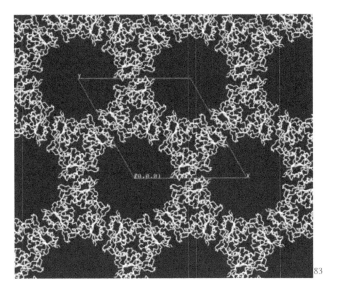

Figure 4. Organic crystalline structure.

The rhombus in Figure 4 is the "unit" that repeats spatially in three dimensions, creating a lattice.

Below is what a crystalline protein looks like three dimensionally.

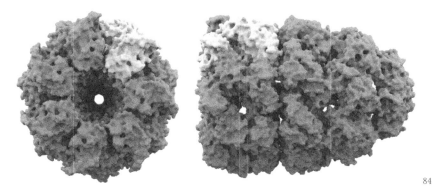

Figure 5. Protein in three dimensions.

It has the "unit" that is repeated spatially highlighted in light gray.

This protein (Figure 5) is named chaperoning, and it's the largest protein molecule that we know of. You can see that it is very porous. In our bodies these porous spaces become filled with water. It is because of this

---

[83] Graphic from http://www.xtal.iqfr.csic.es/Cristalografia/parte_01-en.html

[84] Photo by Thomas Splettstoesser, https://upload.wikimedia.org/wikipedia/commons/6/6c/Chaperonin_1AON.png (released under CC BY-SA 3.0 license).

space that organic crystals are weaker than mineral or metallic ones (and yes, metals are crystalline structures).

What determines the amount of space between molecules is the strength of the bonds between them. The strongest bond that we know of occurs between the carbon molecules of diamond.

I could easily draw a parable here. In our human world, the strength of our relationships depends on our ability to form bonds too. It is no different in the microcosm of the molecular world, as seen in molecular biology or physics.

The more I studied molecular biology and molecular physics, the more I became convinced that the macrocosm was reflected in the microcosm. There is so much to be gleaned from the behavior of these tiniest of units that make up us and our world ... and their message is undiluted, uncorrupted and pure. Up until very recently, no human has been able to change DNA or molecular structure. The laws that govern the existence or function of DNA and the universe had been untampered with. They are, logically, mandates from God, written into the fabric of our existence.

It then stands to reason that by examining these cellular and molecular mandates, we are able to understand many things, not just the functioning of molecules, but the actual functioning of ourselves and the universe. The microcosm and the macrocosm, in black and white.

Getting back to vibrational frequency, I'm going to explain the basis for my theory of a crystal's ability to affect us or help us shift our vibrational fields. I remember growing sugar crystals in grade school by dissolving sugar in hot water. We learned that what causes the crystallization is the fact that these sugar molecules are attracted to each other. Almost all liquids that are heated expand, so the heated water can hold more sugar crystals than cold water. As the solution cools it becomes super saturated, forcing the molecules to precipitate out of the solution. The precipitated sugar crystals attach themselves molecule by molecule to the seed crystal on a string in the beaker, forming a larger and larger crystal. This again is due to the attraction between these sugar molecules.

What held my attention back in the 80s was the knowledge that all the things that make up molecules vibrate. In a crystal there is only one type of molecule, and it is repeated exactly in each unit of the lattice, over and over again. This fact led me to surmise that the natural resulting vibrational frequency in a crystal specimen would be purer and stronger than in substances with multiple constituents (where the vibrational signatures will vary).

Try looking at it this way: consider the ripples caused by a pebble dropped into a pond (Figure 6).

Figure 6. Single vibrational frequency.

This is (almost) a perfect example of what a single molecular vibration, repeating outward without much interference, might look like. Actually, each ring expanding from around the source would be exactly the same height and same width and same distance apart (unless it hit interference of some sort).

Figure 7. Multiple vibrational frequencies.

---

[85] Photo by Koen Emmers, https://unsplash.com/@andreasemmers86 (accessed on 12-25-20).

[86] Photo by Artem Spaegin, https://unsplash.com/@sapegin (accessed 12-25-20).

Now imagine multiple molecular patterns occurring in a substance. The different frequencies would naturally interfere with each other, sometimes weakening the vibrational force of each constituent or even canceling each other out completely. Figure 7 is an example of how something with multiple vibrational frequencies could look. And in Figure 8 below you can see how these different frequencies are creating chaos in the vibrational fields:

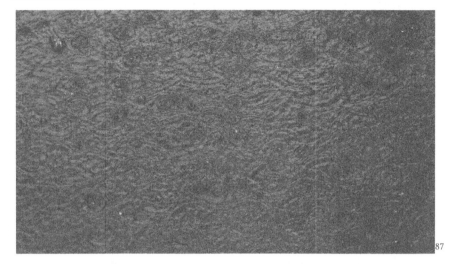

Figure 8. Chaos in vibrational field.

Finally we can see what a repeated frequency that is mostly the same would look like in Figure 9. As you can see, a substance that has a pure, single, vibrational signature produces a stronger emanation, or rippling effect, into the environment. If you put hundreds or thousands of excited molecules together (as occurs in a large crystal), the strength of the frequency would increase. It is just simple mathematics at this point (or so it seemed to me).

---

[87] Photo by Raden Fendyto on unsplash.com (accessed 12-20-20).

Figure 9. Similar frequencies.

We are talking on the atomic level, but nonetheless, crystals should have the strongest unified vibrational frequency of anything occurring naturally on our planet. This vibrational frequency which emanates outward from all matter, I surmised, must be naturally stronger in a crystal. These frequencies are a source of steady low electromagnetic frequencies (EMFs). When I was in college, I was not aware that low EMFs could be beneficial to the human body. Back then the media wasn't talking about strong EMFs being harmful to the body either. What I did know was that people used crystals for healing and I concluded that the reason why certain crystals were said to heal certain parts of the body must be because of a sympathetic frequency between the crystal and a corresponding organ (when healthy).

Scientists have been playing around with crystalline structures since the late 1800s because of their ability to transfer energy, store energy, and refract light. These abilities are of interest to corporations, because they have applications that can be used in big business. Remember experiments and research take time and money. Scientists dismiss low EMF because it is of no commercial use. They are interested only in molecular structures that are excited in a "horsepower" kind of way. Most of the time only

[88] Photo by Jason Leung, https://unsplash.com/s/photos/jason-leung.

things that have a large profit-making potential receive funding. There has not been a much profit in examining the small-scale abilities of crystalline structures.

However, studies conducted worldwide over the last six decades have shown that low EMFs help the human body to heal! For example, in the early 1970s (Levy 1974, Klapper and Stallard 1974)[89] found that, from as deep within our bodies as broken bones to surface skin cells, humans respond positively to low EMFs. We explore this more in the chapter titled "EMFs," but suffice it to say that during this sixty-year span researchers have also established that strong EMFs make us sick.

Getting back to crystalline structure; as I said earlier, I came up with a theory in my early twenties on why crystals could help us heal and how they might correspond to different parts of the body, emotions, or thought patterns. I shared this on a small scale with students and clients for decades, but in 2014 I was asked to give a lecture on Vibrational Frequency and Crystal Awareness at the American Society of Dowsers. I was to be speaking in front of possibly 200 people. It suddenly became important to me that I could substantiate my decades-old theory with current science. I started poring through everything I could find about crystals and EMFs.

Even though the repeated single frequency within a crystal should create a stronger vibrational field than something with multiple vibrational signatures, everything I could find was stating that this field could not be strong enough to be of any significance on its own.

Scientists kept insisting that the molecules would need to be incited to give off any significant level of frequency. Things like light, heat or sound can incite molecules. For example, by passing a light beam through a ruby crystal one can create a super powered laser. So rubies can be used to create a powerful tool, or weapon, but most scientists discount the vibrational frequency of the ruby sitting on your coffee table.

This did not make any sense to me. I knew that it was possible to feel a ruby's frequencies when it was lying on a coffee table (or those of the rose quartz mentioned in Chapter 1). Also something had to explain why so many people believed that crystals had specific properties that they could bring to physical bodies, so I kept looking. I was incredibly frustrated until I discovered three things.

---

[89] Jeanne-Marie Ganne, "Stimulation of Bone Healing with Interferential Therapy," *Australian Journal of Physiotherapy* Volume 34, issue 1,1988, pages 9-20, https://www.sciencedirect.com/science/article/pii/S0004951414605973 (accessed 1-14-15).

First, I learned that the more structured the order of molecules in a substance, the more easily it conducts energy. We have already determined that crystalline structures are the most organized structures on our planet. Therefore, they are able to conduct energy readily. The opposite of this is a highly random structure, referred to as having a high amount of entropy. Entropy is a measurement of disorder. Structures with a lot of entropy do not conduct energy easily. The more random the molecular order, the higher the entropy.

Secondly, I learned what makes a crystal clear. Did you know that there is more space between the molecules contained in a printed page than there are molecules of wood pulp that make it up? If that is true, then why can't we see through it? It's because of the random structure of the pulp molecules. Even though we can't see them with our naked eyes, the tiny movement of the vibrating molecules, a thousand times repeated, makes the paper appear opaque. Of course, the thinner the paper, the more translucent it becomes, because we are eliminating repetition of the random molecular order.

The reason we can see through some crystals is because of the highly ordered molecular structure, with neatly vibrating electrons. This actually allows light to pass through, causing the crystals to be translucent.

This is very important in terms of energy contained within a material. According to classical electromagnetic theory, the photoelectric effect is the process by which light, shining on a metal, causes it to emit electrons. This is attributed to the transfer of energy (or incitement) from the light to the electrons in the metal. Electrons emitted in this manner are referred to as photoelectrons.

I knew that light was an inciter, but now I learned that not only does a crystal's vibrational frequency get elevated from light on its surface, but that its internal molecules must be incited as well by the light passing through it!

If you're having trouble relating the photoelectric effect from a metal to a crystal, remember that metals are crystalline structures, which explains why we use metal wires to conduct electricity, and only orderly structures — crystalline ones — conduct electricity readily.

Lastly, I learned about phonons. Phonons were named in 1932 by Russian physicist Ivor Tamm.[90] The name phonon comes from the Greek word

[90] B. Bolotovsky, "Ivor Tamm," *Physics Today*, 1971, https://physicstoday.scitation.org/doi/pdf/10.1063/1.3022956 https://physicstoday.scitation.org/doi/10.1063/1.3022956.

phonē, which means sound or voice.[91] Long-wavelength (low frequency) phonons give rise to sound, and short-wavelength (high frequency) phonons give rise to heat. (The amount of heat in a substance is determined by how fast its molecules are moving.)

A phonon is a quantum of vibrational mechanical energy, just as a photon is a quantum of light energy. This is important because it means that a crystal sitting on your coffee table at room temperature will be sending out a vibrational frequency. It will have an EM field. Incite that same crystal by heat, light, sound or intention, and the crystal is going to have even more energy to impart to you or your environment.

Did you know that all crystals are considered elastic? It's hard to think of quartz as being flexible, or stretchable, but crystals are. A crystal that is put under pressure actually bends, and when it bends, it emits electricity from its compacted side. This is known as the piezoelectric effect.

> Quartz can produce an electrical reaction. Minerals with this ability are called piezoelectric. The electrical reaction can be created by applying a charge, physical stress, or heat. Quartz is also distinguished as a gem that is capable of triboluminescence, or the ability to create light under pressure. This mystery light is not electricity in the form that we know it, but it is often mistaken as such. The most prominent scientific theory is that it is caused by the separation of chemical and electrical bonds.[92]

The piezoelectric effect was discovered in 1880 and led to the use of quartz crystals in oscillator circuits in 1918. A crystal oscillator uses the resonance of a vibrating crystal to create an electrical signal with a precise frequency. The incredibly precise, stable frequencies of quartz crystals are what we use to create accurate timepieces. Crystals are used by radio stations to allow, for example, WCBS to be found at 880 KHZ AM on the radio dial. Quartz crystals are used in processor chips in computers as well as LCD (liquid crystal display) screens. Ruby, sapphire and alexandrite are used in lasers.

There is a large array of applications for piezoelectric materials, particularly quartz, which can generate thousands of volts of electricity. The most common use of piezoelectricity can be found in the electric cigarette

---

[91] CRS Press, "What causes superconductivity?" https://qudev.phys.ethz.ch/static/content/courses/phys4/studentspresentations/supercond/Ford_The_rise_of_SC_6_7.pdf.

[92] Josie Myers, "How to Make Electricity With Quartz or Diamonds," https://sciencing.com/make-electricity-quartz-diamonds-6456846.html (accessed June 25th 2019).

lighter. Other piezoelectric applications include sensors on electric guitars like pick-ups and contact microphones, ultrasound machines, sonar wave detection and generation devices, engine management systems in cars, loudspeakers, fuel injectors for diesel engines and quartz clocks.

Did you know the shape of crystals also affects their frequency? Scientists have determined that, if quartz is cut into rectangular plates, it produces higher frequencies. The ability to control the frequencies of crystals allows them to be used in a wide variety of applications.

There is a specific, predictable shape to natural crystals in the same family. This is caused by the repetitive, orderly alignment of a crystal's molecules which also allows them to be translucent. This is also what gives them their distinct shape. For example, ruby and sapphire crystals are corundum, which are not only identifiable by their distinct red or blue shades, but also by a distinct shape, different than those of beryl (emerald, aquamarine or morganite), quartz, topaz, diamond, etc. Even in the quartz family, clear quartz has a very different shape from amethyst and citrine or rose quartz.

So if crystalline shape affects frequency, than even crystals in the same family will have at least a slightly different energy from each other, because no two crystals in nature are exactly the same

Our ancestors discerned the energy of crystals without the aid of scientific equipment. But it is not an ability that was unique to them. I experienced this for myself that day in 1980 at the Sunray Meditation Center. (see "Healing a Horse"). Is there much difference between us and our ancestors over the last two or three thousand years? Not physiologically, so whatever abilities they had, we should still have access to. The difference is that for our ancestors there was no "voice of reason" or an "authority" telling them that what they knew, through intuition or discernment, was wrong. Energy was as present back then as it is now and just as involved in life's processes. Perhaps it was easier to more accurately read vibrational signatures back then because there was much less ambient electromagnetic energy in the environment due to human inventions. There were mostly just electromagnetic signatures of natural objects and other living beings, and our ancestors must have been intimately aware of them, at least those who had an interest in such things. So, they were able to "feel" and "see" and "know" the presence and functioning of energy deeply. Knowledge gained in these ways, once you learn to trust the information as well as the process, brings you such a sense of strength, and self-reliance.

Our ancestors were not afraid to use their senses to connect the dots, until groups that wanted to control the populace created "rules" against, and fears about, exploring these things. We will look at this further later in the book.

Suffice it to say that we, for multiple reasons, are not in our ancestors' shoes. Ironically, the science itself that has recently proven that these subtle energies exist was one of the "voices of reason" that convinced people that the knowledge of our grandmothers and grandfathers was useless. In some ways, science actually made that statement true.

Our elders were not quick to pick up new technologies. That is still true today - if you're having trouble with your phone or computer, asking your teenager (or a neighbor's) usually produces the solution to the to the problem. Asking your grandmother doesn't generally help (of course there are technologically savvy grandmas out there); however, youngsters pick up new technology quickly. Everything is new to them, so they are not struggling to unlearn and then re-learn.

It was easy for a new paradigm, one embracing a young science that seemed all powerful, to declare that information gleaned in the old ways was untrue, not valuable or outright dangerous. Derogatory terms like "wives' tales" or "superstitions" are applied to teaching stories or wisdom that was gleaned from experience about the unseen world and that that was passed down for generations.

Our culture turned its back on the traditions of our ancestors and also on our elders. Cultures that held onto their ancestors' teachings about energy for healing and transformation were looked at as backward, all because a young science could not see the bigger picture and therefore could not acknowledge the existence of low EMFs or their role in our bodies and psyches. But our ancestors did.

Although children are born more open to these things, as we grow, we strive to be acceptable in our current culture; consequently, we learn to shut this information out.

Let's just look at this for a moment. If we have crystal in our bodies (our bones are 65% crystal, and there is more crystal in us than just in our bones) and crystals conduct energy readily ... how then is energy *not* affecting us on a daily basis?

Blocking our conscious awareness of these energies does not stop them from affecting us; it simply blocks us from being aware of their direct influence on us and our environment.

Just because you have not learned how to interpret energies clearly or protect yourself from them doesn't mean you are protected from them. For example, if you don't acknowledge microwave radiation or x-rays, you can't possibly develop a shield against their effects ... can you? Stronger EMFs do affect us; there is plenty of research to back this up, but what I'm exploring is subtler energies, those generated by other beings and things in the natural world.

How many times do you feel overwhelmed, sad, drained, or even elated, without being able to directly identify why you feel that way? It is possible that you may be reacting to energy fields around you? It certainly bears looking into.

Discernment and intuition are things that take time to master, as does wisdom. We have lost so many original teachings, and it is clear to me that the path we have been following is not heading in a direction that is good.

How do we find our way? Here are some interesting thoughts; parables if you will. Let's consider diamonds and their clarity.

Coal is organic, the decomposed flesh of plants. These constituents are chemically transformed into coal due to the effects of heat, pressure, and time. So there sits coal. It has transformed from plant to mineral, but it has no clarity. It is consumed easily by fire and it cannot allow light inside itself. Some coal stays that way indefinitely. It formed in an area where, once its initial transformation took place, there weren't a lot of other hardships or stresses. Nothing challenged it or forced it to change.

Other coal didn't have it that easy. It existed in a state of intense challenges, where there was more pressure and even greater heat. The coal that managed not to be consumed by the heat, that did not get pulverized by the intense pressure, that survived this thousand-year process transformed into either graphite or diamond.

Figure 10. Graphite (pure carbon).[93]

Graphite is similar to diamond — they are actually the same chemical formula, but the bonds that hold graphite together are much weaker. You might say its integrity and sense of self are easily shifted. It has some clarity, but nothing dazzling. Internally graphite sheets away from itself easily, leaving it weak and vulnerable. These are the qualities that make it good for pencil lead and as a lubricant.

Figure 11. Diamond (pure carbon). [94]

Diamond, on the other hand, responds to the same pressures, perhaps even more pressure, differently. Its internal bonds are strong (the strongest molecular bonds of anything on the planet), its resilience has been tested and retested until it comes up strong and pure ... a joy for all to behold, with great clarity.

---

[93] Photo courtesy of http://www.xtal.iqfr.csic.es/Cristalografia/parte_01-en.html.
[94] Photo courtesy of https://www.xtal.iqfr.csic.es/Cristalografia/parte_01-en.html.

I don't know if coal had a choice, but I know that people do. How do you respond to stress and pain? Are you becoming clearer? More connected? Life alchemically shapes us all.

It is here on the molecular level that we can clearly see truth of the microcosm being reflected in the macrocosm, the truths of the largest amongst us being reflected in the smallest. Perhaps it is shown more clearly in the molecular, without the diluting (deluding) that occurs in creatures with free will, large complicated and confusing brains ... not to mention intense emotions.

Look to particles, electrons, molecules, etc., to find life's truths. If you were God, would you trust your laws only to man? Until recently, no creatures (other than viruses) could rewrite DNA; the information in DNA was "written in stone." But now humans are playing God, rewriting DNA and molecular structure, and man is frequently not wise.

Interestingly, this whole thing also reminds me of the life of sperm. Sperm are not recognized by their host's body as being part of it. A man's white blood cells see sperm as intruders and would kill them if given the chance. So immature sperm hang out under large "nurse cells" (you cannot make this up!) who protect them from the host body's white blood cells.

Sperm do not mature in this situation (not surprisingly, how can you mature protected from life's hardships? Look at coal!). It is not until the man's body calls for an ejaculation and the sperm cells rush out of the body that they have a chance to mature. The maturation of sperm cells occurs by the cilia present in the vagina hitting them repeatedly on the head. (I'm serious! Look it up.)

So there seems to be a universal formula for attaining wisdom and clarity that involves hardship, pressure, and survival. This is not reserved just for humans.

Only mature specimens have wisdom gained from experience; time is a factor in the creation of higher states. This is why listening to cultures that have not discarded the teachings of their elders has so much to offer us; thousands of years of wisdom that our young science cannot possibly give us. We need to save our indigenous populations; we need to make sure that the information they have is not lost. There are people and groups doing this — Llyn Cedar Roberts is one of them.[95] I urge you to help support her work or that of others like her.

---

[95] See the Olympic Mountain Earth Wisdom Circle, https://www.eomec.org/.

Our ancestors were far more attuned to energy in the world around them than most of us today, so what they knew, and we have forgotten, bears re-membering.

13. The First Law of Thermodynamics

Remember we looked at the fact that thoughts are electrical impulses jumping from synapse to synapse in our brains? (Recall our discussion in the "Our Brains" chapter.) Our thoughts consist of energy. That's interesting, but if you couple that with the next piece of information, it becomes radical. The First Law of Thermodynamics states "Energy can neither be created nor destroyed."

Think about that for a minute. If energy never dies, what happens to the energy that constitutes our thoughts when our bodies cease functioning? Where does it go? Is it still "us"?

Another interesting thought: if energy cannot be created, where did the energy that is our thoughts come from before it was in our body?

This line of thinking opens up a world of possibilities and asks us to re-examine a couple of things. First, we need to re-evaluate beliefs about existence after death. Even in Christianity, there is a continuation of "us" after death, labeled "spirit" or "soul," consigned to heaven or hell (Catholics have a third option, purgatory). Could those entities be comprised mostly of energy, an energy that never dies — the same energy that is our personalities?

Indigenous people from almost all cultures act as though it is a fact that we go on after our bodies die. Many cultures believe the energy that was our ancestors is still very active in influencing our lives today.

Have you ever "felt" someone who has passed, as though she or he were present with you in a moment of joy or sorrow? There are millions of people who believe that not only can you feel those who have "died," but that you can communicate with them and they with you. Even more startling is the belief that people's ancestors influence their descendants' lives daily. The Chinese create elaborate tombs with every modern convenience to obtain the good will of their ancestors. Native Americans leave out "spirit plates" consisting of a small portion of each meal for a year for the newly deceased. The Japanese have small altars on their walls for their ancestors and burn incense daily as well as keep fresh flowers in a small vase, amongst other things.

Have you ever experienced a loved one reaching out to you across the void? I have a friend Nancy whose mom had looked a long time for the site for her interment. The mother was very adamant about being buried under a tree. She saw the tree as making a more pleasant place for her visitors to sit, shielding them from sun and rain. Eventually she found her tree, bought her site, and was interred there when she died. Nancy had been there many times and had really appreciated her mom's selection of a tree-shaded site. One day Nancy went to visit her mother's grave with a new boyfriend, whom I will call Dave. The sky was clear, but there had been snowfall the day before. Nancy and Dave were standing respectfully by the headstone. Nancy was sharing a story of her mom with Dave when "plop" a large wet pile of snow landed on Dave's head and started dripping down his neck! Dave reacted with anger, which is an interesting choice or pattern. Nancy was embarrassed, but couldn't shake the feeling that her mom had done this on purpose ... but she didn't know why. A year or so later Nancy ended the relationship because it became abusive. She thought about that moment at her mom's grave site and realized her mother had been telling her that she did not like this guy! How many times is there help coming to us from "the other side" that we ignore, simply because we are closed to the concept?

The next subject we might want to look at in the light of "energy never dying" is rebirth. If the energy that is us came from someplace before it inhabited the body it is in now, then it stands to reason that it inhabited other bodies before, and will again. The Buddhists believe in reincarnation (literally "re-clothing in flesh"); not only can and do we reincarnate as other human beings, but as animals, plants, and insects as well, even as rocks and the elements.

Have you ever had the sense that you've been here before? Or met someone that you felt like you knew, even though you can't figure out when that might have been possible? If we have lived before, we would have had to live someplace and known other souls. Therefore it makes sense that we could recognize these places and beings.

People sometimes see glimpses of a past life when they meet someone or travel to a new place. In this light, feeling like you know the person or place, even though you haven't met them or been there in this life, makes more sense. Sometimes if you practice being open, you can get a sense of what the relationship with this person or place had been. You might even see pictures or get a strong emotional reaction without knowing why.

That First Law of Thermodynamics starts with "energy can neither be created or destroyed," but then it goes on to say "it [energy] can be converted from one form to another."

What does this mean in our everyday lives? If energy never dies and our thoughts are energy ... then do the thoughts we think have an energy that lingers? Perhaps what we think really does affect what surrounds us. It might actually influence what is present or available to us in our lives.

If energy sticks around ... how would thinking positive thoughts affect you? How would thinking negative thoughts affect you?

Upon realizing you were stuck in a negative thought cycle, if you look at the situation as being energetic, rather than just an emotion or state of mind, could you convert that energy? Could it be that simple? If you become adept at transmuting energy from one form to another, what could that mean for your life? Play with this idea. Entertain it.

Here is another question: are we responsible for the energy we focus on? If energy sticks around, should we be responsible for "cleaning up after ourselves" energetically?

What we focus on grows (it's actually more like we magnetize ourselves to the frequency of that thought or feeling, attracting more of it first into our energy field, and then into our bodies).

If we focus on anger, do we have a moral obligation to go back and to convert or neutralize that energy? I had an Abenaki teacher, Grandmother Nanatasis, who had us practice going back to a moment where we felt great anger. She asked us to observe the area in our mind's eye. She told us to see the energy field the incident created as a colored cloud. We were asked to notice how big it was, how far it had traveled around us (or the spot where we released it) and what color it was.

It was surprising how far these angry energy fields had traveled, left unattended since their point of expression. Mine had grown quite vast. Then she had us visualize transmuting it. This can be done by sending the energy to the sun and seeing it come back as pure energy for the benefit of all. Or you can visualize the color changing until it is pure energy again.

There is so much we do not understand about our universe, our planet, our bodies and the energies inhabiting all of those. Science is uncovering new things all the time. It's hard enough to see something you are not looking for, but it's much harder to recognize something we've closed our minds to. It is so easy to hold onto preconceived ideas. It is my hope that the thoughts and facts I present to you here will open doors in your heart, mind, and soul to allow the greater connections that we all share into your consciousness.

Part II

PSYCHOSOCIAL

14. The Grass Is Greener

I don't think there was ever a 70-year period that changed man's relationship to the world more than the Victorian Era (named for Queen Victoria, who reigned June 20, 1837 – Jan. 22, 1901). Roughly we are talking about the 19th century. During the second half of that century, we saw the long-term effects of overcrowding in cities. Confined in the same places indefinitely, both humans and their livestock experienced an increase in disease. The mortality rate from cholera was at its peak.

It was a confusing time for people. So many inventions were rocking the fabric of everyday life. Anesthesia revolutionized the surgical world. The first vaccines were successfully being administered, and it looked like, through our ingenuity, we would be able to eradicate disease completely. This was the point where we truly began turning away from natural remedies to pharmacological ones. It was almost as though there was a connection made in Western people's minds about disease and nature. "Natural" became associated with poverty and disease. The outcome of this era was for people not only to turn away from all the natural remedies that God literally places at our feet, but to discredit them as well. What a shame.

Gardening changed drastically from manicured natural environments to controlled mass plantings that took continual maintenance from servants. Huge gardens planted to look like giant oriental carpets became the rage. These gardens were so controlled that the flowers were pruned off them daily. This was because flowers fade, are relatively short lived, and susceptible to weather conditions like heavy rains, ruining carefully wrought color patterns. Using just foliage colors to create these ornate patterns insured continuity. Once the living oriental carpet was created, it needed a background to be set in, which was provided by areas of mowed grass in between the beds. These gardens and the large strolling areas in between them were not something the average well to do person could dream of building or maintaining, not even the "lawns." The machines for mowing these ornamental lawns were large and heavy. They were expensive to operate because they required a large indoor space to store, as well as draft horses to pull them.

Enter a new paradigm: useless lawn becomes a *status symbol*. Note specifically, the word "use-less." Fields used for grazing animals had no respect here. If you needed to rely on your patch of land for food or medicine, it set you apart, and not in a good way. You were of the lower class. Elaborate games that could only be played on short shorn grass, like croquet, popped up.

This underlying theme in the Victorian Era in Europe was spurred by man's growing sense of being separate from nature (because of his new-found powers, man mistakenly thought he could control it). As his understanding of the world through science, and the technological inventions it was providing, grew, so did man's sense of separation from the natural world. The successes of the industrial revolution completely fed this misconception. The *BBC Magazine* says this:

> Victoria came to the throne during the early, frenetic phase of the world's first industrial revolution. Industrialisation brought with it new markets, a consumer boom and greater prosperity for most of the propertied classes.
>
> It also brought rapid, and sometimes chaotic, change as towns and cities expanded at a pace which precluded orderly growth.
>
> Desperately poor housing conditions, long working hours, the ravages of infectious disease and premature death were the inevitable consequence.[96]

So while many people's lives were improving, those of others were worsening. The invention of new technologies created a market for the inventors and producers. Marketing became part of the fabric of the middle class. Initially, advertising proved to help create demand but after a while, insidiously, it began to shape our thoughts and beliefs. It created campaigns that helped shift people's habits and create "ideals" that made people wish for things they could not afford, but made them feel that they could not do without.

---

[96] Eric Evans, *Overview: Victorian Britain, 1837–1901, Industrial Revolution,* updated 2011-03-29, BBC, http://www.bbc.co.uk/history/british/victorians/overview_victorians_01.shtml.

There had always been people with the gift of gab, individuals who could sell you anything. If they were unscrupulous, they could harm others by scamming them through charm and wit into parting with their money for nothing or even for something that was actually bad for them. All of a sudden there was opportunity for these folks to reach more than the few people they would normally attract in a day. Advertising allowed mass campaigns to be created, and many of them did not have the consumers' best interests at heart.

We learn from books in school. This in and of itself preconditions anyone who went to school to have faith in the printed word. After enough time you have a population who believes in printed words, which became even more powerful when they gained the ability to travel long distances instantaneously. Twenty-some years into Victoria's reign the telegraph was invented, making that so. A short dozen years later, the first telephone was invented. Can you imagine how much just those two pieces of technology changed everyday life?

Midcentury also saw the invention of the internal combustion engine, which in turn revolutionized many industries and led to the first motorized cars. The lawn mower was redesigned with internal combustion engines, becoming smaller and lighter. This allowed the less wealthy to jump on the "useless lawn" bandwagon. Lawns became the rage as a means of social discrimination.

The development of lawns as a status symbol contributed significantly to our disconnect from nature. Did you know that almost every "enemy" of a trophy lawn is a strong plant that not only has medicinal properties, but is edible and nutritious as well? Dandelion, purslane, plantain, clover, etc., all help heal or feed us, sometimes both.

Our ancestors knew the power of these plants, but we no longer do. Does that make any sense? According to an article at Phytochemicals.info, "During the 19th and 20th century, the main strategy of the scientists was to discover the active ingredients, which had medicinal or pesticidal properties.[97]

It's great that we learned to identify the chemicals or substances in the natural world that help us. But our insights were limited by our developing belief system that a young science was going to provide everything we needed. A belief that everything produced by our technologies would be better for us and cheaper than what individuals could harvest themselves.

---

[97] "History of Phytochemicals," *Phytochemicals.info*, https://www.phytochemicals.info/phytochemicals-history.php.

A whole new concept of mass farming came about because of these new beliefs. Chemical fertilizers were needed to support these massive endeavors, and looking across time we can see the domino effect of this thinking. It always involves dissecting and shaving parts from the whole, thereby drawing a smaller circle.

A century and a half later we are just learning that there are other properties in traditional medicinal plants that help support the specific ingredient that cures a malady. In other words, there is an intricate web of ingredients within a medicinal plant (that we were not aware of) that holistically interacts with the system of living organisms in supportive ways. The whole plant generally turns out to be more helpful most of the time than its dissected parts. Studies are finding that without these supporting nutrients and phytochemicals, some of the extracted or synthesized "medicines" are actually toxic.

That's a strange concept for folks raised in our paradigm, that there is some kind of intelligence in nature that is beneficent to humans. How would it change your life to explore that? To step into each new day looking for how and where the natural world intersects with yours in beneficial ways? Our ancestors lived with these philosophies, and their lives were enriched by these awarenesses. In the face of new technological advances, we threw the baby out with the bath water. We no longer recognize very strong plants as allies or medicine. Instead we have stripped them of their names and their known healing or nutritional properties, and we have label them *weeds*. Weeds have no value. Actually, they do have a value — a negative value. They are hated for their tenacity (the exact quality that tells you they have a powerful medicine to share with us!). They are survivors and and multiply with alacrity, and for this we hate them. Our value system became skewed and we learned to despise anything that threatens the look of our trophy grass.

Today we still practice this worship of useless lawn. Gleefully we poison the medicinal plants that faithfully continue to pop up in our lawns, poisoning our soil, our water, our bodies and our minds at the same time.

We invest time in fighting nature on a weekly, if not a daily, basis, to our detriment. When did our healing plants become weeds? When did we switch from being thankful for a dandelion's incredible healing and nutritional properties and decide that using a strong poison on it (and the surrounding earth) was a good idea? When did our value system become so skewed? It was probably around the same time that our *wise elders* started to become *old people* with nothing useful to offer a young society that valued technology over wisdom and health.

So we have walked down this road for many decades. Do you like where we are? Are you content? Healthy? Peaceful in your skin? Is the earth in a good place? Perhaps it is time for some reprioritizing.

Remember, the questions we ask lead to the answers we find. Since the development of science and the reliance on devices outside our own discernment for answers, the questions we ask have changed. Inventions that help us see deeper and deeper into the world around us cost money. This has always been one of the problems with scientific experiments, and therefore the results. Most scientific experiments take a fair amount of financial backing.

Who is footing the bill? What questions are they interested in? And perhaps most importantly... *What answers are they interested in?* Undoubtedly, something that makes them more money, not necessarily the "truth."

But what of us? And what of the planet? ... If you look around, I would say that "we" matter little to "them."

Our unconscious decision to turn away from nature in favor of our own intelligence and ingenuity is a path that we have followed for so long. Have we come far enough down this path to assess the wisdom of it? Do we need to make some *conscious, intentional* decisions at this point? I would say we do.

> Science cannot solve the ultimate mystery of nature. And that is because, in the last analysis, we ourselves are part of nature and therefore part of the mystery that we are trying to solve.
> — Max Planck, German physicist[98]

---

[98] Max Planck, "Where Is Science Going?" (1932), https://www.brainyquote.com/quotes/max_planck_211832.

15. The Hundredth Monkey

Have you ever heard the parable of "the hundredth monkey?"

The story reportedly results from studies done on remote islands in northern Japan. Several of these isolated islands are populated by macaque monkeys. Macaques are light grey monkeys with bare faces, surrounded by almost two inches of "beard." If you are on social media, you have likely seen pictures of them relaxing in natural hot springs. Their enjoyment is clearly discernable as very human expressions. If you haven't seen them, I have included a link.[99] Because of the macaques' isolation, Japanese scientists have found studying them to be very informative. One thing they learned by observing the macaques is that there are lead monkeys, both males and females. When a lead monkey learns something new and practices it, the practice is adopted quickly by the subordinate monkeys. For instance, sweet potatoes, introduced to the islands by humans in the not too distant past, have become a staple of these monkeys. Sweet potatoes grow easily in the climate and the sandy soil. As the story goes, one day a lead female monkey on one island began washing her potato before eating it. I guess she got tired of the sand .... Within a relatively short time, all the monkeys on her island had started washing their potatoes. The fascinating thing was that as soon as all the monkeys on this one island started washing their sweet potatoes, lead monkeys on a neighboring island started doing the same.

These monkey populations have no contact with each other, at least not visually or through hearing. It is the clearest example I know of one group's consciousness affecting the consciousness of others — a strong vibration rippling out. And why not? Let's look at the physics of crystalline structures for a moment. Entropy is a measurement for disorder, and things with a high amount of entropy do not conduct energy readily. Is it possible that ordered thoughts can contain or carry a greater amount of

---

[99] https://www.cnn.com/travel/article/snow-monkeys-hot-springs-japan/index.html.

energy (higher frequency) than thoughts that are chaotic? Just as the organized molecules in a crystalline substance do? It's an interesting question, one that deserves experimentation, not outright dismissal. It has interesting ramifications in regard to manifesting, as we will explore later. Extrapolating that outward, if one being is focused on one activity or one goal, and others join their thoughts to this cause, could it increase the energy of that focus? Or increase the energy of what is being focused on?

If you can see merit in the concept of group consciousness affecting reality, it can give you hope. Hope that the thoughts you think do make a difference, hope that it may be possible for a percentage of us to create a field that can affect people around us, as well as around the globe.

Let's start a practice of connecting to and creating vibrational frequency intentionally! Let's say that every Thursday, at 7am eastern standard time, we will all focus our thoughts on world peace, on weaving a net of positive healing vibration around the world, on eliminating all suffering, hunger, stress ... Will you join me? If we spend two minutes on each of these, it will take a total of ten minutes. If you can't join me every Thursday that's fine. Join as often as you can. See what you become aware of during this time.

16. Is Ignorance Bliss?

Is ignorance bliss?

Do you really need to think about this one? Of course, there is information that may trigger you emotionally to hear. But the truth is, if something is occurring and you don't know about it, it is still occurring. Take, for example, your partner cheating on you; perhaps not knowing protects you from being triggered in that moment, but you are not protected from the consequences of the hidden event. Whether you like it or not, the event gives you important information — things like the fact that your partner has moved on emotionally, is no longer on the same page as you, is comfortable with duplicity, or does not believe in communication. The list goes on, but all this information is valuable for you to make the right decisions for you.

Ignorance takes away your ability to respond accurately, which could cost you your health or even your life. When is the ability to respond to something actually a negative?

Never.

17. Being Open

Being open is the first and most important step in working with energy in any way. Such openness will also facilitate your ability to connect the dots. If you come with a closed mind, you will leave these pages as you were when you found them. You will not change.

We live in a very exciting time because there is a constant stream of new information now being produced by scientists across the globe. These discoveries support the truth of ancient knowledge involving energy and our bodies, our minds and even our souls. Science is making many discoveries that corroborate information our ancestors lived by.

This information comes from many fields: plant, animal, insect and human biology as well as physics and psychology. Discoveries such as that creatures with brains the size of pinheads, or no brains at all, are able to solve mazes, and that others can recognize the difference between Picasso's paintings and those of Van Gogh. There are new findings about plant biology and physiology that, if we thought about them (and started connecting our own dots), would require us to be open to forming new concepts. Such information supports the truth of ancient knowledge involving energy and our bodies, minds and place in the world. Our ancestors were open and therefore able to receive information directly from the world around them. Max Planck puts it this way:

> The fundamental principles and indispensable postulates of every genuinely productive science are not based on pure logic but rather on the metaphysical hypothesis — which no rules of logic can refute — that there exists an outer world which is entirely independent of ourselves. It is only through the immediate dictates of our consciousness that we know that this world exists. And that consciousness may to a certain degree be called a special sense.[100]

---

[100] Max Planck, "The Universe in the light of modern physics," *Where is science going?* 1932, https://archive.org/details/whereissciencego00plan_0/mode/2up.

Trust me: if you are closed your normal and special senses cannot function to their fullest. Your mind was given to you to use — you *must* take in information from different sources, sift it, weigh it, feel it, and then draw conclusions. You cannot do this if you are closed.

What does being closed look like? It can take the form of someone who believes that there is only one way to view things; people who have stopped thinking for themselves and/or lost their sense of wonder; people who are unwilling to ask questions of established beliefs and systems, or even of themselves.

If you can be open, all will come to you eventually. With openness, all things are possible. Take my life for example.

At the tender age of nineteen I left the USA with a backpack, $500, and a round trip ticket from Los Angeles to Tokyo. I had officially dropped out of college because being an undiagnosed dyslexic was ruining my life. I had gotten a letter from Antioch Collage over spring break notifying me that some (or all — I did not know) of my teachers had made comments about my spelling and punctuation. I was told that if I did not take a re-medial English class, I would not be allowed back. This was like a nail in my coffin. I knew that I could *not* learn to spell. I had suffered too many experiences being humiliated in school already. In high school, my essays were handed back to me covered top to bottom, page after page, with red marks. Teachers who heard me speak and witnessed my vocabulary usage were infuriated by my consistent "disregard" of spelling and punctuation rules. These teachers would not address my thought content, but instead would shake my papers in front of my face saying "Go back and use a dictionary!" and then slap them on the desk.

Trying to use the dictionary sent as much fear and loathing into my small body as a rattlesnake or spider might do for others. Flipping through those pages of tiny words all crammed together was like a nightmare. Even if I could find the word I was looking for (remember you have to know how to spell it to find it!), no matter how hard I tried to transcribe the word exactly letter for letter, every time it would be wrong. The letters would be out of order because *I was seeing them out of order* (but I didn't know that). It was a horrible feeling. I could not succeed. It was degrading to have to endure years of this.

It hadn't started in high school either. When I was in fifth grade, I had a teacher who thought it would be good if we pretended to buy a stock and follow it for the year (an absolute impossibility for me!). Back then the only way to follow your stocks was in the newspaper in those minuscule rows of numbers in columns. There was no way I could copy those numbers accurately. He also had us pretend to write checks and balance a checkbook, something else that I failed at miserably. But the worst by far were the weekly spelling competitions. The teacher would have the two spelling champions of the week before (almost always the same two kids) pick people for their team for these competitions. The class was divided in half in this manner. Not only was I invariably picked last ... but I could never spell a single word correctly! It was so humiliating! I wanted nothing more than to melt into the wall behind me, or die! My inability to succeed in these areas and the humiliation I experienced convinced me of my stupidity.

Maybe that's where I learned to how to endure hard things. Maybe it's where I got the courage to go to Tokyo at age nineteen. It makes a lot of sense. I was such a foreigner in my life for over a decade — New York, Tokyo, Nepal, it really didn't matter where. I was that alone and cast adrift anywhere I was.

It was torture having to get up and show up at school day after day, week after week, all year long, believing that I was a waste of space on the planet and having it confirmed publicly, both scholastically and personally.

So, you see, long before high school, by at least seventh grade, I was convinced *to the core of my being that I was stupid* and incapable of learning. It was not a good perspective to begin my adolescent years with.

Up until that letter home in my second year of college, I had been hiding, doing my best and hoping no one would notice how much of a fuck up I was.

It didn't help that I was sensitive to energy, and saw things and "knew" things that other people didn't. I had no one to teach me the validity of these experiences, and they just served to make me feel more isolated and encouraged my disliking myself more. By the age of eighteen I hated myself for truly being so different from my peers and not being able to fit in or succeed at anything. Being fatherless since I was four didn't help, nor the constant moving around my mom and I did. The letter from Antioch, rather than offering me hope of help, convinced me of doom. I was not going to be able to get a degree. It confirmed my worst fears, and consequently I dropped out of school. I lived in a state of secret despair.

My boyfriend at the time had just graduated from Antioch and was heading to Japan. He was an English major and had heard that you could make a lot of money teaching English in Japan. It was 1982. I decided to accompany him because I literally had *no* options stateside. I was so traumatized by my inabilities that I had developed "deer in the headlights" syndrome and could not even learn how to operate a cash register (because I believed I could not). Consequently, my mind was closed! It did not matter that it was the outside world that led me to believe that. Everything inside me would freeze up when anyone tried to show me something or asked me a question.

What we believe is a powerful activator for what actually ends up happening to us. It's why struggling to stay open is so important.

The moment I got on a plane to Japan, I opened myself, without having a clue what I was doing. Within three weeks of landing in Tokyo I got a job for $12.00 an hour (minimum wage in the US at that time was $3.26). I was hired as an English conversationalist at a Conversation Lounge in Shinjuku. Picture an old-time ISO dance for the troops: a large room empty except for metal folding chairs along the walls and a single folding table with sodas and cups set on a fairly ugly, swirling floor of one-foot square 1950s-style linoleum tiles. My job was to sit in one of those chairs until a Japanese patron came in and sat next to me to practice English.

Talking! I was getting paid to talk! This I could do! I was particularly suited to talking. I was a precocious talker, speaking my first word ("Up") at the age of six months, and according to my mom speaking in full sentences a mere three months later at nine months of age.

Anyway, back in Tokyo, several months came and went, and the more I was exposed to, the more opportunities I found for making money. Given my state of mind and self-esteem, I never would have applied for a "real" teaching job. In the states I would have been laughed at. My boyfriend was teaching at a school in Shinjuku. He was earning about $40 an hour compared to my $12. At Christmas time, his school held a party and invited the spouses of the teachers. I went to the party feeling shy and somewhat out of place, but put my best face on it. As we were leaving at the end of the party, the owner approached me and asked me if I would consider teaching an English class for them! What, *me*?

They didn't ask me how old I was, what level of schooling I had, or what kind of visa I had entered the country with. Based entirely on how I interacted with the students and how I comported myself, the owner felt that I would be an asset to them.

Can you imagine my shock? I told them I would think about it and went home that night with my head spinning. In my short time in Japan I had observed that many Japanese people (at least in Tokyo) had some knowledge of English. They begin learning English in school by at least first grade, some as early as kindergarten. What I saw over and over was their shyness, making it very uncomfortable for them to speak out loud. It is difficult to practice a language unless you speak it. Who better to support them and be sensitive to their feelings of shyness or inadequacy than I? I knew intimately what it felt like to be humiliated in front of a class.

It took incredible courage for me to accept the position. But I did. My first semester I taught three beginning adult classes. My classes were so popular and so well received that the school kept adding classes to my schedule, until I had twice as many classes as my English major boyfriend! By my third or fourth semester I was even asked to teach the advanced English class to corporate businessmen!

I was terrified. Up until then I had been able to avoid writing on the chalkboard. My dyslexia made it impossible for me to do things like draw an accurate rendition of the State of New York, much less where Larchmont was in relation to New York City. Imagine my horror when one of my advanced students asked me that. I was trembling as I attempted to do so, having actually no clue where Westchester fell on a map of New York State. I was dyslexic for goodness's sake and a place's direction (north, south, east, west) eluded me. I was a stranger in a strange land and I was not someone who had succeeded in formal education. It was hard for me to learn anything because I would freeze up inside when I was presented with information.

I did retain information; I just didn't seem to have any control of what information I absorbed and remembered (which happened to be a lot). The facts that I absorbed and retained were odd. Consequently, I had miles of facts and information about certain things (a lot of them scientific or biological in nature), but the schooling or other skills that it would take to put that information to any kind of use in my society was cut off from me. Things like geography, spelling and grammar, directions to a physical location, as well as for operating things or procedures felt like giant holes in what made me up.

I started calling myself "Walking Swiss Cheese" because that's how I felt — like I had all these big holes in me. It was a real challenge to attempt to teach these classes. I have no idea how I actually made it through, yet I did, and my classes were wildly popular. I was soon recommended to other schools and ended up with more work than I could actually accept! How was this possible?

My courage in leaving behind everything I knew opened me. It opened me to new possibilities that were outside my belief system. I believed I could not succeed in the States. Japan was foreign enough that I was willing to entertain a concept of "possibilities" ... And what we *entertain*, or *make space for*, grows.

This is such an important concept. I benefitted from putting enough distance between myself and the belief systems I grew up with that I could open myself to responding in new ways to what came at me and not letting preconceived ideas shape my actions. Leaving the country was a godsend. It saved my life, but it took me decades to understand the processes that were set in motion then.

I was given more opportunities to experience this.

There was an ad in the *Japan Times* (an English-language newspaper) for dancers. I loved dancing and I was pretty good at improvisational dancing. In Tokyo's nightclubs, the other patrons would often clear a circle around me after I was on the dance floor for a while. They would clap and smile and cheer me on. I never saw this happening with other people; it was very flattering. So, when I saw this add, I thought, maybe, just maybe, I could do this. There was no area in my life that dyslexia didn't cripple, and dancing was no exception. It is very difficult for me to *follow* prescribed dance moves (I am fluid when it comes to letting the rhythms within the music originate moves within my body — meaning I am an excellent dancer, at least from an improvisational perspective). Trying to learn anything caused me to freeze ... but I wanted to try! I wanted so badly to have something that I was successful at be legitimatized by the outer world!

I auditioned for the dance troop that "Eddy the Arab" was putting together according to the ad in the *Japan Times*, Eddy was calling the group "Eddy's Blacks."

The English language in Japan is sometimes used in ways that are not literally correct — at least I witnessed that a lot in the early 80s. Also, on top of that it *was* the 80s! Naturally I was expecting that the troop would be always in black, a color I happen to look very good in!

When I gazed around the facility, I was dismayed. I was not prepared to be ... ummm ... the only white person at the audition! Not only was I taken aback by Mr. Arab's choices ... but I was a minority here, and clearly my skin color was going to prevent me from getting this job! "Please, mister, please ... I'll use shoe polish on my skin ... I really want to dance!"

I suppose that it is not very surprising that I did not get a callback for "Eddy's Blacks." Days turned into weeks, and I resolved to let my dream of dancing go. However, three weeks later I did get a call from the producers. I was so excited thinking that my dancing had impressed them.

I came in and guess what? No shoe polish for me! But no, alas, my dancing had not won them over (it's so easy for artists to be misunderstood!). They were not calling me back to dance for them. Instead they wanted to promote me for modeling! What? I was in shock! At 5′ 4 and 3/4″ there was no way I could have contemplated modeling in the States, never mind that I would never have had the self-esteem to try for it. But there it was, I was being called in to shoot a modeling portfolio! I did not even realize that most girls interested in modeling had to pay for their portfolios to be shot (at the time it cost about $500.00). So here was short little curvy me getting mine done for free!

Not long after that I began receiving calls to find my way to this audition or that (another hardship in such a huge city as Tokyo, even if I weren't dyslexic). Trying to juggle my teaching commitments to make it to the auditions and then the gigs that I did get was difficult. But the $400 an hour I got for some of the gigs was not!

So I started modeling and being on radio and TV commercials. I even won the part of a military wife in Japanese soap opera that took place in the Shogun era. Most notably I was in a Nissan van commercial that went to Europe, as well as a Redkin hair care product poster that was on buses and billboards throughout Tokyo. I still have a copy of that one hanging like a trophy on my foyer wall.

So both the modeling and the teaching were things I just fell into. I would never have tried these professions in the States because I was *very* unsuited for them. Yet here I was in Tokyo making a fabulous living doing them. It was a very odd experience — a clashing of realities inside my head. It was sometime during my journey here and after to the Far East that I started playing with the idea *that we could create our own reality.*

My mom and I had been very poor, living off the five to seven thousand dollars a year that her job provided. We never went on vacations. When she met my stepdad and we moved into a posh neighborhood in Westchester County, New York, I had very different expectations than the kids there. Their families would go to exotic places like Bermuda or St. Johns for vacations. I remember looking at pictures of the blue seas and coconut trees, wishing I could go to beautiful places like this and come back with a golden tan and a white Pukka shell necklace around my neck, like them.

My stepdad carefully married a woman who had no expectation of these things, so he didn't need to provide them. Yet even so, I had been taken from my subsistence (mostly farm girl) surroundings and placed in a world where I was a foreigner ... with much less than everyone else around me, including a lack of siblings, a father, or anything resembling fashion or worldly goods. When I started failing at school too, the world closed over my head, like a giant dark wave.

In Japan working on a tourist visa was a little tricky. You had to leave the country for six months after being in the country for six months. I had accomplished my goal of coming to Tokyo to earn enough money to travel for the next six months, until I could return.

I flew to Bangkok where I had heard you could purchase a one-year open ticket with six destinations on it for around $1,200.00 US dollars. It turned out to be true. My destinations were the Philippines, Singapore, Malaysia, Katmandu, India and Japan. In Thailand and the Philippines, I was able to live on sparsely populated, pristine tropical islands for months at a time. It was a dream come true! I rented a charming bungalow right on the water. Being able to swim around untouched coral reefs day after day, all day long was amazing. I visited them so often that the denizens of these reefs accepted me as one of their own.

The only way to describe swimming at night in warm swells teeming with phosphorescence was magical! The light came from invisible creatures that glowed with a bluish neon light when brushed, so that each of my strokes in the water appeared to drip sparks. With my long hair curling around my torso as I swam, I felt like a magical mermaid.

All my meals were from sources collected that day (there was no refrigeration, so everything was freshly harvested). I ate home cooked, delectable foods prepared by native Thai or Philippine people (who by the way prepare some of the finest recipes I have ever eaten). I got to live a dream that far outshone what my Westchester peers had ever gotten to do. And yet, I had *not* gotten there by the prescribed method of my cultural paradigm. I did not have parental benefactors, I had not gotten a college degree, nor had I landed a corporate job that gave me money to do these things. I had manifested these opportunities, without understanding what I was doing — all because my reality back home was so bleak that I had the strength to leave what I knew behind me, literally. When you close one door, others open. Leaving the country of my origin *opened me* as well as opening doors for me.

As soon as I came back to the States two and a half years later, I began manifesting things much more consciously. I had learned how to connect the dots, step outside the boxes of cultural paradigms, and reach for things that should not have been within my reach, given my handicaps.

I still did not have a name for what I was doing. It seemed like I set a goal, and then just jumped from one steppingstone to another that appeared across an expanse of water to reach that goal. Sometimes the "water" in between the steppingstones was actually an obstacle, and it would dictate the next step, but as long as I kept my goal firmly in mind, I would get there!

18. Connection

I want to draw your attention to the word connection ... and beyond the word, to the feeling of connection. What does *connection* mean to you? When was the last time you felt connected? To whom? Or to what?

Think about a time when you felt connected to someone or some place. Close your eyes and visit with this sensation. Savor it, breathe into the feeling, exhale the feeling, surrounding your body with the feeling. See if you can fill the room you are in with the feeling of connection. After spending a few minutes there, come back into the physical place where your body is, and tell me what parts of you feel fed, nourished? Can you identify areas in your body, mind or soul that react to this? Do you have a sense of being calmer? We *are* nourished by connecting.

I believe that our bodies and psyches experience *connection* and *sacredness* in the same "receptors" (for lack of a better word); at least that's how I experience them. Entering into a sacred space or ceremony, I am connecting with something greater than myself. When I deeply connect with anything outside myself, I experience the same sensation. It feeds me in much the same ways. As humans we are hardwired to be connected. Connection is sacred, and not just to humans. In high school I read about experiments performed on young chimps. The upshot was that an infant chimp will live if beaten, but die if deprived of any touch at all.

Our first connection is to our mother when we are in her womb, the drumbeat of her heart ever present in our awareness. A steady drumbeat tells us all is well, a slowed beat lulls us to sleep, and a quickened beat alerts us to danger. Part of this is biochemical because what flows through our mother's veins also flows through ours in the womb.

Once we emerge from the womb, the natural world is what we are supposed to connect to next, along with the rest of our sacred family. The earth is, after all, the Mother of each of us. Not one of us could exist without her. This is the first lesson learned by any being not plugged into an illusion: that we all are dependent on the health and wellbeing of the planet we live on to survive.

If we feel nourished by a concept or experience of "God," it's because we feel nourished through a *connection* with the divine (however you perceive that divine).

I love this quote from Yogi Bhajan: "If you can't see God in All, you can't see God at all."[101] This concept of God in everything is animistic. All first peoples experienced this and had traditions that honored and celebrated it. If God is in everything equally, then we are always surrounded by God, not as a dominant father figure, but as a part of each breath that all lifeforms take. The movement of sunlight on water, water over rocks, the wind in the trees, the roots clinging in the earth — all these things are God, just as we are. I have been told that the Hindu greeting "Namaste" translates to "The God in me recognizes the God in you."

I think this disconnect from the natural world is why we have become so focused on having love relationships in our current paradigm. We have receptors for connection all through our body and being. When we are taught to shut out our awareness of the natural world as connected to us, it leaves these receptors empty and searching, sometimes even starving.

Connecting to the natural world creates peace and bliss inside us, but in our current paradigm we are not taught to pursue connections here. Instead, we search for other things to give us these feelings: love, drugs, acquisitions, speed, dominance, adrenaline, even stress, all become sensory stimulants for our starving connection centers.

Connecting with nature for me is a type of meditating. It can be experienced by slowing down while sitting or standing still in relationship to the natural world and paying attention with all of your senses. Involving all your senses is important, and if you think about it very antithetical to most modern-day work environments where we are asked to ignore our senses. Indeed, shutting out awareness of our senses it crucial to surviving or excelling in most school systems as well. So now it is time to open the shutters. We are fed by connecting, and in order to connect, we must be open and aware. So, when I am engaging my senses I allow things that catch my senses to speak to me. For instance, if I become aware of something like the song of a bird, I stop wherever I am and turn my face toward the song, allowing my heart to open and experience the joy of that moment, connecting to that bird. After doing this for decades, I find that the

---

[101] https://www.lexiyoga.com/yogi-bhajan-quotes (accessed 10/9/2020).

birds seem as if they want me to see them as well. And often they will hop closer or at least into view as I am connecting to them. I do the same thing with a strong breeze or a spot in a stream where the water is gurgling loudly over rocks. I let nature remind me to connect. Sometimes my own states of being remind me to connect. When I am feeling very discouraged, hurt or sad, I reach for connections in the natural world. They are truly what has kept me alive.

There is another great way to experience our connection to nature, and that is by wandering. Have you ever wandered? It's a magical way to connect with nature and the elements. All you have to do is set out on a walk with the intention to be open to experiencing connection. Try not to have preconceived ideas, since they can be walls, or at the very least blinders. Prejudices hinder connection.

You can wander in a park, in the woods, or even on a street that still has trees and birds, squirrels or even insects. Insects will connect and communicate with you, but I find humans tend to have greater prejudices and fears regarding bugs. When I talk about communicating with spiders, for instance, you might recoil. How you feel about a creature probably reflects a lack of connection with, or awareness of, something's true nature rather than something emanating from the creature itself (probably!). But these are exactly the types of experiences/sensations that you need to figure out for yourself. We each have areas we excel in and others where we don't. So what I experience as easy or as a hardship may be the exact opposite for you. This is what we are here for. Figure your instrument out (without hurting yourself or others, please).

As I was saying, being open to the possibility of having a relationship with an insect is hard for some people, because of our cultural preconceptions. But there is one insect that has been embraced in our modern world — the butterfly. Most people have good feelings about butterflies, so let's look at them as our bridge to working with and connecting to insects. Butterflies undergo massive physical changes. Hatching from small eggs, they eat and grow as most creatures do. What makes them unusual is the process of metamorphosis, following their intuition and their ancestors' whispering in their little caterpillar cells. These whisperings tell them to hang upside down and spin walls around themselves. So, with what seems to me to be a huge amount of faith, they spin a cocoon, effectively cutting themselves off from everything they have needed up until that point to survive! Then they sit in darkness as their bodies begin to liquefy so that they can be reformed. I cannot imagine that the process is an easy one to undergo.

Within their caterpillar bodies they carried a tiny pair of wings, that up until then were completely useless. I don't know if they are aware of these vestigial wings. I don't know if they are aware of their destiny ... In the chrysalis these tiny wings grow, emerging from within, and become external. The large body shrinks, short caterpillar legs shrivel, some disappear and new ones grow long. If and when they emerge, everything that that knew will be gone. No longer will they walk the earth or eat greenery. Now they will dance and fly, making love in the sky. And they will drink sweet nectar from flowers.

My Lakota friends would say that transformation was a butterfly's "medicine." What might one appearing on your path have to remind you of in your life that day? Or at that exact moment? It's a great metaphor, and if you encounter a butterfly in your wandering, it may well be a message about transformation. All insects have strengths and skills that you might be needing or need to be reminded to look for or nurture in yourself. It might also be that they are gently reminding you to let go of something that is no longer serving you, or pointing to an aspect of yourself that is out of balance.

You can practice this in your yard if you are lucky enough to have one. Just arrive at wherever you intend to be your beginning point. By arrive I mean more than just physically put yourself there, I also mean to bring your consciousness to this place. Remember that Max Planck said earlier that "consciousness may to a certain degree be called a special sense" [102] — one that you need to practice using! Thich Nhat Hanh describes consciousness from a Buddhist's perspective:

> The second level of consciousness is sense consciousness, the consciousness that comes from our five senses: sight, hearing, taste, touch, and smell. We sometimes call these senses "gates," or "doors," because all objects of perception enter consciousness through our sensory contact with them. Sense consciousness always involves three elements: first, the sense organ (eyes, ears, nose, tongue, or body); second, the sense object itself (the object we're smelling or the sound we're hearing); and finally, our experience of what we are seeing, hearing, smelling, tasting, or touching. [103]

---

[102] Max Planck, "The Universe in the light of modern physics" (1932), *Where Is Science Going?*, https://en.wikiquote.org/wiki/Max_Planck.

[103] Thich Nhat Hanh, "The Four Layers of Consciousness," *Lion's Roar: Buddhist Wisdom for Our Times*, https://www.lionsroar.com/the-four-layers-of-consciousness/ December 26, 2018 (accessed 1-12-19).

If you can, close your eyes for a few moments; if you're not comfortable closing your eyes then leave them open. In either case tilt your face up to the sky. Feel the sun, rain, wind, warmth or coldness on your face. Breathe slowly and deeply several times, just bringing your focus to the natural world around you and how it is touching your body, your senses. Open your eyes. What attracts your attention? Were you aware of a natural sound when you were focusing quietly? If so, follow the sound. Walk slowly, feel yourself opening, relaxing. Notice little things along your way, the movement of leaves in the wind, birds, or squirrels. Notice rocks, pebbles, twigs or fallen leaves that catch your eye along your journey. Pretend, or allow for, the possibility that every being you encounter is there for you specifically at that moment, present to communicate something to you in some way. Allow your imagination to guide you in childlike wonder and openness.

If a rock, tree or animal attracts your attention, focus on it for a minute, or ten. Try not to feel shy about visiting with a tree or a rock. Touch them and see if anything comes to mind, a picture, a feeling; even an unclear impression may be significant. Let go of judgement. If this is a new frontier for you, it will most likely feel awkward, just like learning a new language. You first have to give credence to the possibility that the strange sounds the foreign person is making might actually have meanings; you must do this before you can embark on learning any language. Connecting to nature is a language of our souls.

All of us are dependent upon the earth — she is our Mother. All of her children that breathe share the same DNA as we do. We share many things physically with the mineral kingdom as well (remember we have crystals in our bones and connective tissue). Be open. Wander. Wonder. Try this experiment for at least ten minutes, once a week or once a day. Allow yourself to be drawn, acknowledging that what attracts your attention is speaking to you in some way. See if you can discern the message to you on each particular day. Don't forget that the elements — cloud formations, wind, rain or sun — also connect with us, as do the four directions. What meaning can you draw from them each day?

The most satisfying part of all of this for me is that this rapport is available to us at any time. Such connection is not always available with other humans who may be busy and focused elsewhere. By developing our awareness of, and openness to, the natural world, we can be fed through this connection at every moment.

I know the power of this connection intimately, because the only reason I'm still here in this body is due to my connection to nature. Sandra Ingerman says in her book *Speaking with Nature* that "life shapes us as surely as the wind and the water shapes earth."[104] The course of my life unfolded through decades of repetitive situations that deprived me of connections to other people. I felt the effect of this deeply but had not yet seen the gift in it, or the wisdom and awareness that this path carved into my soul until the last seven or eight years.

When I was in my mid-forties, I gathered with a group of people to build a sweat lodge in the traditional Lakota way in Maine. It felt really good to be participating in returning something integral to the history of this continent that other humans had destroyed and banned.

I myself was trying to recover from the devastation of my marriage which was blowing up and shattering my life. Growing up, I was an only child and moved around constantly. I longed for stability, especially from a significant other. When I met and later married my ex, I believed that he and I were a team who had each other's backs. I operated as though this were true, only to find out little by little that this was very much not the case. My ex was a sociopath and incapable of being a team player. Discovering this fact had been devastating.

Recovering was hard because I had started out desperate for connection, and now after fifteen years of being with this man, I was even more starving. Until that point, I had primarily looked to be fed that way in relationships with men. In the years following my divorce, I was not finding men I could really connect with.

At this particular gathering were two men that I had dated since the dissolution of my marriage. Both were men that I would have liked to be the "right one," but each fell incredibly short of being able to fully connect. Seeing them both here brought up the sense of abandonment and loneliness that had haunted me since the loss of my father and any kind of stable life when I was three. To say I was feeling the lack of being in a relationship deeply is an understatement.

On that day, I chose to separate myself from the group because I needed to cry. I was crying a lot in those days. The path that I chose to wander led through a pine grove and then opened into a field. The sun was shining down on me from a crisp blue November sky. It was a large field, and the grasses that filled it from tree rim to tree rim were autumn

---

[104] Sandra Ingerman and Llyn Roberts, *Speaking with Nature; Awakening to the Deep Wisdom of the Earth*, Bear & Company, Rochester, Vermont and Toronto, Canada, 2015.

pale gold with feathery seed heads. They were rustling gently, stirred by a warm soft breeze. As I was walking, deep in thought, something caught my eye. There was a single strand of spider web stretched taut and seemingly stationary in the middle of the field. It was shimmering in all the colors of the rainbow. It was so straight and so long that I grew curious and traced it from one end to the other. I had never seen such a long spinners' thread in my life. What I discovered surprised me. The web was attached to nothing at either end (not even a tiny spider)! It wasn't simply floating or moving about either, but seemingly held steady, as if by invisible hands ...

I had an epiphany in that moment, and I fell on my hands and knees on the earth. I realized that the "held" spider web reminded me of *me*. I thought about how nature had always *held me*, supported me through my anguish, and shared with me such joy in connection with all of her creatures, whether with an ant, hermit crab, bird, dog or rock.

The earth herself and the small growing green things poking out of her sleeping embrace up lift my spirits with their emergence in spring, as do trees at any time of year. Water and waves soothe my troubled soul. In their presence I feel like my twisted insides are being untangled and cleansed. The wind feels like it unfurls my soul, blowing into all the nooks and crannies, removing any debris that has settled there.

As I became aware of this, and the coolness from the earth radiating up from these points of contact, I had another realization. And it swept through me like an avalanche. She, the earth, was the only reason that I was still here. She was supporting me with invisible hands, like that strand of spider's silk, and always had been. On my knees, the earth beneath my hands, I cried and thanked her, acknowledging for the first time that if it were not for her, I would not still be here ... Alone I would not have been able to withstand the agony of my life, and I am fairly sure I wouldn't have without that connection.

I have never experienced that kind of connection or support from other humans. As a matter of fact, it is often in the company of other humans that I feel the most challenged to stay alive.

That moment in the field changed my life, because I knew that this support had always been with me and would always be there. I was connected! Not in the ways I had looked for (with family, friends or lovers), but in a nourishing way that mattered. It was real.

We need to find the faith to explore this invisible support and aware-ness coming to us from the natural world around us (and within us). In the process we learn how to trust ourselves.

I personally could not connect to the God I found in the pages of the Bible. It was not the God I knew from the fields and streams. And certainly my salvation had not come from the hands of other humans. Yet being connected to this very real force has sustained me. This is a practice that can save your life, yet it is largely ignored or denied in our modern culture. It is what shamanism seeks to do, to reconnect us with nature, both our own nature inside and the larger nature outside. One of the things I re-spect most about shamanism is that it is *a path to direct revelation.* Not a path with absolute prescribed methods that all practitioners use, but a path of direct exploration and revelations; therefore it is about real connections.

In our current paradigm the only times we are encouraged to find this type of connection outside of a love relationship are through very dog-matic religions, where God is seen as a master, a king, a ruler. I have never been comfortable with this view of the one who created nature, and me.

19. Imagination

Of what use is your imagination?

Our current paradigm would have you believe that it serves little purpose for an adult, unless you have a job that involves creativity, which the majority of the population does not.

Interestingly, the language learning center in our brains effectively shuts down after age seven. That happens to us biologically. Our imaginations do not biologically shut down. Evolution or God saw fit to keep our imaginations intact throughout our development as human beings. Think about that for a minute. It *must* serve a valuable purpose.

But this special part of ourselves is shut through parental, peer, scholastic, corporate, religious and cultural pressures. These external constructs cause us to devalue and discredit our imaginations.

What if imagination were an important tool? Imagination is at least a gateway. It is very important in achieving health, abundance, and happiness, as well as developing intuition and a sense of balance in life. The creative process which can find fuel in the imagination is a very important destination for human beings. Check out Steven Johnson's book *Wonderland: How Play Made the Modern World*, or James Hillman's work, which picks up where Jung leaves off.

Imagination is utilized in some very well recognized, documented and effective methods to change your life: manifesting, creative visualization, vision boarding, shamanic journeys, vision quests, positive affirmations, the creative process, and any type of prophetic experience.

Imagination is a canvas for us to work with as we create what we want. It's the petri dish where we combine our intentions with energy and achieve a new outcome. It is also the lens through which we may learn to view different aspects of reality, such as imaginal realms (see next chapter).

Whether you actively, consciously guide this process or not, it happens. As with any tool, the more skill you develop with it, the more the tool enables you to achieve; conversely, the less likely you will be to hurt yourself inadvertently. Just imagine Edward Scissorhands being in denial of his scissors ...

Whether you know what a steering wheel in a car is for or not, it is there. If you're sitting a car that is moving forward (and all our lives are moving), how much better to learn what a steering wheel is, how it works, and start enabling your ability to *choose* where you want to go. A dramatic difference here is that imagination can be like the steering wheel and the environment you are driving through at the same time. Like smoke, imagination can occupy (at least) two separate layers of what we call reality.

20. Imaginal Realms

In the imaginal realm, energy, medicine, science and science fiction kiss, and the resulting children are paths that can lead to deep healing and transformation. In his book *Introduction to Submolecular Biology*, Albert Szent-Györgyi says "The basic texture of research consists of dreams into which the threads of reasoning, measurement, and calculation are woven."[105] I believe he was describing the imaginal realm, which at that time was an as yet un-coined term. In other words, "the imaginal realm is the beginning place of all discovery."[106]

Recent scientific study has revealed startling evidence regarding the effect of thoughts on external reality. We see examples of this in areas like physics, plant, animal, and human biology, microbiology, psychology, medicine, and anthropology. Emerging is a concept of a field that exists outside of human beings, that is as mysterious as it is powerful, and that humans can tap into to access a co-creative power that is life transforming.

This field can be accessed and worked with using a combination of techniques, like intuition and creative visualization. It is not just a place where we can manifest from, or divest ourselves of, emotional and physical burdens that no longer serve us. From this place we can also tune into energy fields of other beings (even those considered non-sentient), communicate with them, and learn from them. What is this place? Welcome to the imaginal realm.

To me it seems as if the imaginal realm is a fertile place where conscious and sub-conscious processes meet and interact. This realm has been accessed by medicine people and shamans throughout human existence.

Looked at another way, the imaginal realm is a petri dish where intuition and science are able to merge, grow together, and become malleable,

---

[105] Albert Szent-Györgyi, *Introduction to a Submolecular Biology*, New York and London: Academic Press, 1960.
[106] Stephen Harrod Buhner, *Plant Intelligence and the Imaginal Realm*, Rochester, Vermont and Toronto, Canada: Bear & Company, 2014.

giving us the opportunity to alter the fabric of our realities. Quantum physics is a perfect example.

The imaginal realm is a place very comfortable to some and extremely uncomfortable, if not outright repulsive, to others (depending on your level of investment in old-school paradigms), and that makes sense. If you cannot access your imagination and your intuition (and validate them — which for most of us takes a lot of conscious work!), you would not even be able to recognize the existence of such a place. For you, the possibility of such a place would not exist; so sad, really. Conversely, imagine being aware of such places of possibilities from birth, but living in cultures that deny their existence. That is sad too; both are damaging in their own ways.

I like how Michael Bogar describes the imaginal realm in his blog:

> The *Imaginal Realm* is *beyond* and *before* human imagination, or imaginary human musings. The two areas clearly intersect because all human 'imaginings' are ultimately connected to the imaginal realm ... The Imaginal Realm is the arena of dreams. It is the Psychic-Sea in which we swim. It is the Realm of Psyche or Soul. It most often takes us into the depths, into the deep, into the abyss, into the labyrinth, into the matrix, into the womb of darkness, into the caverns of Hades. It is the realm of myth and fantasy — but again, these are not humanly constructed fantasies ...
>
> Perhaps most importantly, we must remember that this Realm existed long before the human being, long before the human brain evolved. The Imaginal Realm is NOT synonymous with our neural biology any more than a television's image is the result of the television's internal technology. Both the television and the human brain receive their "images" from a realm that is beyond the container holding the technology, beyond brains and microchips. To identify human bio-chemical cognition (the brain) with the Imaginal Realm may be the biggest and most deadly mistake in modern psychology, and the cause of our modern pharmaceutical culture.[107]

That's a powerful statement, and I agree with him.

---

[107] Michael Bogar, http://michaelbogar.blogspot.com/2009/09/how-is-imaginal-realm-different-from.html.

21. When Men Were Men

Once upon a time, scientists thought we could neatly tack down the corners of the universe as we know it: cows were cows, sheep were sheep, women were women, men were men, particles were particles and waves were waves. Right? So comforting, until one day all that went to hell in a handbasket ... well, at least the particle versus wave thing did.

I remember learning about waves and particles in high school. The teacher explained very clearly how the properties of each were mutually exclusive. I thought the whole thing was super cool. Waves (think light and sound) are energy, and these waves travel, expanding outward from the source where they were generated. Particles, on the other hand, are far more sedentary. Actually, they were not thought to have any energy themselves for a century or more. They travel within the bonds that hold them together (either chemical or electrical), creating matter on our planet and in the universe.

Imagine my surprise when in the very next lesson the teacher told us that light was actually both a particle and a wave! That was mind boggling to me, as well as being very exciting.

I think it was in that moment that I realized that there was room in science for the extra-ordinary ... and that mattered a great deal to me.

In 1937 Nobel Laureate biologist Szent-Györgyi recognized that there was much more to healing than just physical treatment, and he is not alone in this. Dr. Edward Bach in 1933 said in his book *The 12 Healers and Other Remedies*, "Take no notice of the disease, think only of the outlook on life of the one in distress." [108]

Dr. Bernie Siegel, a contemporary surgeon, realized decades ago that he could perform the same level of successful surgery on multiple cancer patients and that the quality of the surgery did not determine whether the patient survived. This awareness made him feel powerless. He realized

---

[108] Edward Bach, M.D., *The 12 Healers and Other Remedies*, C.W. Daniel Co. Ltd. 1952.

that there was something far less tangible that influenced survival rates in his patients. You can read about his findings in his book *Love, Medicine and Miracles.*[109]

He says that love is the most powerful healing force on this planet; but what he describes, the different ways his patients access and interact with this intangible healing force, is, as far as I can see, their accessing the imaginal realms (despite the term not being in use back then).

Penny Parker Lewis, Ph.D., uses that term directly. She is a depth-expressive arts therapy facilitator in Massachusetts. She describes the experience of one of her patients who had previously participated in other types of therapy but had not experienced the success that he was getting from the work he did with her. She writes:

> My patient was clearly not the first individual in history to experience the transformative power that exists in this liminal space. The roots of this phenomenon were depicted on caves by Paleolithic man some 30,000 years ago. For it is in the shamanic tradition that we/man found a link to the numinous world where any imagined spirit, ancestor, animal, or fantastic being could facilitate healing.[110]

Parker Lewis uses the arts to help her patients not just access the imaginal realm, but utilize its unique abilities for powerful transformation. Her work has been shown to help her patients in "valuing and utilization of experience within the imaginal realm."[111] This means that from a psychological perspective, within the imaginal realm we are able to explain something like a fear or a pattern that we are caught in. From this place we can not only "witness" this thing, we can dialogue with it. The imaginal realm grants us some awesome powers, such as the ability to transmute many things, both in the seen and unseen worlds.

The imaginal realm is a place where, among other things, beliefs affect outcomes. This can be readily witnessed by what the medical world calls the placebo effect. Dr. Ted Kaptchuck of Harvard Medical School says:

> The placebo affect is more than positive thinking — believing a treatment or procedure will work ... It's about creating a stronger

---

[109] Bernie S. Siegel, *Love, Medicine and Miracles,* New York: Harper and Row.
[110] Penny Parker Lewis, "The Transformative Process Within The Imaginal Realm," *The Art in Psychotherapy* 15, no. 4: 309–316.
[111] Penny Parker Lewis. "The Creative Arts in Transference/Countertransference Relationships," *The Arts in Psychotherapy* 19, no. 5 (1992): 317-23. https://doi.org/10.1016/0197-4556(92)90027-L

connection between the brain and the body ... When you look at these studies that compare drugs with placebos, there is the entire environmental and *ritual factor* at work."[112]

That's interesting because James Hillman, an influential psychologist who was a student of Carl Jung, said that he sees no difference between *ritual* and *play* and that ritual is healing. (What does ritual have to do with healing?)

Here again we see the devastating results of man's looking at the world dualistically, as opposed to holistically. Holistically speaking shamans have always operated as though there were ways to heal a human being through re-member-ing. This is opposed to dis-member-ing — in other words, even on a small scale, reconnecting to the whole (be it on an individual level or a planetary level) is fortifying as well as healing. Practices of dialoging with inner states, personalities, etc., have been used for thousands of years, and are being used again today in cutting edge psychology. Then and now these healings are all conducted in the imaginal realms.

My first introduction to the imaginal realm occurred long before the term was coined. I used to get really deep warts. I got them on my feet, called plantar warts, and they grow into the body, as opposed to gathering on the surface of the skin. I went through years of painful acid application treatments. I just had to sit there as the acid ate into my skin ... to be followed by tolerating parts of the newly dead areas being shaved off by a razor in the doctor's hands. I dreaded those weekly visits. Then I got a particularly bad one on my heel. It was painful to walk on, and I was told I had to have it burned off. The hole it left in my foot was deep and also hurt to walk on. It felt like torture.

I remember one day when a young dermatologist in New Rochelle, New York told me that I had the chemical within my body to fight warts. He told me all I needed to do was activate it.

"Well, how do you do that?" I asked. I guess I just followed my intuition, which has long spoken clearly to me. So every night before I went to bed, I would imagine these chemicals as lance-bearing knights, riding into battle on swift steeds. In my mind's eye I would see these knights fighting the warts, killing them, driving them out. Within three months, I did not have a wart on me ... and any time I was afraid I was getting one again (which hasn't happened in decades) I just did battle in the imaginal realm. The imaginal realm *is a powerful ally* in healing.

---

[112] "The Power of The Placebo Effect," https://www.health.harvard.edu May 2017.

Would it surprise you to know that new research shows that the ingestion of a hallucinogenic can actually help heal the brain/body/emotional "unit"? Such drugs may be effective partially because they allow us to access the imaginal realms.

Traditional healing ceremonies that often involve the plant healers (some of which contain a hallucinogenic), administered in a safe environment with a teacher/healer, can produce profound effects in remembering broken parts of our ourselves ... and of humanity.

One of the key elements in systemic healing is that you cannot dismember the different aspects of the system to bring about healing (which unfortunately is what most drug therapies focus on, and it is also the perspective of the majority of Western medical practices).

Instead, in order to initiate true healing, you must make whole the entire human being — healing through re-membering. It often takes time, because you re-claim bits here and there, choosing to face what dis-membered you in the first place.

What has caused you to shave off parts of yourself? As you spend time considering this, different things might occur. You might discover that there were parts of you that you didn't recognize. There may be parts of yourself that you had no inkling were buried, cut off. You might experience, joy, anger, rage, sadness, but these are not bad things. Remember we are created to feel. Part of the way to bring our systems back into balance is by reclaiming our emotions. We are dealing with the whole human being — all of you is welcome here. Accepting all of oneself is an important step in the healing process. After all, how can one forgive or heal another person if one can't accept one's own emotions? The embodiment of you is why you are here. Think about it; if you are dis-membered, you will experience dis-ease.

After you have spent time with these awarenesses, I want you to start looking not only at what parts of yourself were shaved away, either consciously by you (in an attempt to fit in better), or by pressure applied by some group. Notice who has asked you to do this, either covertly or overtly.

The imaginal realm is where we can connect to many aspects of ourselves and the world around us. It is the place where inter-species communication stems from. Here humans can open up their other senses to understand more than our modern paradigms allow. Shamanism has been operating in these realms for almost the entire span of human history. Shamanism, which can be seen as a path of direct revelation, is a place where the imaginal realms find acceptance and expression in human beings.

22. Shamanism

My formal introduction to shamanism came when I was eighteen as part of an intensive study at Goddard College called "Vision of the Shaman, Healing of the Dove." I was exposed to many types of healing during a three-month intensive study period. For two weeks we studied different kinds of massage. We were asked to practice the techniques we were learning on our classmates. Unexplainably I started suffering from an odd assortment of maladies: bad headaches, neck pains, knee pain, etc. I could not make a correlation with anything I had done that might have caused these things, so I took acetaminophen and usually the next day these aches would be gone. I was talking to a classmate one day, and she thanked me for relieving her of chronic knee pain. I froze in mid-response, having no idea that she had had a knee problem, much less that I had helped her with it.

Several people told me after that day that they had had a problem which went away after I worked on them. As they started listing their symptoms, I realized these were the discomforts I had been experiencing for about 24 hours after each massage I gave.

Why was this happening? Was there anything I could do about it? I loved helping people, but experiencing their symptoms was wearing me down. Seeking answers to these new questions, I found myself sitting in the waiting room of the Sun Ray Meditation Society in Vermont in the early 80s. It was founded by Diyani Yawaho, a Cherokee medicine woman with a long lineage of healing, providing her, I hoped, with knowledge that might be able to help me. Although I had an appointment, I found myself waiting for an extended period in an empty room devoid of any reading material. This was long before cell phones, so I studied the room. On the table in front of me were some rocks. One of them was pink. My dad had been a miner in the Rockies, and semi-precious gems and minerals in their raw beauty had been a part of my childhood. Because of this I knew that this pink stone was in the quartz family, aptly named "rose." I picked up the rose quartz and had it in my hand when my healer/teacher came in. I spoke with her for some time and, truthfully, I really didn't get any answers from her that satisfied my young self. She gave me some visualizations to do involving different colors and shapes at each of my chakras (we will cover those later), but her suggestions did not resonate with me then. This was partly because I had no idea of the power of energy or colors at the time, and partly because I was looking for an answer, not a practice. So I felt let down as she was guiding me through these visualizations. At the conclusion of our meeting, she directed me "Touch the stone you are holding to the part of your body that it connects to."

What? A test? I hate tests! My mind tends to go blank — you know, that "deer in the headlights" syndrome ...

So, not wanting to fail this "test," I closed my eyes, took a deep breath, and slowly brought the stone to my heart. There was no sound from my inquisitor, so I opened my eyes and found that she was smiling. She said that I was correct, that "rose quartz is a heart stone."

What? My mind raced ... How can a stone be correct for a part of our bodies? How could I possibly have been able to know that!? I came searching for answers and left with more questions...

Even after my study of holistic healing and shamanism at Goddard that year, between where I was personally and where science was, there were no answers that were solid enough to satisfy me. I didn't have trouble holding on to any of the information I gleaned, but I had trouble *believing* in it, because it was so antithetical to the paradigm I grew up in. And that was a dance I did for decades.

Part of my problem was that I am incredibly sensitive. I'm an empath and I'm clairvoyant. I was aware of things happening around me all the time. Having no reason to understand any of this, I developed a blind eye to much of it. The concept was, "ignore it, it's just flights of fancy." Some of it was outright frightening. Why would it not be frightening — I had no teachers! It is hard to find answers when you are discounting the information that leads to the questions, never mind the answers discovered.

Because of my dyslexia, finishing college ended up not being an option for me. Between not being able to spell, reversing numbers, and being more aware (most of the time) of what other people were actually feeling than they were, I was left in a bad place. I couldn't trust myself, which led me to turn to others for answers. I knew I was missing something but did not think that I might have the answer I was looking for!

All these things together led me to believe that I was stupid. That is not a good combination. I hated myself; I hated being alive. I hurt all the time. But I never stopped looking. My answers have been decades in the forming. Before I found answers, I needed to heal, but I didn't know that.

When life teaches you to disrespect yourself and your gifts at an early age, it's a long, conscious road if you are to find your way back. Along my path I discovered that I was not only *not dumb*, but that I was actually smarter than most people. That was a shock!

I have a very keen mind, with an amazing ability to retain a tremendous amount of information. When I focus in a certain way, I can "see" this information spread out in space (above my head), like constellations. I can see how the pieces of information relate to each other, even if they are separated by human definitions. It's hard to describe ... This perspective allows me to correlate a great many random facts and, like astronomers of old, to see pictures within the connected dots. (Although I will tell you, when I look at the actual constellations in the night sky, I do not see how the ancients saw the animals and such in the dots they connected!)

This book is the culmination of part of my quest. I hope that my findings will bring the light of connection to many subjects.   It is meant to bridge the inner human with the outer human, older cultures and information with new scientific findings, and so connect us back to ourselves and the natural world, of which we are an inseparable part and which actually strengthens us when we immerse ourselves in it. If anything I have written here makes you feel more comfortable in your skin, then I will have done something worthwhile.

The information in this book is truly my life's work, and writing it has transformed my life. It is my intention that it will have the power to do likewise for other people.

23. Ancestry

In my family, ancestors did not play much of a part in our day to day lives. You missed some ... others not so much. It seemed very strange to me when I heard of cultures where they honor the dead with daily rituals or believe the dead might be concerned with the surroundings in which they are interred. I remember feeling incredulous when I saw things like toilets and other modern conveniences inside Chinese tombs. This was before I had any idea how advanced the Chinese were at understanding energy and before I knew about the First Law of Thermodynamics. Nowadays I am very reluctant to discount beliefs involving esoteric things coming from a people whose batting average is so high (e.g., feng shui, acupuncture, and martial arts). The Chinese clearly understand energy within the body and in the natural world!

I have stopped being incredulous and scoffing at things I don't understand. Instead I am curious. What reasoning could prompt this lavish treatment of the deceased?

How involved are your ancestors in your thinking? How about in your life? Is that even relevant to you?

Let's review some topics — dots as I call them — we've looked at so far that could potentially affect our understanding. We have learned from the experiments in epigenetics that our ancestors' experiences are not only passed down to us as visceral awareness, but that their experiences can actually change our physiology. So we can say that our ancestors are "with" us in that sense. But is there more?

According to many older cultures around the globe, yes, very much so. But since we have been taught to discredit our ancestors' knowledge and beliefs, let's look at science. New evidence is coming to light almost daily that supports such beliefs (but not many have connected these dots yet). Even if scientists haven't extrapolated their own data in this direction (yet), the conclusion of their findings seems clear to anyone looking. The First

Law of Thermodynamics states that "energy cannot be created or destroyed."

Did you know that the thoughts in your head are electrical impulses jumping from synapse to synapse? Electricity is energy, it has frequency; "Energy does not die." How does that apply to a bioelectric being?

Is it possible that what we call "spirit" may actually be energy? An energy that inhabits a physical body, giving it personality, thought and life? An energy that does not die and (now here's the radical part) that has self-awareness, consciousness. There are many recorded accounts of people who've technically died on operating tables being aware of their surroundings, even seeing their own bodies as they are drawn out of them to a light-filled tunnel, with shimmery loved ones waiting on the other side.

Thoughts being energy that does not die would explain past life memories and even the concept of reincarnation. It would lend credence to the concept of ancestral disembodied spirits having an interest in the lives of the loved ones that they left behind and their descendants.

The Haudenosaunee (ho dee noe sho NEE) — the Iroquois nations — believe that not only are the energies of the deceased around us, but the energies of the yet to be born as well! Think about it: if souls are energy, and energy can neither be created nor destroyed, then those who died, as well as those waiting to be born, would still be around ... somewhere ... as disembodied energy.

Many of my teachers, who are elders from different nations, have told me that it is important to learn about our ancestors. What they believed and how they worshiped is supposed to be relevant to us, their descendants.

I have a great deal of resistance to this particular assignment. I have never felt like a part of any clan. My grandmother on my mother's side, a Harrington, was ostensibly Irish, but she married outside the Catholic faith and so was estranged from her parents. Although there were some branches of her family that reached out to me when I was small, I don't have any real roots there. The man my grandmother married was a German Jew, in denial of his heritage. He kept us away from his side of the family because he had renounced it. My mother, like her mother, married someone completely foreign to her parents. My father was Yugoslavian, and unable to go back once he had fled after the war. I never met any of my relatives from his side of the family. My mother's father never met my father, and my grandmother only met him once. Papa died when I was seven, and I hadn't seen him since I just turned four, so I don't know any of his/my family.

My mom and I moved around so much I never established any roots anywhere ... except of course those I put in the earth and the ones I developed with her denizens (which, looking back on it now, were some pretty deep, significant "roots"!). I always felt close to the Native Americans. When I was little in Colorado, my mom was a social worker. A fair share of her clients were native Hopi and Navajo.

I remember as a child watching westerns, and even though the "Indians" were portrayed negatively, I never believed that they were bad. I never saw them as anything but beautiful, deeply spiritual, powerful, and connected to the natural world. It's quite odd that I could look at the way they were portrayed, as brutal and savage, and not attach any credence to it. I had tremendous respect for their ways, based on my intuition and my gut reaction ... or was it more?

Much later in life, I had a powerful experience studying with a Mashika shaman in the Wewepahtli (Traditional Medicine System from Mexico). I signed up for a five-day workshop with him at the Rowe Conference Center, and was completely surprised at how deeply I fell into the work. What we were learning resonated powerfully with me; I found myself absorbing all the information like it was the first food I had ever eaten in my life! I completely lost track of time, engrossed as one piece of revealed information led to the next. He was sharing with us a system so old that it defied my modern thinking. It contained massive amounts of fascinating and pertinent information, from specifics on diet and sleep to the different types of people on earth. On the last day, we broke for lunch. I was so caught up in the experience that I had not realized we were not reconvening. Of course, I knew the workshop was ending Sunday afternoon, and that it *was* Sunday that day. It just felt completely wrong to stop studying with him. I could not shake that feeling, and as a matter of fact it grew, until at lunch I found tears streaming down my face.

I was experiencing a sense of devastation. I could not stop crying. I knew it was ridiculous, but I was inconsolable — that's how wrong it felt to a part of my being to not continue studying with him.

Honestly, I was not expecting that! I thought about it and the only thing that made sense to me was that I had lived at least one past life (if not several) in my teacher's culture. My soul, or inner being, who was just reunited with these teachings, was devastated at being ripped away again.

I approached Tzen (short for Tzenwaxolokwauhtli Tzatzoehetzin) and through my tears I asked him if he believed in reincarnation. His answer was very important to me. Reincarnation was the only way I could make sense of what was happening inside me. He looked at me and responded, "I don't believe in anything."

I felt a numbness, close to shock begin to settle in my middle ... I took his response to mean "No" and felt so confused, because every fiber of my being knew that this could be the only explanation for the immensity of what I felt. Tzen let me sit with that for probably only a few seconds, but it felt like much longer. I was feeling totally off balance, like someone pulled the rug out from under me. I'm not sure I was even looking at him when he added quietly "I *know* them."

I had to run that round my brain a few times. So he didn't *believe in* reincarnation ... he *knew*. Believing has to do with faith, and knowing is based on experience. I had no other explanation for the tears that would not stop, nor for the sense of wrongness that was present in every cell of my body! What I was feeling was that this was not how things were done. My studies with him were not supposed to stop ... even though I had only signed up for a one-week workshop! I have never experienced anything like that before or since.

A decade later I was studying with an Abenaki Grandmother who told a group of us women in the darkened interior of a sweat lodge that "We are all recycled souls." She said that those of us *called to* what is referred to as "The Red Road," to learn about Native American cultures and practices, had at one point lived Native lives. Recycled souls ... that certainly supported the enormity of what I had experienced with Tzen.

Incidentally, later that same day she said that "God doesn't make trash." Another powerful moment that got me crying. So, for me, it seems like my ancestors from past lives are the ones that I am more connected to than my biological ones in this life. Right or wrong — it seems like my current truth (although I would love to learn more about my father's Yugoslavian Gypsy heritage! Not so easy when you are an outsider ...).

In the Orient they take for granted that deceased family members have a continued existence and that these ancestors take an interest in the affairs of the world. More than that, these ancestors have the ability to influence the fortunes of the living.

Evidence that this belief was in place in everyday life for the Chinese is clearly recorded as far back as 3,500 years ago.[113] What's more is that they are not alone in this belief. Many cultures throughout the world and history have recognized the influence of their ancestors or "spirits" on a

---

[113] Chinasage, "Ancestor worship and veneration in China," https://chinasage.info/ancestors.

daily level. In some Native American traditions, the connection between the living and a loved one who has died is seen as being so strong that the living will not speak the name of the deceased for one year. This is so that the journey that the disembodied spirit needs to make after it leaves its body is not interrupted.

We've been conditioned to be closed to the possibility of communication from our deceased, but that doesn't stop it from happening. As I have said before, if you are not looking for something, it is very hard to find.

Have you ever had something happen that made you think of someone that has "crossed" (died), and suddenly you feel them very strongly, as though they are standing right there next to you? Or something makes you laugh out loud, and you feel the presence of someone you lost, as though they were sharing enjoyment over that humorous event? Or have you gone to a place that was a favorite of your crossed person and felt him or her there?

When people are interested in seeing if they can connect with their ancestors or a loved one who has crossed, the only option they have in our society is to go to a "spiritual medium" or psychic. I will tell you for certain that your loved ones who have crossed are often hanging close to you, just waiting for you to hear them. I know this because when I do energy work with people, I get such messages all the time.

The messages usually come through in the form of pictures — either still images, like I was viewing a photograph, or in short clips of moving images, just like viewing an excerpt from a movie. They most often mean nothing to me.

I discovered a long time ago, in psychic development classes that I took back in the early 80s, that pictures come very easily to me. Because of how readily they pop into my head, it's very easy to discount them as flights of fantasy or imagination.

This is why it's important to practice by yourself, but also with others. You need feedback as to when you are on the mark or when you are not. This allows you to examine the difference in the internal sensations.

Eventually you learn how the things you need to share *feel*, or rather how you feel when you receive something that is not about or for you. When I first started practicing Reiki with clients, I would see or feel things that I couldn't explain while I was working on them. I did not know what to make of it, but it happened with enough regularity that I began to be curious if the information I was receiving might have relevance to the person I was working on. I began asking my clients if they would like me to share anything I "picked up" during their session. Almost all of them said yes. There was one time, fairly early into my Reiki practice, when I was working on a new client. I knew nothing about him; he had been recommended to me by my masseuse (who was also a client). As I worked on this man, I kept seeing the prow of a small boat moving through water. The vision was very persistent. The water I saw moving against the boat had small waves; it "felt" like it was ocean or a salty bay. I tried to ignore this, because it was such a random image for *me*. The image had no personal meaning to me, and it was easy to want to just push it aside. But it kept coming back, so I finally decided to be brave and mention it. When I described the scene I was witnessing, the man began crying. His father had passed just two months prior, and they had sailed a small boat together since he was a boy.

Was I glad I had the courage to share this with him! His dad was saying "Hi, I'm still connected to you, and I want you to know it." Or at least that's what it seemed like to me.

It took a while for me to start to trust the things I saw or felt. Like any form of communication, interpreting such information takes practice. Sometimes (although rarely) what I see doesn't strike a chord for my client. At those times I have to assume that the image is somehow for me. Mostly I've had experiences like the last one, where what I "see" has great relevance to my clients. Such experiences very often involve people who have died, but not always.

Conversely, I have been with dying people and witnessed an interesting progression. As their bodies are starting to fail, they often see a crossed loved one outside their window. As their own time to cross comes closer, so do the loved ones that only they can see, who are apparently waiting for them. The day they tell me that a crossed loved one is standing at the foot of the bed or next to them, I know that their "time" is here, and they will probably die that day or evening.

That is not to say seeing a loved one by your bed means you are getting ready to cross! Children of all nations and races often see loved ones, or ancestors, who have crossed; sometimes they just see unrelated others. Interestingly, most of the time, children are not frightened by this experience. They seem to just accept it. This is because children have not yet learned to tell themselves "this can't be real" or that spirits are bad. Often the children who experience these "visions" speak of them very matter of factly, as if it were completely natural. Interesting, no? It is adults or older siblings who have already turned away from their own truths in favor of the prevailing scientific, cultural or religious views who react negatively.

When children experience something like this and feel comfortable, but you do not, try using it as an opportunity to learn something *from them*. Be open. Dialogue about it. If you feel completely out of your element, seek out someone in the community that is open to, and comfortable with, these types of experiences. There are people who speak with angelic entities on a daily basis, and others who speak with beings that have died, like John Edwards who became well known for his TV series *Crossing Over*. Celtic priests, death doulas, shamanic and Reiki practitioners all have experience in these realms. Choose someone you feel comfortable with, and if you are introducing this person to your children, make sure it is someone they are comfortable with. The more you learn to trust what children intuit, the easier it will be for them to grow into who they were meant to be, with trust and appreciation for who they are. Just as important, if your child is frightened by an experience she or he is having, it is good to take this seriously as well. If you would like to learn about ways to protect a child energetically or to clear space, see Ch. 33 "Intention and Space Clearing."

24. The Alligator under the Bed

As far as I can tell we all have guides of some sort. The world around us, the energy contained within all, communicates with us. How receptive are you?

We have all had experiences we cannot fully explain. It is part of what the Lakota refer to as "The Great Mystery" or "Wankantankan"... which also equates to the Creator or God.

Working with my clients I have seen all kinds of beings, from angelic to amphibian and everything in between. Guides often appear as animate beings, but they can also be inanimate.

The problem with finding your guide may be as simple as recognizing it. If a guide is here to help you work on your fears, it may well be scary looking.

I recently took the Master Shamanic Reiki program with Llyn Cedar Roberts. In this class we were introduced to our Shamanic Reiki Master Guides. Imagine my surprise when what appeared to me was the big alligator who used to be under my bed as a child. I had been so afraid of that alligator! I never saw him with my eyes, but I felt him, I knew he was watching me ... and he terrified me. I was afraid to get out of bed at night. God forbid one of my stuffed animals fell out of bed; I was convinced that it would be gobbled up! My mom tells the story of my asking her when I was five years old, "Mom, I know there isn't really an alligator under the bed ... but could you look anyway?" That is how real he was to me. I could not see him, but I knew he was there. What I didn't know was that he was my ally! Now in my fifties he reveals himself to me. Really?

Imagine what might have happened if my mom had known enough to react to my sensing the alligator by sitting on my bed, holding my hand, and saying, "OK, honey, let's talk to the alligator together." She could have had me close my eyes and picture the alligator, then had me describe him to her. After that, if she had told me to ask it, "Why are you here?" and let the dialogue unfold from there, so much could have been revealed!

Imagine the benefits. For one, I would have learned that there are safe ways to confront fears directly. More than that, I would have had a powerful lesson in dialoging with the "unseen." Dialoging is a process we use in shamanism and Shamanic Reiki all the time, similar to the Creative Arts process developed by Natalie Rodgers. Much is gained from speaking in the imaginal realm to things that are sensed or felt or seen in the body. From this place blocks or intrusions in the energy field or the body can be worked with. They can be neutralized, transmuted and even befriended here with the dialoging process.

My alligator guide wasted no time and started working with me on my fears within 24 hours of my consciously accepting him. Our guides are waiting for us to discover them, as is much of our inner world and a wisdom that is awe-inspiring.

25. The Seventh Generation Principle

I'm sure most of you have heard of the company called Seventh Generation that makes paper products out of recycled materials for household use. It was the first ecologically oriented company here in New York to go mainstream. But how many of you knew that this name came from a principle that was conceptualized by a powerful, aware, eloquent and self-possessed group of Native Americans? Not only did they coin this term, but they did so close to 1,000 years ago!

I cannot touch upon ancestors, or the concept of living in balance with nature, without speaking of the Haudenosaunee, known as the Iroquois Confederacy, and their "Great Law of Peace." This is the oldest living participatory democracy, truly dedicated to what is best for the populace it serves. Research it; it might just blow your mind.[114]

Imagine a governing system where everyone participates in the decisions being made, and where the chiefs or leaders are chosen solely based on a proven record of selflessness and calmness in the face of intense situations. They are chosen by a group of women who are in turn are selected by the tribe, judged on their years of selfless service to the nations that they belong to. This system consists of laws of conduct, designed to keep people in right relationship with all life on the planet and with themselves, as well as with their ancestors (whom they counted as being very much a part of their world) and the *yet to be born*! This meant looking at the effect of their decisions for seven generations to come (about 125 years). Can you imagine? Referred to as "The Seventh Generation Principle," this was a pivotal piece of legislation!

---

[114] Three useful resources: https://www.huffingtonpost.com/jacob-devaney/peace-american-precolonia_b_1932921.html; http://www.ganienkeh.net/thelaw.html; and the book *Debating Democracy: Native American Legacy of Freedom* by Bruce Johansen (Santa Fe: Clear Light Publishers, 1998).

George Washington, Benjamin Franklin and Thomas Jefferson spent a lot of time learning about this governing system, which worked so well that these men incorporated much of it into our constitution. Ironically, although a great deal of our Constitution was based on the Iroquois Great Law of Peace, two of its governing principles were left out of ours.[115]

One was the Seventh Generation Principle itself, a very unfortunate omission. Can you imagine what our world would look like, feel like and smell like if our leaders considered the effects of the laws they passed on our environment for 125 years? If the health and welfare of children yet to come were more important to them than the size of their bank accounts, a lot of the destruction of our planet would not be happening. Prison systems would not be the big businesses that they are. Our lives would not be sustained by the destruction of our planet and the consumption of our resources at the expense of all other inhabitants, including the earth herself!

We think that science has helped us physically, and you could say that the help was greater than the cost to us initially. Now with 70% of our world's water polluted and diseases like cancer, Parkinson's and others an increasingly frightening reality for many (because of pollution and pesticides and processed foods), it is time for the true wisdom of a Seventh Generation system to be used as a guideline for our next steps forward.

Here is one area that would be treated very differently, the use of GMOs (genetically modified organisms). Did you know that the vehicles used to modify cells are viruses? Viruses are injected into the cell and they snip out a part of its DNA and insert their own (or in this case what the scientist has created them to insert). That's how viruses spread within our own bodies naturally by changing our cells into replicas of themselves. Until now, viruses did not move across species, for the most part, and they didn't cross the plant - animal line. But scientists at MIT have been implanting frog DNA in rhododendrons for over a decade now. Can we foresee what the effect of that will be 125 years from now? Will insects that attack rhododendrons develop a taste for frog? And later perhaps fish? Dog? Cat? Human? It is not beyond the scope of possibility.

One of the things we know for sure about viruses is that they mutate; we have seen it thousands of times in cold and flu epidemics. Why do these scientists *presume* that they can control and predict the mutation of the viruses they are using for genetic modification? Can they do that with the ones that make us sick now? Logic and track records say they cannot.

---

[115] Johansen, *Debating Democracy: Native American Legacy of Freedom.*

These experimental products should not be allowed out of the lab for at least 100 years, if it is even worth the risk (at that point) of introducing them into our ecosystems at all. That is what my Seventh Generation "spidey sense" tells me.

Oh, and by the way, the other aspect that was left out of our Constitution was the right of women to participate in the voting process. It was very much a part of the Great Law of Peace. Imagine that! No wonder that the "Founding Fathers" wanted to wipe out the Iroquois nations. Can you imagine ... women with the right to vote? Women with the right to own land! What heathens! Savages!

Part III

INTELLECTUAL

26. Language

Language both shapes, and is shaped by, our thoughts. We talked in "The World is Flat" about how paradigms make it harder for us to look non-judgmentally at the world around us. We learned in "Being Open" that being open is essential to making decisions truly grounded in facts.

In "Is Ignorance Bliss?" we began to look at how a culture's use of language reveals much about its beliefs. At the very least, such usage reveals the ideas it supports and those it doesn't.

Words, whether written or spoken, have the power to alter our states of mental or emotional being. Remember from "Crystalline Structure" that there are several ways to excite vibrational frequency, including *heat, light* and *sound.* Therefore, we are exciting the "molecules" of our intention (whether we realize it or not) in our word choices, with the sound (vibration) of our voice. Spoken words have vibrational frequency added to their innate potency — that's why affirmations and spells are always read out loud. The vibrational frequency of one thing is able to affect the frequency of others. A perfect example would be the Tacoma Narrows Bridge (known as "Galloping Gertie"). Just months after being built, a wind with a particular vibrational frequency started strumming through her cables, and like an aroused lover she responded. At first there were little movements which became incrementally larger, until she was rippling and bucking, only to come completely apart minutes later. You can see the actual footage of the incident online.[116]

Vibrational frequency effects everything, and that should not be surprising. What is strange is that, given how many ways to pick up and decipher these frequencies are built into our bodies and psyches, our paradigms, cultures and religions do not include these teachings!

We experience vibrational frequencies around us daily; they vibrate in our chest cavity, our guts, our ears and on our skin. It would be interesting

---

[116]https://www.youtube.com/watch?v=y0xohjV7Avo.

to study the effect of the frequencies found in the spoken word. Here's what Linda Gadbois has to say about that:

> DNA operates by the same principles as the mind and brain, where the acoustic aspect of information as "words" acts to form a visual holographic image in the imagination that turns the idea inherent in the words into a virtual reality. It translates ideas that are communicated by talking about them, whether through our own thoughts as internal dialogue, or as listening to someone else talk, into visual imagery as living scenarios. It comes as words, sentences, paragraphs, and pages of written and spoken script that forms visual imagery in our mind's eye as we read it (absorb it). DNA works by way of the same principles as the mind and neurons of the brain and body. It decodes words into 3-D realities as the basis for organizing matter into the biological form that corresponds to the image as an archetypal idea. This is represented in Sacred Geometry by the Tetrad (Tetragrammaton), which is the physical outward reflection and projection of the Triad (inner imagining) that emerges naturally out of the Dyad, which symbolizes an interference pattern as the coupling of two wave forms (double helix) of the same frequency to produce a new whole through coherence. Most spiritual texts describe God as the creator calling forth all material life using words as breath that moves across the water (liquid crystal), causing a form to rise up and take shape.[117]

Getting back to our exploration of the effect of words on us, there are three factors to look at: the frequency of the spoken word, the frequency of the thoughts, and of the feelings associated with the word. Because perception is very personal, people experience the same words differently. Those differences should affect the outcome for each individual, and I think they do. However, there is enough commonality within a given social group that the results from a group should be fairly consistent.

Dr. Masaru Emoto from Japan did a study of the effect that words (both spoken and written) had on water. He left containers of water out in heavily trafficked areas. Each sample had a word printed in large letters on a white label placed on it. Students were asked to focus on the word, either silently or by saying it out loud as they gazed at the containers. Dr. Masura later froze the samples so he could study the molecular structure of the

---

[117] Linda Gadbois, "DNA—the phantom effect, quantum hologram and the etheric body," MOJ Proteomics Bioinform, 2018;7(1):9-10. DOI: 10.15406/mojpb.2018.07.00206.

water. What he discovered was remarkable. Water that had had words like LOVE written on it had beautifully shaped ice crystals. Samples that had been labeled with I HATE YOU or YOU'RE UGLY had shortened, lumpy crystals. This is powerful support for the effect words have on our environment, as well as on us (given how much water our bodies contain). You can read about it in his book *The Hidden Messages in Water*.[118]

There was also an experiment in which students in a high school bullied a plant for 30 days and the results were filmed. The experiment was designed to raise awareness of the effects of bullying, but it also shows the effects of words spoken and thought on other living systems.[119]

So how does it affect us when a culture shifts the meaning of a word from positive to negative? Words affect how we look at or feel about things. Changing the meaning of a word that is used commonly will alter our experiences. Let's look at the word "responsibility;" what does that word mean to you? Does it imply a sense of burden? Of work? Of being tied down? Those are the shades of meanings in our current paradigm.

This word comes ultimately from the Latin *responsum*, the past participle of *respondēre*, meaning "to respond."[120] Think about that. Our ability to respond to something, a situation, or a person is one of our greatest gifts! Without it we would be locked into a bubble, with no ability to move toward or away from our preferences. Responsibility is not a burden!

But that isn't how I interpreted responsibility growing up. It felt like a burden when I was younger. For example, my mom made it my responsibility to take the garbage out, and I had to do it before I could go out and play. I had to collect all the trash from each room, then bring it all outside and drag the heavy trash bin to the front of the house. This took some of my precious free time and I resented it.

Now I am thankful when I remember to take the trash out — I don't resent it at all! If I forget, I must live with stinky garbage in my house for another week.

I have a very different relationship to my responsibilities, and that's a good thing because I have many more tasks now that I am responsible for. I have consciously chosen to alter my relationship (meaning my perspective, my attitude and vibrational frequency) to my entire life. It is

---

[118] Masaru Emoto, *The Hidden Messages in Water*, Atria Books 2005.

[119] https://globalnews.ca/news/4217594/bully-a-plant-ikea/. Ikea conducted this experiment using American children.

[120] American Heritage Dictionary, https://www.ahdictionary.com/word/search.html?q= response.

incredibly enriching to form conscious relationships with as many things in your world as you can. You really do get to choose the frequencies that you steep yourself in. What are you soaking in?

George Carlin was the first person who got me thinking about the absurd use of some English words. In one of his skits he points out that we "Park our cars in a driveway" but "We drive on parkways;" we pay for the privilege to drive on "freeways,"[121] and many others.

While none of those examples will affect how you feel about yourself, or about life, others can — for instance, when people use the names of women's sexual parts as derogatory slang words. How might calling someone who is weak or fearful a pussy affect a little girl who hears it, especially if she knows she has one? Vaginas are actually pretty strong; why would you use that word to describe weak or fearful? Calling someone a baby or a sissy would be more accurate and far less damaging to more than half the population.

Start looking at the language that you use, and be aware of how it might be warping your ability to have a better feeling relationship with life. There *is* power in the spoken word.

Here's another example, soil. Good soil meant so much to our ancestors. This might be hard to believe today because we are so conditioned to our food coming to us, delivered in trucks to indoor supermarkets. Our food is so far removed from the earth it was grown in, or having ever been alive, that we don't feel the connection, and this removes us from our actual place in the chain of life on this planet as well.

Our ancestors were connected to the earth and life intimately, and I believe they were better off for it. I find it interesting that most First Nation peoples (across the globe) believed that earth was sacred, and that women were as well. My friends from some First Nations say that this loss of the belief that earth and woman are sacred is the reason that we are in such trouble today. Do you think there could be some truth in this? I do.

Getting back to our use of language and earth: when you think of "earth" what comes to mind? Earth contains a lot of ... *soil.* What impression or feeling arises if I say something is soil-ed? What about when I say that something is dirt-y?

Soil is clean, and so is dirt. Some beneficial microbes that are important for our immune development live in soil/dirt, as well microbes that

---

[121] George Carlin, "A Master of Wordplay," https://www.youtube.com/watch ?v=YSS_PhR9WWo.

affect our brain in much the same way Prozac does.[122] But our use of these names belittles them greatly. Nowadays, we say if something is *soiled*, it is *dirty* (very ironic!) and something that is "dirty" can range from your hands to your mind. Soil and dirt have been denigrated to mean something filthy, contaminated — the same way a woman's body has been portrayed to be unclean. How do these negative beliefs affect you? Do they influence your thoughts around the value of these "things"?

One of my pet peeves is the derogatory use in our culture of the word vagina. Many very strong, beautiful young women whom I know participate in this degradation. If I call you a pussy when you are afraid or weak, then I am participating in denigrating women. Simple.

It is no different if I call you a cunt for being selfish or mean. I have a particularly hard time understanding how this part of a woman's anatomy is labeled this way. Are vaginas mean? Are they selfish? I don't see that. Penises exhibit far more selfish acts and instigate more cruelty than vaginas historically and even today. But having hundreds of thousands of human beings repeating these phrases over centuries has an accumulative affect. And it is not a beneficial one. Remember that frequencies are real and they don't lie. Also keep in mind that frequencies affect things around them. You are affecting the world around you (as well as yourself) with the things you say, do, and focus on.

Have you ever witnessed a woman giving birth? If you had, I am sure you would never associate this organ with weakness or fear. I'd like to see a man pop a watermelon out of his penis and then tell me pussies are weak! Being a chalice of life necessitates that a woman be more aware of her feelings and her intuition. Pregnancy slows you down; in a race for survival there would have to be compensations for this period of encumbrance. Perhaps it's a man's fear of the emotional realm or the psychic realm that causes him to associate an awareness of these two forces with weakness. Or that an expression of fear might in some way weaken a person. In fact, expressing your feelings is a very real process that results in your having more room internally. Such expression can clear the mind and allow thoughts to be more focused and grounded, resulting in better performance, not worse.

---

[122]Jose Glausiusz, "Is Dirt the New Prozac? Injections of soil bacteria produce serotonin—and happiness—in mice." http://discovermagazine.com/2007/jul/raw-data-is-dirt-the-new-prozac June 14 2007.

27. Inference

Referential frameworks, such as paradigms and cultural beliefs, all *interfere* with our ability to see and figure things out for ourselves. They affect our ability to *infer* things, and I see this as one of the biggest problems facing us today. How can we possibly discern anything if we can't connect the dots for ourselves?

Inference is how we draw conclusions: "An inference is an idea or conclusion that's drawn from evidence and reasoning. An inference is an educated guess. We learn about some things by experiencing them first-hand, but we gain other knowledge by inference — the process of inferring things based on what is already known."[123] In other words *what we know (or think we know) can very much affect the conclusions we draw.*

If we cannot take in new information and draw new conclusions from it, then we are doomed *never* to learn or grow. Had we grown up in a world where we were encouraged and or taught how to read the rich stream of information available to us through our intuition, our gut, or even simply our eyes, we would naturally synthesize this information into a holistic picture. The pictures we gleaned from this would differ slightly, or widely, from those of others, depending on our perspective. Each lens that views the universe is shaped differently, so the images vary from lens to lens, from beholder to beholder. We all know that "beauty is in the eyes of the beholder" — but so is everything else; as Jung expresses it, the universe thinks through us.

If we were able to free ourselves from our current myopic and limiting beliefs, our relationship to the world would be very different. For one thing, we would all be more confident. We would not have to wonder if we were in a safe place with the right people. We would feel these things clearly. Other peoples' opinions would not have a heavy emotional impact

---

[123] Vocabulary.com Dictionary, https://www.vocabulary.com/dictionary/inference (accessed 11-4-20).

on us. We would know when someone spoke a truth that resonated with us, as well as discerning when the truth that they were speaking was *their own*. Our knowledge of ourselves and of our place in our environment would grow exponentially.

Let's look at our bodies for a moment as animal vehicles that our consciousness is riding in, not unlike a car. Imagine if we shut our eyes while we were driving. It's not a good idea. How do you think it affects our animal bodies that we ignore their built-in warning systems? Does that produces a good relationship between you and your body? Anything that disconnects us, weakens us. What effect has it had on you? I know it left me feeling afraid of energy and spirits and the world in general.

I believe we are often disoriented, sad, lonely, can't sleep, have anger issues, overeat, turn to drugs, need to be medicated, and so on, because we don't have a clue how to deal with everything of which our bodies are aware, but of which our minds have been trained to be in denial. Our ability to read the "instrument" of our body and connect into the greater web of life around us has been sabotaged.

All types of reasoning that isolate parts away from the whole are inherently flawed. We must struggle to free ourselves from these limiting views. Nothing exists in an isolated bubble. We need to learn to read and trust the instrument our Creator gave us to navigate all of this world.

Because of cultural paradigms, you may be ignoring or discrediting information coming to you on a daily basis, without even being conscious of it. Consequently, you may be having trouble drawing "real," or at least "whole," conclusions. The conclusions you are able to come to depend on your level of experience with the world you can *sense* and your openness to it. I would like you to think about this.

Our current paradigm teaches that we should learn only from what other people tell us is real or acceptable. In the process, we discount much of our own experience and stifle our natural inquisitiveness.

This can be seen in the American school system, which encourages the creation of a "cog," meaning a person ideally suited to fit into an industrial or corporate setting. Such a person is easily controlled and will do or believe what he or she is told. This system also creates a person who is easily misled. It doesn't encourage thinkers or seekers (although I will say that in recent decades the American educational system has begun to acknowledge the importance of individual thinking and creativity). In the 1970s the Nobel prize winning biologist Albert Szent-Györgyi stated, "A discovery must be, by definition, at variance with existing knowledge."[124] And he is not alone. Dr. Edward Bach and Dr. Maxwell Maltz, to name two, published papers or books illustrating the need for us to look outside of our paradigm for answers.

It is not easy to do, because most of us want to conform, to fit in, to be seen as similar to our peers. How comfortable is it for you to step outside your cultures agreed-upon beliefs? To draw your own conclusions? Or to stand up for those?

Here is the other side of that particular coin; is mental *comfort* imperative to your survival? Thinking for yourself may be ....

[124] Albert Szent-Györgyi, https://www.brainyquote.com/authors/albert-szent-gyorgyi-quotes.

28. Recreating the Wheel 1

Humans are strange creatures. Have you ever noticed that we don't learn well from each other's mistakes?

If I did, I would not be working on my computer, sitting outside at a café in Poughkeepsie, New York. I would never even work near a window close to a street. That's because a really dear family friend was killed doing just that at a Starbucks in New Jersey not long ago.

If we learned from each other's mistakes, no one would smoke, do drugs, drink alcohol in excess, eat too much sugar, have unprotected sex, or forget to back up work on the computer. The list is endless. I have coined a phrase for this: "Each person has to recreate the proverbial wheel."

It seems that there must be an inherent value in individuals learning their own lessons. Could it be a form of genetic sifting, life's way of testing how an individual's brain was affected by genetic mingling? Maybe, but there is another possibility too. If, as we learned in the "First Law of Thermodynamics," energy is neither created or destroyed, and potentially our souls are *energy*, why would they (our souls) choose to incarnate?

Would it even be a choice? Would our souls just get sucked into a womb randomly as we floated by? These are interesting questions. What makes sense to me is that the reason for an energetic being to incarnate is to immerse itself in the sensory world and learn lessons from the experiences gained thereby.

In the book *The Divine Classroom: Earth School and the Psychology of the Soul*,[125] Marcia Beachy takes a good hard look at why we are here. She examines different beliefs and offers practical advice for dealing with our time here. She stresses the importance of finding balance or a middle path deep within ourselves in response to our classroom filled with polar opposites, instability and change.

---

[125] Marcia Beachy, *The Divine Classroom Concept, Earth School and the Psychology of the Soul*, Author House 2004.

Have you have heard the term "old soul"? An old soul is generally a person who is very balanced (not distracted greatly by physical sensations) and "wise beyond his or her years."

What behaviors then might a "young soul" exhibit? When first immersed in sensory experiences, a young soul could well be overloaded. It might experience "highs" from every sensory stimulus. It might not be able to differentiate good behavior from bad. It could be difficult for the young soul to raise its conscious awareness above the intense attraction of *any and all* sensory stimuli. It could well take several, or many, lifetimes to refine this young soul's desires to the point where that soul is able to be here for the benefit of others.

If we are here for our souls to grow on their own particular paths, it would make sense that *your* lessons would likely have little relevance *to me*, and vice versa. I would need to experience something to "know" it, to viscerally embody the information.

The bottom line that I draw from connecting the dots is that there is a wisdom guiding everything on the planet. I neither can, nor do, tell my cells how to heal. I am not in charge; there is another force doing this. The lessons that I receive and the road that I walk are mine. The information, the feedback that I receive from any aspect of life is mine; it is in direct response to who I am and what I am doing. Therefore it is not up to another to judge where I am on my path (as long as I am not hurting others). It is given to me to master myself, not others.

Letting go, surrendering, using intention, prayer, meditation, physical exercise, all of these facilitate working towards a good relationship with every being that I share the world with; these are what bring me peace.

We each are here to evolve. This is why a religion that tries to limit a person's experiences, learning, or growth is not truly helpful. Perhaps such a religion will prevent a young soul from experimenting with or practicing something that might damage itself or others — but history doesn't corroborate that. For instance, making sex bad or dirty doesn't stop people from learning about and experiencing sex, does it? No. It just makes people confused about what they are feeling and learning. It actually increases the chance of their making bad decisions around sex and about their partners. This is a huge problem with many of the doctrines promoted by patriarchal religions.

Telling young people that their bodies are beautiful and sacred gives them concrete reasons to value themselves. It provides them with an ability to form a completely different relationship to their bodies than is fostered in our modern world. Individuals who feel sacred find it easier to say "no" when things are happening around them that they are not comfortable with (sex, drugs etc.).

Incorporating the feeling of sacredness into children's cells from the moment they come into our world would ensure that they had these resources in their somatic memories. Such embodiment would go a long way towards making sure that these children made wise, healthy decisions about what and whom they chose to let into their lives, their hearts, and their bodies.

No one that I have ever met is qualified to judge me. No other knows or understands the winds that have shaved off pieces of me, while allowing other parts to grow. "You cannot judge another person's road until you have walked a mile in her moccasins." Many wise people and religions have similar sayings.

Native American cultures created space for diversity. The tribe would employ the wisdom of its elders in watching and interacting with the young, to help determine what path would suit these young members' inner natures. For example, a young person who was easily angered or had high levels of energy that frustrated easily, would be sent perhaps to the warrior society. Or such a person might be brought to an elder to chop wood before beginning to be taught how to direct his energy into a field that was compatible with his or her true nature. Such a youngster would not be considered to be trained as, say, a healer. A child that loved to tell stories would be apprenticed to the storyteller of the tribe (a role of great importance, because all the tribe's inherited wisdom resided in the precise retelling of teaching stories). The point is that there was a recognition that not all people functioned the same way or were able to walk the same path. There was therefore much less judgment about differences. This lack of judgment was apparent in Native American tribes who accepted a concept referred to as two-spirit people, who were a third gender or transgender. People who embodied this two-spirit nature had different roles that they played in the society, but they were very clearly a part of it, rather than judged apart from it. Conforming was not a requirement for being seen as valuable. Acceptance of differences is something we are being forced to look at more and more in our "advanced" culture. Yet "savages" had elaborate methods in place for acknowledging and incorporating differences without damaging the interconnectedness of the community.

Our school systems could not possibly be more different from such a philosophy! Everyone is expected to do the same things, equally well.

Schools do not teach us to honor ourselves, in all our magnificent uniqueness — quite the opposite! They set us up to *compare* ourselves, and to compete to be uniform. Many of us are damaged by this.

Where are you in your life? Do you love and accept yourself? What would it take for you to accept all of yourself?

Take a moment now; after reading this, close your eyes and feel all of you, even the parts you might not be proud of. Look at yourself as you would a toddler. Would you yell at a toddler for making mistakes? Or would you lovingly show her another way of doing or being?

Breathe in and out peacefully for a few moments. As you do, intentionally create space for all of you to be here, in this moment in time, unjudged. Feel yourself expanding, growing into who you were meant to be, embodying, encompassing what you came here to do.

29. Recreating the Wheel 2

Let me ask you this. How much can we learn from other people's experiences? Can you forgo experiencing life for yourself? At some point in the history of humanity, almost everything on this planet hurt or killed someone. So, if we were designed just to be "smart" or stay safe from a survival perspective, there would be so much we would never do or experience.

Other people's information can get us just so far. We've all had a friend whose computer crashes and is devastated by losing all his or her files. How many of you learned from this friend's mistake and ran out and bought a backup system and made sure to back up your files *every day*? Or better yet every hour? Some of you maybe ... but the majority of us probably not.

Does knowing someone that was hurt from drinking too much stop you from experimenting with alcohol? Not for many folks. Likewise with knowing someone who regrets smoking — it probably won't stop you from smoking. In some ways it seems stupid, because many generations make the same mistakes, over and over ... but remember, evolution is brilliant. There are good reasons for how we evolved; we are just disconnected from the wisdom of our evolution. Let's explore this together.

Why would we each need to experience things that others around us have already experienced? There must be some value to each individual undergoing even "negative" experiences. Take for example a sperm's development. Sperm do not mature until they are hit on the head repeatedly by cilia in the vagina — a perfect example of hardship transforming us positively. Or consider an emerging chick dying if someone cracks open its egg to "help" it. Depriving a chick of the life or death struggle to extricate itself from its once safe haven, its shell, that has now become a prison, has detrimental effects on the chick.

Looked at from this perspective, an individual's personal struggle has great significance in her or his evolution; the laws that govern growth and healing are the same whether we are looking at the physical, mental, or spiritual aspects of living systems.

That information should free us to look at our growth from a much different perspective. How relevant is learning from others' mistakes to our soul's growth? Not very. If we are energetic beings, and our essence does not die when our bodies cease functioning, then we should look at our time here differently. Everything becomes an opportunity for growth. This perspective opens the door to explore the possibility that everything that happens in your world has the potential to be purposeful. Open your senses. Clear your energetic pathways, feel, breathe, sense and think.

As spirits, what would be the benefits of becoming incarnate (literally "clothed in flesh")? I have heard some people refer to their time on earth as being "in a classroom." They believe that we are spiritual beings having a physical existence in order to experience all things human, for the purpose of learning. In bodies we experience physical sensations that must have value in our development. On this planet, in bodies, learning is experiential. We feel things through our bodies that we could not as disembodied spirits. This view would support our being fully embodied in this life. Being deeply connected to everything our senses bring to us becomes important. Mastering our instruments, not by shaving off pieces of ourselves but by fully embracing the totality of incarnate existence, would seem to be the mandate.

This is contrary to some major theological views that state we are physical beings longing for a spiritual existence. In these views, our bodies are not divine gifts for us to bond with and learn things through. Instead we are taught that our bodies are born in sin, and we are to not befriend them or learn to listen to them. We are instructed that we have a soul, but it is somehow in constant jeopardy, and we are not qualified to protect our souls on our own.

Others teach that we are all one, connected to our creator as much as we are connected to each other. Some of these teachings, like those from *A Course in Miracles*,[126] state that we are caught in a dream of being disconnected from our creator/God; it is only in the dream that we see ourselves as separate from God and each other. From this perspective, we each have the potential to wake up and remember our oneness.

While all these perspectives are interesting and worth considering, they are certainly not the mainstream view. Our current paradigm does

---

[126] *A Course in Miracles*, Novato, California: Foundation for Inner Peace, 1975.

not encourage individual exploration. Not only are we not encouraged to explore life individually, but that exploration has become more complex. We are not just moving through our own personal issues, but also dealing with centuries of misinformation, and a mechanized world that has grown so complex that we barely have time to catch our breath between one event and the next. This leaves us very little time, excitement or energy for exploration.

Personal exploration is vitally important for any species to survive, but especially so for creatures given free will. Questing for the truth, either personal or universal, leads to enlightenment and self-mastery. Who benefits from self-mastery? Everybody! Children could not walk and birds could not fly without self-exploration and mastery.

The concept that the basic laws of the universe can be witnessed from the smallest atom to the largest creature on the planet is astounding to me. This is evidenced in so many things, from chemical bonding, to molecular structure, to the functioning of digestion or gestation in almost every corner of our universe.

However you view it, there are truths that are undeniable:
- we were not created with a hive mind.
- we were given free will.
- we view the world through different lenses (which were specifically given to us).
- we have more abilities than we are taught to use.
- we are taught to master many things, but not often encouraged to master ourselves.

Our perceptions influence not just the way the world looks to us, but actually affect the world in response (at least on the quantum level).

Why is there a story about the "good" Samaritan in the Bible? Remember back in the day, a Samaritan was not a selfless person, it was Jewish person whose bloodline could be traced back to ancient Samaria. But since God was not emphasizing that we all go out and aspire to be from that country, it seems he must have been trying to elucidate what a "good" person does.

In this it truly does seem that God knows our hearts, because he knew we needed specific reminding not to judge (or turn away) others who are different. We have free will, but if we fall prey to our fears and don't consciously try to understand why we do the things we do, if we allow fear of the unknown, the strange, to close our minds and hearts, then we are not doing as God has asked us.

Does God give us free will so that we subjugate ourselves to others' will? Or that we not use our free will? Or did he give it to us so that we might choose to answer the higher calling that we will each find if we look within?

What if we *are* spiritual beings here to learn from having our own physical existence? If so, judging others for where they are is more than futile. It's potentially harmful to their spiritual evolution. I understand that this can be a hard pill to swallow. However, did Jesus not encourage us to embrace just that when he said "Let he who is innocent cast the first stone"?

People may be exactly where they need to be to get the lessons that they are here to receive. Judging them takes your focus off yourself and your life. Not focusing on yourself will never gain you mastery of yourself.

When someone you love is walking down a path and all you can see is it causing heartache for the individual and for others, it can be extremely hard to keep this principle in mind. But no matter how you feel about it, the truth is we can't possibly know or judge what experiences another soul is here to learn from. If someone you love is walking a path that you don't approve of, you need to try to let go of your judgment. First, not everyone walking down the same path ends up with the same outcome. We all know of people who live a life filled with debauchery, participating in and consuming everything that is bad for them. We would expect that these folks would die young or have a major illness. Yet some live into their late nineties with no repercussions. We also all know someone who lived a healthy life of moderation and ended up dying young of some disease.

Second, we have seen several examples of how hardships, ones that we might perish from, can facilitate powerful growth; they can lead us into a transition, as with sperm or chicks. So no matter how loudly your head is screaming that no good can come from the other person's behavior, learn to acknowledge these thoughts and feelings, but then admit that you are not in a position to predict the outcome. Stop judging and look to yourself! Examine why you are feeling or thinking this; use your strong reactions as your own opportunities to grow and transform! If watching such behavior is too painful for you, you might need to walk away.

What does this bring up for you? Are there areas inside you that are sensitive, tender, hurt or angry? Are they connected to something you gave up? Were there things you censored in yourself or where you gave in under pressure from your family, church or peers? Do you resent that you gave something up? If you had to learn to toe the line, then it's natural to feel resentful seeing someone else do whatever you felt you had to give up. That can make you feel angry. Such feelings, if unacknowledged, get shunted into your subconscious.

If you suffered by walking down a certain path, it's easy to assume that another person walking that path will suffer a similar outcome. You may react strongly to such a situation and come down hard on a loved one, wishing to spare this person the pain that you experienced. However, it was *your* truth that you extrapolated from your journey. The actual truth is that your loved one may or may not have the same outcome, or experience the same emotional impact, as you did from any given path. But in your own life, when you walked down a similar path, did you not learn from your behavior? Eventually did you not learn and grow, making choices that were healthier based on what you learned?

Life is complicated! We are complicated; we need proper guidance and full awareness of our feelings to profitably navigate each situation. When I say profitably, I am referring to profit as the growth of the inner human, not exterior human enrichment.

We are here to learn about ourselves. If you find yourself focusing on someone else, you are off track. If you truly can't deal with where someone else is, then you need to get away. It's harder to do than to say, but if you can't walk away figuratively, or emotionally, from being triggered by what such a person is doing, then you need to walk away literally, physically.

Our school systems churn out people who can more easily follow than lead. Our corporate systems turn out people who have spent their lives following orders. Towing someone else's bottom line is the skill set that allows us to survive in jobs today. We need to work consciously at reclaiming ourselves.

Conversely, how do you think it affects our development to be told that our senses lie to us and that we should mistrust them? If, as evidence supports, we are electrical, energetic beings living in a physical body, then we need to form a pact between these two aspects of ourselves. The emotional, physical, and spiritual needs of *both* need to be addressed and incorporated in our awareness and our daily lives.

We have been told by scientists for a couple of centuries now, and by the church for much longer, that humans are above instincts, that instincts are for baser beings, those without reason. We have also been taught that we are not a part of the natural world, but somehow magically elevated above it. If we look at our physical bodies using a car metaphor, it is like being handed keys to a vehicle that we are told only has three gears. We learn to drive using only those three gears, but our cars actually have five gears. Although the other two are right there in front of us, because we have been conditioned to not look at them, we don't even see them.

Do you think it is wise to ignore your car's needs? A car communicates some of its needs by making unusual noises, at other times by not functioning properly, or perhaps not functioning at all. Your body communicates in those ways and more. We grow up in a society where we are actively taught to discount the information streaming from our bodies from the world around us. How do you think our bodies feel when we don't react to what they sense? We are literally trained not to befriend our instruments ... This process begins our first day in school, if not sooner.

These dismembering practices, that make it easier for those in power to stay in control, are the first in a series of untruths that begin to disconnect us not only from our inner truths, but also from the energy and life of the world around us. This disconnection greatly inhibits our chances of finding our natural, balanced, happy way.

For spiritual beings who come to rest in flesh to grow, learning from others just won't do. Consequently, systems that teach about "reality" rather than discernment are flawed.

"Every person has to recreate the proverbial wheel."

30. Manifesting, Mindfulness and Emotions

It is said that "All that we are is the result of what we have thought: it is founded on our thoughts, it is made up of our thoughts." That's from an ancient Buddhist scripture, the *Dhammapada*, chapter 1:1-2.[127]

I personally find that a little daunting ... downright intimidating, actually. For one thing it makes me afraid to be human, to be real, to *not* be *perfect*. And I am far from perfect, but I have found peace with that. I don't believe we are here to be perfect ... unless you consider the challenge of being *perfectly yourself*.

The statement above makes me afraid to consider my true feelings. It sounds like anything I think or feel is going to be manifested immediately. And so, perhaps I should be afraid to think and feel. What about when I am down? Or feeling insecure? Will that be manifested immediately? Am I supposed to fake it? Deny my feelings, suppress them?

Does that make sense? I don't think so. I keep referring to our bodies as instruments, like clarinets or saxophones. Imagine each key you press on your instrument emits a different emotion, and our emotions are vibrational. Only with full use of your instrument can you produce the vibrational symphony that you alone were shaped to create.

So, if our thoughts and feelings have vibrational frequencies, how do we learn our instrument expertly and not manifest a mess in our lives while doing it? On top of that, how can we possibly manifest something different for ourselves if we don't even know that we *are* manifesting in the first place?

Seeing these things is the first step. We cannot change anything we do not see or feel. Once we have that awareness, how, or what, do we change? First look at what is not working in your life. That will be your guide in

---

[127] *The Dhammapada: The Buddha's Path of Wisdom,* translated by F. Max Müller; http://thenazareneway.com/index_dhammapada.htm.

figuring out what you want to change if you are not manifesting what you want. How much do *you need* to change to affect your life? At what point are you OK?

It is complicated, but it all starts right here inside of us. The more connected we are internally (to ourselves), the more congruently we are able to live. Congruency is when our words match our actions, and our hearts' truths match both of these. Put another way, people who are congruent walk their talk, deeply.

In manifesting, the mind and its thoughts have less strength than our words, feelings and actions do. This is a gift because it means we *can* work stuff out in our heads without having immediate manifestations.

The more congruity you can create within yourself and within your life, the more powerful a manifester you become. Just like in a quartz crystal, the more orderly our internal structure is (i.e., emotions, beliefs, words, and actions), the more internal repetition (congruence) we have, the more concise empty space is created. This in turn allows light to pass through. Orderly structures produce stronger vibrational frequencies, as well as conducting energy more readily.

Remember that the result of our current paradigm has been to systematically strip away our acceptance of many parts of ourselves. The more fragmented we are, the harder it is for us to function. The more entropy or disorder we embody, the harder it is to conduct or direct energy. We need to re-member ourselves, holistically.

The first step on this road starts with discovering who we really are and allowing ourselves to feel all our feelings. (I am not suggesting that you *act out* all your feelings — that is not the point. *Inflicting how we feel on others is not good medicine.* Nor does it indicate strength or demonstrate any kind of worthwhile accomplishment.) Think of a competitive weightlifter, who after lifting an impressively heavy weight throws the weight into the audience, rather than placing it back at his feet on the floor.

Now imagine a different weightlifter who places the weight with shaking, exhausted muscles back on the floor, being conscious of not hurting anyone else with his accomplishment .... It definitely takes extra effort, struggling with exhausted muscles, to control the object he has lifted and place it in a controlled fashion back on the floor. If these two hypothetical weightlifters were in front of me, I know which one I would be more impressed with!

If we *are* that weightlifter, struggling with the desire to throw the weight away from us onto others, we need to acknowledge that this is our

160

challenge. We need to work to shift our goal, and focus it into something that benefits us more. Self-control is not to be confused with self-denial.

Acknowledging the things we do that don't gain us what we really want is the first step towards true self understanding and happiness. This puts us in a position of being able to manifest something different. A weightlifter, no matter how accomplished, who throws his weights into the audience will soon not have anyone who wants to sit anywhere near him.

We all have areas where we are called to grow. Have you noticed this in yourself? For example, it took me decades of looking to others for answers or for guidance before I realized that I always move towards the light of growth and healing. It is the direction I innately move towards, like a plant turning and leaning into the light. Once I realized this, it gave me a sense of inner strength, one that I had never experienced before. I began to realize that not only did I have a process, but that I could trust myself to always move forward, even if others around me were frustrated by my pace. Once I looked back and saw who I was in relationship to growth, I truly began to trust my own personal process. It began to free me from the need to look to others for approval or guidance. It was a surprise to me in many ways. I wasn't expecting it to change my relationship to myself and others as much as it began to.

Discovering what our processes for dealing with things are is a treasure beyond belief. Finally becoming aware of my own very reliable process was a huge step in self-acceptance. It is truly like Don Miguel Ruiz says in his book *The Four Agreements*, "being impeccable with your word"[128] gives you such a strong internal ground to stand on. There is tremendous benefit to conducting ourselves with integrity; it produces a feedback loop within us of surprising strength.

Being congruous embodies being true to ourselves and true to our words. It starts with being aware and allowing ourselves to feel and embrace the full gamut of our emotions, even anger. It means being honest about what is going on for us, mentally and emotionally, without censoring our awareness of where we are at any given moment. In other words, it means self-acceptance. This is a process; it takes time.

Ideally, we would have the support of wise elders in our tribes to help us discover our process. It makes things much more difficult to learn everything by yourself. We need to start groups and communities of people

---

[128] Don Miguel Ruiz, *The Four Agreements: A Practical Guide to Personal Freedom (A Toltec Wisdom Book)*, Amber-Allen Publishing, Inc. July 10, 2018.

who want to become whole again. However, most of us are not blessed with such an ideal situation, so let us start first with ourselves.

We need to entertain the concept that emotional energy is an actual physical product that we are producing all around us. What are you producing? What are you filling the air waves around you with? What do you emanate?

Another way to look at it is: What are you bringing to bed with you? Are you choosing your bedfellows consciously? Or are you allowing circumstances to push unwanted "partners" into bed with you?

Here's what I try to do. Let's say I'm very angry. I focus on the feeling; I breathe into it and try to create (believe it or not) a "peaceful" space around and within my being angry. I don't judge it negatively or try to push it away; instead I aim for "*loving myself*" through the period of time that I am feeling this way.

I let the flame of anger burn true and clear, with no feelings of retribution towards myself or anyone else. Then if I need to address a situation with another person, I turn my focus on how to express my feelings constructively, rather than destructively (a concept introduced in "Language," e.g., "When *this* happened, I felt *this* way" or "When you said *this*, I felt *this*"). These are not inflammatory statements. If someone cares about you, it should matter to that person how you feel, even if he or she feels a little hurt or defensive after your constructive self-expression.

Don't expect people to hear you, or feel caring towards you, if you express yourself destructively. A destructive or inflammatory way to express your feelings would be to say, "You *made* me feel *this way*" or "You did *this* to me!"

Let's use the weightlifter scenario again. In a confrontation, I am struggling like the weightlifter to bear the extended burden of what I'm feeling on my emotional muscles. I must work hard (at least initially) not to drop my emotional state like a bomb, but instead to set that weight down as gently as I can. I say initially because like most things such work gets easier with time.

We are responsible for the emotions we spew. Imagine a world where people were conscious of, and cared about, how they affected others. It's no different than being taught by your mom to clean up your physical mess after yourself. It's not very enjoyable to be around people who leave their stuff all over the place, whether we are talking about their physical stuff or their emotional stuff.

Have you ever been around someone whose emotional state was so palpable that just being in the same space with them feels toxic? That is what I am talking about.

I received a teaching from the Lakota Grandmother I spoke about in "Ancestors." Her name was Grandmother Nanatasis. After working with her for several years, I had decided to commit to a yearlong women's instruction group that she was holding. On our first meeting she had us focus on a moment in time that was very emotional for us. After about three minutes she had us see if we could feel how far out from our bodies that emotion had spread. I experienced mine as having traveled *very* far. She then had us envision neutralizing this energy. In other words, she had us clean up our mess after we were done "creating" or "playing with" it.

I don't always share my feelings. There are times when it feels like it will be productive to share ... and times when sharing does not seem like it will help me meet my innermost goals. Here is where I try to balance awareness between my heart and my brain.

You need to evaluate every situation where you become emotionally charged, look at your relationship with the person or entity that triggers you, and understand within yourself what your goal here is.

Initially your feelings of being hurt might make it seem as though your greatest desire is to strike out and hurt the person back ... but is that truly what you want? A counterstrike rarely makes a situation go away or heals it. Even more rarely does it bring a sense of closeness or warmth; often it just leads to a volley of exchanged strikes.

Deep inside I believe most of us want to feel heard, accepted, and cared about. You can't always achieve all three of those, even when you become very skilled at communicating your feelings (it often depends on the level of skill the people you are communicating with have as well). However, if you just strike out every time you are hurt, you will achieve none of those three — absolutely every time.

Interestingly, constant suppression of your feelings, or a particular feeling (like anger), is just as detrimental to relationships as well. What are you facilitating by denying the truth of your experience? Constantly repressed or despised emotions go to our subconscious where they grow and build pressure, constantly looking for ways out of their "prison." When they find ways out, most often you will not realize this is happening. Why? Because you have a commitment to not acknowledging those feelings. None of our feelings is bad. It's how we handle them that ends up being good or bad. When we do not have a strong community of wise elders around us to guide us, and our culture is invested in division (within individuals and communities), we flounder. We have mutually agreed upon rules of conduct towards prisoners of war laid out by the Geneva Convention, but we have no such thing in our marriages or our friendships. Does that seem odd to you?

Look at it this way: every time we successfully communicate our feelings and help facilitate a situation where we can be heard, we are making the world a better place. Every time ... and so the ripple spreads out.

If you are interested in learning more about supportive communities check out Circle Way.[129] It's a non-profit learning center using ancient wisdom and modern tools to create healthier relationships and communities. The Circle Way was started by a man who changed my life when I heard him speak almost 40 years ago, Manitonoquat (Medicine Story).

Often, we get loud or teary around expressing how we feel because we have been taught that it is *not* OK to feel a particular feeling. Our values (paradigms) are so skewed around the validity (or lack thereof) involving our instrument and its capabilities, including emotions, that we don't have an *expectation* of being heard or responded to kindly or even appropriately. Because of this, the place we come from, inside of us, is automatically on the defensive. This in turn means that just having a *need* can predispose us to feeling grouchy, apprehensive, or even angry.

Expectations are interesting things. In some ways they are powerful manifesting tools. If we expect to be respected, to be treated as though we had value, or as though our feelings mattered, we generally are. Part of this is because when we act as though something is true for us, it becomes true for us. We get into trouble with an expectation when we shift it from ourselves onto someone or something else.

Having an expectation that I will be treated with respect results in my moving *away from you* if you do not treat me with respect. If I expect you to treat me a certain way, and you don't, but I stay with you anyway, expecting (or hoping) that *you* will change, that becomes *my* problem. I can set intentions for what I want, but I need to respond appropriately to what comes my way (like the actions of others).

I do believe that the thoughts and feelings we entertain are vibrational. The vibrations we steep ourselves in are the vibrations that get magnified in our lives, and are ultimately the vibrations that life brings back to us.

---

[129] http://circleway.org/

Conscious manifesting boils down to intention and the energy we are mindful of.

If you can keep returning your focus to *being in right relationship with all your relations* (as my Native American friends are always saying), then your self-esteem grows. You become more comfortable in your skin. As you practice this (and I am not talking about practicing self-denial or being the victim in order to please others), your confidence grows. Your inner knowing grows. You become a powerful force for good in the world. It's an awesome feeling. By the way, all your relations are not limited to two legged beings, but include all of creation and, as the Lakota say, Wakan Tanka "the Great Mystery" as well.

31. Awareness (Inner Light) and Manifesting

We are in bodies that feel, both physically and emotionally, for a reason. It is important not to judge or repress our physical feelings. For example, keeping our hand on something hot, or on something really cold, for too long can result in serious injuries. Sure, you can train really hard and toughen parts of your body like martial artists or football players do, but it is certainly not how we are born. It's the same thing with our emotions. They are there for a reason.

I have a basic premise that reappears throughout this book: if our bodies, through evolution or an act of God, developed certain abilities or awarenesses, what benefit would there be in our denying or repressing them? Both God or evolution are far wiser than we are.

Physical and emotional feelings are available to us to teach us things. Repressing them only limits the playing field from which we learn. But I also believe that there is much more to our emotions than meets the eye.

Did you know that there is a specific angel for emotions? Galgaliel is his name, only "he" isn't really the angel of feelings per se, but rather of vibration, which is what our feelings are, vibrational emanations.[130]

Many people, as they begin exploring this type of energy/thought work, become afraid when they realize how many "negative" thoughts or reactions cross their minds throughout the day. Relax. Not every thought generates a manifestation. Remember that we have to work to manifest something; it takes time and repetition. Beyond that, the most powerful form of manifesting requires thought, combined with intention, focused on a somatic memory, which at its essence is feeling, and all of these are ultimately vibration.

---

[130] "Guardian Angel Galgaliel," *Guardian Angel Guide*, https://guardianangel-guide.com/guardian-angel-galgaliel/.

Occasional negative thoughts alone, on the manifestation scale of one to ten, are like a "one." Manifesting with negative thoughts occurs with repetition, over time, not with an occasional negative thought. Also, as I stated in "Manifesting and Mindfulness," thoughts alone are far more neutral than spoken words or actions.

> While the genetic make-up of our body doesn't change very much throughout our lifetime, our inner constitution as our character and mental paradigm (vibratory structure) can often change quite drastically. As our inner constitution changes, how we see and what we see in the outer world changes simultaneously. This is because the inner and the outer act as two wave forms that resonate with each other forming an interference pattern that activates different aspects while deactivating others, changing how it's configured. We only see in everything else what's of the same nature (frequency) as we are. As we grow, develop into higher states, and transform mentally and emotionally, how things appear to us changes accordingly. You know when you've undergone transformation of some form by the fact that you begin seeing others and the world in general in a different way. What we notice and how we interpret things to give them meaning changes as an outer reflection of our inner state.[131]

Our awareness is like a light. When you become aware of a process, it becomes visible in your consciousness. Until then, most of our processes take place in the darkness of our subconscious. The great news is that as soon as you have "seen" the process, you are 50 to 75 percent of the way to being able to change it. The hardest part is shining the light. Watching your internal connections between a trigger and your response to it is powerfully informative. Some people find it helpful to identify any physical sensations associated with what triggers them.

At first, don't try to change anything, just bring your awareness to a process. For example, how do you react to traffic on the road while you are driving? Do your responses increase your aggravation? Or make you feel more at ease? Watch and see if the outcome of following whatever patterns you are witnessing brings you greater joy, peace, closeness, etc. It is a practice of awareness not unlike the one that Marie Kondo

---

[131] Linda Gadbois, "DNA — the phantom effect, quantum hologram and the etheric body," MedCrave, https://medcraveonline.com/MOJPB/dna-the-phantom-effect-quantum-hologram-and-the-etheric-body.html.

encourages you to develop in her *Tidying Up with Marie Kondo* series on Netflix. She asks you to hold the object and to feel whether it brings you joy. If it does, she says keep it. If it doesn't, she encourages you to let it go. It's the same thing with looking at and weighing our own patterns of behavior. Does your behavior bring you joy? Does it feed you? Do the patterns you enact in response to a trigger increase your unhappiness, disease, or disharmony? If so, you can begin to modify them. It will take time. But this is *your* point of power, to begin making conscious change in your life, to bring you closer to the life you want to live!

Once you recognize a pattern, see if you can trace its occurrence in your past. Notice if this pattern worked for you. Did it bring you the outcomes you desired? If the pattern no longer brings you the results you want, you can change it. Owning your part in what is manifesting in your relationships, jobs, or the world is important, but not because someone else judges that you should. If you cannot see your part in what is playing out in your life, then you will remain powerless to change it.

Don't freak out what with what is revealed to you. Don't judge yourself. Becoming aware of your negative patterns is a gift! Remember that when we see something, we are at least 50 to 75 percent through the process that will free us from this pattern or habit. Keep in mind you have been doing things without awareness up till now, and you survived. Breathe. Sit with yourself and find the place of peace that exists inside every cell of your body.

Try the practice mentioned above and notice either what makes you angry or how you release anger. Most of us have not been taught how to release anger or express it constructively. This means that most likely the processes we are employing might not bring us what we want. Notice things about yourself. Do you release pent up anger by screaming at others? Your kids? Your dog? Your spouse? Notice how that makes you feel.

When I was in my twenties, I realized that I would release a tremendous amount of anger when I got upset with my dogs. I found myself screaming at them sometimes, and I saw that the anger was disproportionate to the issue. I felt awful afterwards, like I had possibly wounded them irreparably, even though they always seemed able to forgive me. I knew I did not want to keep doing this. The interesting thing is that I had probably been doing this for years without realizing it. I don't remember consciously embarking on any prescribed plan to eradicate this behavior, but I noticed several years later that I no longer did it. The light of my awareness was enough to bring about a change. Sometimes it is that easy.

So how do you release negative patterns? Notice them. Send the light of your awareness to them, bathe them in this warm, loving gift of awareness. Remember: our awareness is a powerful tool, and so is our intention. Guilt however is not.

Guilt does not make you a better person; it doesn't right any wrong that you have done. It can often be a quagmire, like quicksand, preventing you from changing the energy or frequency within an issue. Don't indulge in guilt; its redemptive power is a lie, and it is not helpful at all.

Things like negative self-talk will alter your relationship to yourself and the rest of the world — calling yourself names when you make a mistake or putting yourself down when you aren't perfect in some imagined way are excellent examples of damaging behavior. If you find yourself saying that what you are attempting is "stupid" or "won't work" before you even try it, notice these things. Notice where there may be a sensation that can be associated with this pattern. Is there tension in your body? Breathe into it, create space in this area, loosen it, let it go if you can. Create more internal space. In releasing we don't push against things. Pushing against an energy condenses it, making it harder to shift and sometimes strengthening it. I find the image of opening something, or giving it more space, allows the energy to shift.

Let's say you are not someone who is comfortable with anger. I started writing poetry when I was about eight or nine years old. I wrote when I felt overwhelmed and all alone. When I was around thirteen, I showed a therapist my work. She pointed out to me that out of 30 or so poems, there wasn't a single one about anger. This was surprising to me. As it turned out she was right. I had poems about all feelings, except for anger ... how could that be? It was as if I was not allowed to be angry. Anger was apparently not in my feeling repertoire. So what happened to those angry feelings?

We *all* experience anger. No matter how you label it, dress it up, or file it away as inconvenient, ugly, unworthy, or unacceptable, it is still there. What do you do with your anger?

After more years of therapy, I discovered that I was flipping the anger I was experiencing towards someone else onto myself. It was bizarre to watch when I was finally able to see it. Let's say I was having a conflict with a boyfriend. If I felt angry at him, within minutes it would flip, and I would be tearing myself apart internally. I blamed myself for everything, using examples of things had gone wrong over my entire lifetime, leading me to believe that I was never good enough. This was a pattern that took me a long time to shift, but I have.

I saw another therapist decades later, and when he heard my life story, he said he was surprised that I was not a "cutter." I went home and thought about this and realized that I had been a cutter. I was an inner cutter. Awareness of this gave me access to new ways in which I could be with myself; areas to find forgiveness for myself, to love my inner child, to create internal, peaceful, space around ... to cut myself some proverbial slack.

Watch what you do. Become aware. Love yourself. Negativity is a natural part of the whole, as is decay, shadow and darkness. All of these aspects of living are necessary. They are the rich materials that fuel growth. There is really nothing that is isolated on this planet. All of it, us included, is interconnected. Nothing in the plant world can grow without darkness; all babies are conceived and grow initially in darkness. Expose a seed too soon to the light and it can die. All things in their own time.

Be gentle with yourself.

Pay attention if you find yourself generating a lot of energy around other people's behavior. Try to determine why. Very often in these situations it is more about some aspect of yourself that gets repressed (and is not happy about it). For example, if you feel angry or judgmental about someone laughing loudly at a restaurant, look at why it bothers you. Is it because you were made to feel that it was an unacceptable behavior? Did a parent, teacher or peers make you feel badly about doing the behavior that is upsetting you? Were you taught that self-expression was bad? Or jubilant self-expression? When something in someone else triggers a strong response in you, especially a response of wanting to squash that behavior, or wishing the other person would repress the expression of it, those are the times we need to turn our gaze inward. These are moments full of learning opportunities. We are not here to control the behaviors of others — that is not why God gave us free will. Wise humans are supposed to generate laws regarding the major areas of wrong and right, but not subjugate others to rigid rules of conduct.

We had to be given free will so that we could learn about using it to affect the world around us. Can you learn to feel the difference between right and wrong? What is right for you? How do you feel when you do the "right" thing? How do you feel when you do the "wrong" thing? We are here to learn as much as we can, to deepen our experience of being human and being ourselves. Notice where there is tension in your body as you are reacting to someone else's behavior. Notice if it feels good to get upset or yell. What part of this process serves you?

Sometimes it's the experience of feeling guilty after an explosive episode that hooks us into this pattern, because feeling guilty is familiar to us. Or we don't feel we deserve good relationships, so we sabotage them. Sometimes we have so much built up emotion or stress inside us that we just need a release, like yelling. Giving ourselves permission to feel these things allows us to create space for them. This in turn allows us to see them more clearly, to understand them and ourselves, and opens the door for shifts. Once we have embraced these parts of ourselves, we can begin to work on choosing different ways to heal or transform them. We can choose new ways to release these emotions, ways that do not harm others or our relationships.

Breathe; you are not a bad person, you are simply a human being who has not been shown how to operate comfortably, in your fullest capacity, because you have been mis-taught or mis-guided.

Some time ago, there was a struggle for power, and many of the old, wise ways we human beings had established to cope with our very real natures were lost. The loss occurred slowly over time, and in connecting the dots, to me it appears as if it was done on purpose.

Factions who cared nothing for the evolution of humanity, or of the individual, came into power. What they cared about was power and wealth. This happened in different countries and different cultures at different times, but since then, we have been floundering. Lost was the wisdom of elders and of elder generations. Time-tested traditions were strategically stamped out. Inserted in their place were un-natural laws and corrupted thinking, turning us away from who we are and our ability to feel comfortable in our skin, denying us the ability to embrace the totality of who we are. So, breathe. All of your emotions are good. You would not have them if they were not important.

When dogs are frightened, they tremble. Have you ever seen that? It's easy to think dogs are freezing because they are trembling so violently from head to tail. Our knee-jerk reaction is to try to soothe them or cover them in blankets to stop this violent trembling. What we failed to understand for years, and science has only recently shown us, is that this trembling allows dogs to release the intensity of fear that they are experiencing that otherwise would become somatic trauma for them. It is a physical reaction that helps bring their organism back into balance.

Imagine for a moment that there was a community, not of people but of dogs, with a school for puppies. In this school an elder/teacher dog makes fun of his puppy students for shaking. He is a very big dog who has won many fights, so his opinion seems important. What if this elder tells his students regularly that "Shaking is a sign of weakness," or that "Only puppies shake, not big tough dogs." All of those puppies would grow up trying to control their natural reaction, which would cause all kinds of internal mayhem. The spin-off from it would be varied but predictable. When they grew up, they would probably yell at their own puppies for shaking too, because now a whole generation of dogs believed this teaching and because there was unease in their own bodies and minds from embracing this unhealthy belief. Every time something traumatic happened, these dogs would not be able to "shake it off." Trauma would take hold on this community. Signs of emotional dis-eases would appear, such as PTSD, rash anger, irritability, sleep disorders, overeating, and paranoia – all symptoms of self-distrust. I could keep going with this story, but you see where it leads.

All teachings that lead us away from our natural integrity are flawed. Balance always needs to be sought and cultivated, but to turn against ourselves can only lead to problems. There is an amazing beauty and wisdom to our true nature. Nature has a profound ability to self-heal and attain balance. This deep wisdom is within each of our cells. If you listen intently enough, this internal wisdom will surface in your awareness as well.

Carl Rodgers came up with what is termed "Person-Centered Therapy." He states that each individual knows exactly what he or she needs to heal. Three conditions need to be met in order for a person to experience this personal revelation. I will call the person seeking relief the "seeker" and the therapist the "listener." The first condition is that the seeker must feel that the listener regards her with unconditional positive regard. The second is that the seeker needs to feel that the listener is congruous (genuine), and third, that the listener is able to convey that she is listening empathetically. I have watched this process through becoming certified in Creative Arts Therapy, a method developed by Natalie Rodgers, Carl Rodgers's daughter, combining the exploration of Person-Centered Therapy with the creation of art, or more accurately the artistic process. It is incredibly powerful. I have never seen anything like it, and watching this process has convinced me that it is completely valid. Each individual does indeed know what is needed to heal. The knowledge is there, like an inner map.

All you have to do is be supported to step onto that map, and after some few steps, an inner knowing takes over and shows you what to do.

Owning your own process is very freeing. There are no judgments. You do not need to follow anyone else's path. Let your comfort in your own skin be your barometer, along with the outcome of your relationships and your endeavors.

32. Intention and Manifesting

Intention is of the utmost importance. It is also a word that is misused and misunderstood, "The road to hell is paved with good intentions" is a great example.

How we intend something to be received by another has little bearing on how it is actually received. How another person receives what we intended is the truth for them — end of story. The sooner we realize that as a species, the better off we will all be.

For example, because our perception of anything is so personal (the context we put it in depends on our own experience with it) it is possible for us to say something that means one thing to us and can mean something entirely different to someone else. Take the phrase "I love you," for example. When I tell you, "I love you," I might wish you to feel treasured, but that might not be the association you have with the phrase. It might bring up uncomfortable feelings for you. Perhaps it comes with a sense of being burdened, or it might feel suffocating. It might feel controlling to you, or exhilarating. It might give your heart wings, or make you wish you had wings to fly away with.

Your reaction might be based on our relationship, or be something you came into our relationship carrying with you. It doesn't matter which in terms of its validity. If we were raised in enlightened cultures, we would be taught not to react personally to information we receive from another. We would therefore not feel threatened by where someone else is coming from, instead, we would have a sense of curiosity. Dialoguing with others would be conducted with a sense of discovery. Receiving information from another could be viewed as an opportunity to grow closer. Under such conditions, we would not fear being trampled on when we shared how we felt in any situation. Oh how I wish our culture supported this!

On the other hand, when I say "I love you," how in touch with myself am I? Am I saying I love you because I feel like I need you? Or because I love making love to you? Does your sense of humor make me laugh like no other? Or do I feel like I can't breathe if I am without you for too long? Not only might we not be in touch with exactly why we say something, but that meaning, that truth, might change from time to time as well; after all the only constant is change.

So, in these instances you can see that our intention is fairly meaningless. It does count, but only secondarily as to how it is received.

Why then would I say intention is of the utmost importance?

The very fact that intention can be so badly received by someone else should reveal some of its nature and its power. Intending is a process that is deeply personal, because if done properly it embodies the essence of the practitioner, combined with his or her will. Having someone else's will manifest in our lives is not always welcome (to say the least). Think about that. Interestingly, "intentional" is often used in phrases that relate to some form of malice, e.g., "intentional harm."

The more energy we put into harming others, the more harm comes to us and to our relations, even if we don't see it. There are very real laws of energy, just as there are very real laws of gravity, neither of which we can see directly, but we can see the effects of them indirectly.

As a result of my Native American studies, I have come to view everything as having "medicine." Done properly, good "medicine" benefits not only ourselves, but all our relations. Willfully growing and harboring harmful intentions is bad "medicine."

Let's look at "intention" as another one of those words whose deeper meaning eludes us in our current paradigm; The reality is that focusing your intention will create a stronger vibrational frequency, and this has the ability to change your life.

Intention is a combination of your focused thoughts and your will. Your will is the driving force with which you send out your thoughts when you are trying to manifest something.

Intention focuses the thought (energy) you put into something. This is also a facet of transmuting and manifesting. Using this method, we create a space for the thought/intention to dwell inside us. We call this "setting an intention."

To set an intention, simply "think" what your goal is. The clearer you can be in your mind, heart and emotions, including the language you use, the better. Speaking in the present tense adds power — for example, saying "I am exercising and eating perfectly for my body right now" as opposed to "I want to eat better and exercise more" or "I need to eat better and exercise more."

Can you feel the difference in the power and energy of those three statements? In the first one we are stating that what we desire is true for us already. Since this is our goal, phrasing it this way is more closely aligned to what we want. The other two statements are not aligned with where we want to be; they are aligned with where we are now. If your present state is not the one you wish to put energy into, then don't.

Looked at another way, you could say that visualizing what you want as already being present in your life creates a frequency that grows and attracts similar frequencies. The more you create this frequency, the greater the range of altered vibration around you. In the second and third statements we are putting energy into the action of wanting or needing, which actually builds the energy of wanting or needing, not the desired outcome. So we feed our *not* moving forward, instead of vibrationally/intentionally creating the space where we want to be.

In other words, in intending and manifesting, it's OK if the things you are stating are not true for you now. I know this may seem strange at first. We create the space for these things to come into our lives by speaking as if they already exist. You must have heard the old adage "Fake it till you make it." Well, there is real truth in that, and part of it is the intention.

"Practice makes perfect" is another example of intention at work. It works for three reasons: 1. The mechanics of repetitive thinking or acting wear pathways in our brains, facilitating return "trips." 2. Focused intention (a facet of manifestation) is more powerful than unfocused thought. 3. It takes two weeks to create a habit.

We can add intention to any energetic endeavor, such as cleansing a person's energy or a place where one lives. No matter which method you use (fire, smoke, sunlight, water, salt, moonlight or earth), each can be augmented with intention. We will be looking at these more closely soon.

Another way to work with intention is by incorporating intentional vibration. In order to do this, you must be aware of the vibrational quality of what you are intending.

How can you do that? Think about the happiest moment in your life. Close your eyes and revisit that time. What do you remember? Are there specific sounds, smells, tastes or sensations associated with this special memory? Can you recall how it feels in your body to be in that moment? That feeling is the vibrational quality of the event, its vibrational signature.

If you want to create more of that feeling in your life, feel the memory of it as you are setting your intention. Color your words to "paint pictures" of these feelings. Create a vision board of actual pictures or magazine clippings that stir those feelings in you. "Like attracts like" is another adage that perfectly describes sympathetic vibration and manifesting. To visualize well takes conscious awareness, practice and focus.

Our lives are like boats on a river. It can feel like we have no power over our destination. Nothing is farther from the truth. We have the power to steer our boats, our lives; we just haven't been taught how to utilize our abilities consciously. We are sending our crafts this way and that without understanding that we are the ones doing it.

Remember, the people who dreamed up our current paradigm would not benefit from our realizing our powers. If we felt more in control of our lives, from a centered place, and believed that we lived in a universe that responded to us, we would experience life very differently. Our need for things outside ourselves would be diminished, lowering consumerism in general. We would also reduce the need for drugs, both prescription and recreational, as well as the ways we attempt to feed the hunger inside us, like overeating, over shopping, over anything.

Many Native cultures utilized certain plants, recognizing that they had sacred medicine to share with people; these were used in special ceremonies, not recreationally. These plants imparted very real knowledge, because when ingested in a sacred manner, the medicine of these plants opens us, and we learn by seeing differently. Once we experience a plant's vibrational frequency, we can go back to that signature (with practice) without re-ingesting the plant. In much the same way you can revisit a crystal whose frequency you are familiar with. (See Chapter 12 "Crystalline Structures.") In such cases the plant or crystal has shared its medicine with us, and my teachers would say that now "we carry that medicine." In working with intention, the more ways we incorporate our conscious focus into this practice, the more powerful it is. Combining focused thought with somatic experience (feeling memory) plus the spoken word is fabulous.

Another way to work with intention is with written positive affirmations. These are positive statements that you place in your environment where you will see them (and read them), every day. My mom used to tell me as a child that if I wrote something down and spoke it out loud, I would be able to remember it more easily than just reading it. The same is true for positive affirmations. Here are some examples:

I am safe, secure and surrounded by love.

It is safe to be me.

I enjoy my body and love the way I look and feel.

I am enjoying great monetary compensation for work that I love doing.

I live in a beautiful house that I love and can afford easily.

I am a successful writer.

I meet my deadlines easily and well.

Although made popular recently in New Age practices, the use of positive affirmations is not new. They are used in Feng Shui, which developed some 5,000 years ago. The area of your home that is responsible for things like your relationship with bosses, doctors, tax collectors, mechanics, etc. — all the people whose cooperation and good will can make or break your day — is called the "helpful people and travel" gua (area of the house). I will go into this further in Chapter 53, but suffice it to say in order to affect your relationships with these people who have power in your life, you write down affirmations and place them in this gua. The affirmations used could be as follows: "All my doctors are good communicators, knowledgeable, and have my best interest at heart" or "My boss loves the work I do; she sees how hard I work and respects my decisions." After you have written these statements out, you put them in one of three containers you have procured or made for this gua. They need to be silver or gray. One is for now, one is for the immediate future, and the other for the long term. What this means is that for thousands of years, the Chinese have been practicing affirmations to help them have better relationships.

Creative visualizations are another way to work with manifesting and intention, using pictures in our minds that evoke feelings or vibrational frequencies.

A vision board is a collection of photos or pictures from magazines, glued on paper like you would for a collage, that embody where you want to be. You can incorporate words here as well. Looking at a vision board every day reminds you of the good feelings that you associate with the images you chose to inspire yourself like a plant responding to sunlight. In other words, find images that feel like dreams or aspirations.

33. Intention and Space Clearing

We just talked about how we can use our intention to attract what we want more of in our lives, but we can also use intention to clear out, or let go of, what we no longer want in our life. This process is not unlike space clearing. In the latter, we are removing unwanted energies from our physical environment; in the former, we are removing them from within us.

We can utilize intentions in space clearing; as I said, they are very powerful. To use intentions in a subtractive way for space clearing, you simply set a conscious intention of the negative energy in an object or room transforming to positive energy. Speaking your intention out loud, such as "All negative energy must either transform to positive energy or leave my house," adds the vibrational frequency of the spoken word and intensifies the intention. Combined with any of the traditional space clearing techniques described in the following chapters, your intentions will increase the vibrational energy of what you are doing.

34. Sacred Fire

Fire meets all but one requirement to qualify as a living being — I was always fascinated by that. It eats, produces waste, moves, and breathes oxygen. What stops it from being considered a living being is its inability to reproduce on its own. Yet, human beings cannot procreate on their own; women need men (and vice versa). What of the tiny ember that is carried on the wind? Flowers need wind or pollinators to reproduce. So, perhaps at some time in the future we will look at fire differently.

Fire seems to be alive, flickering, moving, breathing. . . . early humans indeed felt fire to be alive. Have you ever thought about the fact that we are the only creatures on this planet to befriend fire? We would not be where we are today were it not for our ability to carry fire, and with that treasured ember light the next fire, over and over again for generations.

In ancient cultures, the fire-keepers held that sacred duty, carrying an ember from even older fires, nurturing it, feeding it, protecting it from the elements, for the benefit of the clan. It is possible that the first sacred ember might still be alive today, burning in some fire somewhere, having been nurtured day after day, month after month, year after year, so that it, in turn, would nurture and protect the people for coming untold generations.

Sacred Fire ... this phrase calls up visions from far back in time, flickering images of ancient people dressed in skins, dancing around a fire. Human community has its roots in fire: cooking; storytelling, ceremonies, celebrations, all performed around a central fire.

Except for the moon (who never consented to be there for us on a consistent basis), fire provided our only light at night — a feature very important for a species that can't see in the dark. Fire also provides us with warmth, an important gift for a hairless, warm-blooded species.

Flame is a powerful force. Like nature herself, flame can be both life-giving and life-taking. Fire is the great purifier, and the only one of the four traditional elements that cannot be contaminated. Water, air, and earth can all be sullied, but not fire.

One can see so much staring into flames: faces, creatures, and more. I believe it is our cellular memory, longing to stare into flames, that gives us our penchant for staring at a TV. We told stories that taught us many things about our interconnectedness with the rest of creation around flickering firelight. Now we watch stories that are sensational but often separate us from our friends and families, on an isolated, flickering screen.

How perfect for both, the symbiotic relationship with early man, who first carried living embers and later learned how to bring flame forth from wood.

Fire is like us; it will consume all that it needs to survive until it extinguishes itself. We are doing this now on our beautiful planet, but while we have the choice to change, I'm not sure fire can.

Fire, in its essence, creation, and being, is riddled with symbology. It is a purifier, taken literally or in an esoteric light. Fire is associated with one's drive, temperament, and passion, as is its heat. Fire consumes, as do all the emotions we ascribe to it. When our bodies are trying to drive out an infection, we get a fever, conjuring a sacred flame within our cells. As a healer, when I lay my hands on an injury or energy block, my hands heat up, as though they were on fire.

Cells remember that in the not so distant past, fire was essential to survival. Whether you are aware of it or not, your cells whisper in your proverbial ears.

As I mentioned in the previous two chapters, intention can be applied to working with any form of cleansing, and fire is no exception. For instance, I like to have a single candle burning when I am working on a client. When I encounter something that is blocking the client's energy, we can both intend or visualize it going into the flame to be transformed.

There are ceremonies where you write down something you wish to release from your life, be it a person, a habit, or an illness, and afterward you feed this paper to a flame, transforming and releasing the energy of your connection to this thing.

Watching fire also purifies the mind. One of my teachers, Tzen, a shaman whom I mentioned in "Ancestry," told me that "We need to watch fire every day." Why would that be?

For as long as humans have been using tools, we have also used fire to cleanse, even if not consciously. Think about how sitting in front of a fire makes you feel. For me it is as though the heat seeps into my bones, warming and soothing tensions away. You can ask or visualize fire to cleanse the stress and unwanted energies from your body as you watch it playfully, seductively dance. Have you ever seen faces or the shapes of animals in fire? It's easy to "see" many things in the dance of both fire and smoke. Perhaps these are some of the reasons Tzen said it is important to look at fire every day.

You don't need to have a fireplace to do this. Lighting a candle each day and spending a few minutes watching it can connect you to this powerful force. Try it and see what you notice.

35. Smudging

Smudging is an ancient technique for clearing unwanted energies from objects, creatures (including humans) and spaces by bathing them in smoke from herbs and substances considered sacred. It is based on the belief that smoke enters the spirit realm — not a far stretch of the imagination when you consider smoke's nebulous qualities, shifting from dense and opaque, then curling, twining and spiraling into various degrees of translucence, always reaching upward. If you stare at smoke it is possible to believe it is at least part spirit itself.

The concept of smudging something is this: by burning a sacred, cleansing, healing or shifting herb, those properties are released and carried into the spiritual realm. The smoke from smudging affects both the physical and the non-physical, because smoke is seen as being able to be in both worlds.

For example, sage is considered a sacred cleansing herb. When you burn sage, its energy acts on your space, physical and non-physical. It helps your body, your mind, and your spirit, clearing unwanted or built-up energies.

The practice of burning sacred herbs or incense for a purpose is not new — it has been done for centuries. What is new is that science recently studied the effect of burning white sage (not cooking sage) in rooms with sick people. Not only did burning the sage rid the room of 90 percent of the germs immediately, but the number of bacteria in the room stayed lower for more than two weeks (in some cases, up to 30 days)![132] I love using sage, I use it anytime I want to get rid of an energy I am dealing with that I am not enjoying, from stress to anger to fear. I use it:

- when I buy a new crystal that I feel something is "off" with.

---

[132] C.S. Nautiyal, P.S. Chauhan, Y.L. Nene, "Medicinal smoke reduces airborne bacteria," National Library of Medicine (NLM), https://pubmed.ncbi.nlm.nih.gov/17913417/.

- after someone touches one of my crystals, and I don't like the energy left behind.
- if I have had a fight with someone, if I'm still in the same room, I smudge myself and the room; if not, I just smudge myself.
- in a room where I am about to conduct a healing.
- on all clients I am going to do energy work on.
- in any space that does not feel right to me.

I have been doing this for so many years that any time I smell burning sage, I immediately ground and center, which is a very relaxing experience!

Once you cleanse an area, person or object, you can choose to bring in other energies by burning an herb or incense that has other properties, but only after you cleanse! For instance, in some Native American traditions, sweetgrass is used to attract positive energies and cedar is used to change energies. There are many references in old texts, including the Old Testament, mentioning the virtue of frankincense. It is thought to be pleasing to deities and is still burned in the Vatican today. Palo Santo wood is burned by the shamans and medicine people of South America to cleanse. You can research different sacred herbs to see how they have been used traditionally around the world.

36. Cord Cutting

Did you ever experience the end of a friendship, love affair, business connection or even a casual acquaintance, when, even though it is "over," you still feel energetically involved with that person? Perhaps your thoughts circle back to this person or to the event(s) that lead to the final straw; your emotional response to this person or situation might remain at a heightened level, despite the passage of time. It is also possible that you feel drained whenever a certain person is around, even though you don't have much of a relationship. All of these scenarios could be explained by a psychic or energetic cord connecting you to him or her. A cord cutting ceremony is one way to correct this situation, or you could do a releasing ceremony as described in Chapter 64, "Play as Healing Ritual." I find that through the releasing ceremony I often discover deeper reasons for being triggered by a situation or person (such as that they remind me of someone from my past with whom I have unresolved issues). In such a case you could then do a cord cutting or releasing ceremony for the past issue or person as well.

Cords between people happen all the time; we just don't realize it. These bonds will affect you differently with each person because we are each in different places in our awareness, our healing, and our evolution.

Imagine children in a swimming pool for the first time. They are very clingy (literally holding on to you, or the edge, as if their life depended on it). It is not surprising, right? But even though it is easy to understand their behavior, if they are clinging too tightly, it could certainly affect your ability to function at peak. Now imagine a more advanced swimmer. If he or she is holding on to you with the same intensity, you have to consider the possible reason for such an action. But you won't know what that agenda is. Both scenarios deplete energy that we could otherwise use for reaching our destination.

Is it good to help others? Yes. But I prefer to help others who ask for help rather than allow others to help themselves to my energy (whether they are conscious of it or not). So here are some simple things that you can do to free yourself from these energetic connections.

When I first learned about cord cutting I was told that you should purchase a knife that was to be used ceremonially. Any knife would do, so choosing one based on your intuition is a great idea. Once you had the knife, you would ground yourself, light sage, and clear your space and yourself of unwanted energies. Then you would pass the blade about four to six inches away from your body, figuratively and literally severing any ties. I used this method for a long time, until I took Shamanic Reiki with Llyn Cedar Roberts. She has a beautiful take on cord cutting (you can find a chapter on this in the book *Shamanic Reiki*[133]) and I have tweaked it somewhat. Today it is the method I employ most often. This method requires that you be aware of where the cord is attached (which many people can feel, once they look for it). First you close your eyes while sitting or lying comfortably, breathe deeply a few times and ground yourself into your body and then into the earth. When you feel ready, grasp the cord at the place where it is attached to your body. I like to begin sending light into the cord now. When it feels correct, pull the cord out of your body and visualize the light filling and then sealing any dimple or blemish where the cord exited. If you like, you can place one hand here until you are ready to move on. Continue sending light. Visualize the light traveling down the cord and the cord dissolving from your end as the light moves away from you. See this progressing until it reaches its source.

If we are creations of God, the Creator or the universe, and we are all one or a piece of that source (as each of the these teachings dictates), then sending light to end things we no longer wish to participate in seems to me to be the correct thing to do. Follow your heart (gut and intuition).

---

[133] Llyn Roberts and Robert Levy, *Shamanic Reiki: Expanded Ways of Working with Universal Life Force Energy* (Winchester, UK and Washington, USA: O Books, 2008).

37. Combining Different Practices

You can combine smudging with intention. Many of my teachers state their intention out loud as they energetically clean a space. Opening at least one window, smudge all four corners of a room and state out loud that "All negative energy in the room must transmute to positive energy. Any negative energy that does not wish to transmute must leave and may not come back."

After you smudge with the intention of clearing, think about how you want to use that space. What is your goal? Do you want to feel safer? Do you want to be more creative? Do you want to step more fully into your own power? Do you want to be able to speak your truth easily? Whatever your desired outcome, smudge the room again, this time with an herb that changes energy or attracts positive energy. If all you have is sage, smudge with that again, using your intention as the flame that attracts what you are desiring. Do this by holding the feeling that you want to experience clearly in your body, heart, and mind.

You can increase the energy of this practice by holding the feeling and speaking the intention as well. "This space has been cleared so that (state name) can feel safe and comfortable and open fully to my/her/his (creativity, voice, power, highest good, and so on)."

I found this "Facebook Energy Prayer"[134] to be said while burning sage:

> Into this sage smoke I release all negativity that may surround me,
> I release all fear that holds me back, I release all energies that do
> not serve me, passing positive energy on to those I cherish.

I think that's lovely.

It might be beneficial to explore what cleansing traditions were used by your ancestors. Working with what you uncover might well increase

---

[134] *Sage Smudge,* "Facebook Energy Prayer," https://www.facebook.com/SpiritTribeCommunity/videos/1208260662578477/.

your awareness of your connections with your ancestors. Be open to potential discoveries.

One of my personal favorites is to invite "Only those that love me" to enter or stay in my personal space. Recently I experienced a situation that regular smudging did not counter fully. I had to keep trying, approaching the cleansing from different angles until I felt clear. These included cord removals (I will explain that in a following chapter) and revoking any and all permissions that had been granted, consciously or unconsciously.

Every person and situation you encounter will be a little different. You need to use your imagination, your creativity, your knowledge, and your intuition to dance with life, whether in the physical world, the emotional, or the energetic.

Before you light your sacred herb or incense, you want to make sure you have a fireproof vessel to transport it in. Large abalone shells are popular for this, because they do not transfer heat readily, but any non-aluminum metal container is good. Just make sure you put a good amount of sand or dirt in the bottom so that the heat doesn't transfer directly to the container as you're holding it. One of my teachers uses a small cast iron frying pan.

Open at least one door or window in each space that you are cleansing; if you are clearing several floors, you may want to open one window on each. If there are really intense energies in the space, you may want to open one or more windows in every room.

Let your intuition guide you. Have you practiced using your intuition? Are you familiar with how it might come to you? It could be a physical sensation that you will realize occurs in certain situations. It could be that you will receive an image or a series of images that flow from one to the other much like a movie clip. You might "hear" a word or phrase that seems as if someone has spoken inside your head, or near you.

We discussed in "Imaginal Realms" how our imagination is like the field that psychic information passes through. Somehow the imagination has the ability to download these invisible signals and transpose them into something our waking brains can interpret. Initially it can be hard to give these translations any credence. They can seem like silly ideas or flights of fancy, especially if you have been experiencing this your whole life and learned to ignore such information. It takes consciously paying attention to this information and figuring out how to test it; by doing so we learn to navigate in this dimension.

As you begin to be comfortable reading energies, you may not feel the need to open any windows or doors (there are very few truly air tight houses after all). As long as you feel comfortable letting your intention sweep out unwanted energies, this is OK as well.

Again, learning first to test your intuition, and later to trust it, is an important part of all energy work.

38. Salt

Salt has been around a long time. There is even an old adage that refers to someone who is honest and hard working as "the salt of the earth."

Obtaining salt was very time consuming, so much so that it was considered precious. As a matter of fact, Roman solders used to be paid in salt (look up the origin of the word "salary"). It was used as a preservative for foods before the invention of refrigeration. Not that our ancestors understood the mechanical functioning of our cells, but salt is necessary for balancing fluids in the blood, which in turn affects blood pressure. It is also an essential part of how our muscles and nerves function. But even if our ancestors weren't aware of why it helped people, they could see that it did. Learning by inference, would this empirical information be enough to draw the conclusion that salt could be used to protect the body on a spiritual level? I don't know. What I do know is that salt has been used in many cultures for preserving one's spirit and physical well-being (we will discuss some of the ways this was done below). So salt was historically very important to survival. It's important to remember that salt is a crystal, so everything we learned about crystals is applicable here.

The Italians provide a great example of the historic use of salt in protection rituals. If you have grandparents from Italy, you are probably familiar with some of these practices. They include placing small open containers of salt (or salt water) above doors and windows to keep unwanted energies out. Salt has also been poured in all four corners of a room for the same purpose. You can pour a ribbon of salt around yourself or an object (and connect the beginning to the end of the ribbon to form a circle). The shape of the circle is sacred in many cultures. It is used both to keep *in* the energy of what is in the circle and to keep *out* the energy of what is outside the circle.

Taking a saltwater bath will cleanse and protect you. Similarly, you can bathe an object in salt water to cleanse it, or put it directly in dry salt. Dry salt is actually safer for some minerals. If you are using salt water to cleanse an object, such as a crystal or mineral, first make sure that it is not water soluble. Selenite, for example, should not be placed in salt water, or water in general; stick to sunlight, moonlight or smoke from a cleansing herb. Also some minerals are toxic to the human body; these should be handled with care and *not* gotten wet. One example is stibnite (or antimonite) — this mineral with the ability to form black crystals is composed of antimony. Antimony has the same effect on the human body as arsenic. Arsenopyrite looks so similar to iron pyrite (fool's gold) that it can be quite hard to tell the difference. While pyrite is inert, arsenopyrite has a content of arsenic of about 46 percent. Some minerals release deadly fumes or dust when heated, so do not leave them near open flame. A great example of this is Coloradoite (discovered in Boulder, Colorado) which is a fusion of mercury and tellurium. It is relatively safe to handle at room temperature, but you do not want to heat it![135]

According to Greek tradition, salt can be used to rid your house of unwanted guests. Just sprinkling salt behind them as they are leaving a room should do the trick. In Greece, before moving into a new house/apartment, people also sprinkle salt at the entrances of each room to cleanse it of unwanted energies.[136] Don't forget to ask elders — including perhaps your own grandmother — what their traditions were (and not just regarding salt!); they might have more to tell you.

---

[135] "10 Pretty Rocks That Are Deadly," BabaMail, edited by Shelly M. https://www.babamail.com/content.aspx?emailid=16792.

[136] Ethel Dilouambaka, "12 Greek Superstitions that People Still Believe," *CultureTrip* 27, June 2017, https://theculturetrip.com/europe/greece/articles/12-greek-superstitions-people-still-believe/.

39. Water

Water is an elemental force. She dances with the moon, forming the tides. She sparkles with sunlight and refracts it upon her surface and within her body, doubling the rays and bouncing them in multiple directions. It seems to me as if water plays with and amplifies the energies of light. Without her, life on this planet could not exist. There are many curious beliefs about water that bear looking into and experimenting with from your own perspective. Belowis a link to a YouTube talk given by Sadhguru titled "The Mystical Secrets of Water."[137] He's a highly regarded Indian yogi, mystic, and author. Sadhguru has many videos where he discusses water and its relevance to us, including "Water Has Memory,"[138] or "The Key to Health, Treating Water with Reverence."[139] He shares ancient understandings about water's abilities to react to us and to our thoughts. Even more, he says water can act as a co-creative force in our lives. I recommend watching a number of his videos.

Adult human bodies are approximately 60 percent water.[140] The water within us follows the pull of the full moon, even if we no longer pay either the water or the moon homage anymore.

How much thought do you give to the water in your body? Remember that Masaru Emoto's experiments with water revealed that water was dramatically affected by our thoughts. What ramifications might this have on our bodies, given the large percentage of water within each of our cells?

Why would water crystals change depending on which thoughts were being directed at it? We learned in "Crystalline Structure" that molecules

---

[137] Sadhguru, "The Mystical Secretes of Water," March 22, 2019, https://www.youtube.com/watch?v=1kKGzCL4D5w.

[138] Sadhguru, "Water has Memory," https://www.youtube.com/watch?v=Z_tg6qZ1hqU.

[139] Sadhguru, "The Key to Health, Treating Water with Reverence," https://www.youtube.com/watch?v=tmqRyVtJEB4.

[140] USGS science for a changing world, The Water in You: Water and the Human Body, https://www.usgs.gov/special-topic/water-science-school/science/water-you-water-and-human-body/.

with orderly structures conduct energy more easily, and that crystalline structures are the most orderly structures on our planet. The fact that the crystals within water became distorted with words like "hate" or "ugly" supports the theory that negative thoughts diminish the ability of energy to flow.

This transformation of water molecules from orderly to disorderly, depending on the words and thoughts directed at them, is fascinating from a spiritual or imaginal realm viewpoint. Is the water trying to protect itself from unwanted influences by altering its molecular shape to not allow these vibrations to be carried as readily within its structure? Given everything that we are learning about consciousness in plants and animals, we cannot rule this out.

Water is a sacred essence, deserving of our utmost respect and reverence. Perhaps water is communicating its preferences to us ... can we listen? Because we are also more than half water, our bodies may have these same preferences. Certainly, if we are interested in becoming clearer channels for energy, we need to strive for less entropy, even within the water in our bodies.

Water can refract the light of the sun or the moon, bending it and even bouncing it around. Light/energy excites the molecules of what it interacts with, so placing objects you wish cleansed or charged under water in moonlight or sunlight is extremely effective. Placing things in moving water is more energetic; just be sure you are not placing them where they could be washed away. Always remember that water is sensitive to our thoughts, so be respectful, mindful, and always grateful.

40. Moonlight

Silvery, elusive, inconsistent, subtle, and yet so powerful. Her full presence tugs on every drop of water on our blue jewel of a planet, including the ones in our cells and our bones (bones are 31% water). Emotions have long been associated with water. It is no wonder that the full moon has the reputation of affecting our emotions and our psyche when she visits us in her resplendent phase.

To older cultures, especially those without electricity, the moon was far more significant than it is to us today. Her magical white light enabled clear vision at night and so facilitated travel and other outdoor activities. If you ever spend the night somewhere without artificial light, you will be amazed at how bright her light is, illuminating every rock, tree branch or root so that you might walk without a flashlight. I experienced this many times when I was living in the Philippines and Thailand, as well as trekking in the Himalayas in the early 1980s.

Our moon's presence graces us with more than just light. Her pull on our planet affects other things as well, something that early humans discovered and exploited in their planting and harvesting cycles. Folks interested in working with energy use her waxing phase to build energies in objects or endeavors. Conversely, the energies available during her waning phase support releasing work or diminishing energy that is too strong.

Moonlight is reflected light, and that energy is different than direct light. To understand reflection from a visceral and intuitive perspective, close your eyes and imagine seeing sunlight hit the moon. See those beams being reflected off of the moon's surface. Sit with that image and tell me what impressions you get. Again, we are not discounting random images, feelings, thoughts, sounds or associations as we contemplate reflected light. How does your inner knowing speak to you? Only by playing with it will you learn. Let your instrument "talk" to you as you think about mirrors, water and the moon.

The moon will impart her light-excited electrons and imbue things like crystals with her silvery reflected light. Placing sacred objects in moonlight is a way of both "charging" them and cleansing them.

41. Sunlight

Sunlight is an active form of energy. It is thought of as masculine energy, like gold (moonlight is associated with silver and seen as feminine). Placing an object in the sun can both cleanse and energize it. If you are working with crystals be careful which ones you leave in the sun. Fluorite, kunzite and even amethyst can fade dramatically if left in direct sunlight for too long.

I remember hiking in the petrified forest twenty years ago. I was following a long-dried-up stream and came upon a fist sized hunk of kunzite. Kunzite's form is so distinctive that I recognized it immediately, but I could not have said whether it was originally pink, green, or yellow; the sun had bleached it completely colorless. I left it right where I found it, for another adventurer to experience the magic of discovering such a treasure.

42. Earth

Sacred ground. All earth is precious. Everything that we depend upon to live comes from the earth. Even man-made things are composed of elements from the earth. Yet our connection to her — *in our minds* — is so tenuous these days that it threatens our sanity as well as our ability to live.

Our ancestors depended upon planting seeds, covering them with soil that they worked with their hands, sometimes patting it into place. They watered, weeded, picked off pests, and protected plants from other predators. A more intimate relationship with the earth, the seasons, the weather, and the plants and animals we ate or simply shared the planet with could not have been created.

What our ancestors needed has been passed down to us in our cellular memory as epigenetics. We need to have our hands in the earth. We need to nurture a plant (and the planet), particularly if it bears fruit that we can eat. It's profound how much of a calming effect this has on us biologically and psychologically. Not only does it soothe us to perform tasks that our ancestors did to survive, but there are also nutritional benefits available in just-picked fruits and vegetables, such as the simple sugars that are essential to our cells' health which begin to convert to starches in as little as eight hours after being picked.

Because the earth provides everything we need for life, most First Nations people refer to her as our Mother.

In addition to nurturing us, the earth can aid in healing us. Did you know that earth will draw off negative energies and balance others? That is one of the reasons it is so good for us to walk barefoot upon her. This practice is referred to as "grounding" or "earthing." An article by James L. Oschman says:

> Multi-disciplinary research has revealed that electrically conductive contact of the human body with the surface of the earth (grounding or earthing) produces intriguing effects on physiology

and health. Such effects relate to inflammation, immune responses, wound healing, and the prevention and healing of chronic inflammatory and autoimmune diseases . . . grounding an organism produces measurable differences in the concentrations of white blood cells, cytokines, and other molecules involved in the inflammatory response. Grounding reduces pain and alters the numbers of circulating neutrophils and lymphocytes, and also affects various circulating chemical factors related to inflammation.[141]

According to an article in the *Washington Post*:

If you think back to the last time you took a science class, you may remember that everything including humans, is made up of atoms These microscopic particles contain equal numbers of negatively charged electrons, which come in pairs, and positively charged protons, so an atom is neutral — unless it loses an electron. When an atom has an unpaired electron, it becomes a "free radical" with a positive charge, capable of damaging our cells and contributing to chronic inflammation, cancer and other diseases. In this case, "positive" is not a good thing. One reason direct physical contact with the ground might have beneficial physiological effects is that the earth's surface has a negative charge and is constantly generating electrons that could neutralize free radicals, acting as antioxidants.[142]

In "Trust Your Gut" we talked about how the vagus nerve is the only way that the gut and the brain converse directly. Well, here's some interesting information on how the earth affects the vagus nerve and how that impacts you, also found in the same article.

Research also suggests physical contact with the Earth's surface can help regulate our autonomic nervous system and keep our circadian rhythms — which regulate body temperature, hormone secretion, digestion and blood pressure, among other things — synchronized with the day/night cycle. Desynchronization of our

---

[141] James L. Oschman, Gaetan Chevalier, and Richard Brown, *The Journal of Inflamation Research,* Journal List, J Inflamm Res, v.8; 2015, PMC4378297.
[142] Carrie Dennett, "Could walking barefoot on the grass improve your health? Some research suggests it can." *The Washington Post,* July 10, 2018 at 7:00 a.m. EDT https://www.washingtonpost.com/lifestyle/wellness/could-walking-barefoot-on-the-grass-improve-your-health-the-science-behind-grounding/2018/07/05/12de5d64-7be2-11e8-aeee-4d04c8ac6158_story.html.

internal clocks has been linked to a number of health problems, as evidenced by research on shift workers. The key may be the impact on the vagus nerve. This is the largest nerve of the autonomic nervous system — extending from the brain to the colon — and plays a key role in heart, lung and digestive function. Strong vagal tone helps you relax faster after experiencing stress, while weak vagal tone is associated with chronic inflammation. Inflammation, in turn, is associated with a number of chronic diseases — including cardiovascular disease, type 2 diabetes and some forms of cancer. Vagal tone is often assessed by measuring the variation in your heart rate when you breathe in and out, and in one study, grounding was shown to improve heart rate variability and thus vagal tone in preterm infants. In another small study of adults, one two-hour session of grounding reduced inflammation and improved blood flow.[143]

So the earth, our Mother, nurtures us, and we need to have physical contact with her to reap these benefits. Does this suggest anything to you? Does it make you question the beliefs and habits that have grown up around this modern world that we humans have created? It should.

Being in contact with the earth also has benefits for animals and crystals. The article above provides examples of animals benefiting in the same ways that humans do from contact with the earth.

To work with the earth in cleaning a crystal or an object, try this: take the object that you feel uncomfortable with and try placing it in the earth. Dig a hole and put the object that you wish to deeply cleanse within it. Cover the object with soil and leave it for a length of time. Use your intuition; it might need a few days, several weeks, months, or even years. Always ask permission before you do this, and always give thanks. You will be amazed at the results. You can also place something that does not feel very badly "off" on top of the earth for a period of time. Here it will receive sunlight and moonlight as well as the energies of the earth and rain to cleanse and charge it.

---

[143] Ibid.

43. Meditation

How do you feel about meditating? If we're talking about Buddhist "sitting," it's not really my thing. I don't get to my bliss by struggling to empty my mind, but I know it works for other people. There is another type of meditating that I do. Instead of emptying my mind, I sit and open myself to the natural world.

In our busy modern lives, we bounce from one thing to the next — not just physically but mentally as well. Unless you go out of your way to create both space and time, you probably don't sit in a quiet place, where you let go of today's "bouncing" and tomorrow's "planning" and just let yourself "be." This kind of "being" feels like becoming a bell that has been rung. You allow yourself to radiate out from yourself, and your vibration begins to mingle with the vibration of what is around you. In these moments, I experience intense bliss. I connect with the vibration of the natural world around me, and it nourishes me in profound ways.

I stated earlier that the experiences of *connection* and *sacredness* are very closely related to each other. As humans we are hardwired to be connected. I believe this is why we are so drawn to being "in love." Our culture has left very few places for us to legitimately connect to other energies on our planet; as a result, we long for connection to another person, because it feeds this part of us. It makes sense that without knowing other ways to connect we would naturally gravitate towards other people for that deep nurturing. If you were lucky, you experienced this with your mother or father. Some of us didn't. Some of us have parents whose connectivity was so damaged in their childhoods that they are ignorant of the benefits of connecting.

How often in the adult world do we experience a connection to another human that is more nurturing than it is damaging? Not often. Why? Because most humans are operating on false, negative teachings and with a deficit of deep emotional/spiritual nourishment.

If this resonates with you, read *The Celestine Prophecy* by James Redfield.[144] It explains how humans take energy from each other and gives guidance on how to get energy by connecting to nature in a cyclical, replenishing loop. Through meditating and being present and aware we can connect to something greater than ourselves.

There is a very interesting phenomenon in physics that may point to why meditating works. In "Crystalline Structure" we learned that a substance that has a regular molecular pattern conducts energy better than one that has a random pattern.

When we are stressed and our thoughts are running in a million directions, this may increase the "randomness" of our frequency, making it harder for us to be clear channels of energy. When we let go of the stressors and sit focusing on our own vibrations, they become enhanced, because what we focus on grows. We "ring out" a more "regular" frequency, which in turn allows more energy to flow into who we are. That's cool enough, but there's more. In "Crystalline Structure" we learned that a very structured, regular molecular pattern allows light to pass through it directly, and it literally becomes clear, like a quartz crystal. Perhaps this is what *enlightenment* is.

Usually people who are seen as enlightened have practiced some form of inner discipline. Could they have achieved enlightenment through a radical transformation — like coal? Coal is dark and dense; no light passes through it. It is a result of the random structuring of its molecules, with high entropy. However, if you put coal under tremendous pressure and high heat, the molecules are forced into a regular, highly structured pattern. The result? A diamond! Can we apply that to the mind or spiritual nature of a human? If we become less scattered, less random, do we become clearer? Better channels for light?

In Buddhism there is a Threefold Path for entering into a state of calmness, oneness, and enlightenment.

The first, called "shila," is comprised of five ethics or guidelines on how to live without harming yourself or others. Buddhists believe that acting ethically affects you deeply — not just others whom you encounter in your life, but you yourself. They are not alone in this. There are similar teachings in Native cultures that stress the importance of staying in "right relationship with all our relations" — which incidentally comprises not just

144 James Redfield, *The Celestine Prophecy: An Adventure,* Grand Central Publishing, Hachette Book Group, N.Y.

humans, but the entirety of creation. This philosophy closely resembles Don Miguel Ruiz's teaching in his book *The Four Agreements*.[145]

On the surface it makes sense; acting ethically un-complicates your life, as well as giving you a clear conscience. So much self-doubt comes from not feeling like we are "good" people. How do we judge whether we are good or not? We are taught to look at external references for answers. And looking for answers outside ourselves leaves us vulnerable to other people, or to institutions that are looking for followers.

There *are* truths. If you look across time and cultures, you will connect the dots and see similarities. All spiritually based paths to happiness advise "right" action for the self. This means not trying to control others, but instead trying to create beauty in every breath and step we take, as in the Navaho "Beauty Way" or striving to "Stay in right relationship to all my relations" as in the teachings from my Lakota and Abenaki friends.

Many Native American Nations chose their leaders from people who had a track record of living for the good of the people and a history of selfless acts. Can you imagine if that were how we chose our world leaders today? Did you know that recent studies have shown that all happy people have one thing in common? They dedicate their lives to helping others.

I can tell you from experience that there is nothing like the feeling of knowing that time after time you chose the higher path of kindness, or awareness of another's personal situation or limitations. It is not easy. It can be exhausting to always search for that higher ground. It does not entail being perfect, or even close to perfect. This is similar to the fact that being courageous does not mean that you are not afraid. It simply means you do not let fear keep you locked up. Taking the higher road means you acted not on impulse, even though you felt anger or frustration, but instead you aimed for an outcome that was beneficial to your relationship.

Our knee jerk reaction is self-preservation; after all, our perceptions are generated from our internal point of view. Since no two people are exactly alike, even twins, all points of view will be slightly different. Animals also have self-preservation at heart, yet they do not practice behaviors that isolate them, if they are pack creatures. They are not disconnected from their interconnectedness. They don't become so enraged that they kill an opponent, not the way they would a creature threatening their young, even in mating season. They have internal stops that they listen to.

---

[145] Don Miguel Ruiz, *The Four Agreements, A Toltec Wisdom Book*, Amber-Allen Publishing, San Rafael California.

We also have this type of information, but we have been conditioned to ignore it, as with so many other subtle inner awarenesses.

You are human. If you judge yourself by how many times you give in to being human, you will be miserable. Aiming for a higher ethic gives you a goal. Like anything else, you work at it little by little. As with training for a sport, it takes time to build the "muscles." We all have our Achilles heel, and that's OK. One of the things that yoga has taught me is to find balance. We do not judge ourselves against others. We judge ourselves by where we are at any point in each given day. There is a Hindu proverb that translates roughly to "There is no point in proving your superiority over another person, but there is much to be gained by being superior to your former self."

The next part of the threefold path in Buddhism is "Samadhi" or meditation. It is seen as the second step in preparing the mind to be clear, in order to be ready for the third part of the threefold path, "Prajna" or developing wisdom — understanding the true nature of our lives and experience.

44. Tonglen

There is a practice in Tibetan Buddhism that I love, called Tonglen. It's a practice of holding the energy "feeling" of a hardship that you have experienced and are deeply moved by. Immerse yourself in this feeling until you fully embody it. Then begin breathing as follows (not that you were holding your breath): as you breathe in, take in the feeling of this issue; as you breathe out, send the antidote to this feeling.

It is a simple yet very powerful exercise. It can be done on a small, personal level or on a planetary level. You can breathe in the pain and suffering of animals, an area, a continent, or the planet, and breathe out the end of their suffering. You can breathe in fear and send out nurturing, peace and safety. You can breathe in hunger and breathe out food and nourishment. The possibilities are endless. The Dalai Lama uses this meditation every morning; he says it brings him great peace of mind.

Tonglen is a practice with which I am comfortable, partly because it has to do with connecting, caring, and expanding. In Tibetan *tong* can be interpreted as "sending out" or "letting go," and *len* as "receiving" or "accepting." Tonglen can be practiced anywhere, as either a seated meditation or as a part of your day.

I see this practice as useful for strengthening one's compassion and sense of connection to *all*. It provides a good basis to begin to understand the principles of transmutation. It will also help you with manifesting. It is said to be a training in altruism, to reduce selfish attachment.

An interesting aside: we talked about humans being walking trees (in "The Earth and Us"). Trees breathe in the carbon dioxide we exhale as a waste product and turn it into oxygen through photosynthesis. Are trees practicing Tonglen on a physical level? All the more reason for us to be practicing this type of toxin transformation.

Taking onto oneself the suffering of others and giving happiness and success to all sentient beings seems a heavy task, especially for a beginner in the practice. It might be appropriate to start out with smaller issues, such as working with oneself to increase one's own well-being, to increase harmony in the family, to open one's own mind to communicate better with other people or to find more peace in doing daily chores.

Try using a small pause after the in-breath to convert the suffering or disharmony to the positive antidote which is to be breathed out.

Taking on suffering in this way does not burden the self with the misery of the world. We are not taking in a brick of static energy and living with it. Instead, as we acknowledge its existence, we transform it; it is no longer in the same form it was before it entered our consciousness. This practice uses many of the same concepts I spoke of in "Somatic Experience." You transform the energy by switching the vibrational signature within you, from suffering to joy, from strife to peace, and so on.

According to Buddhist teachings the rewards of practicing this are to reduce selfish attachment, to purify karma, to develop and expand loving-kindness, among others.

45. Where Can We Get Energy?

Where can we get energy? And I am not talking about the kind we get from eating food. Some answers may surprise you.

What happens when you sit in a place in the woods, near a stream, by the ocean? How does it make you feel? Listening to the sound of the wind in the leaves, the songs of birds, crickets chirping on a lazy sunny day, water burbling happily in a stream, or the ocean, many people feel relaxed and then refreshed. Quite a few folks say they need time in nature to "recharge" their batteries. How could that be?

In *The Celestine Prophecy* (see note 144), James Redfield describes how humans have adopted five strategies for dealing with each other that result in taking energy from another person. It's worth reading because it will make you aware of what these strategies are and when they are being used on you! It might even open your eyes as to when you do it to others. Redfield then describes another way to get energy from the natural world around you, rather than stealing it from others. It's a very simple method that every tree-hugging nature enthusiast does without being conscious of it (and no, I'm not asking you to go hug a tree).

In "Fung Shui" we discover that the Chinese believe that energy follows people's gaze. Redfield asks you to gaze at the same tree every day for several weeks. Gaze at it in appreciation. Appreciate the curve of its limbs, the pattern of its bark, the hue of its spring, summer or fall leaves. When we give positive regard to something, we are giving it energy ... which most living things return. Trees are no exception! Redfield says this is a better way to get energy than "acquiring" it from each other, and I agree. Try it.

Somewhere back in time folks who were sensitive to such things (healers and medicine people) tuned into the essence of a plant and discerned what it could be used for. These qualities were not something that was visible to the naked eye. Yes, there are visual clues such as the doctrine of signatures developed by Dr. Edward Bach (which we get into in Ch. 54,

"Healing Plants") but what we are talking about here is the ability to witness the chi (essential life force) of a plant and be aware of how this affects the chi of a person who interacts with it. In other words, healing properties were accurately intuited or discerned although these could not be explained by the physics of the plant.

Cultures that accept subtle forms of energy in their everyday thinking developed "recipes" for increasing the subtle energy that flows within certain systems, and these have been used successfully for centuries. Some recipes involve physical stances or movements, like Tai Chi, Qigong, martial arts or yoga, some involve breath work, and some involve the mind — like meditation or creative visualization. Some, such as Feng Shui, use the energy of people's gaze, as well as the placement (or removal) of objects, to increase energy flow within one's home, yard or body.

Our bodies get the energy they need to produce muscle movement (and more) from tiny organisms living inside of us called mitochondria. Mitochondria live inside each of our cells that have nuclei (everything except our blood). They don't utilize the same amino acids (the building blocks of life) that we do, but rather produce their own chains of these synthesized from nutrients we supply. Mitochondria are thought to have evolved from independent prokaryotes (single cell organisms) millennia ago. These soft-celled creatures (that look just like a virus!) use the protection of our bodies and have access to our nutrients. In return they produce an energy source called adenosine triphosphate or ATP that they make available to our cells. What is interesting here is that:

1. They respond to our muscles' need for energy by multiplying, thereby creating more energy for us.
2. The failure of our mitochondria to reproduce is now being linked to aging.

So keeping our mitochondria stimulated is very important to our bodies. What if exercise alone is not the only way we can communicate with or affect our mitochondria? Our mitochondria respond to the muscles' need for energy by creating more mitochondria. What if combining different practices doubles or triples the effect on our mitochondria? Looked at in this light, Tai Chi or Qigong takes on a different significance.

Could the breath work in these practices also stimulate mitochondria? What about the positive feelings we bathe our somatic selves with when we practice focused relaxing energy techniques like meditation, shamanistic journeying, or creative visualization? Could part of the reason why these techniques are so effective be because they communicate with or influence our mitochondria in some way? I would say conclusively that we don't know! However, it is possible (and intriguing)!

Part IV

ENERGETIC

46. Can We See Vibrational Frequency?

Frequency is the measurable rate of energy flow that is constant between any two points. It is a wave. We measure frequency in Hertz (Hz).

Thousands of years ago our bodies evolved a complex method to render some frequencies of energy visible. The rods and cones in our eyes let us differentiate the length of energy waves, or their vibrational frequency. These frequencies are contained in the visible light spectrum. Colors, glorious colors! Colors represent the amount of energy in a wave of light. We perceive shorter waves as purples. As the waves become bigger, we see blues, then greens, then yellows, then oranges, and finally reds, the longest wavelength we are able to see.

After that, and before that, we cannot see the energy that light contains, but we know for a fact that there is still energy there. So that brings me to the next question: can things you can't see affect you? What about things you can't feel and have no awareness of? Can they affect you?

Let's look at the energy in light waves, the ones we cannot see. These waves or vibrational frequencies include gamma, radio, infrared and micro waves, referred to as the invisible light spectrum. Are you aware of them? Can you feel them? I know you can't see them ... but they very much *can* affect you. Too much exposure to them can make you sick or even kill you. So, things we can't see can definitely affect us.

Why from an evolutionary perspective would we evolve to *see* a small spectrum of vibrational frequency? It hasn't been studied as far as I know. Even if it had, I doubt it would have been approached from the perspective of energy's *relevance* to our well-being. This is not a question our scientists are posing yet. But perhaps you should.

Why would we evolve to see a part of the frequency of light, and not all of it? Especially why would we develop the ability to see the part of the spectrum that *can't* kill us? That's interesting; I've heard of death by chocolate, but never, for instance, death by purple. It took a lot of evolutionary time and genetic specialization to develope the ability to see the harmless spectrum of light. There *has* to be some major importance in our being able to differentiate those colors.

Visually colors help us identify things. The black snake is harmless, but the black and red segmented one is poisonous. So that's important. As for food, we eat some red berries, but other red ones are poisonous (no help there). It's the same thing with blue ones, so there's no real advantage to seeing colors here. We could learn more from watching other animals eat than from the color coding of food as to its safety. Incidentally, bees see more of the light spectrum than we do; it helps them to see a flower that contains nectar, as opposed to one that's empty.

So, the next logical question would be; Do colors, or more specifically, their vibrational frequency, affect us? We would have to assume yes because we've already established that the frequency of light does affect us at least in the form of the invisible light spectrum. In reference to the visible light spectrum we just need to understand more.

Have there been tests on how colors affect us? Yes. Studies by corporations have been done to establish what colors render their workers more productive, and retailers have studied what colors will make you more prone to buy. Hospitals have studied which colors make a patient more relaxed, discovering in the process which ones affect them in the opposite way.

So, we evolved to see colors, and they affect us. That is proven ... but have we stopped to consider why? What of the vibrational frequency they represent? How do our bodies react to frequency? Perhaps we need to turn our attention to our ancestors' awareness of these things to gain a different kind of understanding.

We spoke about Dr. Fritz Albert Popp's discovery of biophotons (in "Acupuncture"). He says: "We know today that man, essentially, is a being of light."

And the modern science of photobiology is proving this. In terms of healing the implications are immense. We now know, for example, that quanta of light can initiate, or arrest, cascade-like reactions in the cells, and that genetic cellular damage can be virtually repaired, within hours, by faint beams of light.

We are still on the threshold of fully understanding the complex relationship between light and life, but we can now say emphatically that the function of our entire metabolism is dependent on light.[146]

---

[146] Dr. Fritz Albert Popp, "We know today that man, is essentially, a being of light." *Biontology Arizona*, https://biontologyarizona.com/dr-fritz-albert-popp.

47. Chakras

Chakras are energy centers in the body that were mapped out by Hindu yogis thousands of years ago. They were discovered because people were able to feel them within their bodies. As we have talked about often, self-awareness is something that every form of martial arts, yogic practice, or true spiritual seeking encourages. It's more of an Eastern way of looking at life, as opposed to needing scientific evidence to believe in something. We will also be talking about nadis in this chapter, because they are related to chakras but less well known in the West.

The chakras and nadis are part of the same system, the nadis being the almost infinite network of tubular organs or channels of energy flow felt throughout the body, and the chakras being the origins and epicenters of this energy flow. Nadis follow the same lines as all the physical body systems like the nerves, lymph, and circulatory systems, but on top of this there are numerous extra lines of energy (sometimes expressed as extending to the tip of every hair on the body). It is important to retain a tone of spaciousness in order to experience nadis, and this is pointed to by the root 'nad' meaning resonance. While nadi itself means 'a flowing river,' the common description of nadis is as 'tubular organs' through which the energy flow moves.

The truth of science and the truth of yoga do not need to be at odds, as they belong to two different levels of understanding. Chakras (literally wheels) and nadis (meaning energy channels—literally, flowing water) are real experiences reflected [and] expressed through the use of these models. It is not that the nadis and chakras are 'objectively there' so much as they are 'effectively there.' If you like, they are poetic terms that equate to infinite webs of relationships between muscles, nerves, emotions, energy and the psyche. It is perhaps due to the complexity of the experience to which the nadis and the chakras point that more objective language could never accurately describe the experiences felt, not least because of the 'living element' that is involved.[147]

Chakras are sometimes seen as spinning wheels that are on both the front and back of the body simultaneously at specific points. What I see most often is more like a plate or a phonograph album, turning in a clockwise direction at each chakra. I see them as lying horizontal, flat, and spinning, rather than standing like a bike wheel on their sides. These spinning disks are centered in the body, so that they are spinning in the front and back simultaneously, like a record on a record player. What is interesting about this ancient visualization of spinning wheels is that physicists now recognize a phenomenon called a spinning electric field vector (SEV). These vectors are found over turbulent subterranean waters, geo-faults and in corners, to name a few places. There is something about the geometry at these points that causes a phase shift between two vectors and enables the formation of a SEV. Perhaps this is what is occurring at the points of the body recognized as chakras. M. Krinker and A. Goykadosh published a study of these phenomena, where they say that "One of the latest studies confirmed origination of space-time distortions caused by spinning objects."[148]

In the meantime, let's review more commonly known information about the seven primary chakras: the crown, the third eye, the throat, the heart, the solar plexus, the navel and the root or base chakras. There are other chakras, not as well known, throughout the body and you can read about them in different Hindu texts. If you wish to use your chakras to help you evolve, one of the clearest descriptions of them and their significance to us that I have ever encountered was written by Sadhguru in a Huffington Post article. I highly recommend reading it. Sadhguru says that there are actually 114[149] chakras, but for the purposes of this book we will stick to the seven most frequently mentioned ones.

Each of these seven has a color, a sound, an emotional and/or a physical quality that is associated with it, and, in some schools of thought, a shape as well. Interestingly, the colors of the chakras that align with the

---

[147] https://www.vajrasatiyoga.co.uk/nadis-and-chakras.

[148] M. Krinker, A. Goykadosh, *Photonic Aspects of Dowsing and Feng Shui,* SCRIBD, City College of Technology, Department of Electrical Engineering and Telecomunications, CUNY, New York. Nov. 14, 2011.

[149] Sadhguru, *The Seven Chakras and Their Signifigance to Your Life,* Nov. 17, 2011, https://www.huffpost.com/entry/the-7-chakras-and-their-s_b_844268.

trunk of the human body follow the colors of the visible light spectrum from red to purple. The red end of the spectrum aligns with our sacral chakra at the base of the spine. The colors progress, changing at each chakra point, until we reach the third eye chakra, which I was taught was purple. White is the color of the chakra at the top of our head. Some people have even theorized that the circular glow of white light represented as a halo above enlightened beings' heads is what a crown chakra that is fully open looks like.

There is much written on chakras in texts both ancient and modern. One fact, perhaps less well known, is that they correspond to physical nerve clusters in our bodies called ganglia. Remember we spoke about them in "Trust Your Gut." Ganglia resemble small brains, in more ways than just visually.

Of the seven chakras, five correspond to plexus points along our spines, as well as to ganglia and plexus locations in the ENS (enteric nervous system). The other two are associated with major glands. Plexuses are crossroads of major nerves in our bodies, consisting of sensory cells, ganglia cells and their processes. Sadhguru writes:

> The human body is a complex energy form; in addition to the 114 chakras, it also has 72,000 "nadis," or energy channels, along which vital energy, or "prana," moves. When the nadis meet at different points in the body, they form a triangle. We call this triangle a chakra, which means "wheel." We call it a wheel because it symbolizes growth, dynamism and movement, even though it is actually a triangle . . . [150]

There is not much chance our ancestors had visual information about these nerve systems, but obviously they were aware of them energetically, enough so to identify their locations and, in the case of the Chinese, map out their paths and functions in developing the art of acupuncture more than 5,000 years ago.

The most notable plexus is home to the third, or solar plexus, chakra. The solar plexus is said to be so named because of its resemblance to the sun, with many nerves radiating out from a central place. The solar plexus contains three ganglia and three plexuses.

Not surprisingly, the color associated with the solar plexus chakra is yellow, like the sun itself. This chakra pertains to the seat of the will. If you feel vulnerable, like you are powerless to change your situation

---

[150] Ibid.

(especially in a threatening moment), it can often be felt directly here. In these situations, your will is being undermined, and it can feel like nausea, cramping, tightening or pressure in the stomach area. Have you ever been in a situation where someone who has power over you (e.g., a boss, teacher or parent) yells at you? Where in your body do you feel this? Can you remember? Most people feel it in their solar plexus region. Someone who is yelling at you is trying to dominate your will in that moment, and this feels threatening. Citrine and golden topaz are great stones for empowering this area. I like to wear one of these when I know I am "going into battle" with someone. When I have not had the opportunity to prepare for such a situation, I recall the vibrational signature of one of these stones and combine that with a visualized circular shield of golden honey light floating in front of my body at a distance that feels correct. How do I know if it feels correct? One way is that I feel immediate relief from the other's emotions. If you have not flexed these "muscles" previously, you may not be able to feel much, or anything at all. Do not be frustrated by this. We all are created differently, with our own timeline and process regarding our development. Remember, the gift here is you.

Let's explore each chakra in order, starting with the first or root chakra. This chakra, located at the base of the spine, is where we find our ability to ground ourselves physically, mentally and emotionally to the earth. If you are feeling spacey, light headed, flighty, or have trouble making decisions, try starting a practice of grounding. There are many ways to do this, including the use of crystals, minerals and stones. Tiger's eye and hematite are two of my favorites. You can hold them when you practice the next exercise, or you can connect to these stones' energetic signature and visualize them as described above. Try sitting quietly for a few minutes every morning and imagining a taproot coming out of the base of your spine and sending it deep into the earth. This can help balance you, as can walking barefooted on the earth. Do you remember how much you wanted to go barefooted as a kid? Some of us disliked wearing shoes at all. Your body knew how good it was for you to be barefoot. The root chakra is associated with our base needs, like anger and sexuality, and it is seen as being red. There is a practice called Tantra that works intensely with this chakra, and this area is associated with kundalini energy as well.

Traveling upward we come to the second, or navel, chakra. This site houses at least two plexuses, as well as being the home of our naval. This is significant because our navel was where we first experienced connection and being nourished. We received all our food in this chakra for the first nine months of our lives, as well as mainlining the vibrational information our mothers were "digesting."

If our mother endured a lot of stress while she carried us, we can be predisposed to react nervously to stress in our lives, have digestive issues, or suffer from eating disorders. Our relationship to being nurtured or to food can become distorted. You can greatly reduce or even completely release these conditioned responses to stress through energy medicine. I personally recommend Flower Essences for this chakra, but any treatment using energy here can make an amazing difference.

The navel chakra is also the place where we eliminated all that no longer served us when we were in our mother's womb, and this chakra can be worked with as a place to release what we no longer want in our adult lives as well.

The navel chakra is seen as orange, and stones like calcite, moonstone, citrine or coral and some types of jasper will support this center.

We talked about the third or solar plexus chakra already, so let's continue traveling up to the following chakra, known as the heart chakra. Housed within the fourth chakra we have the cardiac plexus. The heart chakra is where we manifest love; the color associated with it is green or pink. So stones like rose quartz, ruby, kunzite, aventurine, mossy agate, morganite (a pink form of beryl which includes emerald and aquamarine), pink-green or even watermelon tourmaline are all good stones for supporting this center.

When we experience a loss, like the death of someone we love or the end of a relationship, we feel it in the fourth chakra — just as we feel a blossoming or opening here when love grows.

Many of my Native American teachers described the heart, which sits in the middle of the seven chakras, as the seat of wisdom (not our heads). It is also described in some cultures and certain spiritual teachings as an *organ of perception*. Its role is to be the mediator between the gut and the brain, having its own ability to weigh matters. My Native teachers said they were taught to sit in stillness, centered in their hearts, to make wise decisions. The men best able to do this were often chosen to be chiefs. People who sit quietly in their hearts are powerful. They do not fly off the handle or get sidetracked by strong emotions. It is especially rare in our modern world for men to practice sitting in their hearts. What a shame!

Continuing upwards from the heart chakra we have the throat or fifth chakra. The throat chakra is the home of our "voice." It often takes girls longer to find their voice in our current paradigm than boys. True use of a fully realized voice is a bridge between the wisdom of the heart and the reasoning head. Women are taught (for the most part) to not speak their truths. After all we were hunted, tortured and burned at the stake for doing so. All women have memories and possible genetic alterations around these issues. Beyond that the only place of relative safety there was for women for centuries was as a sexual object, housewife (literally married to the house!) or a devoted mother. We have been conditioned to be nurturers who do not consider themselves. (There are of course some women who have learned to attend to their own needs, in both balanced and unbalanced ways.) It is our current culture's worship of the purely masculine aspects of existence that has caused many of the imbalances in our world.

A proper relationship to our heart and throat chakras would go a long way towards bringing about balance and harmony in the world and in our lives. The color of the throat chakra is seen as blue. If you were abused as a child or dominated by others in any way, your throat chakra could well be blocked. Here as well the use of energy medicines such as Flower Essences, meditation, singing, Reiki, etc., can be very helpful. Blue stones are good for supporting this chakra.

A word of warning: not all blue stones are naturally blue, whether they are opaque or translucent. Howlite, a white stone with grey veins in it, is often dyed blue to mimic sodalite or lapis lazuli. Natural blue topaz has been so scarce in the last 25 years or more as to be almost nonexistent. "London Blue" topaz is irradiated, and a gemologist I knew showed me on a Geiger counter that it still registers radioactively. I would avoid this stone, especially not wearing it on the throat chakra, which houses your thyroid, a gland that is very sensitive to radiation.

Moving upwards again we arrive at the sixth chakra or third eye. I was taught that this chakra is purple, although some say it is clear. Amethyst is associated with this chakra as are indicolite and sugilite, which are all purple in color, but there are others as well. If you would like more information about the nature of specific stones, a great resource is *The Book Of Stones* by Robert Simmons and Naisha Ahsian.[151]

This sixth chakra houses the pituitary gland, which is responsible for the regulation of several other glands. This is a fun chakra, especially when it opens. It is here that we receive information from sources that come from levels other than the one our physical bodies inhabit. If you see things or experience things like déjà vu, premonitions, etc., this is

---

[151] Robert Simmons and Naisha Ahsian, *The Book Of Stones: Who They Are And What They Teach*, Destiny Books, 4th Edition, Revised, 2021.

where the information comes from. My third eye has been incredibly open as I write this book, feeling almost like a floodlight on my forehead. I am experiencing the sensation of a beam of light with a vast scope exactly where they say the third eye is.

If you have a Christian background, you may have been taught to fear the fact that we can communicate with other levels of reality. You may have received warnings of the potential of losing your soul, or having it corrupted, if you explore spiritual knowledge on your own. (Wasn't that exactly the message in the Adam and Eve story? Do not seek knowledge from nature ....) Look at the scope of wrath and punishment that the men who wrote the Bible attached to Eve's curiosity.

To draw an analogy, let's go back to the invisible light spectrum. We cannot see it, yet it can affect us. Almost all the invisible light spectrum can kill us with too much exposure. Yet how much thought do we give it in our daily lives? We don't (ironic, isn't it, that we equate evil with darkness and light with good, yet light can kill us). Let's look at this dynamic. Do you benefit from not knowing about the nature of invisible light? If microwaves can heat your food, and I share that with you, it might seem miraculous to you. But would I be doing you a favor if I didn't warn you of the fact that they can have negative effect on your body if you expose yourself to them? I don't think so. Wouldn't knowing exactly what their nature was help you? Doesn't *knowing* allow you to look into ways to protect yourself? To respond appropriately? We explored different methods of protecting yourself in Part III, Intellectual.

I can only tell you of my own experience. During 30 years of working with my third eye, developing my intuition and psychic abilities, and working with energy in healing, I have never been harmed by learning to work with these things, nor has anyone I know. There are spirits that might wish to influence you, but in truth they are not that different from spirits in flesh (called humans) who might seek to influence you. How can you tell whether you can or cannot trust someone? It takes time. You need to pay attention to minute reactions in your body, your instrument. Any being that wishes to influence you must first win your trust. If you keep your eyes and heart open, you should be able to discern a being's true intentions. Practice with spirits you can see (clothed in flesh). Can you open yourself enough to read people? Try it. You can use the same awareness of nuances to read animals, insects, the elements, pretty much everything. We are being touched and brushed and affected by energy all the time.

Increasing your awareness of this allows you to interact consciously with so much more of our world than we usually do.

If there are negative energies at large in the world, you are not protected from them by pretending they are not there. My experience has been exactly the opposite. Having knowledge of the energy that I am near puts me at an advantage, not a disadvantage. Knowing how to direct my energy to manifest, to connect, or to clear energy as well as to transmute energies/spirits has helped me. It has not harmed me.

Finally, we come to the crown chakra, at the top of the head. This seventh chakra is seen by some as white. The halo often shown around the heads of religious figures is thought to be the visible effect of an open crown chakra. The crown chakra is where we connect to the heavenly realm. This spot on a human's head is open when we are born. The bones of the skull do not grow over this area until after we have been out of the womb for some time. Perhaps newly embodied spirits need that extra connection to the spirit world, from where they just emerged, in order to complete the transition into a body. We have already established that bone alters frequency. So an infant potentially receives undiluted energy through this opening until the bones begin to close around two years of age.

Stones that can be used to support this center are white: moonstone, quartz, calcite, and agate. Other crystals include selenite, spirit quartz, or apophyllite. Because some see the crown chakra as being purple, stones like amethyst, lepidolite, charoite, or sugilite could also be used. Again, the stones I mentioned for each chakra are just a few; I would encourage you to explore your connection to various stones in regard to each chakra.

Traditionally the chakras are not just stimulated by certain colors; there are also sounds that feed, support or clear these energy centers as well. These frequencies (referred to as "seed" sounds by some practitioners) resonate with the natural, healthy frequency of each chakra. Exposing a blocked or otherwise malfunctioning energy center to these seed sounds brings its frequency back into alignment with the balanced tone, tuning it, charging it, and shaking out foreign matter.

Would it surprise you to know that there are predictable physical ailments associated with blockages occurring in different chakras? I touched on this a little already but here is another example. A blocked crown chakra can contribute to feeling fearful, drained or depressed, all of which can lead to destructive behaviors. You could feel isolated because the crown chakra is where we take in celestial energies, connecting us to our source and the heavens.

As well as being associated with a color, each chakra has an emotional frequency. In some traditions you will be taught that there are also shapes associated with each chakra as well as colors and sounds. I was given a set of those to work with when I was eighteen and traveled to Vermont to consult with Diyani Yawaho, a Cherokee medicine woman who had just opened the Sunray Meditation Society. When I started having trouble releasing the energy of folks that I worked on class, my teacher thought I might find answers with Ms. Yawaho. I was surprised that a Native American tradition would acknowledge chakras, much less work with them!

There are many ways to work with chakras and many ways to balance them. These channels (nadis) and points (chakras) are said to dictate the characteristics of the physical form. It is also believed that through understanding and mastering these subtlest levels of reality, one gains mastery over the physical realm. That alone is reason enough to take the time to learn your instrument thoroughly! By developing a practice of various breathing and visualization exercises one is able to manipulate and direct the flow of energy, to achieve "superhuman" (e.g., in martial arts) or miraculous powers, as with healers or people who can read others' vibes.

In the Orient and southeast Asia it is an accepted fact that energy is a force that moves perceptibly and tangibly within our lives. Much study has gone into understanding how energy interacts with many things to affect us positively or negatively. Feng Shui (which I will go into later in detail) is a perfect example, as are acupuncture and Qi Gong, but there are many others. Energy does not have the same place here in the West. The only types of energy the mainstream paradigm values are ones they can make money from, like electricity and nuclear power. The system also makes money from our lack of awareness of the subtle energies within and around our bodies because our being kept in the dark about these things creates dis-ease. Big business profits by creating modern medicines to counter many of these side effects of our decaying connection to life.

It is my hope that the truths presented in this book will resonate within you, much like the pill in *The Matrix* that Morpheus (Laurence Fishburn) offers Neo (Keanu Reaves), and wake you to yourselves ... and the actual power that resides within you.

48. Can We Feel Vibrational Frequency?

Have you ever made a crystal wine glass sing? It only produces sound when you get the molecules to vibrate at a certain rate — not that you are aware of this molecular level, but you can feel the vibration in your finger as you circle it around the rim. If you have a very large crystal singing bowl, or a brass singing bowl (the original singing bowls created by Tibetans centuries ago), you can really become aware of the feeling of that molecular vibration building behind the movement of the finger (or tool) you use to create the sound. You can feel the strength of the vibration building when you get behind the wave, not unlike surfing. In these moments you are able to "push" the vibrational wave; you can actually feel it. You can hear the sound build as you experience this pushing sensation. If you go too fast and get ahead of the vibration, you can feel the vibration dissipate, as does the sound. Same thing if you fall too far behind the vibration; you cease to "push" it and the vibration and sound dissipate.

I use this scenario to illustrate to students what they might feel as they are learning to work with energy. Such vibrations are what I feel in the palms of my hands when I encounter a block in a client's energy field while I am scanning their aura prior to starting a Reiki healing session. A block may be caused by an emotional trauma, a physical injury, or an intrusion. All of these scenarios can be felt by a trained energy worker.

Remember, all matter is made up of electrons, protons and neutrons, following specific patterns in relationship to each other. This molecular pattern determines what something is.

All molecules are constantly moving and vibrating, except perhaps for things at absolute zero, which means that pretty much everything has a vibrational frequency. We feel vibrational frequency through our gut, amplified and carried to our neurons and ganglia by the vibrational transmitting nature of our intestinal walls.

We feel and translate the vibration through the ENS of the gut and its processing power, with 500 million neurons and its structural similarities to the brain. We also feel vibration through our hands, our hearts and our skin; we hear it as sound through our ears. These are some ways that we absolutely *are* aware of energy as vibrational frequency.

That our culture de-values the existence of this form of information is a travesty. It only harms us. It also feeds the belief that we are not connected to the natural world around us. Hopefully we are learning this is not true.

The vibration of everything around us affects us. Musicians are very aware of this phenomenon. Musicians sculpt and weave with frequency, the way a painter works with color (and while color has frequency and affects us, it usually does so more subtly than music, which can be quite visceral). This is why I think music is the most powerful of the art forms. It can literally "touch" our hearts, as well as every other cell in our bodies!

When we make sounds within our bodies, air moves through our vocal cords causing them to vibrate. All sound is vibrating air molecules. Differing frequencies create different notes. These frequencies flow through our bodies, bringing vibration down into our core. This is why sound healing is so powerful. Different frequencies find harmonic resonance in both the various energy centers in our bodies (chakras), as well as in different organs.

You may or may not be aware of all that, but you certainly are aware that music has the power to change the way you feel. The first great culture to infuse its entire society with the magic of music and dance might have been that of ancient Egypt. According to Joshua Mark:

> The goddess Hathor, who also imbued the world with joy, was associated most closely with music, but initially, it was another deity named Merit (also given as Meret). In some versions of the creation story, Merit is present with Ra or Atum along with Heka (god of magic) at the beginning of creation and helps establish order through music. . . . The pyramids of Giza would have been built to the sounds of music in the same way that people today listen to the radio while they work.[152]

The Irish used dance, with the power of their legs and feet tapping in unison on a wooden floor, to create powerful drumbeats that altered the

---

[152] Joshua J. Mark. "Music & Dance in Ancient Egypt," *Ancient History Encyclopedia*, 19 May 2017, https://www.worldhistory.org/article/1075/music--dance-in-ancient-egypt/ (accessed 2, Jan 2018).

vibrational frequencies in their bodies and for quite some distance around them (watch Riverdance[153] and you will feel what I'm talking about).

Our ancestors sang a lot. They used song and chants in rituals and ceremonies, and the combined vibrational frequencies of their voices changed states of mind, consciousness, and emotions. Such music harmonized groups and brought them closer together.

The Māori battle songs brought power to them and fear to the hearts of their enemies and are still used today at political demonstrations — have you ever listened to one?

Many animals sing, and the vibrational frequencies of their songs can help us heal. How do I know this? Just spend time listening to these songs, and you will see a difference in the states you can achieve. Birds, whales, and wolves come easily to mind as animal singers. An evening of listening to the song of crickets can transform your state of mind and the levels of stress in your body. Did you know that plants sing too? Plants respond to hundreds of things throughout each day with electromagnetically expressed oscillations. According to Stephen Harrod Buhner in his book *Plant Intelligence and the Imaginal Realm*,

> These oscillatory patterns are not random; there are patterns within them. They are in fact songs, possessing melody, movement, communicative interiority. They speak of the life of the self organized system, of how it feels, the interior struggles it undergoes and impact of the exterior world upon it, and its responses to those struggles, those touches. . . . Oscillations in plants have been taken as an 'irrelevant' aspect of plant life . . . Most researchers still treat oscillations in plants as some unwanted 'physiological noise.' Nevertheless, these field oscillations (songs) are just as important on the sonic level as chemicals are on the chemical level. They hold in sonic form the same thing seeds hold, environment captured in one expressible shape. The song is a map of the interaction of that system with both its interior and exterior worlds, the shape of the thing as it has emerged in the field in which it has taken root. And its melody alters from moment to moment as the field shape changes in response to incoming touches (interoceptive or exteroceptive). The genome that is held inside the seed is a map but so is the song that is its oscillating electromagnetic field.

---

[153] Riverdance https://www.youtube.com/watch?v=R9KkbU4yStM.

Everything has a song. And that song is a communicatory description of the livingness of that self organized entity. It is a sonic representation of the nonlinearity of every life form, of the form and behavior that is altering itself continuously.

The blues is inherent in the life of every organism that is, so is the sweet melody of love song. These songs are a multidimensional representation of the self-organized biological systems that generate them.[154]

Would it surprise you to know that First People around the world have been able to learn these plant songs? As ethnobotanist Kathleen Harrison remarks about the pervasiveness of medicinal plant songs in the Americas:

Every [plant] species has a song. If you are granted the song in a vision state, or by just submitting yourself to the presence of the song and opening up, it's a real gift, you are able to remember that song forever and share it when it seems appropriate. That song has power, healing power, and there are some which [are] handed down from one curandero or curandera to the next, and there are others which come to us as individuals. But they are part of an encyclopedia on the sonic level of the same thing that seeds represent on another level.[155]

What does all of this tell me? That we are woven together, with all of creation, by vibration — way beyond anything our current paradigm allows for and far more strongly than we realize. It also tells me that we have the ability with our amazing bodies to develop conscious awareness of such vibrations. Becoming conscious of vibration can help us heal and open new doors of connection between ourselves and the natural world.

Frequencies can be used to heal, to support an organ or a mood. Tuning forks at specific frequencies can help bring the physical, emotional, and energetic bodies back into balance, just as crystals can.

Beware, though too much of a good thing can be harmful. Just the way a low level of harmonic frequency can heal and bring closer, strong harmonic frequencies can potentially break things apart and do damage. These are referred to as harmonic resonances. A perfect example of the destructive power of harmonic frequencies can be witnessed in the case of

---

[154] Stephen Harrod Buhner, *Plant Intelligence and the Imaginal Realm*, Inner Traditions/Bear and Company 5/03/2014.

[155] Kathleen Harrison, *Spirit in Nature*, https://erocx1.blogspot.com/2008/09/kathleen-harrison-spirit-in-nature.html.

the bridge referred to as "Galloping Gertie" (I spoke of her earlier in "Language"). To recap: on November 7, 1940, the wind was blowing at a specific speed around the brand-new Tacoma Narrows Bridge. The wind singing through her supporting cables set up strong harmonic frequencies, similar to plucking guitar strings. The particular frequency created a harmonic episode and tore her apart just six months after her completion.[156]

---

[156] Koyo Kim, Raulca Ifrim, "Galoping Gertie: The Collapse of the Tacoma Narrows Bridge," https://www.youtube.com/watch?v=y0xohjV7Avo.

49. Energy

What is your immediate response to the words "energy" and "healing" in the same sentence? Does it strike you as mumbo jumbo? Make you feel incredulous, suspicious? I get that. For decades, no matter how much I was exposed too, or what powerful experiences I had involving energy, because of the beliefs of the culture I was raised in, I couldn't find a way past my ethnocentric perspectives. That is coming from someone who was constantly inundated by extraordinary experiences. You can only fit a cup of water in a one cup measuring cup ... you cannot put more ...

So, let me ask you this. Is there a valid reason to push ourselves past our familiar, familial perspectives? What if I told you that five thousand years ago, there was a culture so aware of energy that they were able to accurately map its flow through the body — all without the aid of modern technology! They were also able to predict specific ailments when the energy in different pathways grew sluggish, and other diseases when these pathways became clogged.

The amazing development of acupuncture was based on the Chinese being intimately aware of energy more than 5,000 years ago! They called these pathways "meridians." The early practitioners of acupuncture couldn't actually "see" these pathways. As a matter of fact, it has only been in the last 50 years that science has "discovered" them. First identified by Dr. Kim Bong-Han in the 60s, they have recently been confirmed by Korean scientists who were able to inject dye into the pathways Dr. Kim had discovered and follow them using a combination of various imaging techniques and with CT scans.[157]

Suddenly we are able to "see" what the ancients had been talking about for centuries. The researchers saw striking differences in the anatomical structure of the points declared acupuncture points versus non-

---

[157] Kwang-Sup Soh et al, "50 Years of Bong-Han Theory and 10 Years of Primo Vascular System," *Hindawi* 31 July 2013, https://www.hindawi.com/journals/ecam/2013/587827/.

acupuncture points. What is more, they found that the liquid that flows between these meridians aggregates to form stem cells! The Korean researchers refer to this system of vessels as the primo vascular system and it is believed that these vessels conduct energy in the form of biophotons (electromagnetic light waves). The study authors also think that DNA might travel in these corridors as well. With what significance, I am not sure — but I will continue to follow this. So we have light, DNA and stem cells in meridians that we can stimulate by inserting needles at key junctions to facilitate healing — fascinating!

In 1991 Russian researchers at the Institute for Clinical and Experimental Medicine in Novosibirsk, USSR, discovered that these meridians not only carry light, but that they do so even if these corridors are bent or twisted![158]

Scientists have located twelve primary meridians (all of which were identified by the ancient Chinese). Three pairs flow up the body (considered yin by the Chinese), and three pairs flow down (considered yang). Each meridian was found to have a certain time of day when it was most active, as well as being influenced by a season and/or an element. All this is described in the Five Element Theory. It illustrates, beyond a doubt, that at a cellular level we are interconnected to the universe, and that it is absolutely possible to discern or intuit deep truths about the functioning of the universe, and our bodies, without scientific equipment.

Ancient Chinese energy workers were able to determine not just where these meridians were, but also ways to encourage the movement of energy in them. They were not alone. The Japanese developed a form of massage called Shiatsu that works directly with these meridians. It moves blocked energy or Chi in these meridians, as do acupressure and Tai Chi and Qigong. Such exercises can be employed to move and even increase energy in these meridians. The development of yoga in India some 2,000 years ago was based on the awareness of many thousands of nadis (Sanskrit for these energy paths). The Thai refer to them as "sen." Thai massage was developed using a combination of techniques similar to Shiatsu, acupressure and massage to move energy.

Pain or disease can be relieved when energy that is stagnant or blocked is moved. I can tell you personally that it works. In my search for dots to connect, at the tender age of nineteen I found myself in Southeast Asia. That journey lasted for almost three years. During my quest, I picked up

---

[158] https://www.actcm.edu/blog/acupuncture/new-scientific-breakthrough-proves-why-acupuncture-works.

amoebas and some other intruders. The doctors there put me on incredibly high doses of antibiotics. The result, between the two (the amoebas and the antibiotics to kill them), was that for several years I could barely eat because of pain in my gut. I lost way too much weight.

When I got home from my travels, my mom cried when she hugged me, saying that I looked and felt in her embrace like I had just come from a concentration camp. A year after I was home, to say that my digestive system had not recovered was putting it mildly. I had developed colitis, and there was not much that western medicine was doing for me. Not loving the concept, or the reality, of being injected or having blood let by needles left me less than enthusiastic to try acupuncture. As with so many people, I just got to the point where I was willing to try *anything*. After my first treatment, the constant pain I had for over a year was 90 percent gone! I was able to eat more food at dinner that night than I had in a whole day going back for months. I was ecstatic!

I have since used acupuncture for many issues. I have also personally witnessed amazing transformations in other patients I got to know in the waiting rooms of my acupuncturists.

50. Origins of Energy Medicine

For a couple of centuries now, since the advent of "modern medicine," science has skewed our understanding of the human body. This can be traced back to Newtonian physics in the 1700s where we began viewing the body as being only biochemical in nature. This precluded any kind of energy medicine and it has limited our "legitimate" healing sources to pharmaceutical products.

Even though there is evidence that our bodies are primarily bioenergetic, there is still resistance in both science and medicine to change the old paradigm. In its fixation on biochemical treatments, the pharmaceutical companies have profited massively, as have others whose institutional structures make money off our lack of awareness of our own intrinsic holistic being.

To believe that we can understand or impact our feelings and function without considering energy is bizarre. Albert Szent-Györgyi, a Nobel Laureate in medicine and biology, said, "In every culture and in every medical tradition before ours, healing was accomplished by moving energy."[159] Examples of this are acupuncture, Ayurveda, Yoga, Tai Chi, Qi Gong, meditation, all forms of laying on of hands, etc.

In a fascinating paper published in 1956, Szent-Györgyi writes about the dilemmas he encountered trying to understand muscle movement only through only chemical processes (which at that point was the only accepted methodology). In that paper he states:

> The most basic property of the heart is that it is a muscle, and the chief property of muscle is that we do not understand it. . . . The more we know about it, the less we understand, and it looks as if we would soon know everything, and understand nothing. . . . The

---

[159] Albert Szent-Györgi, https://www.azquotes.com/quote/997585.

situation is similar in most other biological processes and pathological conditions such as the degenerative diseases.

He concludes with a powerful statement: "This suggests that some very basic information is missing." [160]

Exactly! Very basic information was missing — energy! As I stated, our current paradigm relies heavily on traditional physics and biochemistry, still mostly ignoring energy. Szent-Györgyi is considered by some as the father of "Bioenergetics" or "Quantum Biology" that describe the flow of energy through living systems. He called this "energy balance" or "energy homeostasis." He wrote, "The first fundamental characteristic of bioenergetics consists in the fact that organisms are open systems, which function only under conditions of constant exchange of materials and *energy* [emphasis added] with the surrounding medium."

Here we can clearly see the presence of a mirroring microcosm and macrocosm. Our cells cannot exist without this energy exchange within our bodies, and neither can our bodies or souls thrive without exchanging energy with the planet and other beings in our environment.

This is not just a human thing. It is also true for every other being on this planet. Yet our current paradigm not only tries to pretend this is not the case, but it also threatens our future. If we kill off enough of the systems we were created to exchange materials and energy with in the natural world, where will that leave us?

Remember earlier I shared Szent-Györgyi's realization in 1972 that "a discovery must be, by definition, at variance with existing knowledge." He goes on to say, "During my lifetime, I made two [discoveries]. Both were rejected offhand by the popes of the field."[161]

This transition we face, into a paradigm where we acknowledge vibrational frequency as a vital part of our physical, emotional and spiritual wellbeing, is such a "discovery," quite at odds with prevailing beliefs. Yet we must make this transition. Our wellbeing depends upon it, and more.

Szent-Györgyi was in a unique position to observe the scientific community and was intimately aware of how it operated. He divided scientists into two categories, the Apollonians and the Dionysians. He called scientific dissenters, who explored "the fringes of knowledge," Dionysians.

---

[160] Albert Szent-Györgyi, *Bioenergetics,* US National Library of Sciences, https://profiles.nlm.nih.gov/spotlight/wg/catalog/nlm:nlmuid-101584924X136-doc.

[161] Albert Szent-Györgyi, "Dionysians and Apollonians," *Science,* 02, June 1972, https://science.sciencemag.org/content/176/4038/966.1.

In science the Apollonian tends to develop established lines to perfection, while the Dionysian rather relies on intuition and is more likely to open new, unexpected alleys for research ... The future of mankind depends on the progress of science, and the progress of science depends on the support it can find. Support mostly takes the form of grants, and the present methods of distributing grants unduly favor the Apollonian.[162]

This is sad for our future, in scientific terms. It means that in the scientific world, like is more likely to beget like rather than embrace something new.

Some scientists, especially those working in biology, and some doctors have been recognizing the dichotomy between the current paradigm and reality. In the early 1900s Dr. Edward Bach, who was a successful bacteriologist and immunologist (having discovered and developed seven strains of bacterial vaccines) left the lucrative "medical industry" in disgust, looking for a way to "serve humanity." He stated:

> The main reason for the failure of modern medical science is that it is dealing with results and not causes. For many centuries the real nature of disease has been masked by materialism, and thus disease itself has been given every opportunity of extending its ranges, since it has not been attacked at its origin. . . . Disease will never be cured or eradicated by present materialistic methods, for the simple reason that disease in its origin is not material.[163]

It is bizarre to me that doctors and scientists find powerful solutions/cures "outside the box" that involve frequency and/or energy and that these natural cures, with no side effects, get ignored despite their success rates. It is because of greed and prejudice. Western science has created a separation between our body's use of energy for mundane functions versus how energy affects our health and wellbeing (the only exceptions being using radiation to kill cancer cells and electrical stimulation to loosen spastic, tight muscles). Remember that Albert Szent-Györgyi said, "In every culture and in every medical tradition before ours, healing was accomplished by moving energy."

The linkage between the two (energy and healing) has been clearly understood and practiced by many, including yogis, Chinese healers and

---

[162] Albert Szent-Györgyi, https://www.science.org/doi/10.1126/science.176.4038.966.a.
[163] Edward Bach, *Heal Thyself,* https://www.bachcentre.com/shop/books/heal-thyself/ (also available as an eBook).

martial artists as well as shamans and medicine peoples in indigenous cultures from almost every nation. Why have we turned our backs on this information? Could the answer be as simple as that no company has figured out a way to profit from these cures? Wouldn't that be horrifying?

We know that our thoughts are energy jumping from synapse to synapse and that our hearts beat through electrical impulses. We accept that energy, in the form of ATP, moves our muscles. Why is it so hard for us to embrace the concept that energy also affects our physical, emotional, mental health?

51. Quanta

Unbeknown to me, the conflict over whether light was a wave or a particle had gone on for hundreds of years. Sir Isaac Newton proposed that light was made of tiny particles. A contemporary of his, the Dutch physicist Christian Huygens, put forth in 1678 the theory that light was a series of waves. This led scientists to describe something they had been witnessing and referred to as "wave propagation"[164] but could not replicate using the particle theory. Huygen's theory was at extreme odds with Newton's.[165]

In 1905 Einstein came up with the quantum theory of light, which states that we live in a quantum universe that is constructed from "tiny discrete chunks of energy and matter."[166] His theory was based on the idea that energy is a wave and particles are made up of up matter; and the two were supposed to act in very predictable, mutually exclusive ways. And they did for the most part. But then there were moments of quantum superpositions (where something exists in two separate states at once) as well as quantum jumps, spins, tunneling, entanglement, randomness and indistinguishability (very much dependent on the state of the observer).

The phrase "the observer affects the observed" was coined to describe some of these phenomena. You could also say "Until observed, nothing and everything exists" (as in the superposition principle, which can be illustrated by an unpleasant analogy referred to as "Schrödinger's Cat"[167]). The point here is that scientists believed for decades that matter was made up of two very different kinds of energy, either particles or waves. The

---

164 Christian Huygens, *Huygens' Principle*, https://www.mathpages.com/home/kmath242/kmath242.htm.
165 If you want to look at this in depth, consult these websites: https://www.bbc.com/education/guides/zsnssbk /revision2 and https://en.wikipedia.org/wiki/Wave%E2%80%93particle_duality.
166 https://interactive.quantumnano.at/basics/what-are-quanta/.
167 Rachel Feltman, "Schrödinger's cat just got even weirder (and even more confusing)," *Washington Post*, May 27, 2016 https://www.washingtonpost.com/news/speaking-of-science/wp/2016/05/27/schrodingers-cat-just-got-even-weirder-and-even-more-confusing/.

nature of each was seen as completely different and mutually exclusive. I remember a high school science class where we learned that particles were different from waves; the teacher drove home exactly how opposite they were. Right after we absorbed these details, we were informed that light, somehow, was both. I remember being struck with wonder and fascination (I know I was not your typical high school girl!).

What happened was that under observation, particles transformed into or behaved like waves, and vice-versa, over and over again. This caused some radical theories to be formed to explain this seemingly impossible behavior. If you want to understand more about this, look up the principle of "Wave-Particle Duality" by Werner Heisenberg (1927) and/or the "Uncertainty Principle." In the ensuing decades two theories have split the scientific world:

1. The Copenhagen Interpretation put forth by Neils Bohr.[168]
2. The Many-Worlds-Theory (or Multiuniverse Theory) supported by Stephen Hawking[169] and Richard Feynman.

My point is that there is much more to our universe than can be tacked neatly down with scientific understanding. For hundreds of years, if you looked at science from above, it would have seemed to be made of long, fairly straight lines. Now those lines are bending and twisting at odd angles, trying to adapt to new information that is changing the foundation of scientific beliefs.

---

[168] Jan Faye, "Copenhagen Interpretation of Quantum Mechanics," *Stanford Encyclopedia of Philosophy*, https://plato.stanford.edu/entries/qm-copenhagen/.

[169] University of Cambridge, *Taming the multiuniverse- Stephen Hawking's final theory about the big bang*, May 2, 2018, Phys.Org, https://phys.org/news/2018-05-multiverse-stephen-hawking-theory-big.html.

52. Electro-Magnetic Fields

The first reference to healing and electricity comes from the time of the Roman emperor Tiberius (14–37 CE), when a freedman named Anthero accidentally stepped on a naturally electrified fish (called a torpedo fish) and was spontaneously cured of gout. In 78 CE a Greek army surgeon named Discorides compiled an extensive pharmacopeia, in which he described using shocks from a torpedo fish to cure stubborn headaches. Six hundred years later shocks were still being used as remedies for headaches, as recorded by Paul of Aegina in Greece. But the true investigation of the application of electricity in medicine was started by William Gilbert (1544–1603), considered the father of electrical science. You can read more about the history of electricity in medicine in a thesis by Jeanette Ann Fourie.[170]

Since then there has been lots of research published on how strong electromagnetic fields (EMFs) can harm us. But you don't hear so much about low EMFs. Did you know that recent studies show that low EMFs actually help healing take place? Low EMFs have been shown to decrease the time it takes a broken bone to knit. Experiments in this area began in earnest after it was discovered that the crystalline nature of our bones allows them to produce electricity when compressed. This is known as the piezoelectric effect and can be seen in quartz and other crystalline structures as well as in human bones (due to their high crystalline content). In a fascinating presentation in 1988 at the international Svedala Symposium on Ecological Design, Professor Bo Nordell proposed that a person's ability to perform accurate dowsing comes directly from the piezoelectricity in human bones.[171]

---

[170] *Stimulation of Bone Healing in Fractures of the Tibial Shaft Using Interferential Currents*, Department of Physiotherapy, Faculty of Medicine, Univ. of Cape Town, June 1994.

[171] Bo Nordell, *The Dowsing Reaction Originates From Piezoelectric Effect in Bone*, https://www.researchgate.net/publication/238094429_THE_DOWSING_REAC-TION_ORIGINATES_FROM_PIEZOELECTRIC_EFFECT_IN_BONE.

The Piezoelectric Effect in Bones

Initially surgeons would implant cathodal electrodes onto the bones at fracture sites. They applied a constant direct current with these. While the healing rates were good and the currents increased bone volume, it was invasive and there was the possibility of infection. It required two surgeries, the first to implant the electrodes and the second to remove them. Even though there is now experimental evidence that unidirectional and alternating pulsed currents placed on the surface of the skin are just as effective, or more effective, surgeons have favored the use of cathodal electrodes inserted at fracture sites.[172]

Well of course they would! Think about it. The cost of two surgeries, versus none. Surgeons generate next to no income from the noninvasive technique.

Surgically non-invasive techniques using pulsed electro-magnetic fields involve attaching a unit to the cast that can be plugged into a household outlet. There has been a success rate of 87% using this method of applied low EMFs to heal un-united (bones that healed over, but did not join) tibial diaphyseal fractures, some of the patients having been disabled for more than two years and facing amputation. The success rate was not based on age, length of disability, presence of infection or previous operative failures. Why is this not the first method of treatment for fractures?

It turns out that a Dr. Nikolova, a scientist in Bulgaria, had been "using surface electrodes with interference currents for delayed, non-union and other fracture complications since 1963, and prophylactically for recent fractures since 1966." [173]

Long before this was discovered, Dr. Royal Raymond Rife developed a theory that every biological or non-biological thing has a unique energy signature that vibrates at certain frequencies (which is exactly what I based my crystal healing theory on — intuitively, because I did not know about his work at that time). In the 1920s he developed a frequency generator.

> According to Dr. Royal R. Rife, every disease has a frequency. He found that certain frequencies can prevent the development of disease and that others would destroy disease. Substances with higher

---

[172] Jean-Marie Ganne, "Stimulation of Bone Healing with Interferential Therapy," *Australian Journal of Psychotherapy* Vol. 34, Issue 1988, pages 9–20, https://www.sciencedirect.com/journal/australian-journal-of-physiotherapy/vol/34/issue/1.

[173] L. Nikolova, "Physiotherapeutic rehabilitation in the presence of fracture complications," *Munchener Medizinische Wochenshrift* (Special English reprint) III (II) 1969, 592–599.

frequency will destroy diseases of a lower frequency. The study of frequencies raises an important question, concerning the frequencies of substances we eat, breathe and absorb. Many pollutants lower healthy frequency.[174]

By the 1930s Dr. Rife had successfully treated close to 1000 people diagnosed with "incurable" cancer. He received an honorary doctorate and fourteen awards. But his success was not good for the pharmaceutical companies, and his lab was ransacked, his records and his frequency generator were destroyed. His work ended and, well, we never hear about him or his work, do we?

In 1992, Bruce Tainio, a plant and soil biologist at Tainio Technology, invented the BT3 frequency monitor. It was an incredibly sensitive machine, originally used only for plants, that registered very low EMFs. Dr. Gary Young (of Young Living oils) convinced Bruce to build a BT3 for him to use to assess the frequencies of his essential oils. Here is a list:

Tainio determined that the average frequency of the human body during the daytime is 62–68 [M]Hz. A healthy body frequency is 62–72 [M]Hz. When the frequency drops, the immune system is compromised. Check out these very interesting findings:

Human Body:
    Genius Brain Frequency 80–82 MHz
    Brain Frequency Range 72–90 MHz
    Normal Brain Frequency 72 MHz
    Human Body 62–78 MHz
    Human Body: from Neck up 72–78 MHz
    Human Body: from Neck down 60–68 MHz
    Thyroid and Parathyroid glands 62–68 MHz
    Thymus Gland 65–68 MHz
    Heart 67–70 MHz
    Lungs 58–65 MHz
    Liver 55–60 MHz
    Pancreas 60–80 MHz
    Colds and Flu 57–60 MHz
    Disease starts 58 MHz
    Candida overgrowth starts 55 MHz

---

[174] Deborah Oke, Royal Rife and Bob Beck, "Can Their Electro-Medicine Defeat Cancer?," *The Truth About Cancer*, https://thetruthaboutcancer.com/royal-rife-bob-beck.

Receptive to Epstein Barr 52 MHz
Receptive to Cancer 42 MHz
Death begins 25 MHz

Foods (fresh foods and herbs can be higher if grown organically and eaten freshly picked):
Fresh Foods 20–27 Hz
Fresh Herbs 20–27 Hz
Dried Foods 15–22 Hz
Dried Herbs 15–22 Hz
Processed/Canned Food 0 HZ (the majority of the foods we eat)[175]

Dr. Young discovered that the lowest frequencies make physical changes in the body. Middle-low EMFs cause emotional changes in the body, and the higher of the low range frequencies make what he refers to as "spiritual" changes in the body. Spiritual frequencies range from 92 to 360 Hz. Other charts showing frequencies for health versus illness can be found in the source given in the footnote below.[176] According to Dr. Young:

Essential oils start at 52 Hz and go as high as 320 Hz, which is the frequency of rose oil. Clinical research shows that therapeutic grade essential oils have the highest frequency of any natural substance known to man, creating an environment in which disease, bacteria, virus, fungus, etc., cannot live.[177]

So these are all low EMFs. For comparison, consider that cell phones in the PCS band emit 824–894 MHz and in the CDMA band emit 1850–1990 MHz.

Those are high EMFs, and if you recall higher EMFs actually do us harm — a high frequency overrides a cell's natural lower frequency, altering it. High EMFs are produced by everyday electronic devices like cell phones, refrigerators, hair dryers and other common devices. In contrast,

---

[175] Susan and Scott Anderson, *Just a List*, https://justalist.blogspot.com/2008/03/vibrational-frequency-list.html.

[176] PEMF frequency charts:
https://www.google.com/search?q=pemf+frequency+chart&sxsrf=AOaemv IMSD5PGUPH2dA8t5-TyTnHvdIqpQ%3A1636643802757&source=hp&ei= 2jONYaXQK92_0PEP-d6F6Aw&iflsig=ALs-wAMAAAAAYY1B6o9KbcbT3gCjHG d9Bv9_MCoCjZsX&oq=pemf+frequency+chart&gs_lcp=Cgdnd3Mtd2l6EAEYADI-FCAAQgAQyBQgAEIAEMgYIABAWEB4yBQgAEIYDMgUIABCGA1AAWA Bg9g9oAHAAeACAAU6IAU6SAQExmAEAoAECoAEB&sclient=gws-wiz.

[177] *Frequencies of Essential Oils: Aromatherapy as Vibrational Medicine*, http://soundhealingcenter.com/shrf/wp-content/uploads/2017/02/SoundHealAroma.pdf.

crystals and human hands, when doing energy work like Reiki, produce low EMFs, just the kind that have been shown to help healing.

What is astonishing is that between 1992 and 2009, when Bruce Tainio died, the BT3 monitor became virtually useless and was retired. Why? According to Teena Tainio (Bruce's widow), it is because the earth became smothered in the EMFs generated by cell towers, power lines and electrical devices — sadly, even in remote areas. The very sensitive nature of this machine made it useless under such circumstances.

This is a warning to us. Our entire planet's air space is contaminated with higher frequencies than are good for us. Can we each take steps to reduce our use of products that produce these? It's a challenge.

What can you give up? We should consider the broader perspective in contemplating "What can *we* give up?" because we certainly cannot give up clean air or water ... yet the choices made thus far are damaging those resources.

I will grant you it's hard to judge the negative impact of high EMFs when we cannot directly see the effect of these frequencies. That is why I am laying out the scientific proof so thoroughly. I hope to make you see, against all odds, that this is real, even though we cannot see it and don't hear much about it.

53. Laying on of Hands and Reiki

Laying on of hands is an ancient technique of applying low EMFs for the purpose of healing. In other words it is an ancient form of energy healing. Does this surprise you? The concept is that when people pray specifically to help another, the Holy Spirit fills them and moves through their hands, easing the pain or healing the receiver. It is not the person praying or laying on hands that is providing the energy that heals. It doesn't really matter what your spiritual orientation is, whether you call this healing force God, the Holy Spirit, Creator, Allah, Universal Life Force, Prana or something else, you can see examples of this kind of healing, on every continent, in every religion, throughout human history.

That is not to say that there are not religions that try to control this ability. Some have tried to "brand" this form of healing (like "Kleenex") and claim that only their version of a higher power can do this. Some have even attempted to make this kind of healing taboo or labeled it evil, but nonetheless, it is a universal and ancient phenomenon.

Reiki is another type of energy therapy, developed by a Japanese man named Mikao Usui in 1922. He taught it to over 2000 students and trained sixteen Masters in Japan before he died in 1926, and his followers have taught it to thousands more since then.[178]

As we have learned that the meanings of words are important, let's look at the two Japanese words, *rei* meaning "divine, miraculous spirit," and *ki* meaning "vital life force, breath of life" or "consciousness."

In some Japanese-English dictionaries, there are additional translations which I think are helpful for understanding Reiki: "feeling of mystery," "an atmosphere of mystery," "an ethereal atmosphere that prevails in the sacred precincts of a shrine," "a spiritual (divine) presence."

---

[178] "Where Does Reiki Come From?," *Take Charge of your Health & Wellbeing*, University of Minnesota, https://www.takingcharge.csh.umn.edu/where-reiki-from#:~:text= Reiki%2C%20as%20it%20is%20practiced,a%20wife%20and%20two%20children.

When you become attuned to Reiki, the energies described above are what fills you before a Reiki session and throughout its duration. Practitioners use special symbols to focus the energy, but once you become familiar with the process you may not need them regularly. This energy fills you and radiates out of your hands and your breath, protecting you from absorbing any other energies, and then flows to the "patient." So it is not your energy that is moving into the person you are directing energy towards. Like laying on of hands, the energy is from a higher source.

There are many reasons to become attuned to Reiki, not the least of which is because it will start you on your own unique journey with energy — which I hope by now, through this book, you are realizing is a fundamental part of our world.

After you become attuned to Reiki 1, you are encouraged to work only on yourself, which is a perfect place for healers to begin. That brings me to choosing a Reiki practitioner or teacher. Since virtually anyone can become a Reiki master and teacher, how do you select someone that you want to work with? Are all practitioners and teachers the same?

No, of course not. We are as different after attaining our certificates as we were before. Do you feel comfortable with everyone? Chances are you don't. There is a myriad of reasons for this, and who I am comfortable with may not be who you are comfortable with.

Here is one thing that is very important to me when choosing teachers or healers. Have they done their homework? (And I am *not* referring to paperwork!) If they haven't, they will not be fully empathetic. There is also a greater chance that they will be judgmental. When we skip doing our internal homework of connecting the dots of our emotional past into the present, we stay largely unaware of what motivates us. Being in that state makes it very easy to judge others. Judging whether or not I am following the path that you see fit to travel has no interest for me.

When people have climbed internal mountains and survived travails and hardships, it opens up their understanding of the human experience. It becomes harder to be judgmental because they have "been there." They understand what causes someone to go to the depths. Such people cut you slack just as they have learned to cut themselves slack. I am open to other people's visions and opinions, but not their judgments.

I spent decades looking for someone else's ideas to explain things (especially myself!) to me and help me heal. What a joke. After years of therapy, self-help groups and books, and studying different religions, I stood back and looked at myself. What I saw was my continued progress over the years, and I saw a pattern.

I realized that I always grow. I kept a steady pace of moving forward through my "stuff." What I saw was that if I appeared stuck somewhere, even if it wasn't a comfortable place or one that directly benefitted me (i.e., was more pain than anything else), I realized that it meant that I was not yet ready to move on. As soon as I was ready, I always moved on. Always.

All of a sudden, I knew on a deep level that I could trust myself. I called this experience "learning to identify my process." Understanding your own process is invaluable. It is truly the only thing that will eventually allow you to be comfortable in your own skin.

I realized that I learned something from all my experiences, and that no one else could determine when I had received exactly what I needed from any given situation. I no longer *needed* anyone else's opinion to help me decide if I was OK.

This is why doing work on yourself is so important. You *can* be a channel for Reiki no matter where you are in your own personal development. Anyone can. But if you want to do more than that, to give advice and share visions that you receive, then you need to do your homework. Otherwise, most of what you will see and perceive will be about you, and when it isn't, you won't be able to tell the difference.

Once you truly see who you are, what your process is, how your learn, how you respond to pain, pleasure, highs, lows, intimacy, isolation, pressure, relaxation, emotions, groups, family, work, etc., then you can begin to relax, because you will know and be able to trust yourself. It does not mean that you will have everything figured out; I don't think we ever get to that point. Nor does it mean that you will have healed every area in your life that needs healing. I'm not sure that's possible either.

It's not rocket science. But it is not an easy path either. Traversing deep emotional terrain takes tremendous courage, partly because our current paradigm feeds us into the world *outside ourselves*.

As I described in Ch. 44 "Tonglen," the Tibetan practice, works with this principle by accessing and dwelling in, not running from or covering up, feelings of pain, anguish, anger etc. It then creates the energetic cure for these feelings, using inhalation to draw in, and exhalation to send out — similar to the way a mother breathing her baby's breath during close contact causes her body to produce antibodies that flow into her breast milk and are passed to her baby when it drinks.

Becoming attuned to the second degree of Reiki, you learn how to do long distance healing and you may begin working on others. Reiki 3 and Reiki Masters receive the final Reiki symbol and no longer need any more trainings, unless they wish to teach Reiki.

There are many other types of energy techniques taught in the States: Karuna, Vortex and Miriel are a few. But many more exist and have existed throughout time. What kinds of healing did your ancestors practice? What can you dig up from your cultural past?

54. Feng Shui

Feng Shui (pronounced "fung shway"), meaning "wind (and) water," is a very old practice that evolved from studying the way energy (chi) moves in and interacts with the physical world. It is built on the premise that the amount of energy, moving or stuck, in specific areas of your body, home, office, yard, etc., affects your health, prosperity, relationships, luck, creativity and more. It also studies the ways we can influence these energies.

We learned earlier that our eyes developed to see certain types of energy as colors (but we don't know why). The Chinese have been employing their knowledge of the distinct energy of different colors to affect their lives for thousands of years! But there is more; in addition, they believe that our eyes can also move or direct energy. Does that seem farfetched?

Remember, this belief comes from a people whose awareness of energy allowed them to map its meridians through our body more than 5000 years ago, long before we developed a process called stereomicroscopic imaging that is sensitive enough to record these meridians.[179]

What if we assume for a moment that the Chinese don't know what they're talking about here? Let's explore that ... Have you ever been sitting somewhere and "felt" something? Only to look up and notice that someone was staring at you? Of course you have, we all have! Perhaps there *is* something to the belief that people's eyes direct energy by their focus....

Such an ability could be a reason our bodies went to so much trouble developing the rods and cones that we now know enable us to see energy. How might these adaptations allow us to direct energy with our eyes? Can we find a scientific explanation for this ability?

Getting back to Feng Shui: according to its principles, what people in your house look at, how their eyes track trough your home, does affect the

---

[179] https://www.actcm.edu/blog/acupuncture/new-scientific-breakthrough-proves-why-acupuncture-works.

energy flow within your house. That's interesting, but what's even better is that you can utilize that energy to your benefit! The flow of energy from people's eyes can be used to address deficiencies in many areas of your life. So, naturally, one of the techniques Feng Shui employs is the artful placement of objects throughout your environment to draw people's eyes. But it doesn't end there.

Though careful observation over the course of centuries, Chinese wise men created a template of the actions of energy in the physical world. This is referred to as the Five Element Theory (which I will cover in greater detail in the following pages) and was perfected during the Han dynasty (around the first century BCE). It describes the relationships and interactions between phenomena. The understanding it provides gives insights into traditional Chinese medicine, astrology, geomancy, martial arts, and Feng Shui. It is employed in every aspect of life in China — military strategy, politics, business plans, weddings, music, purchasing property, etc. Think about that for a minute. There is no way the practice of cultivating specific energies would have been followed for centuries in so many important aspects of Chinese life if doing so did not produce consistent positive results. And yet, how thoroughly we (here in the West) have rejected even granting these traditions the smallest amount of credibility. Does that make sense to you? I know that some of us are tired of drawing lines in the sand, diminishing those who are different, or whose practices are different. But I also know others who still feel the need to cling to these distinctions, allowing them (in their minds) to claim superiority.

Understanding the Guas

Each of the nine guas represents an area of your life; together these are referred to as the bagua (which actually means "eight areas," and these surround the center or health area, which is not technically a gua, although it is treated as one). In some schools of Feng Shui, the bagua is represented as a circle, with each of the eight guas being shown as equal slices, like a pie, with a circle drawn in the center, representing health. Such a representation illustrates how your health gua affects all the other guas equally. But for simplicity we will use the tic tac toe grid. There are many different Feng Shui schools or "sects." We will cover two of the primary ones, the Black Hat or Modern Method, and later the Compass Method. But for now, let's look at the guas and learn about what kinds of things they affect, as well as how you can create remedies or cures for guas that are not functioning in your life as well as you wish they would.

I also want to point out that, just as with the chakra systems, there are particular shapes, colors, or objects that have their own energies and correspond to each gua. The guas are also given an image (or trigram) from the *I Ching* ("The Book of Changes"), an ancient Chinese book of wisdom and divination.[180] Guas are also associated with a direction, a season, a number and the essence of yin (contractive, feminine, dark, restive energy and the moon) or yang (expansive, masculine, light, active energy and the sun). Each gua is associated with natural elements (earth, water, fire, metal and wood) which make up the five-element theory. (I will explain this after I introduce the guas.) Adding or taking away any of the things just mentioned will stimulate or slow the energy in the guas and therefore your life as well.

Because our thoughts also contain energy, any images, words or objects that make you think or feel a certain way can be employed in each gua to enhance it (or detract from it). Here is an example: in China the word for the number four sounds very similar to the word for death. So the number four is considered unlucky. Purchasing a house with that number in its address would be considered bad luck, because every time someone spoke the address, he or she would hear the word "death."

In the States the number four has no such association, so a house with this number in it would not bring bad energy with it. Here again the strength of personal association is important, just as it is in manifesting. Ultimately, that is what we are doing in Feng Shui, manifesting what we want more of, and minimizing or neutralizing what we want less of.

Skills and Knowledge (Gen)

This is the area to enhance if you are looking to develop contemplation, wisdom, and intuition. It is also the energetic birthplace of good communication, critical thinking, self-motivation, determination, persistence, flexibility and time management. Skills and Knowledge is important for every area of your life, such as managing your money, health, relationships etc., which makes this a very important gua.

If you have the ability to do so, it is a great place to locate your office. But do not worry if the space in your home or apartment does not allow for an office here. There are many ways to augment this area.

This gua's element is earth, specifically yang earth. Its *I Ching* Trigram is mountain. Its number is eight and its direction is North-East. Objects

---

[180] The *I Ching* uses hexagrams (symbols made out of six horizontally stacked lines) read from tossed coins to provide general guidance or even answer specific questions.

that are flat or square work well here. For the Chinese the color representing this gua would be dark blue. Sometimes you will read that dark green or black are good here as well. Use your own intuition to guide you in cases like that. You can add the energies from these colors by painting them on the walls or adding objects that are these colors. You could add actual water (as in a fish tank or a fountain or depictions of water) as a way to increase the energies as well. Books on subjects you would like to become an expert on, or a computer, would be good here.

I had the opportunity to build a house back in the early 2000s and I used Feng Shui to design it. My office was in the Skills and Knowledge gua. I paid someone to paint a sky on the celling, representing "the sky is the limit" for me. I also found a lamp for this space that was a shaped like large light bulb. This was to stimulate "bright ideas." You can see how incorporating personal symbols works here, and this can be applied successfully in other guas as well.

Career or Life Path (Kan)

This is an area to enhance if you are not happy with your career or are looking to establish a new one, want improve your working conditions, or you feel that you have not found your calling or life path yet. It is not just about employment; it is also about job satisfaction.

The element here is water. It is represented in the *I Ching* Trigram as water, and its number is one. Its season is winter and its direction is North. Objects that work well here are wavy, undulating or round. The traditional color to energize this gua is black, which for the Chinese represents water. Mirrors also are seen as bringing the water element to any environment in which they are placed. Glass objects in these shapes are also good here. You can add any of these to this gua to energize it, including using the sound of water.

Helpful People & Travel (Qian)

This gua is where you turn if you need more support from the people around you, such as benefactors, bosses, parents, mentors, doctors, police, tax collectors, building inspectors, loan officers, teachers, electricians, etc. It is also the place to energize if you wish to travel more. The element of this gua is metal and it is seen as male or Yang. The *I Ching* Trigram is heaven; its number is six and its season is autumn. It is North-West and objects that work well here are round or circular. Colors are grey or silver.

In addition to bringing in any of the above-listed energizers for this gua, you could also add the sound of metal chimes or bells here. This is also a great place for statues in the home or garden of spiritual benefactors such as Jesus, Mother Mary, the Buddha, angels, saints, etc.

As I mentioned earlier in "Intention and Manifesting," we use written affirmations in this gua to gain the help we are requesting. Place the affirmations in a metal box — silver-colored is best, and yes, painting them works great! — or silver or grey file folders. I was taught to write the affirmations in red ink.

Family & Ancestors (Zhen)

This gua may surprise you — it is not just about family or ancestors! With its spring-like energy, it can facilitate new beginnings in any area of your life. I was also taught that this the gua to strengthen if you need more money in your life; specifically, this is the gua that produces the money you need to support your family. This gua's element is wood (Yang). Its *I Ching* Trigram is thunder, and its number is three. Its season is spring and its direction is East. Objects that are tall, square or rectangular work well here. The colors that stimulate this energy are green, blue or teal. You can also activate this gua by bringing in living plants or hanging pictures of your family in wooden frames.

Health / Center (Tai Qi)

This gua, as I stated before is not technically a gua; however, being in the center, it touches upon all the other guas equally. It is also seen to be connected to your health and wellbeing. Its element is earth. It doesn't have an *I Ching* Trigram associated with it. It corresponds to the number five, and its direction is center (and yes, center is considered a direction in some cultures — cultures that place a value on internal growth or see a distinction between inner and outer aspects of human existence). Objects that are square, flat, horizontal, rectangular or octagonal stimulate energy in this gua, as do earth tones like yellow, orange and brown. You can stimulate the energies using any of the things mentioned above or you can bring in crystals or stone, as well as a square earth-toned rug.

Creativity & Children (Dui)

This gua relates to creativity, projects or offspring and supports your sense of joy and completion. Its element is metal and it is seen as yin. The *I Ching* Trigram is Lake (Marsh) and its number is seven. It is the autumn season, and it represents the West. Objects that are circular, round, oval or arched do well here. The colors of this gua should be white or pastel.

Along with any metal, white or pastel objects in the above mentioned shapes, you could bring in fresh flowers in those colors, or use things that represent the area you wish to be more fruitful in.

Prosperity & Abundance (Xun)

This is the gua to energize if you are looking to increase your wealth. This gua generates the extra money that one would need for non-essential activities (as opposed to basic needs). It can also stimulate your sense of worth, as well as increase generosity. This, above all other areas in the ba-gua, is not the place for anything broken. The element for this gua is wood (yin) and the *I Ching* Trigram is Wind. Its number is four, its season spring and its direction South-East. Objects that are columnar and things with movement are appropriate here. The colors for this gua are purple, red, green and sometimes blue. Expensive items that are beautiful, especially ones with movement like fountains or chimes, are particularly good here. It is also a great place for amethyst crystals.

Fame & Reputation (Li)

This gua is an important one to balance carefully. Receiving too much notice and developing a strong reputation are not always desirable ... even if the attention you receive is good. Naturally, this gua also affects your future and the recognition you receive. The element here is fire, and we all know that fire is powerful and almost has a life of its own. Its *I Ching* Trigram is Fire, and its number is nine. This fiery gua's season is (not surprisingly) summer, and its direction is South. Objects that are triangular, pointed or representations of flames work well here. This gua's color is primarily red, but I have seen orange used as well. An actual fireplace, candles, or things representing fire are good here.

Relationship (Kun)

This gua influences the quality of your relationships, love, marriage, partnerships, and friendships. (No surprise there, but it may be surprising that it also affects your relationship to yourself and the feminine in general. As far as I'm concerned, the entire world could benefit from having a better relationship with the feminine aspects of ourselves, other creatures and the planet.) This gua's element is Earth, its *I Ching* trigram is earth, its number is two and its direction is South-West. Since it is associated with earth, like the Health gua, the objects that work well here would be flat or square. The color for this gua is primarily pink, but red will work too, and some books even include white.

You can bring in representations of pairs of things, like figurines, sculptures, paintings or photos of couples — they don't have to be human, they just have to represent the quality of connection that you are missing or wish to encourage in your life. Pairs of pink or red candles, if placed with the intention of "heating things up," are a good example of how to influence this gua's special energy.

Applying Black Hat, or Modern Method, Feng Shui

Here's how you can apply this method to your life. First draw a rough representation of the space you want addressed. It does not need to be blueprint accurate. In the picture below (Figure 12), I have not labeled each room because I put furniture in the rooms to identify their use. But if you are drawing empty boxes to represent each room, it is a good idea to label each room (bedroom, bath, kitchen, etc.). The reason for this is that we will need to look at the area in terms of how it relates to the bagua. The Feng Shui bagua (grid or map) is divided into eight sections, and I will get into that more in a moment.

After you draw the space that you wish to diagnose and label each room, the next step is to draw a tic tac toe grid over it. The grid should contain nine boxes, three up and three across. Each box should be the same size. After drawing these you need to label each gua as shown in Figure 13 below.

Figuring out how to place the grid is easy in the Black Hat method; the most-used entrance to the space is always addressed as the "front," whether it actually is the front of the building or not. The reason for this is simple — the frequent use brings in or moves energy in the area being diagnosed.

In the Black Hat Method, Skills and Knowledge is always the first box on the bottom left. The middle box in the same line is Career, and the one on the right is Helpful People and Travel. The entrance to your space will always fall into one of these three guas.

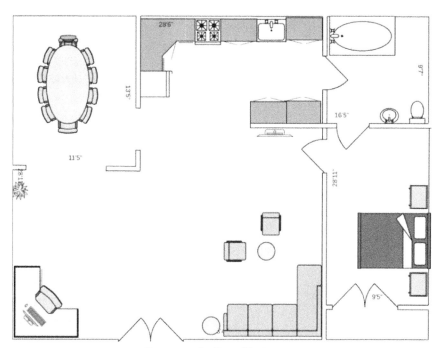

Figure 12. Outline of living space.

Prosperity	Fame	Relationships
Family	Health/ Center	Creativity/Children
Skills & Knowledge	Career/ Life Path	Helpful People & Travel

Figure 13. Bagua grid with labels.

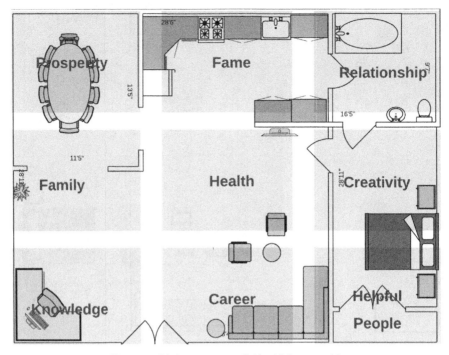

Figure 14. Living space overlaid with bagua grid.

Just a note: the house I have created above has an ideal layout. I have also added all the furniture in the best gua for it. For example, the desk is not just in the Skills and Knowledge gua, it is also in the skills and knowledge corner of the room. The stove is in the Fame gua. In that same gua, the kitchen sink should have been switched with the last cabinet on the right. Doing so would have put the water in the relationship gua, which is a better place for it than in Fame (fire). Bathrooms can cause a drain on whatever gua they are in (the energy litterally goes down the drain!). The ideal place in a house for a bathroom is the relationship gua (which I have done). I placed a tree in the family gua. There is no staircase in the health gua, as stairs also cause energy to move out of or into a space very quickly, creating imbalances. The bed is in the perfect position in regards to both doors in the bedroom. There are also two matching night tables on either side of the bed, which is good Fung Shui. The dining room table is oval, which is considered to be the best for creating abundance. The computer didn't allow me to place a bowl of fruit on the table, but that is a good thing to do as well.

An important place to start in any gua is to clean, dust, get rid of clutter (which blocks energy), and remove any broken objects as well as any object you don't like. So if you cannot do anything else, just doing this will begin to change the energy flowing or stuck in any of the guas. Another rule of thumb is to make sure all doors open fully, without having things blocking them which restricts the flow of energy

I have created a quick reference for each gua in Figure 16 on page 256.

The Five Element Theory

The five elements are Wood, Fire, Earth, Metal and Water. Each of the nine guas is governed by one of these five elements. The elements have a relationship to each other, either destructive (as fire is to wood), or constructive (as water is to wood).

In this theory, which is visualized as a wheel turning clockwise, the element before it feeds or creates the following element. The building or feeding phase of this cycle is referred to as Wu Xing, (short for *Wu zhong lauding ahi qi,* meaning "the five types of energy dominating at different times"). In this view wood feeds fire, fire feeds earth, earth feeds metal, metal feeds water and water feeds wood, cycling back to the beginning.

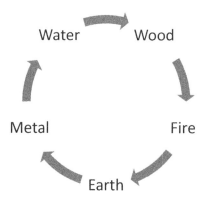

Figure 15. Five element wheel.

For the destructive cycle, use an alternating element (still going clockwise); in this situation an element destroys or controls the one before it. E.g., look at the top one, wood, and the third one, earth; wood eats or destroys earth. Earth (skipping metal) eats or destroys water. Water (skipping wood) eats or destroys fire. Fire (skipping earth) destroys metal, and metal (skipping water) destroys wood.

BACK OF SPACE BEING ADDRESSED

Prosperity & Abundance **Wealth, Extra Money**	Fame & Reputation **Passion, Visibility**	Relationship **Love, Marriage, Commitment**
Element: Water (Yang) I Ching: Wind Number: Four Season: Spring Shapes: Square, cube Direction: South-East Colors: Red, purple, green, blue Items: Expensive things, fountains, chimes, mobiles	Element: Fire (Yang) I Ching: Fire Number: Nine Season: Summer Direction: South Shapes: Triangle, cone, pyramid Color: Red, Orange Items: Fire, candles, fireplace furs or skins or animals	Element: Earth (Yin) I Ching: Earth Number: Two Season: Autumn Shape: Square Direction: South-West Colors: Pink, Red, White Items: Pairs of things, pictures of couples, candles, mirrors
Family & Ancestors **Community, New Beginnings**	Health or Center **Health, Healing, Unity**	Creativity & Children **Descendants, Completion, Joy, Pleasure**
Element: Wood (Yang) I Ching: Thunder Number: Three Season: Spring Direction: East Shapes: Tall; square or rectangular Colors: Green, blue Items: Earth-tone or yellow rugs or flowers, crystals, stone	Element: Earth (Yin/Yang) Direction: Center Shapes: Horizontal, square or rectangular items, cubes, or octagonal objects Colors: Yellow, gold, brown, orange Items: Peaceful, sun, mountains, rugs, flowers, stone or earth	Element: Metal (Yin) I Ching: Lake (Marsh) Number: Seven Season: Autumn Direction: West Shapes: Circular, oval, arched Color: White, pastel Items: Photos of children or art in metal frames
Skills & Knowledge **Self-cultivation, Wisdom, Skillfulness**	Career & Life Path **Job Satisfaction, Calling**	Helpful People & Travel **Benefactors, Mentors**
Element: Earth (Yang) I Ching: Mountain Number: Eight Season: Winter Direction: North-East Shapes: Flat or square Colors: Dark blue Items: Books, computers	Element: Water (Yin) I Ching: Water Number: One Season: Winter Direction: North Shapes: Wavy, undulating, round Colors: Black Items: Water or its sounds, glass objects, mirrors	Element: Metal (Yang) I Ching: Mountain Number: Three Season: Autumn Direction: North-West Shapes: Round, circular Colors: Silver or grey Items: Statues of spiritual benefactors, travel photos

ENTRANCE TO SPACE BEING ADDRESSED

Figure 16. Gua reference chart.

256

Diagnosing Your Chosen Space

So now that you understand a bit about the guas, let's look at how to diagnose an area. Remember that you can address a desk, a corner of a room, an office, an apartment, a house or a yard, etc. Whatever type of space you are addressing, you will need to place the tic-tac-toe Fung Shui bagua grid over it. I created a "cheat sheet" for you (Figure 13) that you can use as a quick reference for diagnosing spaces.

When you apply the bagua to your residence or workplace, it would be wise to examine how each of the areas discussed above is functioning in your life currently. As you examine these aspects of your life, you decide which areas need augmenting.

Applying Cures

I love the adage "If it ain't broke, don't fix it." So, if you are doing fine in your love life, then there is no need to change anything in the relationship gua. However, if you are single and want to be in a relationship, or you have rocky relationships, then you may want to augment this gua. To do this you could either use the objects that represent the element of this gua; or bring in pairs of things, or red or pink objects (including painting furniture, trim or walls these colors). You could use pictures on the walls that employ these colors or contain pairs of things. Hang curtains in pink or red. To attract a relationship, a popular cure is to hang a photo of red or pink peonies in this gua. Just be sure to remove it after you are in a relationship; otherwise it can lead to unfaithfulness.

Or you could use the constructive phase of the five-element theory to augment an area of your life that corresponds to that element. In the case of the relationship gua, earth is its element, and fire nourishes or creates earth, so adding a candle here would be good. A pair of pink or red candles would be even better.

Here's another example. If your career needs boosting, you would want to add water elements. To the Chinese black represents water, as do mirrors. So add things that represent water; objects that are black, wavy, or made of glass would work well. Paint your furniture or all the picture frames in this area black. Hang a mirror. Depending on where that gua falls in your house you could buy a black couch, black throw pillows, etc.

If you couldn't add these things, the next cure or augmentation would be to add things that build water (in this gua's case, metal objects) to this area of your home, room office or desk to build the water element.

As final example, the Fame gua is seen as fire. Wood feeds fire, so placing wooden objects in this gua will stimulate it if you could not add actual fire.

Cures for Missing or Augmented Guas

Ideally a house would be a perfect square (or a circle like a yurt), which would ensure that each gua started out equal. You can deal with areas that are missing from the square or rectangle in two ways. Look at the picture below. See how the second bedroom juts out by itself? In Feng Shui you could say that the empty space that is under and above the second bedroom on the grid is missing. Since the space that is devoid of a physical building is affecting two separate guas, you would have to create cures (or augmentations) in each of those guas to help balance the total energy of your living space.

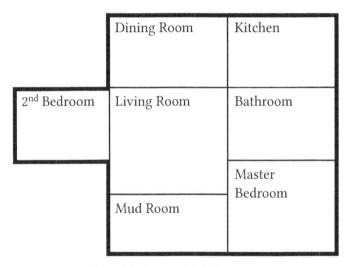

Figure 17. Asymmetric living space.

The second way you could look at this scenario is that the second bedroom is an augmentation to your Family gua, not that the other two are missing.

Which way you chose to view this scenario will help determine how you deal with it. For instance, if you see/experience this gua as being an extension, then you would not need to cure anything. If you view/experience the other two guas to be deficient, one cure would be to create an outdoor feature where the house would be if it was a perfect square or rectangle. For the empty space above the second bedroom, a fountain in the far corner of the missing piece of house would be an appropriate cure.

For the other missing piece below the second bedroom, you could place a light in the far-left bottom corner, shining back towards house. Again, this would be placed at the exact corner where the house would be if it was a perfect square or rectangle.

How you diagnose this or any situation will partly depend on what it feels like to you, but more importantly it should be based on how you are doing in each of these areas of your life. It will be apparent to you if your life is suffering in some way due to a deficit. Similarly, you will most likely be able to tell if a particular gua is over-stimulated, because we all know that there can be "too much of a good thing."

If this is a space that you are not currently living in, then you won't know how these things will affect you. In this case you could implement cures in anticipation of deficits, or you could wait and see. Remember, there's no need to change what is working.

Using the Destructive Phase of the Five Element Theory

As I stated earlier, the destructive flow within the elements are as follows: water destroys fire (or creates steam, which is a very powerful force, so use this one very carefully), fire destroys metal, metal destroys wood, wood destroys earth, and earth destroys water. There are degrees within this cycle, from weakening an element to completely nullifying it. All of these elements are used to balance the energy within different areas of your home, just the way acupuncture is used to balance energies in your body.

Employ the destructive cycle if there is too much energy in a gua of your life. For example, if you are attracting too much attention at work or school and wish a more private life, you might want to control the energy in your fame gua. If your business is growing too quickly you might want to control some of the energy in your career gua. If, due to the structural layout of your home or office, you have too much of an element in a gua that you can't change, like a bathroom in your career gua, you could bring in potted plants (not trees), or any of the colors (yellow, brown, orange) or shapes (squares or cubes) that represent earth.

Sometimes you need to correct situations where the layout of your house employs the destructive phase.

If you have a bathroom in your Fame gua, for example, this is not considered favorable because Fame is connected with the element fire. Water destroys fire, so you would need to add flame-like symbols, candles, triangles, and flame colors to stimulate this energy. Be careful here though because fire and water create steam, which is very powerful. Make sure you are powering up the aspects of this gua that you want, if you employ these cures. There are plenty of types of fame we would not want! A safer way would be to bring in the element of earth by adding brown, yellow, orange, or gold, flat, square or rectangular objects (like a carpet) which represent earth, to reduce the potency of the water element. You might find or make a painting with these shapes and colors. Also, you could add a decorative square or rectangular container filled with soil and place some crystals, or some other artistic touch (to give the soil a visual reason to be there). But you would not want to add a tree here. While the tree would help mitigate the water influence, trees in their growing phase deplete the power of earth. Those are examples of bringing balance by reducing the influence of an unwanted energy in your space.

Going back to the augmentation we discussed earlier in the relationship gua: ladies, let's say your juiced-up relationship gua worked really well and you just got married. However, you notice men keep crawling out of the woodwork. They just won't leave you alone — old boyfriends, men at the supermarkets, the office, bookstores, men everywhere, they are blowing up your phone and your new hubby is getting jealous. I know it's an interesting problem, but if this were the case, you would need to remove some of the relationship-enhancing objects or colors from your relationship gua (slowly, until you find a balance). You could also apply the destructive phase of the Five Element Theory. Since earth is the element for the relationship gua, you could add water, trees, or representations of trees.

The art of Feng Shui is very complex and takes years to master, but anyone can use it to address specific issues in his or her life. Many people find it enjoyable.

Once you start studying Feng Shui, you will notice that people often employ cures, without even knowing that they have done so. For example, a toilet in any gua can cause the energies there to be "flushed away" too frequently for the space to function well. When you go into a bathroom and see that someone without knowledge of Feng Shui has placed a plant on top of the toilet tank, that is a cure for energy that is being drawn too quickly out of your house.

The Compass or Traditional Method

I'm going to throw one last wrench into this complicated subject. I have mentioned that there is another method for practicing Feng Shui, one that I personally never used. The one I have described here is called the Black Hat or modern method. There is also the traditional method, also known as the Compass method.   This method uses a compass to place the bagua over your space. You do not orient the position of the guas according to the entrance you use most often. Instead, you would address your space with a compass, as illustrated in the diagrams below.

I had never been drawn to use this method until very recently. I am moving into a house where my normal way of laying out the guas just felt completely wrong. It was clear to me that using the Black Hat method was not working. I was so frustrated. I was working on this chapter and saw a traditional layout using the Compass method on one of the sites I visited and, just for kicks, I applied it to my new house. It fit and made so much sense. So I will be applying the bagua as shown in Figure 18 below.

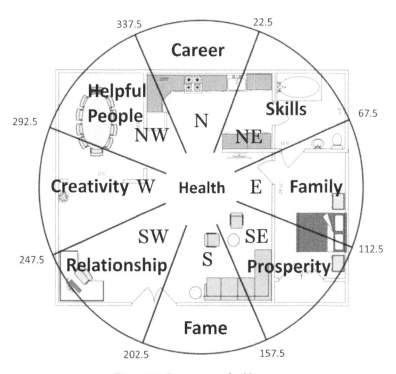

Figure 18. Compass method bagua.

As you study, you will notice that there are some discrepancies in the colors suggested for the guas in the Compass method, compared to the Black Hat method. For instance, the color of the Skills and Knowledge gua in the Black Hat method is blue. Blue reminds me of water, and water muddies the energies of earth. I never stopped to think about until this moment, but that doesn't really make sense. Since Earth is the element of this gua, earth tones make so much more sense and (luckily for me, already correspond to the color in that section of my new home!).

You will also find that there are schools of Feng Shui other than just the ones I have mentioned. Feng Shui is so complex that even though I have studied it for almost two decades, I still consider myself a novice.

There are many good books on the subject, as well as much material on the internet. So with a sense of openness, enjoy exploring this ancient technique for moving energy in your life!

55. Healing Plants

Let's look at healing plants. How did our ancestors know what plants to use? They undoubtedly learned a bit from watching other species choose certain plants to eat. But since they would not have been aware of specific ailments of most of these creatures, they would not have been able to discern what plants healed what ailments. So how did they learn? Trial and error? That would have led to a lot of death and illness. It would have made people afraid experiment with plants. There had to be a fairly consistent success rate for primitive people to continue to pursue using plants to heal. So how did our ancestors know?

If you talk to people from any culture that still has a lineage of using herbs for healing, they will tell you that people were "guided" by the plants themselves. Does that sound outrageous to you? In many cultures it is said that medicinal plants "shared" the knowledge of their use with people attuned to them.

Remember I talked about Dr. Edward Bach, the successful bacteriologist and immunologist in the early 1900s who left his successful career to pursue energy medicine. He became the father of Flower Essence medicines, known as "Bach Flower Remedies." In fact, his formula called "Rescue Remedy" is the number one selling remedy for stress in the world.

How did he figure this out? He began studying plants. What he discovered was that plants had very distinct traits, strengths, or "medicine" that they could pass on to us. He learned to identify these strengths by simply studying a plant's nature, where it grew, the conditions it needed to survive, its disposition, if you will. He used these characteristics, as well as the shape of its leaves, flowers, and roots to tell him about what these plants could help people (and animals) with. He called this information "The Doctrine of Signatures." It's profound stuff, and very accurate. He wasn't the first person to be aware of this — he was simply the first successful Western doctor to document it. Ethan Vorly writes:

. . . plants having healing properties that may not be explainable through the actual physics of the plant. There may seem to be no interaction on a physical level but the chi of the plant can affect the chi of a person, which leads to healing. Understanding the astral forces and resulting chi energy of plants is where healers and medicine men of various tribes and civilizations gained their knowledge. It was not a trial-and-error science but one of feeling the essence of a plant and knowing what it may be used for.[181]

Many cultures believe that the plants themselves reveal their "medicine" to those who are paying attention. Take pulmonaria or lung wort, for instance; its leaves are shaped like lungs and are spotted, giving the appearance of diseased lungs — remarkably, that is the area of the body this plant affects. Pulmonaria has been used to successfully treat chest conditions. It is especially helpful in treating chronic bronchitis. Another example is mullen, with large lung-shaped leaves that are velvety. Mullen has been used by native Americans for centuries to ease asthma. Oddly enough, smoking these leaves improves this condition of the lungs.

It is not easy to accept from our current paradigm that plants might actually be able to communicate with us. I am an herbalist, certified in Flower Essences, as well as a landscape designer, an organic gardener and an energy healer. I have no doubt that plants communicate to us. I know that trees in particular have wonderful senses of humor, at least some do. They also make great teachers and confidants.

I was talking with a fellow Reiki master the other day and she shared a powerful story. She is a runner, and one day not long ago she was on a run and got an important text. Normally she would not run and text, but she thought she could just respond to this one quickly. So there she was running and texting, when suddenly she heard an intense voice, "I'm here!." Startled she looked up to see a tree less than a foot in front of her and was able to avoid it.

I was working with a wonderful woman and one of my favorite teachers of all time, Penelope Smith. Her claim to fame, I suppose, is that she was the first person to teach animal communication in the 1970s. But Penelope teaches so much more than that these days. And you can learn more from her than just by listening to the words she uses. She embodies a connection between nature and herself that can be absorbed just by being

---

[181] Ethan Vorly, "Chi/Etheric Body, Alchemy Realm," http://alchemyrealm.com/etheric-body.html.

in her presence, if you are open to such things. At this workshop, Penelope told us to choose a tree to ask four questions of it. I began to wander and ended up by the lake. There was one tree, a medium sized maple, that called me. We were instructed to approach the tree from each of the four directions and ask it a specific question at each cardinal point. I had never asked a tree a question and really did not know what to expect.

I started with the North and silently asked the maple tree the question Penelope had given us for that direction. I was surprised how quickly I began receiving pictures in my mind. The questions were along the lines of "What is my purpose?" or "Where did I come from?," so you can imagine that the answers (as pictures) were complex. They were metaphorical images that left me spinning! After I had asked my four questions, I thanked the tree and, as I was departing, the image of a bright shiny red apple appeared in my mind. That was odd. I stood there for a moment considering what the image meant ... and it seemed to me that the tree was asking for an apple. "OK," I said out loud to the tree, "I will bring you an apple."

I worked with Penelope for the better part of that week, and when our time together was finished, I remembered my promise to the maple tree. After our closing ceremony and lunch, I brought the maple tree a red apple. The tree had a crotch about eye level and I sat the apple there as I hugged her goodbye and expressed my thanks. A picture of a maple tree covered in shiny red apples appeared in my mind. OK, I thought ...? and a moment later a huge wave of mirth washed through me. I had the distinct impression that the tree was laughing, and not just giggling — what I sensed was a huge belly laugh. As it laughed, it imparted this information: "Why would a maple tree wish to be an apple tree?" This was not spoken in words, either in my head or in my ears. Yet still the information was clearly placed ... almost in my heart. The utter assuredness of the tree's reaction and the strength of its humor was profound. Never had information imparted to me by another been so somatic or deep. What a great lesson for my life about self-acceptance. I was just as I was supposed to be. I had come to the tree asking questions that I had been given to ask. I think the tree saw me, my insecurities, and I guess it wanted to share its own teaching with me.

Dr. Bach said that for hundreds of years medical science has been off the mark. What does that mean? It means that we have been misled, intentionally or not. It means that there were things that our great great grandparents knew, that had been passed down to them from their ancestors, that were rejected by "modern" medical science. The reality is that our current medicine is no better than what Dr. Bach saw more than 100 years ago.

Since the same beneficent forces that were in effect back then are still here, we just need to tune into them. Our ancestors, however unsophisticated from today's perspective, knew how to discern truths in the natural world around them. Do we?

For example, willow bark tea has been used for centuries to relieve pain. Scientists come along recently and are able to "find" or "prove" which exact ingredient is responsible for this healing effect. So they extract it and create Aspirin.

Our current paradigm believes that "more is better," so medical or pharmaceutical scientists extract from a plant the single ingredient that they identified as being the healing component. They then market this single ingredient for human consumption, touting it as "the cure." Only now we are seeing that many of these ingredients, separated from the whole of the plant, are actually toxic to the human body without the presence of other ingredients found within the plant.

What is sad is that the advent of modern medicine caused people to turn away from the old ways and from the wisdom or knowledge keepers in each culture ... everyone drops the herbal healers to run to these scientific improvements.

Are we really smarter than what created us? Than what created the world? I know I am not. I am just a humble follower of the proverbial crumbs ....

56. Mouse Medicine and More

"Medicine," according to native and ancient cultures around the world, is an intrinsic strength that a being has, that can be shared or imparted. Pretty much everything has medicine.

How do you determine something's medicine? You study it. We can learn a great deal from watching anything. There is much medicine in nature. Chinese martial arts masters studied nature and learned quite a few fighting forms or styles from animals, like the Tiger, Crane, Leopard, Monkey and Snake styles. In watching these styles performed, you can often recognize the animal that inspired the moves.

In QiGong we practiced what is called "Five animal play." Here again masters looking to improve the human condition turn to nature for guidance. Does it surprise you to consider that animals might practice specific moves to help them heal and enhance their life force? Or that their practices could help us too? If this is a hard concept for you, to me it indicates that your mind is prejudiced with information you were fed from the outside. If you were open to information based on your own awareness, you would see this is true. For example, let's look at what is probably the most widely known yoga move, downward dog. Dogs are not the only animals that practice this (cats are another), but it is wonderful for humans as well.

Getting back to mouse medicine: when I was five or six I wrote my first book, a short story with my own illustrations. It was called "The Lonely Little Mouse." What I am about to share with you has nothing to do with either of those facts, but it does have to do with mice ....

I have always loved mice (ergo the book). I love their family values, their curiosity, their boldness as well as their utilization of everything around them. As a child, the more animal beings I could have around me the better. I was blessed with a little dog I named Happy, but I craved more! We were very poor, so the only other pet I could have was mice, and they became very dear to me.

What a surprise, decades later, when I realized I had Owl medicine and was told to study what owls ate to better understand the medicine this totem imparts. Owls see in the dark. Having Owl medicine, I see inside people, in their darkness and confusion, where their feelings hide, and in the darkness of space between the stars. My Owl medicine is part of what enables me to connect the dots, for individuals and on a planetary scale. What has this to do with mice? The primary food for owls is mice, so they are intricately and intimately connected. All birds of prey depend on the greens their prey has eaten to get a full spectrum of nutrition. Any time you suspect you carry traits or medicine from one creature, you should look at what it eats to tell you more about other medicines you might have.

Mice are detail oriented; they notice much in their immediate environment. This blends very well with Owl's gifts of triangulated hearing, totally silent flight, and the ability to see the larger picture — not so large a picture as eagle, but much larger than a mouse's view.

Native Americans do not see the other creatures on this planet as being less than we, to be dominated or controlled. In their belief system we are all equal. There is language to express this concept in many Native American Nations. Here are a few examples:

In Lakota people say "Aho! Mitakuye oyasin," which roughly translates to "Hello! Yes! All my relations!," literally including all beings, two legged, four legged, winged, scaled, plant or rock, elemental, seen or unseen. In Algonquin, "Nogomaq!;" in Anishinaabe, "Gakina-awiiya!;" and in Cherokee, "Ea Nigada Qusdi Idadadvhn!"

It may be hard to comprehend, if you have not experienced communicating with any of the other beings we share this planet with, but all beings have medicine. Just because you may have been conditioned to disregard or even scoff at such notions does not make the reality less real.

I am proposing to you that if you have not had these experiences, it is *only* because you have not tried, or you are so predisposed to disbelieve that you do not see the truth. If you have ever felt that a dog or cat has communicated to you, then you have experienced this. There can be as much to learn from a crow or ant as from a tree, rock or fellow human.

Indeed, when you are able to open to receive lessons or teachings from all beings around you, it is an amazing feeling. It is both humbling and expansive at the same time. This connection truly feeds my soul as nothing else does.

There are different ways to work with animals or other beings. Simply begin by watching them. You can learn about the medicine of animals by observing moments of their lives. Eagle flies higher than any other bird. Its wing beats are steadier up high than any other bird I have ever seen, enabling an eagle to appear to truly be master of the sky. If you are gifted with the ability to really see the larger picture, while also being able to focus on smaller things, you may have eagle medicine. Squirrel medicine can teach you about working hard, but never forgetting to have fun. If you were in abusive situations as a child, you may have adopted Opossum medicine. Opossums survive by being able to play dead. Their breathing and heart rate slow dramatically, and they even produce an odor of death when they need to. If you freeze in a fight or lose your voice, these are gifts of Opossum medicine. They could help save your life when you are powerless, so that you don't antagonize you abuser.

At the same time, *sometimes the methods we adopt as children to survive end up not benefitting us as adults.* If you recognize that you adopted Opossum medicine at a time you had no other defenses, you can work with Opossum by asking it to release you from this medicine as a "first response" in the here and now. Ask it to share its medicine in a different way, so that you do not lose your voice now as an adult; tell it that you are stronger now and no longer need help that way. Always be thankful for medicine, even if you have outgrown it. There are great books on the subject: *Animal Speak* by Ted Andrews, *Medicine Cards* by Jamie Sams and David Carson, and *Speaking with Nature* by Sandra Ingerman and Llyn Cedar Roberts.

I first found my animal totems twenty years ago by doing the spread described in the *Medicine Cards* book. The instructions in the book state very clearly to do the spread only once. I honored that teaching, even though I was surprised and initially disappointed at who my totems were. They were not creatures I felt immediately connected to. But as the years have unfolded and I have gotten to understand myself and the animals better, they actually all make perfect sense and have helped me to transform my relationships to the world and myself.

But make no mistake, medicine comes to us on a daily basis. Just open your eyes and your hearts; there is much to learn and much joy to be felt.

57. Dark Matter

Remember when I said that my Owl medicine allows me to see in between the darkness of the stars? Well, it is there that I first "felt" what might be called dark matter and dark energy, and learned the medicine of these forces, without even knowing that they existed. Does that sound strange? It is exactly how our ancestors discerned and intuited much about our universe! My experience was before I had heard about dark matter or energy. So I had no outside knowledge of them.

I was participating in a Lakota sunrise pipe ceremony. The pipe carrier told us that we should ask Wakan Tanka (Creator, or more precisely "The Great Mystery") to show us what our color was. Imagine my surprise when all I saw was translucent darkness between the stars, and starlight. "What kind of color is that?" I thought sarcastically to myself. "There must be *more*".... So I sat with it. The translucent darkness had a palpable density and incredible depth. It had a light viscosity that felt ... intelligent ... or wise ... peaceful ... hard to describe. I decided it fit me after all. Starlight and the translucent darkness between the stars. Yep, that's me!

It wasn't until almost a decade later that I learned of the existence of dark matter and dark energy. Dark matter and dark energy make up 95% of the total mass–energy content of the universe (68% dark energy and 27% dark matter; the remainder is less than 5%, yet scientists call this 5% normal matter). That's a huge amount, especially when you consider we are talking the whole universe, not just our planet or galaxy!

By the early 1990s scientists were fairly sure that the rate of expansion of the universe was not slowing (as one would expect so long after the big bang). In 1998 the Hubble Space Telescope relayed observations of a very distant supernova illustrating that long ago the universe was actually moving slower than it does today. They realized there had to be something powering this increased rate of expansion. There are three theories that may explain this and you can read about them in an excellent, easy to read article put out by Nasa Science whose link is below.[182]

So, what would the "medicine" of this force or forces be? How would we discover the message in them? The best way is to study them and uncover characteristics that make them special or unique.

We will call them dark matter and dark energy for convenience. They cannot be seen, not with the naked eye, nor even the most powerful telescopes or microscopes. Because of that they went undetected for centuries. So how were they discovered? Their effects could be measured! Their presence was *inferred* because of gravity and electromagnetic radiation detectable with radio telescopes.

Dark matter and dark energy are the explanation most scientists have today for why the universe is not only still expanding, but doing so at an accelerated rate.

Pretend you are watching dark matter and dark energy. It's hard because you can't see them with your physical eyes, but you can visualize them from what we know about them and from their effect on the materials of the universe. They are pushing things apart, expanding. Why? What does it *feel* like to you? Sit with that a few minutes before reading further.

After sitting with it, to me it became clear that the medicine of the most prevalent energy in the universe is *opening*. Expansive energy is the medicine of these two. Not closing or withdrawing. Expansive ... opening, growing, radiant.

If you can truly connect to that and *feel* it, it is incredible. Feel it through your heart chakra. This is the medicine of dark matter and dark energy, and it is the most prevalent energy in our universe ... perhaps there is a message here for you. What would change in your life if you consistently followed the path of these energies? Always opening further. Opening to your own perfect radiance, to your own particular vibrational frequency. Opening your heart wider and wider ....

---

[182] https://science.nasa.gov/astrophysics/focus-areas/what-is-dark-energy.

58. Anger

Anger is very misunderstood in our culture. It is seen as a negative emotion. I want to restate that *none* of our emotions is bad. In a highly evolved society, a child would be taught to communicate his or her anger *constructively*. Do you know what that would look like? It would be someone saying, "When *this* happened ... I felt this way." Or "When you said *this* ..., I felt this...." That is what owning what we are feeling looks like. It is *not* about attaching blame to the other person for our feeling "it."

Anger in our culture has been reduced to a competition. The prize is seen as "winning" an argument, as opposed to growing closer or getting our needs met. Who can be the loudest? Who can dominate the situation? "Let the angriest man win!" We pursue this, as opposed to learning to listen, which promotes others' feeling heard, creating understanding and closeness between both parties. What we are taught instead is that the most abusive person "wins." That way, the winner feels vindicated, but there is not a sense of being held in love and respect. The relationship does not grow, nor does a sense of closeness. Instead the other person usually feels abused, often shutting down. Eventually the love in a relationship like this will wither and die.

If we can agree that we each want to be heard, to sense that how we feel matters to the other person, then we can consciously begin to hold space for each other in our attempts to create this. It can be done. It takes practice. I am committed to this way of communicating.

Anger is not of darkness. Anger is more like clean quick lightning, if it has awareness (light) and wisdom-guided channels to travel. If we are taught how to communicate anger constructively, it is a tool to bring people closer together as well as to protect our boundaries, and boundaries are important.

To handle anger constructively there are two basic premises that need to be met. One is that you believe that your feelings matter, and are valid — because if you don't, then you will be trying to convince everyone (including yourself) that they are, and the actual reason for what you are angry about will get obfuscated. If you can work on yourself to the point of fully accepting this, then explaining what made you upset becomes much easier. Because very few of us grow up believing this, it is helpful at first if you believe that the person listening to you has an interest in hearing you, that she or he cares. But ultimately, we can't control whether another person cares about our feelings. If we believe how we feel matters, we will be much more centered, less off balance, in any situation. As many martial artists can attest to, when we are off balance, we can easily be thrown. It is we who need to care about ourselves enough to give ourselves permission to feel exactly as we feel.

You then need to consider what you want the outcome to be. It takes as much co-ordination and practice as a martial art form. If we were instructed in this from the time we were infants (and we witnessed adults around us doing it), it would come very easily. We would know that expressing our feelings should never come to a battle. In a battle one person seeks to overpower the other. But what has the aggressor ultimately "won?" What is the defeated person giving up? A piece of his or her "peace" (sanity, joy, sense of being cared for, openness, etc.)? How does that affect the quality of attention that the loser is able to give you? Repeat this scenario enough times and you will destroy whatever was beautiful between you. You have not "won" respect, admiration, a sense of trust or more love and affection. What do you want?

During the exchange you need to stay focused on your desired outcome. Do you want to feel heard? Do you want to feel closer to the person you are addressing? Or more comfortable in a working or living environment? We all have boundaries and preferences. If we do not feel able to express them and have them be taken into account, then anger and resentment build.

What happens to anger that is not expressed? It is sent to the subconscious. What happens to it there? For one thing, you are no longer aware of it. So it might seem like the battle is won, but it is far from over. There is an interesting relationship between the conscious and the subconscious. When we relegate something to the subconscious, our consciousness wins a "free pair of blinders" that automatically screen those unwanted acts or feelings from our sight.

It might actually feel as though you have completely removed yourself from these stirrings. But that is not how it works. Whatever we send to the fertile, dark fields of our subconscious continues to grow, all without the light of our awareness. On top of that, it has an unwritten "get out of jail free card" in the form of these "blinders." We literally have chosen not to see this behavior in ourselves. What do you think happens? It doesn't get expressed consciously, where we would be able to work on how we express it, as well as be directly aware of the affect of our expression. Instead the anger leaks out of us. One common way anger relegated to the subconscious leaks out is passive-aggressive behavior. Our anger can just ooze out of our pores; I call this being "stinky." We might experience having a very short fuse — small things trigger big responses. People often refer to someone like this as "being toxic" and in a very real sense they are.

John Bradshaw describes this as process of denying feelings as putting them in a sack on our backs. Like the antithesis of Santa Claus, the bigger our sack grows, the heavier it becomes and the less jolly we are. One day, the sack splits open and all that unexpressed emotion comes tumbling out. It's simple physics, folks, not rocket science (what goes up must come down, and what you bury will resurface, often when you least expect it or want it).

It's not easy to begin this process of reclaiming your authentic self, but if you don't do it, who will? And if you don't, what kind of life are you consigning yourself to? What kind of life are you consigning your children too? Just look at all the shootings by children that are occurring in our schools. Do you need a stronger statement that how we are handling our emotions is not healthy?

59. Zooming

I remember zooming along the road, moving easily towards my destination, but I was running late to teach a class. Well ... I wasn't technically late ... not yet, but I didn't leave myself a comfortable enough margin that my commute would be stress free.

It's a commute I had done dozens of times before, so my mind was only peripherally on my course. I was pushing the pedal to squeeze every second I could out of each mile.

The traffic slowed noticeably, causing me to focus on it. Feeling annoyed, I looked around and saw that if I moved into the farthest right lane, I could skirt the thickest part of the traffic jam. My focus had been on the slowing traffic, not on where I was. As I started to change lanes to enable me to resume zooming, I noticed the intersection I was in. In mid lane shift I realized that changing lanes would cause me to miss my turnoff — the traffic had slowed right before my exit. I quickly switched my blinker back and made the turn that I had almost missed towards my destination, the school. The traffic had alerted me, by forcing me to slow down, that I was about to miss my exit. If life hadn't interacted with me, I would have zoomed past my destination, without a clue.

After that incident, I started paying attention to how life might be communicating with me. There is Medicine even in the flow of traffic.

What if?

Have you ever tried playing this game yourself? Instead of feeling annoyed about something that slows you down or interrupts your plans, take a deep breath and look around you. You might discover that something put in your path which initially seemed like a hinderance actually ended up helping you.

It's hard to keep that focus all the time, especially at first. Like a mindfulness meditation, let certain feelings — irritation, anger, annoyance or fear — be your reminder to look around. Look to see what *you* might be missing, what gift this possible moment could hold, that your speed and trajectory might be causing you to overlook.

What if something — your life or a higher power (angels, God, ancestors, the creation itself) — is interacting with you? Looking at and experimenting with whether these things could possibly be for your highest good or are messages worth heeding is powerful and has the potential to change your relationship with the life you are living.

Did you hear stories of folks who, for varying reasons, missed the bus or train on that fateful day the Twin Towers fell? I bet initially they felt nothing but annoyed at whatever circumstance caused them to miss work or be late that day; but when they learned what happened ... they were awed. Many of them will tell you that whatever stopped them from arriving at the Twin Towers that day had never happened before. That moment of realization forever changed the way they looked how the world interacted with their lives.

Perspective is everything, and it is a choice. You can choose to change your perspective, or you can choose to close your mind. Why would you want to choose something different? I always tell my clients, if you are completely happy with your relationships, your job, your health and your life, then don't change a thing. But if you are not, then changing yourself is the only solution.

Looking at the interactions in your life is an interesting exercise. For me, doing so cut down on the angst I experienced on a daily basis. You might even say that being aware of such interactions allowed me to feel the hand of God in my life. If my life, and the world around me, can interact with me, it opens up an amazing number of potential connections, as well as mystery and intrigue. It is not a mystery that other people hold the answers to; rather, I myself do. My world reacts to me and communicates to me. I only discovered this by opening the door of possibility and by paying attention. Life can interact with you in the form of plants, animals, insects, water, wind, clouds, rocks, missed taxies, interrupted plans, traffic, etc. The more you open to possibilities, the more you hear and see, the more you can feel connected. It *is* worth the effort to get there.

I'm driving to work today on a twisty mountain road. I come around a corner and see a squirrel in the road up ahead. He is standing perpendicular to the road smack in the center of my lane. There are no other cars. This squirrel definitely seems to a have a message for me. He is on all fours with his tummy as far off the ground as he can get it (squirrel tiptoes), his back is straight as are his head and his tail sticking straight out in front and behind him. He looks stiff and uncomfortable and he is taking up as much physical space as he possibly can, "blocking" my way. I slow down; he is looking at me from this stiff position, making no move to flee. I open myself to receive what information he has for me. "Go slower than normal up ahead" is what I get. "OK, message received, and many thanks" I think back at him, and he takes off, like a rocket.

Mindful of his message, I keep my speed well below what I would normally be driving on these familiar roads. I am curious as to what lies ahead. Within two miles I come around a corner to see a deer family with young ones crossing the road. There is a car already stopped in the oncoming lane waiting for them, so if I had had to swerve, I would have had no choice but to turn off the road, hit the deer family, or hit that car, and quite probably drop off the side of the mountain. Thank God I was going so slow.

I would not be here, alive on this beautiful planet, if it were not for my ability to see these incredible connections.

How might this type of awareness affect your life?

60. House Hunting

I was getting a divorce, and that meant looking for someplace to live. I enjoy looking at real estate, so it wasn't *all* bad. I had brought my mom with me on this particular occasion. The real estate agent, a nice older woman, had showed me several places. I was looking forward to the next house because it had a stream — I love the sound of running water. We arrived at the site and from the outside the place looked charming. It was a salt box colonial, set on a small rolling parcel, with not just one stream, but two!

The layout was close, but that's to be expected with a salt box, and I could not afford something modern with an open floor plan. We headed upstairs, and looked at one of the two bedrooms. It was on the smallish side, but was well suited for an office with a nice view of one of the streams. We walked into the master bedroom, and I was overcome with a sense of heaviness and despair. I studied the room and could discern nothing obvious about it that would cause me to feel this way. It was painted a light blue and had two windows that were letting in the beautiful spring light. But in the room it felt like the sky was a dark leaden grey, and this heavy feeling permeated the entire room. I couldn't wait to get out. Just based on the feeling of that one room, the house was immediately off my list.

Several houses later, we were finished with our house hunt for the day, and we gathered in the parking lot to go over how the places we viewed had met my criteria. When that house with the two streams came up, I was honest with the realtor. I told her that it had felt like a woman had been trapped in that house in a terrible abusive marriage, and that she had died in that room. Surprisingly, the realtor said she had felt the very same thing! My mother chimed in that she also felt like a woman had been murdered in that room. We didn't have any confirmation of those impressions, but I didn't need any to know that I did not want to live there!

It's not just people who pick up on these things. Several years before, I had rescued a horse named Solo Flight. I moved her to a barn close to my house and on the second day she was there, when I came to visit her, she was standing in the stall she had been assigned, all lathered up. Horses usually have to run very hard to work up a lather like this one. I asked the barn manager if anyone had taken her out and she said that Solo had not been out for hours. I went back to her stall intending to walk her until she cooled down. As I was putting on her halter, I had an idea jump into my mind. It did not originate from me; rather, it was a clear thought/feeling that I perceived and it seemed to come straight from Solo. She expressed to me that a woman had died in that barn, and that she (Solo) was very distressed about it.

I took Solo for a walk and cooled her down, all the while playing the scenario over in my mind, trying to decipher what had actually happened and what I should do about it. After several hours, I put her back in the stall; she seemed OK about it, and I left. On the way home I decided to stop by the local tack and feed shop to ask the woman who owned it what she thought. When I told her about Solo being upset and what had transpired, she stopped what she was doing and turned to look me straight in the face. She hesitated and then told me that the woman who had built that barn had been murdered there, by her boyfriend.

Oh my gosh! Solo knew! Not only did she know, but she communicated this to me! I was in shock. I didn't doubt the possibility of it happening .... But to be the recipient of such a strong, clear communication, non-verbally from a different species, floored me.

I made arrangements to get her out of that barn the very next day. In all the years Solo and I shared time together, she was never in a lather again while in a stall. That incident, however, was the beginning of many communicated images/feelings from her to me, none of which I ever questioned the validity of.

There was one dirt road that we rode on where Solo showed me clear pictures of British soldiers and farmers in work clothes fighting. There were bodies as far as you could see, scattered and fallen like forgotten toys. It was amazing how clearly Solo communicated these past events to me.

61. Parking

My mom had an amazing ability — I would defiantly call it her super power. Whether she could have developed this ability in any other area I don't know, but in a parking lot she was an oracle. I can't tell you how many times this happened, but it was in the hundreds. Entering a large parking lot that was full, we would drive up and down four or five lanes of parked cars when Mom would announce, "Stop here". Then she would clarify, "One of the next three cars will be leaving, but I think it's the ..." (and she'd identify it by its color). She was *never* wrong.

When I asked her about it, she said it was like she would find herself looking down on the whole parking lot from above, and at the same time the words or information would just pop into her mind. She reckoned she somehow picked up on the thoughts of a person leaving a nearby shop, who started thinking about where he or she had left the car.

I often wished she had taken up playing lottery.

I find her description very interesting because she seemed to be describing something similar to how I connect dots across time, space, and disciplines. This process starts with an odd sensation in the area of my third eye, right where the pituitary glad sits. I associate this sensation with my third eye opening up. Everything here is translucent blackness like smoke or space. From this somatic/visual place, I am able to "see" things or get the gist of something in my body. All I have to do is focus on something I am pondering, and information opens up to me ... kind of like in layers. Information spreads out like constellations in the translucent depth of the night sky.

I wonder if I am accessing what people call the Akashic records. It is spoken of as a place where the entire timeline is stored; everything that has ever happened, and all that is yet to be, are recorded here. Some people can access this place at will. Some must struggle to get here, while others never come close. There is a particular quartz crystal that is said to actually store the Akashic records, and people working with it are able to facilitate accessing this information. They are referred to as tabular crystals, identifiable by their thin profile. They can be a quarter of an inch thick, yet their sides are faceted in quartz-like formation, and they have a termination point, just like regular quartz. I happen to adore tabbies (as we have affectionately nicknamed them), especially double terminated ones! I was crazy about them the first time I ever laid eyes on one, without having any idea about what they were known for. I have never sat down and tried to work with these particular crystals. But I do not doubt that having all these tabular crystals around me for so many decades could have attuned me to this layer of stored information.

So I don't know that accessing the Akashic records is why I am so drawn to these crystals, but I am very attracted to them. What I do *know* is that the sensation in my third eye when I am experiencing this type of awareness is a unique feeling.

Focusing on your memory of the feeling of a place, a being, or an object allows you to connect at that moment, no matter where you are. It also will allow you to manifest similar energies. Recreating the exact vibrational signature of a crystal that you have held, an animal that you have connected with, a stance in martial arts, a yoga pose, or an internal emotional "space" is the key. Awareness of the sensations of these things grants you access to them.

62. Joy and Gratitude

I was asked to co-present a talk that focused on joy. In thinking about joy and how to manifest it, I had a kind of epiphany: "We don't struggle our way to joy!"

Think about how that *feels* for a minute ... "We don't struggle our way to joy." How does it feel to try to wrestle yourself out of sadness? Or depression? Or lethargy? It's not easy to struggle against the tide. The stronger the tide ... the harder it is to fight it.

So what do we do? Some philosophies encourage us to surrender to the force of the tide, saying that we need to stop pushing against it and go with the flow; and I think that's good advice. As I have said before, the macrocosm reflects the microcosm. Here's an example.

When I was living in the Philippines and in Thailand in my early 20s, I was swimming and body surfing in vast oceans with no lifeguards, and maybe ten people in a square mile. When body surfing (as opposed to using a surfboard) I stay in water that comes up to my waist or chest. I stand on the ocean floor and gauge waves coming towards me. Some reach me at the perfect moment to ride them in towards shore. With these, I turn my back and jump up into the wave and, if I have timed it properly, the swell continues my upward movement and propels me forward with the wave. That is going with the flow.

If I judge that a wave will not reach me before it breaks, I attempt to meet it by swimming to it. Sometimes I am able to reach the incoming wave, but at other times one of two things happens: the wave will break before it gets to me or it will break on top of me. The former is disappointing, and the latter is downright dangerous. As a wave breaks above me, it creates a sort of sideways tornado and the force of the water crashing down reaches all the way to the ocean bottom (when you are at the depth I am). I learned very quickly that if I tried to out-swim a large wave that was breaking above me, I would get sucked into its powerful undertow. This invisible force would pull me down to the rough ocean bottom and drag me tumbling against it. It was very hard to extract myself, since a person seems to have about as much strength as a rag doll in this situation. I could easily run out of air while being buffeted about, struggling to get out of the forceful undertow.

What I discovered was that if I dove into the side of wave that was crashing above me, I could avoid being sucked into the undertow. Instead, I would literally catch the force of the undertow from the previous wave which was rushing back out to sea. It is amazing how powerful "going with the flow" can be, riding the undertow out underwater, shooting straight like an arrow with incredible speed, and come up easily on the other side of the wave. A human cannot move that quickly underwater unassisted.

This is a perfect example of allowing the forces that are assailing you to be added to your force, aiding you to get out of a scenario (even though it is carrying you away from your ultimate destination — in this case the shore). Once I learned this technique, it was *fun* to swim in a turbulent sea, even without a lifeguard!

So getting back to joy, what if we change the tide? Well not exactly ... what if we dive through the feeling into a different feeling? "We don't struggle our way to joy," "WE JOY OUR WAY TO JOY!"

This clearly shows why it is a good idea to memorize feelings that are beneficial to us. Memorizing in this case simply means fully embodying the feeling, to the point where you can recall it in detail.

Humans employ this process in other scenarios, often without consciously understanding what they are doing. For instance, children may cry not when they are hurt, but are anticipating getting into trouble. Actors also utilize this process to cry or to express strong emotions.

Tuning into a vibrational frequency and sitting with it begins to alter our frequency. If we stay with that sensory memory it begins to ripple out from us, like ripples in a pond. Because we are now sending this frequency out, we attract more of it. Like begets like. What does that mean to me? It means ...

When I am down, I search out something that brings me that feeling of joy and grab onto it. I focus on that warmth, no matter how tiny or faraway it seems. I don't know about you, but I feel joy inside my chest, like a sense of something opening there ... or I have a sensation of tangible warmth spreading out from there, as though it were a tiny flame. I fan it, I feed it ... and it grows.

Part V

PSYCHOSPIRITUAL

63. Art and Play

Humans did themselves a great disservice when they shifted the focus and value of creative expression from the joy and benefits of creating to placing singular value on the product. Concepts such as art versus craft or good art versus bad art divide creative expression as well as demean it.

Prior to this paradigm shift people used creative expression to identify their domain and express themselves; they made their tools, their clothing or their dwellings "special." That "special" was like a signature. The impulse to create, to make special, is a fundamental part of human beings.

In an interview for her book *The Creative Connection*[183] Natalie Rodgers quotes anthropologist Angeles Arrien: "the creative spirit within an individual is that impulse which is deeply connected to a spiritual essence that is *relentless* about being expressed."

All children, if not suppressed by their cultures or their families, explore this type of expression freely, with no fear or judgment. Children do not question the validity of creativity; it simply feels good. It is as natural an extension of finding their way in the world as is exploring movement and sound. Most young children have not yet learned to mistrust or judge their feelings/impulses. This creative, spiritual impulse shouts with joy when they splash a color on paper (or on the wall, or the floor!).

Dots, dashes, squiggles, shmears — it all feels correct as it is happening, because their impulses are not tampered with. The lines on the paper to them imply dog, cat, tree, or house. It doesn't matter to them that it might not be a perfect illustration, or even recognizable by another. What is important is their experience in creating the piece, and their relationship to it now. There is value in creating, which the child intimately *knows*.

One day, someone — a teacher, a parent, or someone they look up to — tells them "You're doing it wrong," or "It's not good," or "It's not good

---

[183] Natalie Rodgers, *The Creative Connection: Expressive Arts as Heling*, Science & Behavior Books, Palo Alto California, 1993.

enough." Perhaps they are told "That's not a dog" (cat, house, etc.). Immediately a duality is created. From that day forth the child will begin to recognize that the man-made world around her does not validate any connection to this inner world.

These authority figures say something that hurts the creative impulse, and the child realizes that her work is not about the joy that she experiences creating it... Further she begins to realize that is unacceptable. She learns that what *is required* is strict adherence to certain rules, not self-discovery or self-expression. These acceptable paths that art is herded down, quite possibly, like illustration, embody rules the child does not yet have the eye-hand coordination to fulfill. Her world is thrown into turmoil because she is being told that finding joy in self-expression is not good enough (knowing what brings her pleasure is bad ...). And either little by little, or suddenly, she is afraid to create again. Sadly, that fear of creating badly often remains well into adulthood or even follows her to the grave.

Natalie Rodgers says in *The Creative Connection,* "It seems the creative bud in each of us is very delicate. Although the urge to express ourselves is powerful, it seems to be easily squashed in childhood."[184]

This part of us is so easily shut down because almost everything in our modern world tells us that what is inside us is valueless, that we need to shut out anything generated internally in favor of what others tell us. And what those others have been telling us, is to look outside ourselves ... and to copy what is outside, as opposed to rejoice in self-discovery and expression.

The creative impulse is one of the last strongholds of internal guidance semi-allowed to us in our modern world. Most children *are* allowed to play, some are even encouraged to be creative, but think about this. Children don't have to be rocket scientists to see that the majority of the adults around them do not indulge in creative expression. So they begin to question the validity of pursuing such endeavors. Unfettered creative expression begins to be considered "childish," and so another layer of discomfort gets added to this very natural healthy process. If the adults around these children are being creative, for the most part they are "coloring inside the lines." This focus on things being predictable, perfectly rendered, in appropriate colors, immediately connotes a value judgement that children are very quick to pick up on. There is not much room for true passionate self-expression while coloring in the lines. Although those lines have

---

[184] Natalie Rodgers, *The Creative Connection: Expresive Arts as Heling,* Science & Behaviour Books, Palo Alto California, 1993

meaning and value for the mind, they harm the voiceless part of us that can only give expression through unfiltered creativity.

We are getting the message all over the place to *not express ourselves*, to "fit in," "follow orders," or "be more like everyone else." So when this one last vestigial window gets closed on our delicate little creative spirit fingers, this part of ourselves resigns and withdraws.

We have already gotten the message: conform, be quiet, deny joy, freedom, wild exuberance ... don't express our inner essence. And because of this, we come once again to the path of our current paradigm, of soul loss, dispiritedness, depression, heart ache, heart attack, dis-ease, drug dependency or addiction, even suicide.

I love that we are finally attempting as a society to make space in the world we have created for folks who live outside the box, whose promptings don't fit into the "acceptable" pocket of personal choices. We are realizing that there cannot be a one size fits all rule book, however much that throws a wrench into the proverbial machine. There are support groups and rallies and protests for small groups of people who are different, and this is needed! However, there is still so much to be accomplished to heal humanity. More than fifty percent of our population – women – is still treated as second class citizens (and that treatment gets worse if you add another "minority" definition, e.g., if you are not white, married, from an acceptable religion, attracted to "acceptable" people, etc.). However, the creative impulses exist in all humans. (I am not saying that it is not evident in nature as well. In her book *Love Is in the Earth: A Kaleidoscope of Crystals* the author Melody says, "Crystals are the highest expression of the earth's imagination." I thought that was a lovely concept.)

I tell my students all the time that if they have not tried playing with clay or paints or pastels since grade school, they owe it to themselves to play with them now. Most of us were exposed to art as children at a time where our eye-hand coordination was undeveloped. We compared our efforts against grownups' works and felt inferior. In this process we embodied a sense of shame, and most people file this away as a failed area of their lives that they never intend to revisit. And this is a mistake, as it only values the product and places no value on the amazing wisdom that resides inside of each of us, which can speak only through the creative process.

Many people are pleasantly surprised by their abilities when they try being creative as adults. People who truly believed that they had zero artistic talent discover that they do! Eye-hand coordination has improved so adults are able to have more control of the media they explore. People discover that this part of themselves, which they cut off so completely in childhood, has grown and developed without their working with it. This is something I have witnessed in my own relationship with my creative work, as well as with clients. There is some *je ne sais quoi* involved in the process of creation. It is much larger than us, or at least our consciousness. I liken it to another creative process, birth, even something as specifically birth-oriented as postpartum depression! Many artists experience this after they complete a piece (if they can get themselves to the point of calling a piece "done"). All the phases of a pregnancy can be experienced in any creative process. And in these, one single fact shines through: we are not in control of the process. We never are. Sure, we can abort the process, or we can support the process, but we are not in control; we are along for the ride. This is why developing a relationship with your instrument is so important. We require the wisdom within to be able to manifest good medicine in the world. Have you ever thought about making that a goal?

Even though I am encouraging you to explore your adult relationship to art and different media, and reassuring you that your abilities will be greater than when you were a child, I want to be clear. The most important thing you could take from allowing yourself to play with being creative is not the *product*. If you can firmly set in your mind that the goal is the process, and your relationship to the process, as well as what the process reveals, you will reap tremendous rewards.

The process of being creative involves the whole body. It is not just about what color suits a particular moment. It's also about what rhythm feels best for applying the color. Does it feel good to lay the pastel on its side and glide it across the paper? Or does it feel better and more in alignment with internal guidance to bang the pastel on the page over and over again? Different colors will inspire different movements. Aligning to these subtle inner promptings is how we begin to reconnect to ourselves, and subsequently to something greater that exists outside us. Yet the path to that something greater is through us.

How do you start? Get access to a box of pastels. Sit for however long is necessary for you to get in touch with something that is bothering you. You can focus on a question you have; perhaps you are frustrated about some juncture through which you are unsure how to move forward. It can encompass a situation with another person that is difficult, or some other challenge that is looming. If you want to write down a few words about it, that is OK too. Perhaps you want to start with words on your page and then move to colors. Many people find that moving to music for a few minutes before sitting in front of your medium(s) is helpful as well. In the next chapter we will learn that modern psychologists say that ritual is healing, so do not be afraid to create a sacred or safe space to invite your inner wisdom to come out and play.

How many of you indulge yourself in a hot bath? Do you light candles? Put a scent in the water, turn off the lights or put on relaxing music? These are all ways that we create ceremony or ritual. Setting the stage if you will, play, experiment, feel good. When you are present for yourself in a meaningful way, go and sit before your piece of paper and box of pastels. Pick a color that seems like it most closely expresses how you feel at the moment: red, blue, black, yellow, whatever. Begin moving the pastel against the paper. Don't judge what you do. Remember the most important thing you can do here is *play*. If "play" is too threatening to your inner critic at this juncture, than focus on sensory information. Notice how the pastel feels in your hand. How does it feel to interact with the material you are drawing on? Does the pastel move easily? Is there resistance, perhaps a slight vibration as the pastel moves across the page? Focus on that; where does the sensation take you? Not judging is difficult, but is a very worthwhile endeavor.

Remember our commitment to practicing something until it becomes true for us? Pay attention to inner guidance. It may come very clearly, or it may express itself as subtle urgings. Do you feel like soft languid scribbles, trailing the color across the page? Or do you want to strike the page with your color, over and over again? It is a very personal process, and *there are no rights or wrongs.*

As the medium touches the paper, it's a moment by moment exploration, getting lost in the process; this open the door to creative spirit and spiritual essence.

Psychiatrists speak of art as an enabling mechanism and state that it is through the process of creating that we experience the power of control over our inner environment. They describe it as "self-soothing," "pleasurable," and "surprising." Those are qualities that we could all use more of in our daily lives. They also state that through the creation of art we can connect to our "spiritual essence" — which is not at all the impression we were given as kids....

If you have trouble expressing yourself at first, do not get frustrated. Try not to let the inner critic shut you down (again). Remember that the inner critic was nurtured by your culture whose sole purpose, it seems, is to ridicule your efforts. It developed when you were a kid and does not serve you in your adult life, except to suppress you. Find a Creative Arts Therapy class or individual practitioner. Lucy Barbera, the woman I became certified with in Creative Arts Therapy, is an extraordinary guide for rediscovering your creative impulse and giving it voice. In her classes she provides many exciting media and a safe place to explore creativity in a group setting. If you are in the New York area, her program information is below.[185]

---

[185] https://arttherapycertificate.com/.

64. Play as Healing Ritual

"Ritual is healing." When I first heard my Creative Arts Therapy instructor Lucy Barbera read those words written by Dutch historian John Huizinga,[186] it stopped me dead in my tracks. I tend to shy away from the word "ritual" because the first time I ever heard of ritual; it was paired with the word "satanic." And especially because I could feel energy, these things scared me. Later in my life the connotation changed slightly as I became friends with Pagans, and Wiccans, yet still an underlying current of fear remains for me around being associated with the word. Perhaps it is an epigenetic inheritance from a long-dead ancestor burned at the stake for "witchcraft," or even from a past life memory.

Whatever the cause of the discomfort, it is present for me as a sense of having to look over my shoulder. I find myself experiencing a strong desire to hide when I hear that word.

I am however very aware of the profound healing power of "ceremony," a term I borrowed from my Native American teachers and friends. Ceremony is a word that feels so much safer, or at least more acceptable in our culture. After all, we have graduation ceremonies, wedding ceremonies, and even award ceremonies. But when it comes right down to it, ceremonies are not fundamentally different from rituals. It is just the stigma against "ritual" that makes me uncomfortable.

I love creating ceremonies for clients that help them release attachments to patterns which do not benefit them. I find it interesting that we can be aware of a pattern that is not serving us positively, and yet it can be so difficult to stop repeating it. A ceremony can work wonders for letting go of something that we have been struggling to have power over. For example, there may be an old relationship with someone that you have tried many times to make work, and each time it ends badly, with you

---

186 John Huizinga, *Homo Ludens: A Study of the Play Element in culture*, Martino Fine Books, September 23, 2014.

being hurt. Yet now, here is that person in your sights again. You know you should not let him or her into your heart and mind again. But you feel it starting and no amount of talking to yourself helps. That is a perfect time for a releasing or cord cutting ceremony.

I love participating in releasing ceremonies. One of the reasons for this is that positive effects often begin immediately, if you have done it right.

To begin, set out a candle or start a ceremonial fire in a hearth or fire pit. Remember fire is cleansing and transformative, so bring in your intention to have it help you. Sit down and write about the situation that involves such repetitive behavior. Be as clear as you can. The more of the situation that you can own, the more powerful it will be. What do I mean by "own"? Taking ownership of what your reactions are, not placing blame, and just stating what happens, i.e., "When this person says or does this, it trips me up because it makes me feel *this* way." While you are writing this down, you might find that there is already a clarity beginning to take place.

You may become aware of a dynamic in the situation that was not apparent before. Often the situations that we repeat have great lessons for us. When you become aware of a pattern, hold it in your consciousness, examine it, have gratitude for it. Most patterns we have originated as a protective mechanism during times we were otherwise powerless to change the things we were experiencing, as when we were children experiencing a trauma, or as adults during war or enduring captivity. Traumas can cause the formation or reformation of our personalities, and even of our brains (due to their neuroplasticity). We have even learned that trauma can be passed down genetically (see Ch. 4, "White Mouse").

As you go through this process, if nothing seems to have altered yet, it is OK too. Each time it most likely will be different. After you have finished writing down everything that wants to be said, stand or sit in front of your fire, read what you wrote, either out loud or silently. If you have found a resolution already, you may not have a need to release the issue into the fire for further transformation. What you wrote may be important for you to look at later, in which case just appreciate the fire, and thank it for its illumination into your process.

If you need to complete the process of releasing a pattern from your life, fold the paper up while holding the clear intention of releasing this stuck, swirling energy back into the universe to become free-running universal life force again. When you feel that this intention is held in your mind and heart, put the paper in the fire. Be open to feelings that come up, as well as images or even interactions from nature, a change in the wind or clouds. Take note of these. The cardinal directions have different associations in different cultures. For Native Americans this includes colors, traditionally black, yellow, red, and white (some see these as representing the four different colors of mankind). The directions also carry within them the vibration of different times of life: birth and beginnings, youth and growth, adulthood (maturation), and elderhood (wisdom and completion or death). The four directions not only are imbued with unique energies, but each has its own elements, animals, insects, and plants as well. The Chinese also associate the directions with energies (as is apparent in Feng Shui), and Pagans work with others. Consequently, if a wind stirs from the east during your ceremony, look up what East symbolizes. Also make sure to open your senses to be present for these occurrences.

A bird, a squirrel or an insect might appear. Each one of these has its own medicines, its own strengths and weaknesses that may have relevance to your quest or shed some reflection on where you find yourself currently. These beings may or may not interact with you personally; just make note of how these appearances feel to you, and be open to any messages they might have for your situation. When you feel you are done, thank the fire, your Creator, and any angels, guides or animals for energies or messages that visited you during your ceremony. Then, with thanks, put out the ceremonial fire.

Remember to be open to the spirit of play and symbolism as you enact your ceremony. Science has confirmed that ritual play is healing! Donald Kalshed said in his book *Trauma and the Soul*, "the core of self is sacred innocence and wisdom";[187] this is your birthright.

You are the horse; you are standing in front of water. The question is "Will you drink?"

We can also create ceremonies for opening ourselves to new energies, jobs, love, wealth, housing, or relationships (including to ourselves). When we open to something, we are creating space for it in our minds by visualizing what we want as already existing for us. We open up to something vibrationally in the same manner, by feeling the frequency of what we want. In this moment we are both inviting the energy of what we want, while we are also growing it. For what we focus on grows.

A ceremony can be as simple as consciously repeating a positive affirmation. Feng Shui rituals, especially for the Helpful People and Travel

---

[187] Donald Kalshed, *Trauma and the Soul: A Psycho-Spiritual Approach to Human Development*, Routeledge, 2013.

guas, remind me very much of New Age positive affirmations. I told you about them in the "Feng Shui" chapter.

There are many ways to create rituals. Rituals consist of stringing together actions, thoughts and even sensations in a way that has meaning for you. And truly they are healing. But we are not taught this, nor anything like it. There are very few ritualistic experiences that we create for ourselves with conscious awareness.

That is one of the reasons smoking is so attractive/addictive. The act of smoking incorporates so many ritualistic elements: fire, smoke, deliberate breathing, a desire to relax, an intention to enjoy the moment. When we smoke, we create a ritual. The place where we enact the ritual probably varies, but the steps do not. The smoking ritual involves slow deep breathing. When else in our day do we consciously focus on our breath, except in yoga, martial arts, meditation, etc. Most of us breath shallowly, not deliberately. As we take a drag from our cigarette, it's a slow, long deliberate inhalation. During this phase we open ourselves to the moment, we engage our senses, allowing us to savor the taste as we feel the chemical reaction in our bodies (inhalation is one of the fastest ways to get a chemical into the bloodstream). Such exquisite awareness, deliberation, expectation, and then we release the smoke in a long, conscious exhalation. Pure ritual. Why do we not allow ourselves this combination of elements in other, healthier ways? All it takes is conscious determination.

Have you ever smoked? I did. I remember I would get a ten-minute high after smoking a cigarette when I first started. I smoked Newports at the time and the menthol may have added to that sensation. Because I experienced a high or a change in my chemical state, when I smoked I expected the act to create a change in my day. I expected to feel different, better, each time I partook, and you know what? I did! Between the slow, conscious deep breathing and the chemical effect, as well as my expectation of a positive change in my chemistry, those aspects were amplified, and I continued to experience positive effects from smoking. This is similar to what I shared with you about my learned reaction to the smell of sage burning, which is to become instantaneously relaxed. A consciously enacted ritual can help you more than an unconsciously performed habit.

What I am saying is that often when we have an expectation of something, we will experience that. Rituals help us set up situations where we can experience internal states that we choose.

In a way a ritual can create a habit. Addictions and habits are not the same as rituals, although it's a slippery slope because habits can be ritualized, and addictions, well, they control you. A ritual should never control you.

People perform morning rituals that are important to them with different levels of awareness. Coffee, using the john, showering, all of these can become habits, with not much thought given to them. Even in that state, your day just doesn't feel right without them. But imagine if you thoughtfully wove elements of greater peace or joy into these activities. Remember that an essential ingredient in ritual is consciousness — making conscious choices and assigning these a meaning that is uplifting for you. The final element? Practice!

Imagine the outcome of consciously putting together rituals, of adding elements to your routines. Because rituals heal, you would undoubtedly bring more healing into many parts of your life! As my Creative Arts therapy instructor was fond of saying, experts like John Huizinga *see no formal difference between play and ritual.*

Well then, if both play and ritual are healing, let's incorporate as much of both in our lives as we can, shall we?

This brings me to consider the wealth of information our ancestors intuited or discerned without the benefit of modern scientific study. They were able to ascertain the benefits of practices like these. Being able to discern what feels good, what facilitates growth and healing, is not extraneous like rocket science. No, it is completely natural for humans to have and utilize these awarenesses.

If not being culturally predisposed to ignore such things, almost every human being would develop a relationship with these gifts, naturally, just as an infant reaches for things with its hands without being taught. Who knows exactly why; is it instinct or epigenetic inheritance? There is only one reason that I can see why someone might want to tamper with these natural abilities, and that is to make it easier to control an individual or a population.

However, there are those of us who discovered by accident this ancient methodology of finding our way by discerning, intuiting, and connecting to the natural world. We clung to this methodology without any guidance or confirmation from the outside. Why? Because it fed us in a way no modern methods did. We experienced what it feels like to believe in our senses while almost everyone around us scoffed, laughed, was incensed, or abandoned us. Those of us who clung to these shores without guidance or support, and without being able to explain why, are vindicated by modern findings! Ritual is healing! (Well of course it is!) Psychologists such as

Carl Jung, James Hillman, Sigmund Freud, Melanie Klein, Jean Piaget and Lev Vygotsky state that play is necessary for human development. They assert that all *play means something*; it is not a random act. This is evidence yet again of an innate wisdom that resides in each of us. James Hillman says that "Imagination is the ally of the child."[188] Through ritualized play, the child reenacts an issue or trauma, until eventually she saves herself.

Adults have lost much of this. Our induction into "adulthood" has circumcised our ability to feel our needs as authentically as the child does.

We are taught to ignore, trivialize, fear or resent our personal wellsprings of natural reaction and creative expression, and yet play can still lead us to a release of unwanted energy or to an awareness of ourselves as the generator of our own answers. It's a shame that our sense of comfort with these things has been almost eliminated. However, it is not eliminated from our holistic makeup. We just have to dig deeper for it. Knowing that it exists means all we must do is look for the experience of it.

Our need to create is as much a part of our digesting and integrating psychospiritual material that we ingest as our alimentary canal is for the processing of the food we eat. Creative expression could be compared to defecation of the psychospiritual body; and as such, it is just as detrimental if constipated. In modern Western culture we have become massively constipated in this area!

Nowhere can you see the healing power of creative self-expression more clearly than in Creative Arts Therapy and Sand Play. I was lucky enough to be certified in this. The curriculum created by Natalie Rodgers is an incredibly powerful process that anyone can use to tap into what Carl Rodgers identified in his groundbreaking "Person Centered Therapeutic Approach"[189] as connecting to that inner space where each individual knows exactly what he or she needs to heal.

All it takes to locate and connect to this inner sanctum of wisdom is the willingness to try. Working with a trained listener and observer who listens with unconditional regard, congruence, and empathy is key. When these conditions are met, I have witnessed very profound results for the sharer. It reminds me of the saying from the Bible, "Whenever two or more are gathered in my name, there shall I be." (If God is love, then God is also the path to healing.)

---

[188] James Hillman, *Re-Visioning Psychology,* Harper& Row Publishers 1976.
[189] Elizabeth Hopper, "An Introduction to Rogerian Based Therapy: The therapeutic legacy of psychologist Carl Rodgers," ThoughtCo, updated Aug. 20, 2018, https://www.thoughtco.com/rogerian-therapy-4171932, accessed Nov. 24, 2019.

In trial after trial Rodgers found that as long as the "clients" felt that the "therapists" were congruous (real/consistent), present for them non-judgmentally, and held them in positive regard, each and every "client" was able to find the way to exactly what was needed to heal. This is the magic of compassionate presence.

Shamanic Reiki pairs beautifully with the Creative Arts Process. Shamanic Reiki involves the client as a participant in bringing balance to the emotional, physical and spiritual systems. In traditional Reiki the client is passive and just receives energy. During a Shamanic Reiki session, I encourage the client to use her somatic intuitive self to tune into energy blocks or intrusions that either she or I sense. Together we work with these energies. If the client is having trouble accessing, changing or dialoguing with any aspect of this process, I will often offer a short session of Creative Arts as a way to help the client gain a different perspective and be able to resolve the issue internally. It has been one hundred percent effective every time I have incorporated it in such a situation.

We live in a time when modern medicine (at least here in the States) has reached a pinnacle of commercialism. For example, doctors are forced to join groups to reduce insurance costs. In the group it becomes paramount that the doctors' time is maximized and that a profit is made. The results? Doctors are so overbooked that they can spend only ten minutes with their clients. Our medical system is starting to feel more like an assembly line experience, devoid of much warmth or of patients truly being heard or cared about. And those missing aspects, we are discovering, are important components of healing.

Just as surely as our soil has become depleted of certain nutrients from over-farming, so has the fabric of our modern society been depleted of many psychological and energetic "nutrients." Why has our culture developed so many constraints around acknowledging simple basic human needs? I have touched on my conclusions regarding these many times throughout this book. How can we change this? Let us gather those who feel the incorrectness of the current modalities our cultures apply. Let us together consider and discuss this. I do not think we can make changes quickly on a large scale, but what I do know (and yes, anything is possible recall "The Hundredth Monkey") is that we can quickly set up support groups on the local level. And what begins on the local level, if it truly feeds folks, creates internal strength for both the individual and the group. Vibrational frequencies ripple out. Balance influences balance.

But let us not forget Chaos in this equation. Remember in "Trust Your Gut" I shared the old Norse creation story that opposites were injected into chaos and the world crystalized from these? Chaos is raw force. All creation comes from raw force, from chaos; ask any artist. Self-mastery is required to sit with chaos and consciously coalesce (manifest) something beneficial.

Make no mistake, transmuting emotion is not the same as suppressing emotion. It is a process that I find easiest to teach or learn somatically and that is similar to manifesting. Consciously changing emotions does take practice. And please note I am talking about actual transmutation, not denial.

These are some of the many reasons we all need to practice using our entire gift. This amazing instrument we were blessed with is able to connect in mystifying ways to the planet around us. All you have to do is try.

65. The Inner and Outer Human Being

When Europeans first came to this continent, they encountered people who had spent their time focusing on the growth and prosperity of the inner human being for generations. What these colonists were leaving behind was a culture that focused on the growth of the exterior human. On the outside, a culture that has devoted decades and more to developing technologies will seem far more advanced than a culture that has practiced inner arts. However, if you step back and look beyond the surface, you will notice that the Natives on this continent had cultures, trade, and good lives with much time for the pursuit of self-mastery, play and pleasure, with wise elders to guide them. Working side by side with nature, there was little disease, and no toxicity in the environment.

We can see examples of this in-depth awareness of inner human nature, as well as very concrete ways to work with these potent human aspects, in many First Nations' ceremonies and practices. For example, in the sweat lodge and sacred pipe ceremonies of the Lakota, the practitioners pray mostly for others, rarely for themselves.

The purpose of your sweat during a lodge is to give back something to the mother. You pray as you sweat into the earth you are sitting on. Being a Pipe Carrier requires hours of selfless work, every day, as well as attending to anyone's request for a pipe ceremony for healing. Another example would be the Sun Dance, which is such an intensely spiritual practice of giving away that it is massively humbling. All of it is done as a very long, very arduous prayer. Please note that, among the Lakota and many other nations, no one would ever charge for ceremony. Ceremony comes from spirit. Like the earth, it is not ours to sell.

Bringing a chicken or firewood as a gift, to relive the healer or shaman from everyday chores so that he or she would have time to do the healing work, was the custom. The Northwest Coast Indians conducted a ceremony where a person would give away many of his or her belongings, called a potlach ceremony. Can you imagine doing that? What might be the benefits to a human being from freeing ourselves from our possessions? My mother had a saying that I thought quite brilliant, "To the spoils goes the victor." So you can see why shedding possessions is like fasting for the interior human, an emotional and mental cleansing.

A great example of an elevated form of prowess in warfare was developed by the Great Plains Indians. During skirmishes, getting close enough to your opponent to touch him and dance away unscathed was the mark of a very skilled warrior. Accomplishing this earned you great prestige. Because your touch could have killed, but it didn't, and you moved in and out of range before your opponent could respond, you had bested that particular warrior. This was called counting coup.[190]

One of my favorite examples of elevated human thinking is the amazing constitution of the Haudenosaunee (ho dee noe sho nee), also known as the Iroquois Confederacy.[191] Jacob Devaney of the *Huffington Post* describes it as follows (quoting Bruce Johansen in *Forgotten Founders[192]*):

> The Iroquoian system, expressed through its constitution, "The Great Law of Peace," rested on assumptions foreign to the monarchies of Europe: it regarded leaders as servants of the people, rather than their masters, and made provisions for the leaders' impeachment for errant behavior. The Iroquois' law and custom upheld freedom of expression in political and religious matters, and it forbade the unauthorized entry of homes. It provided for political participation by women and the relatively equitable distribution of wealth.[193]

The Haudenosaunee have a form of record keeping involving shell beads that were handmade and sewn in a particular order on a belt. Each bead represents an Article of the Great Law of Peace that is meticulously memorized and handed down from generation to generation. I have heard that it takes four days to recite the entire Law. Can you imagine having to commit that much information to mind word for word? The beads that represent each article are called Wampum. Here for example is Wampum 24:

---

[190] Evan Hawkins, "Counting Coup on the Plains (and Over Seas)," Center of the West, July 21, 2016, https://centerofthewest.org/2016/07/21/counting-coup-on-the-plains-and-overseas/ (accessed Nov. 24, 2019).

[191] https://www.indigenouspeople.net/iroqcon.htm.

[192] Bruce Johansen, "Forgotten Founders," https://ratical.org/many_worlds/6Nations/FF.html.

[193] Jacob Devaney Hufpost THE BLOG 10/03/2012 04:55 pm ET Updated Dec 06, 2017.

The chiefs of the League of Five Nations shall be mentors of the people for all time .... they shall be proof against anger, offensive action, and criticism. Their hearts shall be full of peace and good will, and their minds filled with a yearning for the welfare of the people of the League. With endless patience, they shall carry out their duty. Their firmness shall be tempered with a tenderness for their people. Neither anger nor fury shall find lodging in their minds and all their words and actions shall be marked by calm deliberation. [194]

Can you imagine if our leaders here in the States were held to such high standards? I can, and when I do, it *feels* really good.

If you look at the happiest humans on this planet, they are folks who are *not* obsessed with the growth or status of the exterior human being. Bhutan is a perfect example. Bhutan considers the happiness of its population to be so important that it has created an index to measure the collective happiness and well-being of a population, referred to as the Gross National Happiness Factor.[195] Can you imagine if our happiness mattered here in the States?

Unfortunately, when you are obsessed with the exterior human world, it is easy to mistake people who are not similarly obsessed as being backward or uneducated. You need to consider what your value system is based on: Material wealth? Mechanization? Institutionalized industry? How do those words feel to your soul?

By contrast consider a culture that is focused on attaining inner wisdom, finding deep connections, happiness, integrity, and peace. These concepts *feel* different, don't they? Yet how many of us get up in the morning and say ... *this* is what I choose? Do we attempt to make a choice? Or does our modern world have us chasing *its* dreams? Does it have us running so much that we do not even realize that there is a choice we could make?

Decide that you value the growth of your inner self, and that of others, breathing into who you are, rather than what you look like or own. Make little choices each day to be happier, to figure out what "happier" looks like to you. This is how you begin to foster positive changes. Remember, "What we focus on grows." What are you growing?

[194] "Kayanerehkowa, The Great Law of Peace," http://www.ganienkeh.net/thelaw.html.
[195] "Bhutan's Gross National Happiness Index," World Government Summit, Youtube, April 6,, 2017 https://www.youtube.com/watch?v=E9IAIlLuq9M accessed July 21 2017.

Strands of indigenous wisdom remain and are still strong in many areas. Is the world ready to embrace indigenous wisdom? Placing the health of the whole above the individual and taking care of the environment are values from native culture worth emulating.[196]

We have been seduced, narrowly educated, beaten and bullied away from our natural abilities. If we use our bodies as the instruments they were designed to be, they would transmit the full awareness of the vibrational states of the things around us, so that we could innately know right from wrong within us and around us (unless we are damaged and cannot feel the difference). For most individuals, being taught to use our inner abilities as our guide would bring us more awareness than just what was right and wrong for us; we would know deep peace, because we would not walk down paths that were wrong for us.

Now we have no clue. We can't tell what vibrations mean, so we experiment with lovers, family, friends, careers, work situations, etc. Without the guidance from within, we are almost sure to end up in situations that don't suit us, that don't support our unique radiance or our vibrational frequency. It is no surprise we get hurt, and in response our light gets dimmed. We shut down. We quite understandably lose our way.

"When human beings create and share experiences designed to delight or amaze, they often end up transforming society in more dramatic ways than people focused on more utilitarian concerns," says Steven Johnson.[197]

A modern example of this would be Gene Roddenberry's *Star Trek*. The communicators of that 1960s show strikingly resemble the first flip top cell phones. The famous starship *Enterprise* had replicators, and we now have 3D printers that can replicate small objects perfectly. All the *Star Trek* crew members could access the ship's computer by speaking to it. Voice activated computer systems like Siri, Alexa, and Google are the beginnings of this technology.

Star Trek's universal translators, which evolved into the com badges of the various *Star Trek* spinoffs, allowed all species to be understood by crew members. There is now an app, "Voice Translator" by TalirApps, that will translate 71 human languages; you say something, and the app will repeat it in the language you selected (no Klingon yet). Personally, I'm waiting with great anticipation for apps that can translate the language of horse, dog, cat, whale, dolphin, and tree into human. And on that note, regarding

---

[196] Jacob Devaney, *What is the Great Law of Peace? The Native Roots of Democracy,* Sunday September 6th, 2015, https://uplift.love/what-is-the-great-law-of-peace/.

[197] Steve Johnson, *Wonderland: How Play Made the World,* Riverhead Books, Nov. 15, 2016.

human versus animal intelligence, who learns whose language? In our current paradigm, humans do not know how to speak any animal language. No, instead we expect "dumb animals" to learn ours. And they do! (And don't think that animals don't try to communicate, both by body language and vocalizations, as well as their vibrationally transmitted emotional states, because they do. We just have too many blinders on).

Our computer tablets were first seen in *Star Trek: The Next Generation* where they were called "Personal Access Data Devices," or PADDs. Other examples include tricorders, holo-decks, hypo sprays, phasers, communicator badges and even tractor beams, all of which have been or are being developed in some fashion, all based on Mr. Roddenberry's imagination ... or was it precognition? Who knows, but there can be no doubt that during our visits to the imaginal realms we can bring back new inventions.

Just as with all visionaries, no one in his time looked at any of those devices as anything but science fiction. Carl Jung said, "The dynamic principal of fantasy is play, which belongs to the child, and as such it appears to be inconsistent with work. But without this playing with fantasy no creative work has ever yet come to birth."

Steve Johnson found evidence of this as far back as 760 CE. He describes learning about the golden era in Arabia. It began with a dream beheld by Abu Ja'far al-Mansur. This great man had a vision of a unique city that was clean and held learning in the highest regard. He set about to create this city, which he named Mandinat al-Salaam, Arabic for "The City of Peace." In a hundred year span the city grew to house close to a million people! Within those walls he founded a great library called "The House of Wisdom" dedicated to the translation of all pre-existing texts in science, mathematics and engineering from Greek sources. If not for this library, much of the translated information might well have been lost during the following centuries.

The Book of Ingenious Devices was compiled from any past explorations into mechanical inventions up to that point. In the House of Wisdom, these inventions were studied and improved upon resulting, two hundred years later, in its next generation, *The Book of Knowledge of Ingenious Mechanisms*. Of this book Johnson says:

> [it] reads like a prophesy of future engineering tools: crankshafts, twin-cylinder pumps with suction, conical valves employed as "in-line" components — mechanical parts centuries ahead of their time. ... The two books contain some of the earliest sketches of technology that would become essential components in the

industrial age, enabling everything from assembly-line robots to thermostats to steam engines to the control of jet planes. . . . The overwhelming majority of the mechanisms illustrated in the two volumes are objects of amusements and mimicry ... The revolutionary ideas diagramed in these ancient books would eventually transform the industrial world. ... Those ideas first came into being as playthings, as illusions, as magic. It can lead to only one conclusion. Play and imagination fuel change. [198]

This is proof that imagination and wonder, as well as play, should be encouraged not just in childhood, but in our educational systems and in the adult world as well. We need to realize there is value in dreamers and become more accepting of individuals who embody these qualities.

Our masculine-dominated social structure makes it much harder for creative individuals, those of high imagination, to develop their gifts, and that is a detriment to humanity's growth, if indeed, *"Imagination is the birthplace of everything."*

---

[198] Steve Johnson, *Wonderland: How Play Made the World,* Riverhead Books, Nov. 15, 2016.

66. Nature, Women, Cats, and the Church

This chapter contains a number of different ideas that I feel are important to look at and that I am going to attempt to weave together. I am organizing the various ideas as their own sub-chapters. Amongst my own musings you will find pivotal pieces of papal bulls, writings from other cultures, and parts of the Bible. I was aware of some of these growing up, but many I had never read or even heard about. Yet I was affected by them. And I could see their affects across cultures and time as well. As soon as I was made aware of these pivotal pieces of writing, I saw the dots that were connected to them, like dominos. These underlying structures that our cultures are built on affect us today and do so in ways that we have grown so used to looking at that we do not see them.

This is why it is so important to take them into our awareness. What you do with them at that point is entirely up to you; the onus is on you to choose wisely. Think about the effect of your thoughts, words, and actions on the next seven generations. Make decisions as if their lives depended on it ... because they do!

I did not grow up in the church. I was still affected by these Christian teachings in the culture around me, perhaps as much as those people who grew up in a church community. As an outsider who constantly moved, I longed for the type of community represented by Jesus' teachings. How did I know what Jesus' teachings were? My mother was an atheist, so I did not learn about them from her. Whatever my dad believed he took to the grave with him long before I was old enough to contemplate such things. Yet I knew about kindness and support through the teachings I received from the vibrational world around me, through my heart. Does that surprise you?

Not only can I tell the difference between right and wrong from within my heart, but there is no doubt there. In my head I vacillate, endlessly. It does not seem that there is a single thing that my head cannot find a sound reason to doubt from time to time (if not constantly). In my heart there reside no words, only the language of vibration. When I drop into my heart I find such peace. I exist in a state of connection. My heart swims in the vibrations that are emitted by every living thing (and by everything that has molecules ...). My heart teaches me somatically about many things. And so I came to know Jesus' teachings from the perspective of being a "heartist." Through my heart I learned about love and compassion and, as I grew, I kept expecting to meet other people who existed on this empathetic level — loving and caring, aware of the impact of their words and actions, loving their neighbor as themselves. I expected that churches should actually attempt to help people attain this internal state.

But this is not what I found. It wasn't until after my dad was gone that mom started going to church. I did not experience love in the churches we attended. Instead, people would dress up, form cliques, and gossip. I was sorely disappointed.

I did not find folks living Jesus' teachings in the churches we attended, at least not at my entry level. But I did begin to receive teachings, and they were odd. Money in the mouths of fishes and Jesus' turning water to wine ... none of it made any sense to me.

On a heart vibrational level, these stories were empty to me ... I was not told of a deeper meaning to the stories. There were references to parables, but I could not find these things somatically. Nothing caught my heart. But what I could feel viscerally was these stories' condemnation of women. It wasn't just the stories like Adam and Eve, it was also the fact that no parts of the Bible were actually *written* by women. I became aware of discrimination on a personal level, because I was a woman. I found it very disturbing. It made me feel like an outcast in much the same way that, years later, the parents of a Jewish boyfriend made me feel — not good enough as I was.

Have you ever considered how growing up with these messages makes a very large percentage of our population feel? Or how these ideas, whose adoption by our societies occurred thousands of years in the past, might shape young minds and hearts today?

Might Makes Right

I think it gets confusing for humans when we start claiming that "might makes right." As soon as folks within the church started believing that God condoned his followers committing genocide on the inhabitants of lands that they wished to occupy, what effect did that have on the teachings of Jesus?

Unfortunately for all of us, when the Church began crossing the line from being purely a religion into being a political entity, it attracted businessmen and politicians, some of whom were there because they truly believed in Jesus' teachings and some because they saw an opportunity for power. Power corrupts. There is a fine line between having a vision and trying to force that vision on a large populace, especially one made up of people from disparate and conquered nations.

Interestingly, before Christianity was adopted as *the* religion of Rome, a wide variety of religious practices was allowed within Rome's borders. Rome even allowed women to hold certain positions of power, such as the Vestal Virgins, which I talk more about in "Managing Ourselves Better."

The Importance of Recognizing Underlying Structures

There were so many ideas that were set into motion back then, ideas that, like snowballs rolling down a mountainside, have increased in size exponentially. Some of them have grown so large that they have become like mountains themselves on which we have built our cultures and our homes. These slopes feel solid to us, because, for one thing, we expect them to be. Remember, what we focus on grows, and a group belief naturally has more energy than that of an individual. So there is good reason that these things feel solid to us. They also feel solid because they have been in place for such a long time that we do not realize that they are human constructs.

Because of this, we cannot see the underlying thought structures that cause our present day "lay of the land." We see, instead, the vague shapes of the original thought forms under many blankets of snow (time and acceptance), and so we proceed with our daily lives, accepting constraints and beliefs that we have not actually looked at. I would like to share with you what lies under many premises that have shaped our current beliefs, without our conscious knowledge or consent.

I say to you that this should not be! Oh, I support you in believing what your heart calls you to follow. But you must *look*, and you must think about what you find, in order to be able to decide what you are called to believe. It is not always comfortable to see the truth. But that doesn't negate the tremendous value of doing so!

Let's first look at the type of leaders that these European systems chose. Pope Gregory IX came into office in 1227. He had practically grown up in the business of the Church (being the nephew of Pope Innocent III) and was described in an article in the *Encyclopedia Britannica* as follows:

> It was his quickness to anger and his impatience with opposition that marked the character of his pontificate. When Ugo ascended the papal throne as successor to Honorius III on March 19, 1227, he had already lost patience with the moderate policies of his predecessor.[199]

This is not at all the type of person that would be a good choice to follow Jesus' teachings such as the meek shall inherit the earth. Nor was he a man that would have been selected to lead using the guidelines put forth in Wampum 24 of the Great Law of Peace.

Were you aware that the Church has been linked to an event associated with a resurgence of the black plague in Europe? Let me introduce you to the *Vox in Rama,* put forth by Pope Gregory IX on June 13th, 1233, as his first Papal Bull. I want you to really look at it because the attitudes underlining this Bull are still affecting women today, as well as cats! The *Vox in Rama* describes a satanic ritual as follows:

> When a novice is to be initiated and is brought before the assembly of the wicked for the first time, a sort of frog appears to him; a toad according to some. Some bestow a foul kiss on his hind parts, others on his mouth, sucking the animal's tongue and slaver. Sometimes the toad is of a normal size, but at others it is as large as a goose or a duck. Usually it is the size of an oven's mouth. The novice comes forward and stands before a man of fearful pallor. His eyes are black and his body so thin and emaciated that he seems to have no flesh and be only skin and bone. The novice kisses him and he is as cold as ice. After kissing him every remnant of faith in the Catholic Church that lingers in the novice's heart leaves him. Then all sit down to a banquet and when they rise after it is finished, a black cat emerges from a kind of statue which normally stands in the place where these meetings are held. It is as large as a fair-sized dog, and enters backwards with its tail erect. First the novice kisses its hind parts, then the Master of Ceremonies proceeds to do the same and finally all the others in turn; or rather all those who deserve the honor. The rest, that is those who are not thought worthy of this favor, kiss the Master of Ceremonies. When

---

[199] James M. Powell, "Gregory IX," *Encyclopedia Britannica*, https://www.britannica.com/biography/Gregory-IX.

they have returned to their places they stand in silence for a few minutes with heads turned towards the cat. Then the Master says: "Forgive us." The person standing behind him repeats this and a third adds, "Lord we know it." A fourth person ends the formula by saying, "We shall obey." When this ceremony is over the lights are put out and those present indulge in the most loathsome sensuality, having no regard to sex. If there are more men than women, men satisfy one another's depraved appetites. Women do the same for one another. When these horrors have taken place the lamps are lit again and everyone regains their places. Then, from a dark corner, the figure of a man emerges. The upper part of his body from the hips upward shines as brightly as the sun but below that his skin is coarse and covered with fur like a cat.[200]

I doubt very much that statues actually came to life back then, any more than they would today. It seems likely that these tales were concocted, like fairy tales, to install fear in a populace. This type of fear gives certain elites the ability to gain, or maintain, control of the masses. But fear, like a fire, can burn out of control. Another element of fear woven in here is that the accounts of such rituals were produced under torture. The inquisitors did not stop until they heard what they wanted to hear.

This was the first time that the church implicated cats as being in league with Satan, and the effect spread like wildfire. Here is one historian's view on the *Vox in Rama*:

Its long-term effect, however, was to reshape the view of the cat in European society in general, morphing it from a pagan sacred animal into an agent of hell. This demonization led to the widespread, violent persecution of black cats in particular.[201]

It is interesting to note that cats were sacred to the Pagans. Pagans and many First Nation peoples were animists, as were the Celts according to the scholar Miranda Aldhouse-Green, Professor of Archaeology at

---

[200] "Vox in Rama: Pope Gregory IX on the Witches of Stedingerland (1232)," https://pages.uoregon.edu/dluebke/Witches442/442Week02.html.

[201] Natasha Sheldon, " 'Thou Shall Not Suffer a Cat': Why Pope Gregory IX's Vox in Rama Implicated Cats in Devil Worship," *History Collection*, https://historycollection.com/thou-shalt-not-suffer-a-cat-to-live-why-pope-gregory-ixs-vox-in-rama-implicated-cats-in-devil-worship/.

Cardiff University.[202] Animists believed that all aspects of the natural world contained spirits. They saw communicating with these spirits as natural as communicating with another human. They were a people who *saw* and *felt* God in every blade of grass, every rock, every tree, every being. They did not separate themselves from their own nature, much less the nature of the world around them. They, like many indigenous people, saw themselves as interconnected with the natural world, which included considering animals, plants and rocks as possible teachers. With this world view, they had reverence for all beings, including women and the earth. This did not fit into the Catholic institutional world view at all. The Church taught that lay people cannot possibly judge anything from the "spirit" realm and that anything nonmaterial should be feared.

Why? I want you to think about that. I also want you to really take in the absurdity of the logic in many of the stories that were used to create fears and prejudices that we have inherited.

Why would it be important for an institution (including a religious one) to make us uncomfortable in our own skins? I have talked about that before. If we are afraid to explore and learn, how can we possibly find our way and utilize all the abilities of our instruments if we are frightened by not just our own natures, but the nature of the world?

We can't, because fear shuts down many areas within living creatures. Our muscles tighten, our breathing becomes shallow and rapid. We stop analyzing and we become reactive. Unless we are taught, we cannot remain open when we become afraid. We need teachers, but many of our teachers were burned at the stake centuries ago. So most of us relinquish any discernment that we may have in favor of compliance and promised safety, and who can blame us?

Another story that has shaped our thinking, perhaps without our noticing, is the story of Adam and Eve. This is a complicated story that people have attached many meanings to. It gets really interesting when you start looking at the etymology of the important terms of the story (which we will do later). No matter what else you see in it, this story has been used by men to subjugate women throughout the centuries.

Woven into the scary tale of harsh consequences of making a single mistake is an evil snake who talks Eve into eating the forbidden fruit. Eve is often portrayed as being weak for following the snake's promptings, but

---

[202] Miranda Aldhouse-Green, Ancient-Origins, 8 Febuary, 2013, https://www.ancient-origins.net/opinion-author-profiles/miranda-aldhouse-green-0010270 (accessed 2 June 2017).

the story can be seen from another angle — communication with a being from the natural world. An interesting coincidence is the creation of this tale at a time when talking to the spirits was regularly practiced by animists across the globe. This frightening tale of devastating, everlasting retribution from an almighty God illustrates the dire consequence (according to the men that wrote the Bible) of talking to a spirit or an animal. It also conveniently casts an evil pall over the snake which, with its ability to shed its skin, had long been the symbol of fertility and rebirth often associated with the Goddess-worshiping religions.

The whole thing bears an uncanny resemblance to a tale concocted to deal a heavy blow to those who believed differently. The effect of this story was to forever cast women into the position of being the lead sinner, in need of constant supervision and strict rules. And this is seen as reason enough to condemn her sex and strip her of any power. How convenient in a patriarchal society.

The Church taught its disciples to deny their true nature, which does nothing to teach a man how to channel his very real energy. If a man did succumb to its "evil pull," all he had to do was come to church, repent, and be absolved. I don't recall any stories from the Bible where Jesus suggested any of those things. I also don't see that there is much personal growth attained from this paradigm. If it did work, there should be more peace in the world, and far fewer "sinners." The priest is not helping the person to come to terms with his "inner demons," but rather to suppress and deny them. What are "inner demons" after all if not facets of our true nature?

Power of Groups

Many things happen when groups grow very large. There are predictable group dynamics as well as environmental issues that need to be addressed (like waste management).

These dynamics grow in magnitude as populations swell. I do not envy those that wish to govern, because there are no easy solutions (at least none that this humble dot connector can find). And unfortunately, when one is in a position of power over others, the temptations are great and many: temptations to force your vision on others, especially if you have passionate convictions; temptations to favor your family, friends and causes that you hold dear; temptations brought on by others who want to usurp your power, as well as by others who would attempt to lead you astray for their own advancement. Power like this should not be handed over to un-considering, unfeeling, unkind, judgmental, or righteous men because the power will be abused.

We should all be required to study the Great Law of Peace of the Iroquois Nation in America's schools (see Ch. 25, "The Seventh Generation Principle"). I highly encourage you to read it. It has a great deal of concrete wisdom on how to effectively run a functioning democracy, including strict guidelines for choosing officials, as well as rules of conduct that those officials must adhere to stay in their position.

Women, by the way, were an integral part of this system. I bring it up now to illustrate the differences between this Law put forth by "savages" and the laws being written in Europe by "civilized men." Consider the Decretals, the Papal Bulls, and the Papal Inquisition which all were put in place by popes around the same time that the Great Law of Peace was evolving. The difference is striking. Only by making yourself familiar with these things can you hope to truly see the real lay of the land, under the blankets of time and total acceptance.

Our Subconscious

As I have stated before, suppressing, denying, or rejecting any part of ourselves does not rid us of it. Doing so simply shoves the offending feeling or thought into our subconscious. It is dark in there, simply because the light of our awareness is focused other places. Shoving things in there places them out of sight (awareness), but it does not neutralize them or transmute them. Remember that energy never dies, so something you push away from yourself still exists. All you are doing is giving yourself a break from it at best. At worst you are relinquishing any control you might have over the expression of this energy.

There is a reason we have an inner world that is dark, and it has *value*. Our dark matter asks to be tilled, not ignored; it is rich with material that, if we utilize it, helps us to be whole, healthy human beings. No seed can germinate but in moist darkness, and nothing can bloom without the light of the sun. We are a reflection of nature, the inner and outer microcosm, both yin and yang.

But we have been taught to fear darkness as well as ourselves. This is especially true for women. The concept of yin and yang illustrates the interconnectedness of light and dark beautifully. In the heart of the darkness is light, and in the heart of light is darkness. In the East it is recognized that one cannot exist in without the other. So, what becomes of a culture that insists on instilling unbalance in its populace?

Our Connection to Nature on a Molecular Level

It seems that in the West we wanted to come up with our own understanding of the world. We wanted nice little tidy scientific theories, nothing mystical, and we proceeded to invest heavily in these as they were produced. If something didn't quite fit, we tweaked the scientific theory until things were re-contained in these nice tidy explanations. This has been going on for several centuries. But recently spirituality and mysticism have been discovered under the microscope, e.g., Quantum Theory with its assertion that the smallest particles of matter behave differently depending on who is observing them. Ergo "the viewer affects the observed."

The more I study these things, the more I am convinced that there are universal truths evident in the smallest building blocks that make up the world around us, and that these laws also operate in the universe at large.

Nature, or these laws, exists inside all of us, and it exists outside of us. We are not above nature; we are deeply connected to it. Think about the mitochondria living inside all the nuclei of your cells. Not just inside of *us*, but *every other living thing* on this planet whose cells contain a nucleus as well. This is just one more way in which we participate in the circle of life on this planet. We are truly connected, not just to our mitochondria, but to everything. We share most of the same DNA as a banana does.

Contemplate the flora and fauna living inside your gut helping you digest and assimilate nutrients, or your circadian rhythms that respond like a plant to light. All of these are nature living inside you, but there is also another layer of our "true nature," something that exists at the core of each of us and connects us individually to the natural world outside us.

People living close to the earth, "First People," all were and are intimately aware of this connection. Animistic cultures believe that everything has a spirit and that those spirits can communicate with us. Some of these spirits were seen as benign, some helpful, while others were viewed as pranksters, and some as menacing. This is really no different from our fellow humans.

Back to Cats

Getting back to women and cats, the medieval view put forth by the *Vox in Rama* was not how either had been viewed in other cultures, or even in Europe initially. In Egypt cats were so revered that there were severe penalties for killing them. I wish that were true for women as well ....

Cats have very acute senses and superfast reflexes. Some people saw these attributes as active in multiple dimensions, the psychic as well as mundane, so it makes sense that anyone dabbling in the psychic realm would be interested in befriending a cat. In these circles happy cats are felt to be psychic protectors, a feature welcome in any animistic, magical household.

In a medieval game of *phone*, the fear of cats promoted by the Church spread across Europe. Cats are mysterious; unlike dogs, they are not afraid to stare into your eyes. Cats are hard to train, independent, willful. Where a dog will cower and submit to your will (whether he has done something bad or not), a cat will run or squirm, claw and bite to avoid submitting.

Due to its fierce independence and some twisted flights of fancy occurring to someone in power, the cat became officially associated with evil, witchcraft, vanity, and even female sexuality. Do you think any of that silliness is still at play in our lives today? Black cats are thought to be bad luck in some circles. Consider the superstition about a "black cat crossing your path" ... probably that doesn't happen very often in your daily life. But we women are regularly reminded of this association. A woman's sexual organ is still called a "pussy."

So a woman's sexuality was cast in league with cats and the devil ... and at that period in time, it was a dangerous association. Consider *brûler les chats* (burning the cats) which was a French form of medieval entertainment that employed several ways to hang a cat over a fire until it died. Until 1817 cats were hurled from belfries onto the streets below and then set of fire in a ceremony called *Kattenstoet* in Ypres, Belgium. There were even cat chasers called *courimauds* who would pour a flammable liquid on a cat, light it on fire, and chase it through the streets. These all originated from the Papal decree.

So, what was up with the church turning against cats? Did the Pope really feel that cats were that much of a threat to his mission? Or perhaps the real question is *what really was his mission?*

As far as I can tell, this fuss was not so much about cats as it was about the Catholic Church as an institution, seeking to increase its power. After all, having a terrifying reputation is a good way to intimidate and control people. Humans have known that for thousands of years — look at the scary creatures of fairy tales, created to frighten children into obedience.

Using the concept of God as a masculine punishing force, the church turned people's fears of disease, pestilence, and bad fortune into "God's righteous retribution" for "sins" that the church *alone* defined. Doing so enabled it to wield this force against any individual or group that would not comply. Instead of encouraging the practice of Jesus's teachings such as "Love thy neighbor as thyself" or "Let he who is innocent cast the first stone," the Church leaders played on people's pettiness, ego, jealousy, competition and self-righteousness. In some cases this resulted in turning neighbor against neighbor, son against father, and everyone against the women or natives who listened to their true natures.

Getting back to the *Vox in Rama* and its consequences: there was a massive negative side effect to the eradication of cats in Europe. It led to a surge in the population of mice and rats and, not long after, the black death (bubonic plague). Europe lost 45 to 60 percent of its population during this time. Some people feared it was the end of the world. As the death toll rose so did the mistrust of "outsiders" and cries of "witchcraft." Many wise men and women were tortured and burned at the stake. There were murders of Jews as well, because they were not believers and refused to be converted; therefore, they had to be in league with the devil.

I don't know how the Catholic Church managed to reverse its decree that cats were evil and still maintain credibility, but it did. The return of cats to homes and streets helped rid Europe of the rats and mice that helped spread the bubonic plague.

It was not the first time, nor the last, that a major religion used its power to attempt to manipulate facts to its benefit. But recognizing a deadly mistake did not deter such practices.

Another Power Play

On June 18th, 1452, the very next Pope, Nicholas V, issued the Papal Bull *Dum Diversas* authorizing King Alfonso V of Portugal to attack, conquer, and subjugate Saracens, pagans and other enemies of Christ wherever they might be found. In 1455 Nicolas V wrote a second Bull also to King Alfonso, the *Romanus Pontifex*: "It extended to the Catholic nations of Europe dominion over discovered lands during the Age of Discovery. Along with sanctifying the seizure of non-Christian lands, it encouraged the enslavement of native, non-Christian peoples in Africa and the New World."[203] This implied God's blessing and the support of genocide and slavery.

Then in 1493 the next Pope, Alexander VI, wrote the Papal Bull *Inter Cetera*. The purpose of this Bull was to protect one Christian-dominated land from being conquered by another. This with the previous two Bulls

---

[203] "Dum Diversas," *Doctrine of Discovery*, https://doctrineofdiscovery.org/dum-diversas/.

created the Law of Nations and "came to serve as the basis and justification for the Doctrine of Discovery, the global slave trade of the 15th and 16th centuries, and the Age of Imperialism."[204] This is pivotal to understanding the structures that underlie our current paradigm — three Popes in a row contributing to the church's attempt at dominion of lands outside Europe.

I have not encountered any spiritual teachings, from any enlightened being, that say: "to rape, pillage, maim, kill, or subjugate is good practice for spiritual growth." Quite the opposite, actually. So how has this twisted and insidious belief come into being? It has gotten into our thinking without our noticing, because the concepts have been around us our whole lives (and those of our parents, their parents, our great grandparents, etc.). So long has this information been whispering in our ears that its shape is honored in our everyday lives. We don't question why we think certain ways or why we have come to believe the things we have — so much so that we are literally clueless as to how many areas of our thought process are even today colored by this way of looking at the world.

The idea that native peoples needed to be purged of their "heathen" ways by being tortured was common. It is truly horrifying, and it was employed not all that long ago in our own country, as you can see from the following letter written by General Robert E. Lee:

> The blacks are immeasurably better off here than in Africa, morally, socially & physically. The painful discipline they are undergoing, is necessary for their instruction as a race, & I hope will prepare & lead them to better things. How long their subjugation may be necessary is known & ordered by a wise Merciful Providence. Their emancipation will sooner result from the mild & melting influence of Christianity, than the storms & tempests of fiery Controversy.[205]

Might makes right is not what we need to base our spirituality on. Nor is it the philosophy upon which we should run our relationships, our families, our communities, or our governments. In my opinion it is wrong thinking, it is not good medicine. It is not a foundation that we can base healthy societies upon, nor is it a way to grow closer to Jesus's teachings.

---

[204] Ibid.

[205] Adam Serwer, "The Myth of the Kindly General Lee: The legend of the Confederate leader's heroism and decency is based on the fiction of a person who never existed," *The Atlantic*, Jun 4, 2017, https://www.theatlantic.com/politics/archive/2017/06/the-myth-of-the-kindly-general-lee/529038/?google_editors_picks=true (accessed Sept. 2018).

However, it is an excellent philosophy for domination and, as history reveals, genocide.

The Church Focuses on Women as Evil

Animals who foul their nests don't survive long. Successful parasites do not kill their hosts; instead, a balanced symbiotic relationship must be formed. We humans have very much participated in both practices!

All older cultures across the globe recognized our interconnectedness with the natural world, both inside and outside ourselves. In Western civilization, by denying our place in the web of life, we confuse ourselves. We think that we can live by our own ingenuity ... but can we? Do you tell the cells surrounding a cut how to mend the damage? No, of course not. Do you personally create clean water and food for yourself out of thin air? By demeaning femininity and the earth, we create no measures to preserve them. Honor and respect are needed to preserve things. We will not survive if we keep dismembering the web of life that we are a part of, as we have been doing.

To illustrate the level of poison that has spread through such teachings — and I can't help but feel this slander — let's look at the *Malleus Maleficarum, Maleficas, & earum hæresim, ut phramea potentissima conterens* (*The Hammer of Witches Which Destroys Witches and their heresy as with a very powerful sword*).[206] It's a fifteenth century manual that not only describes how to root out witches and sorcerers, but spells out (no pun intended) specific instructions in using torture to produce confessions, along with details on what to do after a confession is procured. Who under horrifying, gruesome torture would not confess to *anything* to make it stop? The document specifies death as the only way to put an end to the witchcraft. *Significantly, it was the first treatise that defines women as being the most harmful in their abilities — male magicians or sorcerers are actually marginalized in this document.* This was a devastating blow to women, if Adam and Eve weren't enough. It also elevated sorcery to heresy, which made it a criminal offense for the first time, and secular law condemned heretics to being burned alive at the stake. (Interestingly, the church's stance on witches, for all but the last two centuries of the Middle Ages, was that they did not exist; it was sinful even to claim they did.)

---

[206] https://sites.google.com/wztbook.42web.io/djawhead19/pdf-download-the-hammer-of-witches-by-heinrich-kramer-full-books. This translation by Christopher Mackay is the most recent and reliable.

This document was directly responsible for the heinous death of hundreds of thousands of women. And for what? If you read this stuff, it's so far out there as to be beyond ridiculous! Written by Catholic clergyman Heinrich Kramer (under his Latin name "Henricus Insititoris") and published in the late 1400s in Germany, it was, according to Rosemary Guiley in 2008, "a bestseller for 200 years, second only to the Bible."[207] (Ladies, can we say, "epigenetic trauma"?) So, women, the next time you are afraid to speak your mind, or afraid to shine, or to open yourself to the full beauty and power of who you are ... give yourself a hug and hug your ancestors as well for the unspeakable circumstances under which they were forced to live and die. You are *not alone* in your struggle to find and free yourself or in attempting to move through centuries of inherited fears.

The early modern British and European historian Brian Levack says:

> Explanations for the predominance of women as witches often focus on the treatises written by demonologists, many of which comment on the fact that most witches were women. This literature is in most cases intensely misogynistic, in the sense that it is demeaning, if not blatantly hostile, to women. The common theme in these demonological treatises is that women were more susceptible to demonic temptation because they were morally weaker than men and more likely, therefore, to succumb to diabolical temptation. This idea, which dates from the earliest days of Christianity, is expressed most forcefully in the *Malleus Maleficarum*, but it can be found in many places, even in the skeptical demonological treatise of Johann Weyer.[208]

Levack presents the patterns of witch-hunting in the British Isles. He says, "A Scottish woman was twelve times more likely than her English counterpart to be executed for witchcraft." He points out that at a time when there were less than a million people living in Scotland, 1,500 were executed as witches, compared to 500 executions of witches in England, whose population reached four million by 1650.

---

[207] Rosemary Ellen Guiley, *The Encyclopedia of Witches, Witchcraft, and Wicca*, New York: Facts on File, Inc., an Imprint of Infobase Publishing, 1989.

[208] Brian P. Levack. *Witch-Hunting in Scotland: Law, Politics and Religion.* New York: Routedge. 2008.

The Fear of Women?

What I find fascinating about all this is that the *most heinous crimes throughout history* have been perpetrated by men, not women. If women are so evil, so easily led astray by demonic forces, then why are they not at the forefront of every bloody, dark thing that has happened here? Nine times out of ten, men are the perpetrators.[209]

One of the common complaints of men was that women's sex drive was insatiable and that they were weak-willed. OK men, let's take a poll, how many of you have actually been in a relationship with a woman like that? This sounds like many men's fantasy of a very good time. So why would you complain or try to destroy such women?

Most men I know complain of women not wanting sex enough! So the attitudes just described don't make sense to me. Perhaps a man might feel used after such an encounter, or feel diminished because of the insatiability of such a woman? Or is her ability to have multiple orgasms something that provoked jealousy? I am simply trying to understand here ....

Traditional stories in Christianity are not always factual. Look at the fact that there were no serpents in Ireland for St. Patrick to banish. Yet he is famous for ridding the island of them! All of these stories need to be reexamined. Stories whose wisdom we took at face value are damaging to a large part of our population. Like let's look at women's stability. The fact that men not only commit the majority of violent crimes, but also perpetrate more sex crimes by far than women, is undeniable. This was as true throughout history as it still is today.

Correct me if I'm wrong, but those statistics don't support the kind of restrictions that have been placed on women. Instead, this information supports that women tend to be far better able to "keep it in their pants" then men, and proves that women can keep their heads, even when aroused.

For some combination of the reasons above, men just could not stop messing with women in some essential ways. Men embellished these stories to place women in the worst of lights. I am really speechless at statements such as the following from the *Malleus Maleficarum*:

> What shall we think about those witches who somehow take
> members in large numbers – twenty or thirty – and shut them up
> together in a birds' nest or some box, where they move around like

---

[209] James Allen Fox and Emma E. Fridel, "Gender Differences in Patterns and Trends in U.S. Homicides 1976–2005," *Violence and Gender*, Vol. 4, No. 2 Published Online: 1 Jun 2017 https://doi.org/10.1089/vio.2017.0016.

living members, eating oats or other feed? This has been seen by many and is a matter of common talk ...

The absolute ludicrousness of keeping a severed penis alive in a nest fed with oats is mind-boggling. The fact that the *Malleus Maleficarum* led to the torture and death of thousands of women is horrifying. We must learn to think for ourselves even in the face of first, our fears, and second, mass propaganda.

Figure 19. Penis tree mural.

This massive mural was discovered in 2000, inside a public fountain in Massa Marittima, Tuscany, Italy.[210] It is clearly a penis tree, with "ripe" or erect penises for the "picking" (damn ... we have been cast out of Eden).[211]

I find it interesting that men seem to universally have a fear of women stealing, shriveling, or rendering invisible their penises. You find it in

---

[210] Sailko, CC BY-SA 4.0, via Wikimedia Commons; https://commons.wiki-media.org/wiki/File:Massa_marittima,_fonte_e_palazzo_dell%27abbondanza,_al-bero_della_fecondit%C3%A0,_1265_circa_05.JPG.

[211] If you want to read more about it, here is another link with more pictures of the Tuscany mural: *Massa Marittima Mural*, https://www.atlasobscura.com/places/massa-marittima-mural. In the following link are paintings of different penis trees: Elizabeth Wilson, "Can't See the Wood for the Trees: The Mysterious Meaning of Medieval Penis Trees," April 9, 2007, https://culturised.co.uk/2017/04/cant-see-the-wood-for-the-trees-the-mysterious-meaning-of-medieval-penis-trees/.

different cultures even today.[212] Despite their fears, very few men lose their penises to women (with the very rare exception of incidents like that of Lorena Bobbitt[213]). However, removing a woman's clitoris is performed *hundreds of times daily*.

An article from the World Health Organization on female genital mutilation reports that "More than 200 million girls and women alive today have been cut in 30 countries."[214] How does reading that make you feel? It makes me feel ill.

So men have this underlying fear of women mutilating them ... and because of their fear (and various other reasons) they have subjugated, massacred and mutilated thousands of women across hundreds of years. Why? What have we ever done but give birth to you? And nurture you as best we could, feeding you from our own bodies, while you are in the womb and after you are born. What have we done to earn such treatment?

And why, may I ask, when women are being sexually mutilated and emotionally scarred daily, don't they have this same cultural fear whispering in their collective cells? Dismemberment for women is a reality, and yet women do not retaliate, while for men this is an abstract fear, yet they act out on it. What makes any sense here? Men, can you imagine if cutting your penis off to keep you from straying were a common practice? How would you feel about that?

Women do not often have an orgasm from vaginal stimulation. So if you remove a woman's clitoris, where does that leave her ... aside from being violated ... and yet she is still capable of servicing a man ....

Let's get real.

The Importance of Awareness

If we are fully responsible, we stop moving forward like automatons. We become aware of how life is interacting with us, and the dozens of small ways nature reaches out and responds to us. If we can be awakened to

---

[212] Sunday Ilechuwu, "Magical Penis Loss in Nigeria: Report of a Recent Epidemic of a Koro-Like Syndrome." https://www.researchgate.net/publication/247741243_Magical_Penis_Loss_in_Nigeria_Report_of_a_Recent_Epidemic_of_a_Koro-Like_Syndrome?_sg=I2q4iFMWcJe_TObCSntYW8VQZmXiME1CwZBXNnXK2rWhMg-ZEBqwz4gbabf_pxDFelz6yDXUV3Cn32s0.

[213] Biography, A&E Publishers, April 2, 2014, updated April 16, 2019 https://www.biography.com/crime-figure/lorena-bobbitt, (accessed December 5, 2019).

[214] World Health Organization, "Female genital mutilation," January 31, 2018, accessed March,1, 2018, https://www.who.int/news-room/fact-sheets/detail/female-genital-mutilation.

these awarenesses, it will be a gift to ourselves, to the planet and to our co-inhabitants. We need to revive these intrinsic gifts within each of us in order to find peace, be healthy and survive.

From my experience, if you open yourself to feel these energies and connections, it is like the difference between eating a meal that makes you feel sluggish or unwell, versus one that leaves you feeling light, satisfied, and energized.

"Whenever two or more are gathered ... there shall I be." Have you ever given this statement thought? I am going to push the envelope here (because that is what I do). This dynamic, of two or more gathering in the name of God (of love) must be important, or it would not be included in the Gospel of Matthew. Why? Is it because of the same principal at play in the concept of the hundredth monkey, that like vibrations support each other? *But here's a million-dollar question: does that other have to be a human?*

"Love thy neighbor as thyself" ... That speaks to me of feeling intimately connected to my fellow humans. And now I'm going to push the envelope again. Experience has shown me that there are many more beings on this planet that I am neighbors with than just humans. Are not the rocks, trees, streams, and fields also my neighbors? Being aware of these energies increases my connection and makes me stronger. As I keep stating, with these connections in place, we are less likely to fall prey to the things that cause us to want to leave this world, like depression, anxiety and self-doubt.

If you don't feel connected, then you are much more vulnerable and will probably seek guidance outside yourself. Since teachers outside the accepted modalities have been killed for centuries, you will most likely rely on an institution such as the church to inform your beliefs.

When you can tune into your gut and honor this level of discernment, then you will also honor the validity of others receiving their own information This is essential for our evolution. If we believe only in "truths" we are taught, then personal information is devalued.

Our instrument is highly personal. It picks up and reacts to energies slightly differently than anyone else's does. Perception is unique. Hence each individual will experience what is right and wrong in her or his own way. The teachers I respect the most have realized that "What is right for me is not necessarily right for another."

It is interesting that some religions feel the need to impress upon their practitioners that one's very soul is endangered by discerning. These same religions attempt to dictate what is right and wrong, as opposed to sharing teachings that allow people to find their own way. Once you tell people they are bad, or their bodies are bad, or what they feel is bad, you cripple them. In my opinion the only teachers that do this are looking for control.

Of course, there are always exceptions, but much of human nature is predictable. What I respect and honor the most about Native American cultures is the way they studied actual human nature. Through trial and error, they discovered practical ways to incorporate these behaviors into ceremonies and rituals, allowing human energies to be expressed and integrated for the benefit of all. How much better is this than repressing and condemning?

Robert Mirabal, a famous Native American flute player and maker from Taos Pueblo, New Mexico described a predictable time in a young man's life as "When the blood boils." He was addressing a powerful time in each young man's evolution, a time of hard to control internal forces. Naming it "When the blood boils" gave it an acceptable place in society. More than that, it allowed elders to address this phenomenon. Wise people determined ways to help young men channel this energy to benefit the community as well as themselves. Awareness is good medicine!

Lack of Awareness

As we have discussed, pressure to deny parts of ourselves can be exerted through cultural, spiritual, peer, or family paradigms. When we deny things – feelings, desires, emotions – we are *choosing* not to address them or even see them. They get relegated to our subconscious. Once there they are almost invisible to our awareness. This does not mean that they are gone or neutralized – far from it. Here they are free to run amok, expressing themselves in cloaked ways. It may take weeks or even years before they start leaking out of us, but they always do. Passive-aggressive or victim-martyred behavior, paranoia, anxiety, psychosomatic illness, or being enraged become almost a part of our personalities. Therefore we have no ability to control or change them when they begin to emerge from their prison. We won't allow them to pop their heads up cleanly and clearly in our consciousness. We have decided that "you are not acceptable" or "I don't want to deal with you." And so it is. We don't see these emanations, but eventually the people around us end up dealing with them as they are expressed without our awareness in the behaviors I mentioned above.

Denial

The other invisible effect of this process is that anything that you are in denial about makes you feel resentful when you witness it in someone else; it can make you feel angry or even enraged. This depends on how much pressure is building internally. This pressure can motivate you to try to control others' behavior (after all, what they are doing is making you very uncomfortable)!

This is why it is vital to look at yourself when you experience judgement or anger towards another. Self-denial and repression create a sore spot within souls, and when someone brushes against that spot (by doing the thing you deny yourself), you feel discomfort and may lash out. The *un*-understood pain and subconscious reaction to it causes us to focus on the behavior of others.

We mistakenly interpret our discomfort at what another is doing as an indication that he or she is doing something wrong. Discomfort can indicate a great many things, but it is not, in and of itself, discernment. It is instead a natural reaction to suppression. We have talked about the symptoms of suppression and denial. Un-suppressing yourself begins with the light of your awareness. Like carburetor cleaner, your light begins to de-gunk your engine. Just start a practice of self-observance. It's not about right or wrong. It's not about good or bad. It's about reality. How does your instrument function? Become curious; it has the potential to set you free.

There are other lures that entice us to walk the path of losing sight of the self. One is the natural desire to be included in a group. That is why we need *respected* elders to point out to us when we step off a good path. "No man is an island," and groups are seductive. There is a sense of strength in a group; look at how easily we rally around our favorite sports team, or scream and stomp in unison at a concert of our favorite band. We *are* tribal. We benefit in so many ways by sharing this type of energy. Playing on a team with a common goal is a positive way to experience this shared consciousness. But think of all the parents of young children who get vicious over their child's game.

This over-reacting doesn't make sense to others. But it makes perfect sense to the organism (our instrument) because it is so overburdened with repressed emotion that, in its infinite wisdom, it looks for any excuse to bring balance to itself. This type toxic dumping brings balance to the system by releasing pressure. But at what cost? Such a person will not be likely to advance in the self-mastery arena.

Groups are seductive, and so is self-righteousness; when you combine them, look out! Folks who are in various stages of their own repression find comfort in numbers. And in such groups, there never will be anyone suggesting you look at yourself. Instead, the group's energy is fed by focusing on the behavior of others. This gives rise to judgment and gossip. It also nullifies our potential to become self-masters and shifts much of that energy into controlling others. Not good medicine — not for yourself, for the other, or for communities. Yet this has been the accepted paradigm for centuries.

Interestingly, as many of us are becoming more and more uncomfortable with our paradigm, we see a rise in leaders who encourage us to point fingers at our neighbors who are different. Never would these leaders think to look at themselves, following the maxim "Become the change you wish to see" as opposed to bashing others into submission.

Waking Up

I think this is what Jesus was talking about when he said, "Let he who is innocent cast the first stone." The implication: look within, know thyself. None of us is perfect or without blame. Jesus wanted us to recognize these inherent human "flaws." How can we love our neighbor as ourselves when we don't even know who we really are? Do we truly accept ourselves? Can we? We certainly do not trust ourselves, not when we must suppress parts of ourselves to fit in.

How well do you understand why you operate the way you do? We can't have the lives we want, the beautiful relationships, happiness, joy and fulfillment, with an internal structure that is built on the denial or the repression of part(s) of ourselves.

So now that we are waking up and we find ourselves in this giant sacred hoop of life, let us consciously join hands. Across continents and time zones, let's join together energetically. Let's have the intention to help each other on the various paths to self-discovery and mastery. Let these be clear, conscious goals in each of our minds at the start of every day. At the end of the day, imagine placing some joy or gem of new understanding of connection into the circle, the great spirit hoop of life that holds us all. In this way we will build positive energy for ourselves and for creation.

After learning all I have about energy and manifesting, I can say this: even if you do not believe, simply *try* by hold these intentions in your mind. There are wonderous possibilities in our world at this very moment.

Think about this: why would God have gone through all the trouble to create energy radiating from everything, tie it into our emotions and thoughts, and create abilities within our bodies to read these energies if it was something God did not wish us to do? And the same is true if you don't believe in God. Why would evolution have gone through all the trouble to allow these abilities to develop within us if they were not important?

Begin this practice. Discover thyself so that thou mayest truly love thyself, and only then canst thou truly love thy neighbor.

67. Women's Bodies

Women's bodies ... are they blessed or cursed? Historically and culturally, a stigma has been attached to women's bodies. At best, they are viewed as powerful sexual lures, at worst as dirty, sinful or cursed. Where did this come from?

I like to look at how things *are* for clues as to where they originated, as well as to give me a sense of where things should be. Here's what I see. Many female creatures can carry offspring fathered by multiple males in one pregnancy. This is dependent on multiple eggs being in play, and on having more than one partner during the time the eggs are released from the ovaries. Multiple partners during the expression of more than one egg in a woman's cycle can result in fraternal twins.

The simple fact that human females evolved in this manner (or that God created women this way) points logically to inheritance passing from the mother's line. At the moment of birth, we all know who the mother is; it wasn't until recently that blood testing could reveal paternal lineage. So lineage descending through women makes sense. That is how it is in Judaism, as well as in Hispanic cultures (as evidenced by the mother's last name or *apellido materno*[215] being included in the name of the offspring).

The conclusion I draw is that we were designed to positively know who our mothers were. From an evolutionary standpoint, knowing who fathered us was not obvious and therefore could not be very important. (Sorry guys, I'm just following the clues.) Look at chimps that depend upon a tribe or clan. The father's identity is irrelevant to the survival of the offspring; only the mother's relationship to the hierarchy of the clan and to the child matters.

It looks to me as though at some point human males decided they didn't like this. These males came up with rules to empower themselves

---

[215] Aron, "Spanish Naming Conventions," *My Heritage Blog*, July 18. 2011, https://blog.myheritage.com/2011/07/spanish-naming-conventions-%E2%80%93-part-1-the-basics/ (accessed 5-9-21).

in this admittedly one-sided arena. What is sad is that eventually religion got involved and, as we have seen, religious justification for dominating others can get pretty ugly. Let's look more closely.

How can you insure whose seed sparks life in a woman's eggs? You could attempt to control all access to that woman sexually. This would of course involve controlling the woman as much as possible. Making her chattel, or property, with no rights would help a great deal.

That is what I see going on in our patriarchal history, as well as in the Bible. Like it or not, the Bible was written by men, and "the victors always get to write history." Of course, they are going to paint a convincing picture as to why *they* commit the horrors they commit to attain whatever spoils they are after.

I am focusing on Christianity because it is the cultural paradigm that has touched me personally. I am addressing feelings about a system I have felt repressed by, so I can speak to that system more easily. We grow up accepting being suppressed by the unquestioned structures around us. In order to survive this world created by men, we women, perhaps more than other disadvantaged groups, are forced to dismember ourselves to fit in.

In the battle of the sexes, men won for a long, long, time. They are the conquerors, they wrote the Bible, and they made the laws. Here are some translations of Genesis 3:16, a text originally written by men in the 5th or 6th century BCE.

> New International Version: To the woman he said, "I will make your pains in childbearing very severe; with painful labor you will give birth to children. Your desire will be for your husband, and he will rule over you."

> New Living Translation: Then he said to the woman, "I will sharpen the pain of your pregnancy, and in pain you will give birth. And you will desire to control your husband, but he will rule over you."

> English Standard Version: To the woman he said, "I will surely multiply your pain in childbearing; in pain you shall bring forth children. Your desire shall be contrary to your husband, but he shall rule over you."

I cringe every time I read the last sentence of that one. "Your desire shall be contrary to your husband, but he shall rule over you." That sounds like rape is being condoned to me. It makes me furious.

New American Standard Bible: To the woman He said, "I will greatly multiply your pain in childbirth, in pain you will bring forth children; yet your desire will be for your husband, and he will rule over you."

King James Bible: Unto the woman he said, I will greatly multiply thy sorrow and thy conception: in sorrow thou shalt bring forth children; and thy desire shall be to thy husband, and he shall rule over thee.[216]

Once this type of thinking became accepted, women were sunk! Think about it. A possible interpretation of this passage is that *easing a woman's pain in childbirth could be seen as directly in opposition to God's will and used to punish women!* So anyone trying to ease a woman's pain in childbirth could well be called a heretic! And the cry "witches" could now be turned on the traditional healers, a label that was punishable by torture followed by painful death.

Imagine how much worse things became then for women, as midwives and healers could be cast out during childbirth? Horrifying. The plight of women seemed sealed in suffering — but by *human action*, not God's will.

We cycle back to "Might makes right", and the belief that whoever wins, by whatever means, meets with God's favor and support. It is so sad that, after all this time, we have not evolved beyond this.

Thinking that women (or pagans, dark skinned people, etc.) deserved to be treated as sub-human (human in this case equals *white male*) became an underlying structure in our current reality. See if you can recognize this thread and trace it forward; how might it be affecting us today? Anything associated with traditional healing, herbology, energy work or reading energy would suddenly become sinister. All of which made it inevitable that we would turn our backs on natural healing. What else has been affected by this trickledown effect over thousands of year?

What a terrifying time to be a woman in Europe. Women truly became chattel. This was to me the beginning of the dark ages. Women's bodies, their thoughts, their actions, all were controlled by the men in the village.

We would not hesitate to condemn Chairman Mao for removing doctors from their positions and replacing them with farmers. The elimination of traditional healers in Europe was just as bad.

I see so many baseless tales coming from the popes and others in the church back then. One can easily assume that more than one male in

---

[216]All translations from Bible Hub, https://www.biblehub.com/nlt/genesis/3.htm.

power within that institution touted the higher mortality rate from untreated complications in childbirth as "God's will," using the direct results of their having removed medical help during childbirth as proof.

Women are to be silent in the churches. They are not permitted to speak, but must be in submission, as the Law says. If they wish to inquire about something, they are to ask their own husbands at home; for it is dishonorable for a woman to speak in the church .... (I Corinthians 14:34–35)

A woman must learn in quietness and full submissiveness. Do not permit a woman to teach or exercise authority over a man; she is to remain quiet. (Berean Study Bible Timothy 2:11–12)

Women had to relinquish and endure so much!

I remember as a child of six or seven not being able to understand why, on a hot summer's day, I could not take off my shirt when I was out bike riding with my friends, as the boys did. After all, at that point we all looked exactly alike from the waist up! I resented that so much. I also remember having to wear dresses to school, even in the harshest of Vermont winters, while the boys got to be comfy in their long pants and long johns. The first day that girls were allowed to wear pants in my public school I was so excited! I cannot imagine living in communities where there were far greater restrictions on women.

As female individuals needed to learn how to hide, to dim their glow, their intelligence, their sacredness, their wisdom and their insights in order to escape torture and death, the pressure to comply must have been suffocating. Denial of self and connection to nature was now forced on women who grew up in cultures that had embraced these things. To remember freedom ... joy ... wildness ... but be denied them, must have been a torture in and of itself. As with caged animals, *what happened to all that was repressed?* As we have discussed, things forced to the subconscious take on a life off their own. So, for centuries, at least half an entire population globally (because patriarchy and religious persecution of women happens in many religions and many countries) could not be themselves.

Competition

The young of any species are always looking for ways to compete. It is a natural extension of the will to survive. In what ways were women allowed to compete? What powers were allowed to women outside the home for centuries? Some not very helpful ones.

In a world where women were not allowed to speak their minds or follow the dictates of their cells, what could they do aside from menial labor and being brood mares? They could compete at needle work, house cleaning and cooking, but women are born with the same drives to leave their mark on the world as men. How could a woman gain a positive reputation under those circumstances?

Did you ever hear the tale of "The Little Boy Who Cried Wolf"?[217] It is about a shepherd boy assigned to watch the flocks in a field. He was told to call "Wolf!" if the flock was attacked, and the villagers would come running to help. In boredom one day he decided to try it. He ran towards the village crying "Wolf." As promised, the villagers dropped everything and came running. The little shepherd felt very powerful. He did this several times, and one day, when a wolf really did attack the flock, no one came.

Normally when we look at this story we are concerned with the moral that liars are not believed when they tell the truth. But I want you to look at it as an example of how humans who feel powerless may seek to grasp more power. A woman could gain a lot of attention by singling out one of her sisters as a witch. She would be called on, probably multiple times, to recount her story. It would be a unique opportunity for a woman to gain a sense of popularity or power.

By pointing a finger at others, we gain the attention of many people, including the powerful. Perhaps that gives us the only sense of power that we can experience in our very proscribed world. Also, causing a fuss about someone else might be welcome relief from the monotony of repression. Misery loves company, so if I have had to endure a lifetime of repression, perhaps I would be more comfortable if you had to as well.

Trying to dim the light of our sisters or control them does not benefit us ladies. We expend so much energy trying to be "good" women, taking care of everyone but ourselves. We, as much as anyone on the planet, need the warm nurturing that women are capable of providing. We must learn to rise above these epigenetic fears and victim-martyr tendencies to embody all our sacredness. How can we recognize and support the sacredness of other women if we cannot find it in ourselves?

Consequently, a young woman growing up under such extreme pressure would be struggling with how to function in the vary narrow parameters set for her. She would be divorcing from herself her natural tendencies towards self-exploration, creative expression, curiosity, connection,

---

[217] "The Little Boy Who Cried Wolf," http://read.gov/aesop/043.html.

physical prowess, sexuality, and intellect. Walking in the woods to blow off steam or to facilitate thinking things through would be viewed as unseemly for a girl or woman. Connecting to a tree, bird or other creature could be a death sentence.

We have learned that the phytochemicals released by trees both heal and sooth human nervous systems, lowering blood pressure among other things. Let's also not forget that bacterium in the soil, *Mycobacterium vaccae*, that affects the brain like Prozac (see "The Earth and Us"), and there are possibly dozens of other benefits that we have not yet learned about.

Historically all of these benefits would be available to boys and men. This gives them even fewer excuses to be the most aggressive and violent animal on the planet.

Women were cut off from the ability to help themselves through nature. This stifling set of constraints had to produce resentment, rage and fear all mixed in a pressure cooker, with no accepted way to release these feelings except by gossiping, being "holier than thou" or finger pointing. And these carefully developed skill sets are still at play today. How are women supposed to emerge from this in any kind of a healthy fashion?

From an epigenetic perspective, every woman may still have these fears and these dictates whispering through her cellular and emotional memories. Under pressure, women of all ages may well resort to those same ways of releasing pent up energy.

The Sins of the Father Shall Be Visited upon The Daughter

Have you ever thought about the saying "The sins of the father shall be visited upon the son?" That applies to women as well. There are great truths in the Bible. I believe this saying is referring in part to epigenetics. But there is another factor at work here. Remember that psychologists have determined that trauma is not stored only in the mind, but also within the cells of our bodies. I talk about that in the "Somatic Memory" chapter.

It seems we cannot escape these internalized memories. Look at the fact that most child molesters were molested themselves as children. Without help from a strong, supportive community, or therapy, the wound festers and spreads, leaving twisted, confusing, terrified emotions behind. In an effort to feel more powerful (against a situation where they had no power) the child victims of sexual abuse begin to identify with the abuser. It's a sad truth, a part of human nature which our ancestors understood. For example, ceremonies and rituals were created to help reintegrate warriors into the community after fighting was over. We need to borrow this wisdom to help own soldiers. There are also ceremonies to help return parts of the soul that have splintered off due to trauma. Sandra Ingerman wrote a wonderful book called *Soul Retrieval* that demonstrates some methods for doing this.

For the child survivors of sexual abuse, not talking about what happened causes these experiences to be sent to the subconscious, either immediately (because of the degree of trauma) or some time later due to resistance from adults in supporting the victim. Either way, the effect is the same. I go over what havoc traumatic memories relegated to the subconscious wreak in several previous chapters, and in greater detail in the following chapter.

Domination

Another thing to consider in terms of ways women were conditioned is this: if I intended to dominate 50% of the population, I would not want them to band together. So I would want to create a dynamic in my female population that kept them isolated from each other.

In researching the biblical passages cited above, I ran across another strange set of decrees in the Bible about women's hair. To understand the import of these passages, think about how many years it takes hair to become long. Imagine a village of women who have grown their hair since they were born. Everyone would have hair that was long. If you were forced to cut your hair at any point, your hair would *always* be shorter than that of every other woman in the village. It would be a stigma that followed you, possibly for your whole life. (Which raises the question of what's up with hair anyway? What it so powerful about hair that a woman needs to cover it? We will explore that later).

Here is I Corinthians 11:6 in two translations:

But every woman that prayeth or prophesieth with her head uncovered, dishonoreth her head: for that is even all one as if she were shaved. (Webster's Bible Translation)

... but a woman who prays or prophesies with her head uncovered dishonors her Head, for it is exactly the same as if she had her hair cut short. (Weymouth New Testament).[218]

---

[218]Bible Hub, https://biblehub.com/1_corinthians/11-6.htm (accessed 1-23-17).

And the punishment for this, if I understand it correctly, was to have your head shaved: "If a woman does not cover her head, she should have her hair cut off." (Berean Study Bible)

Looking at this, as far as I can tell, it's all about subjugation. Not even her own hair belongs to her. She is made to keep it long, but should she fail to keep it covered, her head is to be shaved as a public humiliation that will last for years!

God Made Them in His Image

Can you imagine the pressure this placed on women to conform? It also was an invitation to practice judging others and harming others based on those judgments. This was the opposite of what Jesus was trying to teach. Instead it was about absolute control. The degradation of women continued for centuries.

In various Bibles it says "God made *them* in his image"... both man and woman are created in "his" image. Interesting. But women are not to ever think of themselves as equals ....

Yet which ones create life within their bodies? Which ones give birth? Women. It seems to me that producing life from one's body is closer to a godlike power than anything I have seen a man do. A man can take life, but he cannot bring life into the world.

Again, let's consider how things might exist naturally by looking at how they operate. If you lose enough blood you will die. It is not surprising that many cultures consider blood precious. A man bleeding from a hole in his body for a week would need medical attention. Not so women. Only females bleed copiously without dying or becoming ill. What is more, that they do it once a month! That is a powerful phenomenon.

Blood has powerful symbolism throughout history on every continent. In the Hindu tradition once a year a person, family or business will sacrifice the largest animal they can afford and spill its blood on what they are dependent upon or most grateful for. This is done to give thanks for their blessings and to insure continued blessings. For example, taxicab owners will spill blood over the engines of their cars. People who are lucky enough to have a home spill blood over the threshold. At this time in Katmandu, the streets literally run with blood, despite the fact that they're dirt (at least most of them were in the early 1980s when I was there). Imagine what it feels like for a woman to be on her menses during this time. She is bleeding, but has not had to harm anything to shed that blood. It's powerful. I experienced it personally when I was in Nepal.

Traditionally blood is considered sacred, and when people were closer to the earth and less squeamish about such things, so was a woman's menstrual blood. I don't know how foreign a concept that is for you. There is much to be learned about women's teachings regarding the sacredness of a woman's blood during her "moon time." As a woman do you feel this sacredness at all? Is there an epigenetic whispering in your veins during your moon time that hints at such things? Or have your ancestors long since given up trying to remind you?

Many young women I know are far removed from entertaining even the possibility of anything positive about their periods, never mind feeling anything sacred about them. As a man, can you?

In our culture a woman is so disconnected from the natural world that there is little to herself or to her family that is sacred about her bleeding. Look at the words we use to describe it. The curse, period, being on the rag; all of these reflect negativity. A period ends things. A woman who is married and gets her menses has, in essence, failed. She has failed to get pregnant. Period.

I remember many years ago reading a book called *Circle of Stones: Woman's Journey to Herself* by Judith Duerk[219] — I cried when I read it. It's very short, maybe a quarter of an inch thick and a very easy read. It paints pictures of how things were in the past in many cultures and it's *powerful*. The traditions described in this book are so opposite to our current attitude towards women and a woman's moon time as to be almost shocking. I highly recommend it for both men and women; it should open your eyes to choices that have been made and the resulting structures.

For the Lakota, a woman in her moon time is considered to be the "walking sweat lodge." The sweat lodge is sacred, so that conveys much respect for a woman in her moon time. Unless you understand the symbology and the sacredness of the sweat lodge, it will not mean much to you.

Men traditionally enter the sweat lodge to give back to our Mother the earth, to honor her, and to pray. The belief is that nothing on this planet is ours to give; everything came from the Mother (earth) except our sweat and our blood. So, when you really want to offer something back, you offer your blood or your sweat.

In the sweat lodge, you crawl into the dark space on your hands and knees, pressing your forehead to the earth at the entrance saying "Mitakuye Oyasin!" (All My Relations!). This phrase acknowledges your

---

219 Judith Duerk, *Circle of Stones: Woman's Journey to Herself*, New World Library, Novato California.

337

interconnectedness to everything large or small, scaled, barked, furred, finned, winged, two, four, six, or a hundred legged. Then you continue crawling to your place in the darkness. You sit around the central pit where the glowing rocks, called grandmothers and grandfathers, will be placed, and you prepare to pray and offer your sweat to the earth, upon which you sit.

Many wise elders from different Nations have expressed that there is a link between the regard women are held in and the regard the earth is held in. The earth is our Mother, and women are mothers. Women and the earth need to be cherished, respected, nurtured. Many elders have said that one of the reasons the earth is in the state it's in is because women have stopped the practice of giving their blood back to the earth. That is a foreign concept in our culture. But let's look at this. We have been concretely establishing the existence of deep wisdom in older cultures. They understand the true functioning of complex systems in realms both seen and unseen. Don't you think that there is a chance we might gain something through exploring these concepts, these energies? From my experience, there may be profound, surprising opportunities for healing.

A women's moon time is very special. Our culture has no place for this. It's a great example of cultural paradigms affecting not just beliefs, but physiology as well. Women in our culture often have very painful menstruation because they do not have a spiritual connection to this event. They do not have a sacred connection to their bodies. Menses are seen as an inconvenience at best, and as something dirty or a "curse" at worst.

Sometime during my college studies my experience of my menses changed. They stopped being extremely painful (nothing that a couple of Motrin couldn't take care of, whereas previously I was prescribed codeine for the extreme pain). As I settled into my body more, I realized that at these times I had a sense that I existed out of phase with the rest of the world. It was a very cool feeling. It lasted for the first couple of days of my menses each month, but it was always the strongest in the first 24-hour period (no pun intended). It felt *right* to slow down, be peaceful, connect to the deep energies I was feeling. I loved it! It helped me to attune, not only to my own energies, but to those of the planet and nature as well. I would steep in those feelings as much as I could.

You can learn more about this from a modern phenomenon called the Red Tent, or Red Tent Temple, movement. Its philosophies have been around for thousands of years, but were brought back into mainstream consciousness in 1997 due to a novel by Anita Diamond called *Red Tent.*

Reclaiming the Sacred

Around this same time, I started taking a Psychology of Women class at Antioch College. I had been protected in some ways from being exposed to women not being treated equally because I was raised by a single mom who was very intelligent, well educated, and quite capable. She was not religious, so I had no idea of Christian views on women's roles or their unparalleled "sins." So it was quite a surprise when I learned about the atrocities committed against women for thousands of years by different religious factions. What fascinated me was that farther back in time women had been venerated. Witness the Venus of Hohle Fels, an Upper Paleolithic sculpture carved from mammoth ivory dated between 35,000 to 40,000 years old. It is generally considered the oldest sculpture of a human being, and it is of a very robust, well endowed, female figure, a goddess.

Does it surprise you that the first religious sculpture created by "man" was of a goddess?

Every time I think about this I have to ask ... why? Not why would man sculpt the great goddess, but what changed? Why would men grow to hate or fear women so much that they would need to go from worshiping us to treating us like chattel? The fact that it had not always been this way intrigued me. After all this sculpture was created long before the Bible was written. And we have determined that the goddess worshiping religions were still going strong long after Genesis was written. So why and when did all this shift?

I am so upset by the things I hear from women raised in the Catholic church; they talk about how they were taught to look at their bodies as dirty. A large percentage of the human population feels horrible about their inner nature and their bodies. What is wrong with this picture? Women are taught to be ashamed of their bodies, the way they look, the way they smell, their passions (the actual drives that the Bible says they should have in order to procreate). And yet men crave them. They crave everything: the body, the smell, the passion. How much sense does this make?

If a woman's body is dirty, how could a child be conceived and grow — much less thrive — in a "dirty" vessel? Let that sink in for a moment. Evolution, if not God, would have seen to the vagina and uterus being beautifully clean, as the place to conceive and carry young. How could any child be disease free if it was incubated in filth?

A man pees from his penis. Urine is excrement. Women do not release any waste products from their vaginas, except once a month, when the beautiful nourishing lining of the uterus is shed, if a child is not conceived, in order for a new one to take its place. The vagina is a holy, sacred, clean vessel, created by the creator, to be the chalice of life! That is clear if you connect the dots!

I think all this negative propaganda boils down to men trying to keep control of whose seed is quickening inside the woman they chose to produce their offspring.

Human women, like other mammals, are capable of having twins, fathered by different partners. This makes it difficult for a man who wants to control access to his chosen "breeder" and therefore the purity of his offspring. In cultures where clitorectomies are performed the procedure is done so that the women will not stray from their husbands.

To gain even more insight into the way women are taught to look at their bodies, look at something as simple and basic as potty training. I worked at a day care center for a year. Very different messages were given to little boys about their bodies than those given to little girls ... all without conscious volition (as far as I could tell). As soon as a little girl can get up on a toilet by herself, we can trust that she won't be making a mess that we have to clean up. Not so a little boy. He has to be coaxed to hold his penis and aim. I saw countless examples of this and was even coached in how to train the kids. Girls were sent in by themselves or placed on the potty and left. We were to stand outside, in case they needed help, but if they didn't, as they were leaving, we would ask them, "Did you wipe?" and then "Did you wash your hands?"

Little boys were escorted into the room, and we were to watch them from behind. If they touched themselves to aim their urine stream, we clapped! Sometimes there were multiple adults clapping (depending on how long the lack of aiming had been going on for a particular boy).

Can you imagine, girls, if anyone ever clapped enthusiastically as a result of you touching yourself? I am still waiting .... Such divergent messages for boys and girls are clearly absorbed by young minds.

I got my menses when I was quite young, around nine years old. I remember being so embarrassed by the whole process. Having to purchase sanitary napkins publicly was mortifying. I also used to have horrendous pain. As I mentioned earlier, my relationship to my moon time changed during college. But I didn't have anything but my own inner promptings to guide me. The reality of how I felt was undeniable, despite my culture. It was not until I was in my late forties and early fifties that I really understood why I had felt what I felt during my moon time. I began studying with Grandmother Nanatasis, an Abenaki elder, and she taught us sacred women's teachings. I was lucky enough to still be having my menses during the training with her. Grandmother instructed us on how to create the Moon Lodge, which was a special place for women. If a woman was in her moon time she could come here and be tended to. It was also a place for teachings and stories while others were involved with the sweat lodge.

I remember being in the Moon Lodge with Grandmother Nanatasis and about fifteen other women. This Moon Lodge was a tent within the circle of the sweat lodge ceremony. Grandmother was guiding us in traditional Moon Lodge teachings. She asked at one point if there were any women in the lodge that were in their moon time. Of the fifteen, there was only one amongst us who was. Grandmother asked this young lady to step out of the lodge and stand fifteen to twenty feet away. I was so surprised because I could immediately feel the difference in the energy within the lodge! The woman who was menstruating created an aura of warped time around her that had allowed me to feel that gateway myself, just as though I was menstruating! They didn't teach that in Sunday school! Nor in high school. We need these teachings! We need, as women, to feel the power and sacredness of our bodies, of our processes, and we need guidance to help us validate what we are feeling.

When women are in balance, they are able to enter a different phase of existence during their moon time. If you are tuned into your body you can get a sense of that other-worldly space at those times. I was aware of this long before I received any formal moon time teachings. Our ancestors recognized that for women who are in their moon time the veils between the worlds were thinner. Among the Lakota and other First Nation peoples across the globe, women would seclude themselves during this time, be cared for and nurtured by other women. They were not to work or prepare food. Often, they came back with a prophecy or a solution to a problem that was facing the clan. Grandmother Nanatasis told us to prepare nourishing foods for ourselves before our moon time, so that we could sequester ourselves in peace and have a sense of being nurtured during this special time.

Moon time is a powerful time for a woman, one that is so misunderstood and maligned that young women often "hate" this time as opposed to feeling the sacredness of it. When we are not taught and nurtured, we are out of balance and therefore uncomfortable. When we understand that something feels wrong but we don't have a sense of what balance looks or feels like, we spin. As women we seek what looks and feels like power in our sexuality by being as sexually alluring as possible. This is our current cultural paradigm. It is not balanced, and it backfires, because most of us want to be loved for who we are, not for what we look like. It also backfires because what we focus on grows, so if we are feeding being sexually alluring and becoming charged energetically by others' reactions to our efforts, then we are encouraged to continue ... and yet in the end, what have we amassed? Usually not anything that causes us to feel essentially valued. Our culture — TV, movies, music videos, all of it — is like the whisperings of a serpent from the garden of Eden telling us that there is power in sexuality, and there is. But it should not be the only power we reach for.

At some point all women grow older, and the ability to possess this kind of power fades. We are left scrambling to find an awkward balance between perceived cultural prowess and complete obsolescence. It's a path that leads to a kind of spiritual death as well as depression, for if we are no longer mothers or potential mothers, and no longer plump skinned, toned and dewy eyed, what are we?

If we have steeped ourselves in our own sacredness, learned to respect our bodies and honored our inner calling for self-nurturing and peace, then we age gracefully into wise women whose beauty is much deeper than the skin and whose power has anything but diminished.

68. God, Sex, the Church, and Issues of Control

Is Knowledge Bad?

I remember having a conversation with a Hasidic Jew one day while designing a garden for his older brother's wife. This man, my client's brother and a rabbi, was sitting in a patio area I had created in the shade. I was deadheading daffodils nearby. He had been chatting to me as I worked. The rabbi's fifteen-year-old daughter walked by us and he grew quiet. After she passed out of earshot, he leaned towards me and said quietly and conspiratorially, "I have to marry her off soon." I was taken aback by the intensity of his comment. I asked, "Why the rush?" He replied, "Before she touches herself and becomes ruined."

I was very aware that in days not that far gone (and still today in some areas of the world) it was not uncommon to marry off a daughter at age thirteen. But I knew and respected many Jewish families. In them the mother was a person of consequence. They were definitely *not* folks who would marry a daughter off young or be upset with her for discovering herself. What was I hearing here? That for Hasidic Jews, if a girl masturbates, she is considered "ruined"?

I'm sorry, I'm having trouble wrapping my brain around this .... Is knowing what brings you pleasure somehow bad? And for whom would it be bad? For the woman? Because somehow it will harm her? (Well, I don't know anyone who's gone blind yet!) I can't even imagine where that originated from biblically unless it was extrapolated from God's command to "go forth and multiply." One could potentially claim that a man masturbating was thwarting God's command because orgasm for a man results in his spilling his seed. If he does it by himself, then no multiplying is possible (a child cannot be conceived). However, women do not shed their eggs through orgasm, so I fail to see the implication of sin in a woman orgasming (especially by herself).

Adam and Eve Revisited

"Knowledge is bad" could be one interpretation of the story of Eve and the apple in Genesis, at least regarding the knowledge of good and evil. But there are also arguments that knowledge is power, and we will get into that later.

For now, I would like to scrutinize this story in Genesis. There exist internal inconsistencies that are as fascinating, as confusing and as controversial as one can find. These inconsistencies become evident as one delves into details of etymology and translation. Another reason to examine this story is because it has been used to control women for thousands of years.

If there are inconsistencies along with changes in the meaning resulting from translation, then how can we create anything honest and true from those beginnings? We need to examine these dots carefully. Remember that Albert Szent-Györgyi said:

> A discovery must be, by definition, at variance with existing knowledge. During my lifetime, I made two. Both were rejected offhand by the popes of the field. Had I predicted these discoveries in my applications, and had those authorities been my judges, it is evident what their decisions would have been.[220]

Albert Einstein said, "We cannot solve our problems with the same thinking we used when we created them."[221] In other words we must look at old things in new ways to change our paradigm. If you think the world is fine, and man is fine, and the earth is fine, then please, don't push yourself to look at anything differently.

But if you don't think that everything is fine, then perhaps we should heed these two great men, who believed there was real value to humanity in examining things that we take for granted in a whole new way. Einstein also said that "Unthinking respect for authority is the greatest enemy of truth." So please indulge me in looking at these things unconventionally. Although I am pushing the envelope, the inconsistencies and translation issues in the story of Adam and Eve *are* there. I ultimately hope to draw

---

[220] Albert Szent-Györgyi, "Science Quotes by Albert Szent-Györgyi," *Today in Science History,* https://todayinsci.com/S/SzentGyorgyi_Albert/SzentGyorgyiAlbert-Quotations.htm.

[221] "80 Albert Einstein Quotes to Inspire You for Life, *Addicted 2 Success,* https://addicted2success.com/quotes/80-albert-einstein-quotes-to-inspire-you-for-life/ (accessed 6-5-20).

not just your attention to the inconsistencies (although they are worth noting) for their own sake, but more so that you begin to see the consistent thread woven throughout the last several thousand years, reflecting choices and directions taken by the men in charge of our most powerful institutions, that all support disenfranchising women and maintaining them in cages, not just in the world, but within their own minds.

Both the Hasidic Jew's view of a girl touching herself and Eve's knowledge of good and evil raise the question: who exactly is knowledge bad for? Certainly, for beings with free will, the ability to discern right from wrong, good from evil, would be an important awareness. What is that saying? "Knowledge can set you free" but apparently not in this case ....

Snakes

Eve listened to a snake and ate fruit from the tree of knowledge (knowledge of good and evil, but let's put that in a different context). How would a woman touching herself and bringing herself pleasure have been viewed in those days? Could it have been similar to the view expressed by the rabbi brother of my client? If so, could we be talking about knowledge of what felt good to Eve sexually? And whom would that threaten?

It's also interesting to note another part of Genesis, specifically verse 1:22: "And God blessed them, saying, 'Be fruitful and multiply and fill the waters in the seas, and let birds multiply on the earth.' " God decreed that all creatures should do this, including humans, right? So God is, in essence, telling us to follow our inner urgings to procreate, is he not? Genesis doesn't include any negative stipulations regarding sex at this point.

So where did rules such as that sex can occur only inside marriage come from? And why? In Genesis God gives specific instructions on how humans and animals should live, including what they should eat. He tells us to go forth and multiply, but he never specifies marriage. He tells us to go forth and multiply, he causes sex to feel good, and women to be not only capable of multiple orgasms, but of carrying children from multiple fathers in one pregnancy. What is the real message from God here?

Let us peer into the garden again through the window of Genesis. It is unclear how much time passes between when Adam was created, when Eve was created, and how long after that the apple transgression occurred. But it seems as though time elapsed between these incidents — time for Adam, who is wandering around Eden, to feel lonely enough to ask God for a mate. And then time for Eve to become familiar with the Garden and the beings that dwelled there. But not much is mentioned after the initial creation story. We are left to wonder until Eve has the bad judgment to listen to a being of the Garden and eat of the fruit of the tree of knowledge of good and evil.

Obviously, this story is pivotal in Genesis, but it gets more intriguing if you look at the etymology of some of the key words. In Hebrew (the original language of Genesis) the "serpent" who beguiled Eve was *nachash*, which can be translated as an "angel of light" or the "shining one."[222] That's very interesting. Do you know what Lucifer means in Latin? Light-bearing. Now that's a twist from what we have been taught! Was Eve seduced by God's most beautiful angel instead of a slithering, scaled creature?

Why would it be important to change who tempted Eve from an angel of light to a serpent? Perhaps because some religious leaders didn't want us to have any sympathy for Eve? It is hard to empathize with a woman seduced by a snake! However, being seduced by an angel — many of us could sympathize with that!

Clearly the men who translated the Bible from Hebrew decided to substitute a snake for a light-bearing being. Why would they do that? Let's look at what we know about snakes for clues. They are cold blooded and they have slit eyes, like a cat. They have scales instead of skin, fur, or feathers. This makes them seem more foreign to humans compared to warm-blooded species. So, if I were looking to discredit women, a snake would be a far better choice of coconspirator than an angel.

Another interesting factor to me is that snakes resemble erect penises more than any other creature; more than worms, for instance, whose bodies do not have defined "heads." Was this a coincidence? Or is it a warning about giving in to sexual temptation? Were the translators implying that a penis led Eve astray? With what? Good sex, and *knowledge* of what turned her on? And what did the men who wrote the Bible say the snake presented Eve with that tempted her so much? ... "Knowledge."

Then we come to the snake himself (who has a distinctly masculine energy to me, although its gender is not specified). His actions are addressed by God in Genesis 3:13–15:

> The LORD God said to the serpent, "Because you have done this, cursed are you above all livestock and above all beasts of the field; on your belly you shall go, and dust you shall eat all the days of your life."

---

[222] "The Nachash in the Garden of Eden," *Freedom From Delusion*, https://freedomfromdelusion.blogspot.com/2014/12/the-nachash-in-garden-of-eden.html.

So God cursed snakes after the "apple transgression," proclaiming that snakes would "eat dust." Now I might take this whole thing a lot more seriously *if* snakes did in fact eat dust. However, not only do snakes not eat dust, but they are not confined to the ground (where I would keep a creature I intended to "eat dust").

Even though this point is not key, it illustrates the dichotomy between those that view the Bible literally versus those that view it allegorically. Whichever way you approach it, neither is accurate. Even though snakes are legless, they are actually able to swim and climb very well ... almost *as if they had been designed to do so.* In actuality, being legless gives snakes advantages over other legged reptiles — enough so that other creatures have evolved to be legless as well, including some lizards![223]

Have you ever seen a snake with vestigial legs? I have. It was bizarre to see a set of miniature (but not functional) legs shrunk tight against the reptile's body. I'm assuming it was a snake; there are more lizards with vestigial legs than there are snakes (and it can be difficult to tell the difference between them, at least for humans, but one would expect not to God).

There are no stories in the Bible about lizards offending God, yet both lizards and snakes have become legless. God knows all the creatures that he created; he would not punish a lizard for no reason. So being legless cannot be a punishment for snakes, while it is an advantageous adaptation for lizards.

If I was seeking to control people, using the legless reptiles as an example of God's ability to punish living beings would be the perfect teaching tool. Also the translation from light-bearing being to serpent was most likely chosen to show Eve in a bad light. And that bears sitting with. But there are other curious factors at play here, aside from a snake's erect penis resemblance.

Because of their ability to shed their skins, snakes have long been associated with rebirth and the feminine — possibly because of their resemblance to an umbilical cord, snakes were often seen as connecting humans to the earth. Snakes have had a long history of duality, being viewed as both healers and killers, benevolent and wrathful. This duality can be found in many cultures from the Near to Far East, in the ancient past as well as present day. The Egyptian goddess Mut, also referred to as "the resplendent serpent," and the god Atum (an Egyptian primeval creator deity) were sometimes found in snake form. In a fascinating article Andrew

---

[223] Mike Wall, "Are Legless Lizards Snakes?," https://www.livescience.com/40810-are-legless-lizards-snakes.html October 30, 2013 (accessed 5/12/17).

C. Skinner proposes that he has found testamentary evidence of both the dove and the serpent being linked to the Messiah. He goes onto say the dove was the only symbol that the devil cannot come in, so to try to pose as the Messiah, Satan assumes the shape of the serpent.[224]

In modern and post-modern Hinduism, Nagas and Nagini are respectively male and female deities whose lower half is a snake. They are viewed as nature spirits and are associated with water, protecting springs, wells, and rivers.[225] They are considered rain bringers and are thus connected with fertility. Nagas can also be either entirely in human or snake form[226] and are thought to become dangerous (capable of creating both droughts and floods) to humans that have harmed them or what they are protecting. They are also associated with dragons in the Orient.[227]

Snakes were the symbol of the Goddess-worshiping religions in Europe for centuries, as well as a symbol of healing adopted long ago by the medical profession — the Rod of Asclepius (a serpent entwined around a stick). This symbol evolved a bit, becoming two snakes wound around a rod, with wings. This symbol (the Caduceus) is still used by the medical profession.

Here's another interesting twist. If snakes were not seen as good, why would Christian European doctors have adopted the snake as a symbol of healing? Especially if a snake betrayed the Creator. My point is not really why, but rather to ask you to consider how often the men in charge of Christianity have picked and chosen the interpretation that serves their interests.

What Was God's True Goal?

Here is another curious part of the Genesis story. I just have to ask, "What's up with putting information in an apple anyway?" Why on earth would an almighty Creator have put knowledge that no one should access in a fruit? And then, to make matters worse, leave it hanging from a tree?

---

[224] Andrew C. Skinner, "Savior, Satan, and Serpent: The Duality of a Symbol in the Scriptures," *The Disciple as Scholar: Essays on Scripture and the Ancient World in Honor of Richard Lloyd Anderson*, https://scholarsarchive.byu.edu/cgi/viewcontent.cgi?article=1288&context=jbms.

[225] "Naga," *Wikipedia*, https://en.wikipedia.org/wiki/N%C4%81ga.

[226] Constance Jones and James D. Ryan. *Encyclopedia of Hinduism*. Infobase Publishing 2006, p. 300.

[227] "Indian Nagas and Draconic Prototypes" in Ingersoll, Ernest, et al., *The Illustrated Book of Dragons and Dragon Lore*. Chiang Mai: Cognoscenti Books 2013.

I could think of much better places to put it; a crystal would be a cool place. Or a stone; nobody eats those. Putting information inside food, information that is *forbidden,* strikes me as more than odd.

Think about it — God would have had to be pretty sure of controlling all the creatures in the world: ants and wasps, not to mention fruit flies (who can keep fruit flies away from any fruit? ... They just magically appear when you leave fruit out anywhere). What about birds, squirrels, rabbits, deer, and bear? Those are just few of the creatures I know that relish the taste of apples. Or did God not care if these other creatures ate the fruit of knowledge of good and evil?

As I write this, another possibility occurs to me. Has God evolved in all these centuries? Was the Creator of all a bit of a bully back then? Or were these stories about God altered to fit into a business plan (if you will), being used purposely to make people afraid to disobey (what they were told was) "God's will?" Or did humans' need for God as a frightening, controlling force change? Did they no longer need God to be so domineering? Perhaps churches were losing followers with such a harsh God?

If we take the story at face value, putting knowledge in a fruit hanging on a tree can be seen as a form of *entrapment* — thereby baiting not just humans but all the other creatures on this planet. Was God daring us to go against his word?

If it was a test (and if God loves us as his children), then why would he punish all descendants of those involved for eternity? Where is the value in such a process? Don't we evolve and grow from having made mistakes?

God is supposed to know our hearts; there is no hiding that we are rife with faults. Why bait us that way? The dots just don't connect for me.

Why give us free will, if God ultimately wanted complete subservience?

And what about Adam? He was older and therefore supposedly wiser than Eve. If he knew and respected God, why would he listen to Eve? Is he not responsible for his own actions?

So if we take this passage at face value, Adam could get away with no changes to his body because he *only* listened to Eve (even though he also ate of the apple). But Eve, who (only) listened to the snake (the Shining one, or a penis), was not only cast out of Eden, but made to suffer pain in childbirth as well as total subservience for eternity!

And what did the shining one seduce Eve into? Taking on knowledge. And what is the knowledge of good and evil if it is not the ability to judge the difference between the two. So Eve was seduced into taking steps to secure her own autonomy, and she wished to share this with Adam. I think it's interesting that she did not attempt to keep this knowledge to herself.

If Adam's listening to Eve made him less culpable, than why is the fact that Eve listened to the snake worse? Especially if the snake were actually a light-bearing angel?

Wasn't it ultimately the snake's fault? Both Adam and Eve were weak, but the men writing the Bible used this story to focus on women as the perpetrators of "evil." Eve's punishment doesn't end with her complete subservience to her husband in the home. It extends into her public life where she is not allowed to speak in church, ask questions, or grow into any positions of authority, not even being allowed to teach.

Also woven into the story of Eve being created from Adam's rib is the ability for a man to consider women property, with little to no say over their bodies.

Masculine and Feminine

We have already established that Genesis is fraught with inconsistencies, but how we interpret these can be quite different. For example, in the King James version Genesis 1:26 reads "Then God said let us make <u>man</u> in *our* image, in *our* likeness, ... and let <u>them</u> rule over ... " In 1:27 it continues "So God created man in his own image, in the image of God he created *them*; <u>male and female</u> he created *them*."

This is quite confusing. I had understood that Adam came before Eve, and that she (almost as an afterthought) was created from his rib; certainly not that God created them together, male and female in his image.

Remember, I look at the natural order of things to get a sense of how things actually are (before man's meddling) as well as how they are supposed to be. Let's face it, God or evolution has created an amazingly complex system of life and functioning here in our universe that we certainly do not have the ability to recreate. In other words, we do not understand how it all works or fits together, so every time we tamper with that order, we are playing Russian roulette! However, if we study how any organic system functions, it will give us clues to the natural order, which we are supposed to participate in. Again, it boils down to going with the flow or against it (the only difference here is that man has created his own order within God's natural order). Consequently we find ourselves having to go against mankind's flow, or order, to seek God's true order. We can see this order not by studying the words of "God" as written by men, but through the order of the universe, that man is only now beginning to tamper with.

Looking at life on our planet, these are the truths I see. The majority of life, whether plant, animal, insect or human, requires a male and female counterpart to reproduce (with some exceptions like amoebas). If everything on the planet were made in some fashion using the principles that God used to create, then the logical conclusion indicates that conception or creation in our universe requires masculine and feminine elements. The coming together of these two opposites is the easiest way to manifest or create on our planet.

Since there are truths within truths, let me ask you this: what does it mean for humanity that not only are our males and females at odds with each other, but so are the masculine and feminine sides of ourselves? Perhaps this rift has more far-flung effects than we have been looking for, and are therefore unaware of? This would be evident especially in our ability to manifest (create).

"Let us create them in our image" (Genesis 26 and 27). So let me ask you this: how is God "us" if God is just male? If we are created in God's image, then it does not seem likely that God is purely masculine — if God is *not* both male and female (or more than one being ...) How could man and woman be in God's image?

Again, I draw your attention to the rest of the creation that we are a part of. Unless you are an amoeba you will need a male/female counterpart to go forth and multiply. The King James Version in 1:22 says "And God blessed them, saying, Be fruitful, and multiply, and fill the waters in the seas, and let fowl multiply in the earth." God is telling the fish and fowl to breed, meaning presumably that "he" had created them as male and female as well.

Here is another thing I find interesting:

1:29 And God said, "Behold, I have given you every plant yielding seed that is on the face of all the earth, and every tree with seed in its fruit. You shall have them for food. 1:30 And to every beast of the earth and to every bird of the heavens and to everything that creeps on the earth, everything that has the breath of life, I have given every green plant for food." And it was so. [228]

This seems to be indicating that all creatures were designed to only eat vegetation! Two questions arise from that statement. Have the bodies of carnivores altered so drastically from the time Genesis was written till

---

[228] Genesis 1, English Standard Version, https://www.biblestudytools.com/esv/genesis/1.htm.

now? From empirical biological information, it looks like God created omnivores and carnivores ... not just herbivores. And second, if we are not supposed to eat other creatures, wouldn't this place them in a different light? If we followed this rule from the Bible, we would not have done the horrible things we have to our fellow inhabitants. Do you see where I am going with this?

Inconsistencies also exist not only in the translation of individual words but also in deciding which statements from the Bible should be observed. The men involved in creating church rules have chosen to focus not on God's word regarding diet but instead on who you can or can't have sex with, which is not included in Genesis at all.

Who gets to decide which translations are acceptable and which are not? One thing I notice is that keeping women down always seems acceptable. If these things are all open to interpretation, then why are only certain paths of interpretation that are acceptable?

Am I supposed to listen to Genesis as God's word? What about the fact that Eve didn't show up until 2:22? This leaves us scrambling to understand who was the other person included in "them" in the passages cited above.

Because *they* were instructed to go forth and multiply, we would logically assume that "other" is referring to a woman ... but not Eve. So this first woman would have been made exactly as Adam, in God's image, from earth. Equals they would have been, because unlike Eve, she was not a second thought. She was not a part of Adam; she was not created to be his helpmate.

Back in that "Psychology of Women" class at Antioch, our professor said that the original Hebrew word that had been translated as virgin actually referred to a "woman who was one unto herself," meaning she did not need a man to support her. *It did not refer to her hymen being intact.* So how did that interpretation change? And whom would the change benefit?

While we are on the topic of translations, did you know that the name Adam is derived from the Hebrew word *adamah*, meaning ground or earth (just as in Latin the word *homo* is linked to *humus*, also meaning earth).

Why would that be? Just because they (Adam and ...?) were made from earth? That's possible; another possibility that occurs to me is, was God naming mankind "from the earth" or "of earth" because man was supposed to be reminded of his inseparable connection to the earth? How would our lives be different if we honored that sacred connection?

It's obvious from how badly we have polluted the earth that we need to be reminded of this sacred, indivisible connection. But there are other possibilities; for instance, did God label this specimen "from earth" because he had created humanoids on other worlds that exist without soil?

Do we know for sure that we are God's only creation? I realize that this is not the way most people view these stories ... but it is interesting to look at facts and ask questions! Keep in mind this saying by Albert Szent-Györgyi, "A discovery consists of seeing what everybody has seen, and thinking what nobody has thought."[229] So consider me your outside the box thinker!

Who Actually Was the First Woman?

If we are sticking to the story as told in the Bible, then who was made with Adam? Who was the other part of "*them*"?

There *are* stories about Lilith. Have you ever heard of her? Lilith supposedly came before Eve. There are many who believe that Lilith was the second half of the "them" that is referred to in Genesis.[230] According to what I have read, Lilith was made, like Adam, from the earth itself. (This, by the way, is accurate. We are all made of minerals from the earth. Ultimately those minerals came from the stars, making Joni Mitchell's lyrics from her song *Woodstock*, "We are star dust, we are golden, and we've got to get ourselves back to the garden" almost prophetic on more than one account ... the stardust part, and our need to get "back to the garden" [in so many ways — remember how science is just discovering the benefits of things like forest bathing!].)

Just an aside here. Look at the depiction of Lilith in Figure 20 (page 354). Imagine that instead of the python wrapped around Lilith's body, there was a perfect, eternally young, glowing, well-endowed male body. I bet you would have a very different reaction. This was my point about the choice of changing light-bearing being to serpent!

---

[229] Albert Szent-Györgyi, https://www.brainyquote.com/authors/albert-szent-gyorgyi-quotes.

[230] Sampson Books, 3.9 *A Helpmate was Shown to Adam before Eve*, http://www.bitterwaters.com/bw_12_21_2018/the-case-for-lilith/the-biblical-case-for-lilith/3-9-a-helpmate-was-shown-to-adam-before-eve/.

[231]

Figure 20. Painting of Lilith by John Collier.

Getting back to Lilith, one story goes that Adam was not able to control Lilith, and she, being a strong and self-sufficient woman, left him and made her own way (perhaps she too was a "virgin," a woman one unto herself}. She supposedly even left Eden and refused to come back (not having been "cast out" at all). She imagined "outside the box" and made love to an angel. And not just any angel ... the Archangel Samuel. That's very interesting. Did both Lilith and Eve sleep with an angel?

It's also interesting to note that there are stories in the Bible of angels mating with humans. The offspring were claimed to be giants and many of them were reportedly violent. What's even more interesting is that there were many skeletal remains of giants found throughout the old and

[231] *Lilith* by John Collier 1892, public domain via Wikimedia Commons.

new worlds at the turn of the twentieth century.[232] Were these the result of angels mating with humans? That is what the Bible says.

Here's another strange twist on statements made in the Bible. Remember in Genesis we are told to go forth and multiply? And we (both males and females) are capable of finding great pleasure, as well as stress relief, through sex. Despite both these incentives, God did not give us any restriction as to whom we should have sex with. That is very interesting, is it not?

"God created them in his image," yet despite there being references to "them" later in Genesis, Adam complained to God about being lonely and needing help, and in an act of mercy (or to shut him up) God created Eve from Adam's rib, perhaps hoping that doing so would make her more pliable than his first female creation had been.

After Eve was created things seemed to go along fine, for ... days? weeks? years ...? Until that damn snake ... .

How to Create an Institution

None of this really makes much sense to me. Looking at the whole scenario, between Genesis and history what does make sense to me is the existence (throughout time) of enterprising human beings — people trying to make a profit off a good thing. God is a good thing; Jesus is a good thing. Manipulating the interpretation of the words of Jesus and or God could be very profitable if done right.

We have witnessed atrocities due to power plays throughout history ... wars that were started over land, resources and riches. If you were starting an empire and you needed followers and resources to support you, the more you could attain, the easier it would be for you. It's not too difficult to imagine some clever, power-hungry people manipulating the teachings of a humble spiritual leader, as well as events, to their advantage. We saw that in Hitler's Third Reich not so long ago, and I believe we are seeing it again here in the USA right now.

Natural disasters happen all the time: floods, droughts and years of pestilence. If I can convince you that your own actions are causing these things, then I can get your attention (who doesn't want good weather, plentiful crops, food on the table, and vibrant health?). The law of averages would make it so that at least 50% of the time these negative events would

---

[232] Watch "Giants Emerging Everywhere – They Can't Hide this,"
https://www.youtube.com/watch?v=sVmOnwng6gs.

correspond to someone doing something wrong (according to my teach-ings). I would just need to convince you that the other 50% of the time, *you* were still messing up on some level ... *or your wife was* ....

The next step would be for me to give you a list of what you needed to stop doing in order to prevent bad things from happening. Again 50% of the time following these practices would appear to positively affect your life. If this were coupled with some practices that actually benefited both you and the community, then I would gain creditability and begin to be-come very powerful indeed.

If I were smart, I would create celebrations that coincided with local religious holidays to help my religion find acceptance more easily. Many of Christianity's holidays fall on ancient pagan holy days. Christmas co-incides with both the Winter Solstice and Saturnalia (a popular holiday when, among other things, masters and slaves swapped clothing and the wealthy would pay rent for those who not afford it). Some other "coinci-dences" are Easter and St. Patrick's day, which fall close to the Vernal Equi-nox, and Halloween and Samhain.

In the search for ever-increasing control, once I had the elements men-tioned in place, I could fill your head with all manner of things, and you would not be able to tell truth from fiction. Especially if I wove in universal truths, then things I said would ring true. The more people I got to partic-ipate, the faster the ball would roll. A community of believers has its own force. If what was important to me was "winning" at any cost, then I would play off people's human nature — jealousy, fear and greed, as well as their sense of inadequacy, hurt, righteousness, etc. I could begin to influence large groups at that point.

It would take time and work to attain this status, but if I were quite brilliant, and got charismatic speakers/ministers who truly believed in my plan (or religious philosophy), and we used the teachings of a truly in-spired humanitarian, altering them just slightly ... I could create something powerfully evocative.

It's so easy to exploit people's weaknesses, rather than trying to edu-cate them into the arts of self-mastery and self-control (but where would a ruling class built on the backs of consumers be in a world like that?).

Gossiping

People have such deep seated needs to gossip and to judge others. Why is that? Does it make them feel better about themselves? If you are focusing on what someone else does, it takes your own and other peoples' focus off you. Using this facet of human nature within a group, the group itself would become dangerous to others who did not practice what "*we*" preached.

Hitler used these facets of human nature to forge a powerful, ugly, tool out of his followers. Unfortunately, from my perspective, Christianity has done the same.

It is such a shame that pointing a finger at an outside person or group, and labeling them "bad," is such a binding force in the human psyche ... and yet ... In the Bible it states, "When two or more are gathered in my name, there shall I be." Where exactly is God in the former? Jesus did not teach any of these things. Neither did the Buddha, nor is this type of behavior condoned in the Bhagavad Gita, nor in the teachings of Islam.

Sex as a Bargaining Chip

As an adult I can look at the views of some religions and say "What a brilliant business plan it was for someone to come up with the concept of controlling sex!"

I will absolutely grant that, if you have sex with someone who loves you, knows you, and cares for you, then you will be in a much better place than if you share yourself with someone who cares nothing for you.

However, that being true, if we take that truth and twist it a little, saying that it is against God or a "sin" to have sex out of "wedlock" (a ritual *only I* or my ministers can perform). Wow, great business plan! What a great way to gain lots of power. I would need to convince you that I had a secured pipeline to this God that I reported to.

Once that bit was in place and accepted, what would be next? Well, I would not want the populace to feel as though they could just dissolve these "contracts." That would weaken my position. I would need to make it another "sin," if you break this bond that I tell you that God has established with my ritual of "permissible joining."

Back in those days, living in a community made survival a good deal easier, so a great punishment would be *being cast out* ... not only of this community but from the God whom I have a direct pipeline to. Depending on where and when you lived, that could literally be a life or death sentence that I was threatening you with. That's pretty powerful.

The authors of such a plan would just have to be patient, clever, and willing to be cruel and devious to make it work. They would have to care more about power and the success of their institution than for individuals and humanity.

In order to make it seem reasonable to ask a populace to divest itself of its natural sexual tendencies, the people I ordain to "minister" my plans and rules would need to be even more pious than the folks I was looking to convert. So making the ordained ministers renounce their "human nature" completely looks good on the outside. Yep, my ministers are so pious and so committed to God that they never, ever have sex!

Brilliant! Except ... Telling ordained ministers that they cannot have sex *at all* turned out to have serious negative consequences. It's a perfect example of what happens when paradigms suppress human nature, and illustrates what happens to these denied feelings in the subconscious. It's rarely pretty, and often completely opposed to what people strive for in their conscious lives.

69. Managing Ourselves Better

Free Will?

We really *can't*, and *shouldn't*, attempt to cut ourselves off from the gifts that we were created with. It is not why we were given them. Denying them causes problems. Learning to understand them, to work with them, to focus them with intent, to direct them, these lead to better societies. It is better to give them viable avenues for expression that do not hurt the individual or the community — while leaving out judgment —as long as no harm is done. This is what we should strive for. In the Bible we are told, "Judge not lest ye be judged." Why would God give us free will if he wanted strict adherence to authority? It would seem more logical to assume that God saw a value, a purpose, for humankind to use that free will. How can we use free will when our cultures and our religious institutions preach that there is only one way to do anything correctly? How can people find their own wisdom in that? If we are children, then learning the difference between good and evil, right and wrong, would help us become better people. If we grew up in cultures where we were shown different outcomes of choices that were in our power to make, this would ultimately create wise people who considered their actions in terms of consequences, not in terms of immediate gain.

In many cultures we find statements that a person's true wealth is within. Which way did God intend humankind to achieve spiritual maturity? By it being beaten into them, making them afraid to trust themselves? Or by self-awareness?

What if instead of using guilt, our teachings presented the lessons through sensory awareness and example? I believe this is why Lakota children were cradle board trained. Having periods of time where they were not allowed to explore their world through touch and taste caused them to focus on their other senses. This created calmer, thoughtful young people, fully aware that there was much more to life that just its physical side. This fosters right conduct, which naturally includes the consideration of the quality of life for all beings.

Children raised in such a manner would see the benefits of self awareness and would begin to examine themselves and their motives in direct response to any unwanted occurrences in their lives. In time they would see clearly that they were the generators of much of their reality.

All of the practices in this book help to bring one closer to self-mastery, but they are not the only ones. Remember all roads teach us something. But no matter which path you take, you cannot have self-mastery without self-awareness. And as you have probably gathered by now, I am not talking about self-deprivation or super-intense discipline to attain this state either (although those are paths one can take.)

Honest self-examination (without condemnation or guilt) allows one to take the necessary actions to create the life one wishes to live. Knowledge is power.

Knowledge of self includes honest assessment of one's drives. Learning to deal in a healthy manner with strong drives takes a lot of work, not unlike flexing a muscle for the first time. If you have ever had a muscle atrophy due to injury or surgery, you know it is not easy to get it back in shape. At first it can seem almost impossible to get it to move at all.

Dealing with Our Inner Nature

It takes practice to become strong enough to channel the really powerful stuff in a productive way. Powerful stuff includes anything that triggers an intense inner emotional response, like pain (physical or otherwise), rage, passion, etc.

The opposite of this is denial. In denial, there is no practicing, nor gaining mastery of anything — except the mastery of keeping ourselves in the dark. Remember what I've said about anything that divides us weakens us. Denial divides you from recognizing your true self. If you can't see it, you can't possibly develop skills to deal with it in a productive way.

So, what negative side effects would there be from an institution who insisted that its highest-ranking members deny their sexuality?

As we looked at in "Manifesting and Mindfulness," our awareness is like a light, shining in the darkness. Imagine then the conscious removal of that light, of that awareness, from our sex drives. Doing so sends that strong stirring into the dark, fertile fields of our subconscious, where we have *zero* control over what happens. The very name subconscious tells you that this area operates *below our conscious awareness.* Why would you develop a practice that routinely sends strong unwanted, socially undesirable, unacceptable drives/emotions here? It's a sure recipe for disaster.

Some men who wanted to dedicate their lives to God and had to renounce sex in order to do so have committed horrible atrocities because of the way this denied drive, relegated to the subconscious, expressed itself. It is a perfect storm, creating people who act out subconsciously, as well as for creating "out of control" appetites.

The antidote? We need to be taught and we need teachers! Teachers who know the power of these drives and have had personal experience channeling them creatively and positively. Leaders who can lead by example (a good example). These teachers/leaders could guide us in how to sit with the intensity, channel the energy, fight the good battle within ourselves and become strong and whole.

We also need to place value on this practice as a society, as well as have communities where all parts of us are accepted. I don't just mean that every type of person is accepted, but that the whole you is accepted. "All of you is welcome here." How did it feel to hear that spoken in your mind? How did that feel in your heart? Did you feel like crying? I did when I first heard those words spoken. For human beings to be able to heal and move on, in therapy, in relationships, in life, we need to feel deeply as though every part of us is accepted. And then we need to self-assess whether how we act around these different parts of ourselves is creating the responses from the world around us that we desire. If our lives are not reflecting back to us the scenarios we crave, then we need to look at our behavior.

This is the difference between older cultures and ours. Some of our ancestors in the not-too-distant past (and probably all cultures if you look back far enough) utilized the in-depth study of human nature to help its people transform or transmute issues. They depended on tribal cohesion to survive, so their intention was to help bring people into balance with themselves and their environment, because this led to health of the individual as well as the group. It was very good medicine. For example, many of the Native American Nations had rituals for warriors returning from war, to help them reintegrate into their former lives.

Conquest-era Aztecs believed that the cosmos and its human inhabitants were connected by a self-generating and regenerating energy that is sacred. "Knowledge, truth, value, rightness, and beauty were defined in terms of the aim of humans maintaining their balance as well as the balance of the cosmos. Every moment and aspect of human life was meant to further the realization of this aim."[233]

Beltane (discussed later in this chapter) is a great example of an ancient ritual that allowed human nature to freely express itself once a year. Even the gladiatorial arenas of Rome were designed release parts of human nature so that folks could coexist in larger communities.

Today, with few to no wise men or wise women to teach us the techniques to master these powerful emotions, we flounder. Removing teachings that show us how to control (with the goal of channeling) sexuality, anger, passion, etc. and replacing them with instructions to ignore these powerful energies ensures that we will run amok.

There are no stipulations by God in Genesis regarding sex except that we should "Go forth and multiply." Given that humans usually enjoy sex and were given free will ... What does that suggest to you? I imagine that there must have been a lot of sex taking place back then. Apparently even sex between angels and women is mentioned in Genesis, resulting in the Nephilim (large people or giants).[234]

Sexual Energy

We discussed the various reasons why it was advantageous for men to control sex, but are there any actual benefits to renouncing sex? The concept of divesting yourself of sexuality to attain a heightened spiritual state did not start in Christianity. It has been touted as giving men greater energy for centuries. In early Rome the Vestal Virgins[235] were chosen between the ages of 6 and 10. As part of their training they were required to dedicate their bodies to the goddess for thirty years and remain celibate during that time. On a positive note they were paid a salary by the state for their services and received a pension for the rest of their lives at the end of their thirty-year term. Unlike Christianity's lifelong celibacy commitment for male clergy, these Virgins had a chance to be human after their service.

Having those benefits at the end of a long period of self-denial would probably make those deprivations easier to bear. Still, the punishment of

---

[233]James Maffie, "Aztec Philosophy," *Internet Encyclopedia of Philosophy*, https://iep.utm.edu/aztec/.

[234]"Who Were the Nephilim?" *Christian Standard Bible*, https://csbible.com/who-were-the-nephilim/.

[235]Elda Biggi, "Rome's Vestal Virgins: Protectors of the City's Sacred Flame," *National Geographic History Magazine*, https://www.nationalgeographic.com/history/history-magazine/article/vestal-virgins-of-ancient-rome.

breaking that oath was death — a pretty harsh sentence for falling prey to one's inner nature, instilled in us by our Creator.

So although Christianity took the whole virgin thing to a new level and created rules around coupling not found in Genesis, the concept of an energetic or spiritual benefit to celibacy came long before, as did the idea that energy generated sexually could be used for other things. But we will address that a bit later; for now, let us look at why some advocate renouncing intercourse. And is it actually intercourse or is it the orgasm itself?

Is there a benefit to not orgasming? Is there a difference between orgasm and ejaculation? The benefits in abstaining from sex in general are fairly obvious; you don't have to worry about conceiving, for one thing. There were times in history when survival has been so tenuous for humans that not conceiving would increase the chances of survival among women, and ultimately the family or tribe. The other benefit is not having to worry about STDs. But you do not hear that being discussed in any spiritual textbooks. What you do hear about in textbooks on Kundalini, martial arts, and yogic teachings (to mention a few) is that especially for a man, participating in sexual activity, becoming aroused, and not ejaculating, imbues the body with extra energy that gets depleted when he ejaculates.

Think about it for a moment. When a man ejaculates, his sperm and his energy shoot forth from his body, like a suddenly exploding fountain. Where do they go? We can see where the seed goes, but what about the energy? According to traditional teachings they are "wasted."

It is different with a woman. When a woman orgasms, she does so within her own body. Occasionally liquid is released forcefully, but not her eggs. A woman's energy stays more within her body, building with each orgasm. Unlike a man, she does not deplete her fertility with orgasm. A man depends on orgasm to produce offspring. Not so a woman. If that were the case, a woman would never conceive from rape.

So there are some real reasons why orgasm in men and women is different. Only men ejaculate, but would it surprise you to learn that the ancient texts teach that both men and women can orgasm, without losing this essential energy? What these ancient teachings are implying is that celibacy in and of itself would not produce the same benefits as if the man were arousing himself and stopped from reaching the point of ejaculation.

For a man, the conscious, controlled use of this method produces a storehouse of energy within his body that he can learn how to utilize in other ways. Martial artists cultivate this energy for the express purpose of increasing their abilities, both offensively and defensively. This energy can be used to heal, and it can be used to harm. Using our energy to harm hurts us in many ways that we have not been made aware of. You have heard of Karma, the concept that what we do comes back to us? Wiccans who consciously build and use energy daily operate under the motto, "Do as ye will as long as ye harm none." They also have a saying that what you do to others comes back at you three times greater. Many spiritual or mystical teachings emphasize the consequences of the energy we put out, since this energy magnetizes and shapes the reality we experience. We explored this in the "Manifesting" chapters earlier. So conscious use of our energy, our thoughts, our actions and our words helps us create our now. Does it make any sense to turn a blind eye to all this?

Also, if God created these abilities, and if the act of sexual arousal builds energy that can either be used consciously (with training) to heal or harm, are we wasting a gift from God by not receiving these trainings?

By continuously "throwing" the spun-off energies of orgasm in women and ejaculation in men to the wind, are we sinning? If sex and sexual energy can be used to heal (and believe me they can), is it not a sin that these sacred practices have been reduced to base acts, and even capitalized upon?

Sexual energy and anger are the only energies we are taught to run through our bodies here in the West. It is actually funny; our society accepts a person who displays anger inappropriately, and it encourages a focus on unbalanced sexual energy, but people who use their energy for healing are looked upon with suspicion! Honestly, how bizarre! It's on a par with sacred healing herbs being sprayed with deadly toxins so that we can have useless ornamental lawns!

But no matter how you feel about it, energy is energy, whether it is negatively charged or positively charged. Energy can neither be created nor destroyed, yet it can change form (as we learned in "The First Law of Thermodynamics"). Sexual energy is released through an orgasm, and unless this is done with intention, the energy simply dissipates from here, wasted (just like a man's seed). Or it can be allowed and encouraged to move up through the energy centers of your body, your chakras.

Sexual energy is created between your lowest two chakras, your root chakra and your sacral chakra. Do you remember which chakra is next in line after these two? It is the solar plexus, the seat of our will, so if you have a weak will, or your third chakra is out of balance, you will not have much luck in generating enough willpower to transmute or direct this energy, and most likely it will rule you.

The same thing is true of your second chakra. According to Scott Jeffrey, author of *A Practical Guide to Sexual Transmutation*:

> When the sacral chakra is in balance, this drive for sexual pleasure stays in moderation. But when something obstructs and weakens this sexual energy center, it leads to all kinds of problems like sex addictions, perversions, porn addictions, and aggressive behavior.[236]

Learning to work with this energy so that you can incorporate it into your other energetic systems has many benefits. Sexual energy that is shifted into your other chakras will give you raw power to manifest, create, and maintain the things you want in life.

Cultures from around the world work with transmuting sexual energy; Kundalini Yoga and Tantric Yoga are two examples. Wiccans use sexual energy to manifest things consciously, creating rituals with partners for specific purposes.

In Egypt there were temples dedicated to healing with intimacy achieved through lovemaking. The holy priestesses that resided there and administered these healing rites were highly regarded. If you think about it, it makes a lot of sense. There are very few times in our lives, especially for men, where we can open ourselves as wide or let our guard down as much as during intimacy with a sexual partner that we trust. Being held, comforted, stroked, soothed — most of us only experience this with our parents or with lovers. The "problem" with our lovers is that unless there is a great deal of conscious commitment to treating each other as sacred beings, the day to day relationship dynamics creep in, and very few people can stay focused on *healing* as the ultimate goal.

When you incorporate being held tenderly and you experience being regarded in a sacred way, it allows you to take these feelings in deeply, at a cellular level. When you incorporate all of these elements, with intention to heal, into a ritual or ceremony it is so very powerful.

Remember a natural healer is highly intuitive, sensitive to energy, and loathe to cause harm. The priestess of these temples (sometimes referred to as "sacred whores") were natural healers who had received training in many healing techniques. Being intimate with such a woman who is completely present for you, to heal you, and nurture you, would be powerful indeed. There are so few experiences in our world where we simply

---

[236]Scott Jeffrey, *A Practical Guide to Sexual Transmutation*, https://scottjeffrey.com/sexual-energy-transmutation/ (accessed February 15, 2020).

receive energy and attention from another person ... with no strings attached. That is one of the things I love about giving and receiving Reiki.

A warrior coming back from the front line could benefit greatly from the wholistic healing he would receive at a temple like this. So while some humans saw sex as something to rise above, or to control for their personal gain, others used sex as a healing vehicle.

A semi-modern-day equivalent might be found in Japan, in the form of the Geisha, women who are highly trained in many art forms and in all aspects of intellectual pursuits. Just being in the presence of these women is very healing because they are so gracious and aware.

If we are not being prudish about our human nature, it is so much easier to establish acceptable healthy outlets for it. For example, Beltane was a holy day for the Celtic pagans where fertility was celebrated. It was a ritual performed by every eligible member of a village to return the fecundity to the earth in the spring. All celebrants were masked and anonymous, dancing around the Beltane fire. After a time, couples paired off to copulate in the fields. The concept was to renew the fecundity of the earth by coupling upon her and allowing the energies to mingle and rise. Even if it is not your cup of tea, you will have to admit it served to allow some very real sexual tensions that built up in small villages to be released once a year. Both men and women had a chance to experience this freedom of sexuality, with no judgements, no pointing fingers, just an opportunity for human nature to crawl out from the intense restraints our complex societies force us to wear.

Incidentally, children conceived at this time were considered blessed, and the identity of their biological fathers was of no consequence. How does that make you feel?

As the guiding forces of our cultures have moved us deeper into the belief that we are separate and removed from, as well as being "above," the natural world, they needed to remove us from our own internal nature as well.

People committed to, or locked into, living in such communities couldn't afford to admit to having these natural reactions. So men who wished to believe (or pretend) that they could divest themselves of unwanted erections would need to blame them on an outside force. Women are safer to blame, than, let's say, the *devil* would be ... (there was a period of time when admitting the devil had gotten into you might not be good for your health) although we still hear cries of "The devil made me do it."

It was convenient for a man with "impure" thoughts to blame the woman walking by for his arousal. It was *her fault*: the way she dressed, walked, or talked. We still hear this type of scapegoating in rape cases.

Conclusion: Self Responsibility

Can we switch our gaze from the seduction of judging others and learn instead to gaze upon ourselves? Can you look at yourself with love, forgiveness, and acceptance, as well as being honest about where you require your own healing?

None of us is perfect. But if you can learn to love your wounded self as you would love a child, or at least begin by looking at yourself as a child, then looking at yourself becomes not a judgment, but a moment full of potential and a gift. "What?" you say ... "Looking to myself is painful. Growing and changing is painful, as well as being fraught with insecurity and discomfort." Sadly, this is true; it is why judging others is so seductive. It is a wonderful distraction from our own need for growth and healing.

All I can tell you is that a babe feels the same way about leaving the womb. Yet we all know the consequences if it stays there too long or gets stuck in the birth canal ... it will die. We also know that there are incredible opportunities for unimagined growth, happiness and fulfillment for the babe that lets itself go through that vastly uncomfortable, unfathomable process that represents the cessation of all that it has known — birth.

As always ... you have a choice.

70. Trust versus Faith

Trust really has to do with "knowing." You can't fully trust without *knowing* that you can count on something. Faith is more based on "feeling." You have faith in something because you believe in the principle, or you believe it exists.

You can have either faith or trust because you have had positive experiences that lead you in that direction. You can build trust and faith in similar ways, and they can be destroyed in similar ways ... except:

You can have a leap of faith, but not a leap of trust. Similarly, you can have blind faith, but not blind trust. Faith is an unknowable quality. You may never be able to prove to another the existence of what has caused you to have faith.

You can be blind to truth, and so trust unwisely (that happens a lot) but there is no blind trust. Likewise, we can make a decision that we are going to move forward with someone or something (based not on what we intuit or discern from them) but rather from an idea of a desired outcome. In such cases we can feel that our trust has been betrayed, but really we are pulling the proverbial wool over our own eyes.

Trust is something that forms with time, and requires concrete knowledge of what you are trusting. There is an aspect of judgment that goes into true trust. Not so with faith ... Faith requires closing your eyes and allowing yourself to be guided by something else — the proverbial leap of faith.

True faith can connect you to a deep source of peace. It is hard to describe but it is both nebulous and solid as a rock at the same time, like possessing an unshakable awareness that does not reside in the mind. It's funny, because in the West we have a bizarre reverence for the mind and believe that it is our one source of trustworthy information. We distrust the heart, as well as other organs of perception like the gut or the third eye. This mind that we have such reverence for, however, is easily led astray. Its perceptions are not based solely on facts, but also on cultural and familial beliefs. This is further complicated by the fact that an individual's perception of any event can be radically different from that of another individual standing several feet away. These perceptions are created by personal experience as well as preferences. How can we balance this? We need to be still and calmly observe what is around us. It is not an endeavor that many of us have the luxury to pursue with our hectic, modern lifestyles. And I believe the trend towards extreme busyness that we are forced to adopt just to survive is harmful to us. It creates at the very least an exhausting fog that we must strain to peer through. At worst it creates unthinking cogs, who plod along, one foot in front of the other, doing as they are told, perennially asleep.

As we discussed earlier, it's hard to find something if you are not looking for it specifically. So if you encourage a population to be asleep, who benefits? Not the individuals who are asleep! They are very unlikely to see anything new or out of the ordinary. Similarly, if you are asleep, you cannot respond appropriately to outside stimuli. This can cost you dearly, even sometimes your life.

Faith can connect you to much more than yourself. But the worlds it connects you to are the unknowable ones, the un-seeable, untouchable ones. For me, the physical location in my body where faith resides fluctuates slightly between my third eye and heart, but it's mostly in my heart area. For many it is predominantly in their gut, their heart, third eye, or some combination thereof.

So yes, faith and trust are different. Trust starts in my head, and then if my trust is proven accurate, it begins to grow.

Once trust is destroyed, there is only one way of getting it back, and that is *if* whoever damaged your trust becomes consistently 100% trustworthy. The person needs to be impeccable with his or her word and subsequent actions. He or she needs to do this for a long time, remaining completely consistent in words and actions. And that does not happen often.

Trust grows, but it also can wither and die. Trust is mathematically inclined. You can add to it or subtract from it, but once it is gone, hard, diligent work is the only thing that can reestablish it, one inch at a time. Such an endeavor could only be possible if the transgressor became 100% trustworthy from the moment that he or she asked for forgiveness.

Faith is different; you can have your faith shaken but somehow not broken. It goes back to that intangible sense of unshakable awareness that does not reside in the mind. To become more fully seated in one's faith can sometimes require a proverbial leap of faith.

Faith can move mountains, but trust cannot. Why is that? Trust cannot move a mountain because it is connected to your expectations. Expectations are not clear. We have all kinds of expectations that we are not even aware of. For example, we may have been abandoned as children, and deep inside we have an expectation of being abandoned again and an expectation of love hurting. When we attempt to trust, the energy is muddled by our expectations.

Faith is more elusive; it does not reside in the mind. It is a more intuition/heart/feeling based sensation, that can be focused through thought and intention. It is a stronger vibration than thoughts alone. In the realm where faith operates, all things are possible.

You certainly cannot develop your intuition without faith. Faith, discernment, and intuition feel very similar to me. They are connected. It makes sense; why would our source/God/Goddess *not* be connected to our ability to have and experience faith? Like a muscle you need to work the concepts and the sensations of these three (faith, discernment and intuition). This is how you develop a relationship with them and they with you. After some time, you will learn to trust these things for, as a relationship to them builds within you, so does your trust in them.

Trust only occurs in relationship. Trusting your own process is one of the greatest gifts you could ever give yourself. And it does mean living a life that attempts to be "impeccable with your word" as Don Miguel Ruiz says in *The Four Agreements.*[237]

When we operate in life without actively digesting the wealth of information coming into our instrument, through our vibrationally sensitive gut material, we don't feel well. When we don't learn how to interpret this information, we lose so very much. Likewise with the wisdom that resides in our hearts, or the intuitive information shared with us by spirit, that is available to us in our third eye.

I don't believe God asked us to turn our backs on this information. Why would our Creator have gone to all the trouble to give us those abilities if we were not supposed to use them?

Or, if you believe in evolution, why would our bodies have evolved in this manner if it were not important to our survival? I believe it was people (men), who wanted to control others and make money off them, that labeled these natural gifts as bad. They created stories about how dangerous it was to experiment with being open to this information. We have

---

[237]Don Miguel Ruiz, *The Four Agreements*, Amber-Allen Publishing, Inc. July 10, 2018.

been told that our soul is somehow threatened by learning to open ourselves to our gifts and to connect with nature around us (and within us). But let me ask you this. If you can't control your thoughts and don't know how to open and close your energy centers, how can you be any safer from negative energy or spirits than if you practice developing these skills?

71. Placing Value, A Choice

Is it really surprising that it is so hard for us to learn to trust ourselves? From my perspective, we have been carefully trained to fear these built-in early warning parts of ourselves. Organized religions saw the benefit in having followers who were afraid to think or discern for themselves. The Church has a long tradition of opposing many things that might cause people to question its authority and theology. When Galileo proved that the earth revolved around the sun, the Church wished to discredit him. Its first response was to publicly burn his books. When that didn't shut him up and ruin his credibility, they banned his books. When that did not prevent his theory from gaining followers, they placed him under house arrest for life, labeling his work as suspected heresy. Why? Because the church leaders proclaimed that everything revolved around the earth. Any time something threatened the security of the position they held, they tried first to absorb it or control it, but if they couldn't, they labeled it heresy, the devil's work, and destroyed it. If the church had never done such things, I would have no problems with it as an institution. But I cannot forgive the church its past any more than I can the Nestlé company (as discussed in "The Earth and Us").

Do you know why modern-day descendants of Europeans have next to no teachers for energy work and intuition? It's because they were almost all burned at the stake for being heretics and witches. This happened so many times to cultures who lived close to the earth, people who never lost sight of the value of the growth of the inner human. These cultures didn't invent massive tools of war, because *what value is war to the growth of a human being?* They focused instead on competitive forms of self-mastery, as opposed to weapons of mass destruction. Not that there were not wars —it's just that they were very different. For example, according to a Lakota friend of mine, their war parties were usually smaller than 30 braves. The skirmishes were also mostly hand to hand combat, where each person's strength, speed, stamina, as well as grace and skill, were called upon. This is much different from folks blowing their enemies up from afar, or shooting them from a distance with high powered rifles.

War's value lies in acquiring wealth, land, or resources. Hand to hand combat, jousting, sword fighting, wrestling, these are all arts that require personal mastery to become proficient. There are codes of conduct with each of these forms, and in a single duel, no matter what the type, there can hardly be the spoils that would result from taking over an entire city.

Naturally the cultures that valued warfare developed more and more ways to kill from a distance, even to level armies or towns. They never had to acknowledge the beings that they were killing, making it easier to demonize (or at least de-humanize) them.

Some cultures valued nonmaterial qualities such as wisdom, traditions, arts, healing; these were considered most important and granted the practitioner prestige. These cultures did not value war as highly, as can be seen in the Great Law of Peace written by the Haudenosaunee. The Great Law included many checks and balances to ensure that disputes ended in deliberations, rather than war, for the six nations that participated in it.

Our current culture places most value on the growth of the outer human. On our entire planet I believe that Bhutan is the only country that actually counts the happiness of its population as a gross national product. That's pretty cool, and you can bet that their joy in life is not derived from the amassing of material status or products. There is a wonderful talk by Gaur Gopal Das called *Looking for Fulfillment from Life,* that you should watch. Below is a transcript[238] of his talk (imagine this being delivered in a melodious voice with a heavy Indian accent).

> Whether you drive a Volkswagen or you drive a Bentley, the road remains the same, isn't it? Whether you speak on a Samsung or you speak on an iPhone X, whoever you are calling remains the same, isn't it? Whether you're flying economy or you're flying business, the destination where you are heading remains the same, isn't it? Whether you are wearing a simple Fastrack or you wear an Omega or Rolex, the time remains the same, isn't it?
>
> It's quite amazing how we work ourselves up so much with increasing the standard of living that we forget to increase the standard of our life. And which is why wherever I travel, I make

---

[238] Gaur Gopal Das, *Looking For Fulfillment,* https://ganeshgpks.blogspot.com/2018/06/gaur-gopal-das-video-with-script.html?m=1. To watch the actual video, see https://youtu.be/Mxnf9YNoIR8.

an appeal to people, there is nothing wrong with an Omega, there is nothing wrong with a Bentley, God bless you with that and if you have it drive it — no problem.

But in trying to enhance and increase and improve the standard of your living, please, please do not compromise with the standard of your life.

It's not the standard of your living that makes you happy, it's the standard of your life that makes you happy.

And very often, we forget to give attention to those things that can truly make us happy, those things that can make us happy which is why I always say things that I am talking about have utility value, right? Not happiness value.

Travel business class or first class, travel — no problem!! Drive a Bentley — no problem! But in doing so, never ever compromise on those problems that also improve the standard of your life. And therefore, I always say, some people are so poor, so poor, so absolutely poor that all they have is MONEY. That's all they have! If all you have is money, you are the poorest person in the world. I consider that life a poverty-stricken life.

Because there is more to life than money and there is way more to life than what money can buy. And therefore, I many times say, if you truly want to know how rich you are, drop a tear and see how many hands come to wipe that tear.

Ladies and Gentleman, our happiness, our happiness and our increased life of standard are not the things, it's in people. It's relationships. It's meaningful, heartfelt deep bonding of love that bring fulfilment to the heart. It's those meaningful exchanges of love that we share with each other in relationships that bring true joy to the heart. And isn't it the greatest irony, that something that brings the greatest fulfilment, we very conveniently neglect in just running after increasing and enhancing the standard of living.

In order to be truly happy, we have to start in our skin. We cannot have the relationships we crave when we are so confused by mass propaganda. Instead of understanding ourselves (which gives us empathy to understand others), we are encouraged to work a forty-hour work week (or more). When do we have any time to look at or "fix" anything? We don't; we just get wound tighter and tighter. When our culture and our history support disconnection, we are at a distinct disadvantage.

Not having our inner reality validated, we turn to the outer, man-made reality for everything. We are told that if we follow the mandates for "success" in this outer world, we will find happiness. But many of us accept empty years of hard work and unfulfillment in the pursuit of the outer world's promise. What do we end up with? Accumulated layers of gunk and junk, and an internal loneliness or emptiness that can eat you alive if you are not careful.

We can't express our needs; indeed, we don't even feel comfortable with or accept many of them. We spew anger when we are in pain because we have such a buildup of unexpressed emotions. Anger is wielded like a weapon, because we have not been taught how to communicate anger in a constructive way. Most of what we learn in this society about anger is how to "win" at being angry.

We are not taught to navigate the inner worlds that dwell within all of us, because up until now, our society's paradigm did not value or even recognize them. So as we fumble through life, we wonder why we are miserable, why we don't like ourselves (many have no concept of true self-respect, having been driven by trying to attain the sexy car, Barbie-doll trophy wife, or MacMansion). We are surprised when our relationships fail. We don't understand why we are attracted to the wrong people, we overeat, enjoy losing ourselves in drinking or drugs or sex. We are left drifting, feeling empty, and somehow cheated, after closely following society's mandates for decades.

And this is all because we have been trained to look for immediate results, and/or we have been told that there are plateaus where we will experience "having arrived." I always imagined this place would feel safe (financially secure, healthy, with 2.5 kids and a house with a white picket fence ...). Yet any time I have reached any one of these goals, there was no "seventh day of rest." Maintaining the things I worked for required more work to maintain — an endless cycle of stress. When do we arrive at these plateaus? When do we find these breathing spaces of ease? Most of us don't, because they cannot be attained by chasing them, but rather by making the conscious choice to include them in our daily lives. Again, this is not something that is handed to us from the outside, but instead something we choose to create and steep in.

How far down those paths are you? When did you realize it wasn't working for you? Sometimes it takes a shattering of one of the major facets of our "dream life" for us to wake up. Departure of a spouse, loss of a job that you thought was forever, loss of health, or a realization of loss of youth, all these can eventually lead to waking up.

But then where do you go? Many of us are waking up, but we awaken alone, without a safety net. We are getting strong feelings that we need to change what we are doing, but the solution can mean walking away from everything we have been taught will protect us. Incidentally, these teachings have mostly been lies, and we know it. But knowing does not mean it is comfortable to walk away from what we have been promised will take care of us.

Are you aware enough of your feelings to get anything out of therapy? Therapy is very worthwhile if you are committed to getting to the bottom of why you are where you are and if you have a good therapist.

Medication? It has its place for sure, but has side effects as well, and while it can give you a break from the intensity of what you experience, by itself it doesn't really heal you (sometimes we really need that break from intensity though). Yoga? Meditation? Both of these are good. What is best is whatever takes you inward and connects you outward at the same time. Sit with a tree, or many. Be by the ocean, listen to the birds; what do you feel when you do that? You may find tears leaking out of your eyes or streaming down your face. You may feel peace or joy. You might feel as if you are being held. Look at these experiences as views through a new door that has opened. Look and listen with new expectations, and have faith. The creation, of which you are a part, has always been here for you. God is in every tree, rock, blade of grass, and creature. Open up to feeling this connection — it can sustain you when the human world lets you down. I know this because it is the only reason that I am still alive on this planet.

You have, most likely, faithfully listened to those around you and followed the recipe for happiness and success that our culture teaches. Most likely you have not found what you needed because our current paradigm was developed to adapt humans into cogs, creatures who don't know how to find their own way. If we can't find our core and be grounded there, we are easy prey for big businesses like the pharmaceutical companies and for religious institutions.

I am writing this book to help shed light on how we got here and how we can find our way back. Look at history with new eyes. Look at our bodies, neurology, biology and psychology the same way. Science has finally developed sensitive enough equipment that it can, and is, validating what our ancestors discerned about the world around us. Ask new questions. Why are we here? What are the actual physiological abilities designed into our bodies? What were they developed for? Who actually benefits from our current paradigms? What actually makes sense to me? These are great places to begin.

72. Developing a Relationship with Your Sixth Sense & More!

I find it interesting that mainstream paradigms lead us to question the existence of a sixth sense. I don't just work with my sixth sense; I work with my seventh and eighth as well! The senses I am referring to are not assigned a number permanently. In other words, you could switch the numbers around and it would not change a thing. So for now I will call the sixth your intuition, received in your third eye. The seventh would be information coming through your gut, or what I refer to as "discernment" (see Ch. 2, "Trust Your Gut?"). The eighth is your heart, but I will get into that in the next chapter.

Intuition is information that you receive and decipher through your third eye. Working with my third eye, sometimes I actually see still pictures, as if I was looking at a photograph. Other times I see short clips of moving pictures, like an excerpt from a movie. These moving scenes most often loop, like seeing the same section of the movie over and over again. I have come to interpret the repetition as an indication (like a push) from spirit to share what I'm seeing with the person I am with.

More rarely, I might "hear" a word spoken, but not with my ears. It is a strange experience, hearing words around you, but in your mind too. The first time it happened to me, I was looking in the bathroom mirror at a small grey kitten sitting on my left shoulder. I had invited her into my life two days earlier and had not come up with a name for her yet. I was discovering that she had a penchant for sitting on my shoulder as I moved around the house. So there we found ourselves in the bathroom, me looking at her reflection, she looking at mine. "Bu" said a voice out of nowhere. The word reverberated inside my mind. It was a strange word for me. I had never heard it, except as "boo," to scare someone. You wouldn't think that hearing a word that wasn't spoken out loud would give you an awareness of how it is spelled. But I suddenly possessed that information. "Bu" was the word I heard. I looked in some shock at the tiny face reflecting back at me and realized that I had just been told the name of this adorable creature. Just like that! Months later I learned that "Bu" means "best friend" among younger people. How appropriate!

I did not have many experiences such as this one before being trained in the three levels of Reiki and becoming a master and teacher. No one told me that taking Reiki would increase my abilities in other areas of my life; I was only expecting to help people. However, shortly after being initiated, I started having more experiences like the one with my kitten.

Now I recognize that Reiki can accelerate your awareness of energy and open you to new experiences. Here's another example. I was studying a large amethyst crystal that I had just purchased. What's odd is that I was not consciously working with the stone. I was simply sitting with it at eye level, turning it slowly, appreciating its nuances and its beauty. While studying it closely, I had a vision. It appeared in midair about seven feet in front of me. I saw a white swan in a most unusual position, as if she were standing on her feet and walking upright like a person, but she was floating in midair. Her wings were outstretched so that her body resembled a cross, with her neck straight up. She floated silently like this, coming closer to me; I had no fear at all. When she was an inch in front of me, she wrapped her wings around me, embracing me. At the same time she nestled her neck close to my face and then I felt/sensed her face brush mine and our chests touch, but not exactly like a physical touch. At that moment I heard the words "I am Swan Woman." In the next instant she disappeared. Just like that! It was as if she exploded; there was a sense of a burst of light, but at the same time it seemed as if she melded right into me! You can imagine my surprise. When you experience something like this, it is overwhelming because it happens so fast. Afterwards it can be hard to determine if you heard the words through your ears or not. I guess it's because we are not used to listening through our inner ear or third eye.

For the next couple of months, I spent a lot of time trying to decide if Swan Woman was now with me ... or ... if *I was* now Swan Woman?

In all such instances, it takes practice to learn to pay attention to the information and learn to trust it, or not. I get "premonitions" all the time about there being an animal in the road in front of me. Most of the time I do not encounter it. Whether I am picking up on an animal that crossed the road earlier in the day, or one who died on the road and whose spirit lingers because of the trauma involved in its passing, I do not know.

Even though I do not necessarily see an animal every time I have a premonition, I still take it seriously when I have one; on occasion such a warning has saved my life or the life of another (as well as my vehicle!).

On the other hand, when I pick things up either visually, audibly, or energetically when working with a client and I share the information with him or her, it is almost always very significant to that person.

It's so easy to discount information of this sort. Ironically, those of us accustomed to seeing visions since childhood find it hard to believe this information is real because first, it happened all the time (which makes it easier to reject) and second, we are conditioned by family, peers and schools (the "real" world) to discount or reject such information.

Taking classes in developing your intuition or psychic abilities is really helpful in learning how to work with and trust such phenomena. Becoming a Reiki practitioner connected me to the universal energy I call "Source" in a way that I did not anticipate, and I have since seen it facilitate the same type of experiences in my students. I highly recommend it.

Some people are born into a family where psychic awareness is accepted. Even so, it can be difficult truly to accept this facet of oneself because of cultural attitudes.

In our current paradigm, "sixth sense" has come to refer to something supernatural or abnormal. You might even have been taught that it is something to fear. Given how our ancestors' fears can be passed down to us through epigenetic inheritance (see "White Mouse"), it is not surprising that we can have an innate fear of anything that makes us stand out from others or that is not accepted by our culture. For the people alive during the period of the witch hunts, just like for that white mouse in a Lucite world, spiritual mediumship, connecting to the earth's powerful energies, participating in ceremonies, or working with energy in general, became the scent that was piped into our environment, that got our feet shocked — only worse, in this case it got thousands of women burned at the stake! Recall what Brian G. Dias wrote in his studies cited in "White Mouse": that reproductive biology is impacted by stress or trauma, and parental legacies of stress or trauma influence offspring.

So there is good reason to experience fear around non-mainstream beliefs, on top of the fact that we have precious few people to guide us. Note that in the realm of priests, doctors, lawyers, teachers, mediums, healers, etc. there are people who are healthy enough to take on a position of power in their field and stay balanced, and therefore able to serve their clients well. There are others who cannot. Just because someone has a title does not mean that the person has done the work on him- or herself. A title only means that the person has successfully followed the system. It doesn't speak to morals or discipline. Any type of person can attain any position. Do not assume anything. Listen to how you feel while you interact with someone, whether a healer, a shaman, a doctor, a teacher, a boss, or a parent. Trust your gut. Tune into your intuition. Experiment with processing all this through your heart. These forms of awareness are your best friends; they will never lie to you, but you do need to learn their form of communication.

This is why developing our eight senses is so vital. They give us much richer information. Imagine looking at something you have always known and all of a sudden you realize that instead of seeing twenty colors now you see a hundred, and each of those colors has a distinct feeling to it, as well as a taste or a sound. You may also discover that you are able to find more places within yourself to process this information.

Will you make mistakes? Of course you will! No one learns anything without making mistakes. We have all trusted the wrong person at least once, and it led to varying degrees of heartache or regret. But those are *learning experiences* and, as such, they should be welcomed. If wisdom is the true gold in life, then anything that we learn is valuable.

When someone tells me something that hurts me, I take a deep breath, and I know. What I know is that what they told me is good information about them — who they are and how they process things. I will look honestly at what they say (especially if I hear anything similar from someone else, in which case I realize that it might be a pattern I am repeating and therefore something I want to address within myself). If it is the first time someone is telling me such a thing (you are selfish, controlling, etc.). I will place a marker in my mind (to be pursued further should I hear this again from someone else) but I will not jump on their words as something I need to take ownership of. In such cases, I acknowledge that this other person is in fact experiencing the emotion, but the reaction is not of my doing. It is about the other's perception, not me.

Again, the relationships we have with others reflect where we are. If I am not satisfied or happy, then I need to change some internal process, or I may also need to leave a certain person or situation behind. This is how I truly become the master of my own life.

It should not be any different in the realm of energy. Go slowly, as I said, and listen to how you feel. If you stay open, you will find a guide or a book that you can trust.

Energy is around you, as it has been your whole life. Internally, from your instrument's point of view, all of this is familiar. What is unfamiliar is the brain wrapping itself around these sensations and concepts. If we are not taught about the reality of energy and we experience its influence in a strong way, it can be very disconcerting, even frightening. Not only do these taught fears become magnified, but we also can end up feeling like all those fears and warnings were justified.

The Native Americans had a very different perspective; was they were not raised with a fear of the unknown. Far from it; in Lakota, "Wakan Tanka" (one of the ways they refer to God), translates to the "Great Mystery." They humbly welcomed this aspect of their creator's all-knowingness. They did not feel the need to understand everything or to pretend that they did. True humbleness means not pretending to understand what plans your creator has set in motion and accepting that you are only a small part. It also means admitting and recognizing that there is a natural code of interdependence, a web of life of which we are all a part.

Needing to pretend to have all the answers is only valuable for those who wish to impose themselves as the ultimate authority. To pretend you have all the answers reflects deeply on you. People taking this position will not like it if anyone questions their authority. Being comfortable in the darkness of not knowing can be very hard for some. Being comfortable with your humanity and its animalistic natural state, as well as its spiritual state, is the mark of an enlightened being.

Teachers that I am interested in learning from do not presume to share anything that they have not experienced themselves. What they do experience for themselves, they share as a story, with medicine, confident that the medicine will reach the ears and hearts it is supposed to ... and not others. And they accept this with peace in their hearts.

The concept of a Great Mystery (which implies both the existence of, as well as the revelation of, a plan) acknowledges the impossibility for human consciousness to grasp all its complexities and its magnitude. It also implies that each of us has our own relationship with this great mystery. Unlike some insects, humans do not partake in a hive mentality. Our creator did not make us to function that way. So then why do certain factions of humanity try to enforce a hive mentality on us?

We still have only scratched the surface of understanding the universe's, or even our own, functioning! Armed with the deep belief in the smallness of human beings in the scheme of life, the existence of an awe-inspiring interconnection as well as a guiding plan that is beyond our ken but that responds to each and every one of us, the natives of this continent were far more open to new ways and new ideas than those brought up believing that there is one right way or that humans are superior and do not need the good will of the rest of creation.

Take the world of flowers. A sunflower must live in full sun and it follows other inner promptings its creator bestowed specifically on it. Imagine if one day this sunflower looked at itself and thought "Look at me, I am tall! So much taller that the other plants that grew up with me. My flower is bigger than theirs! It is golden and radiant! Wow, I am like a small sun on earth! Surly this means that creator has blessed me above these others. I need to tell the shorter plants, who do not live as I do, of my ways so that they can become beloved of creator like me!" So the sunflower sets of on a long journey to tell other flowers about what he feels has been revealed to him. Others can see the accuracy of sunflower's claims, and some believe that there might be truth to what sunflower was saying, so they began to follow sunflower and do as he does.

But sunflower sees only a small section of life (as each of us does) and does not realize that there are flowers who were created to live by the ocean, with salt tangled in their toe roots. Nor does the sunflower realize that there are flowers who were meant to live in the deep shade, for whom stepping into the full sun, day after day, would mean sickness or even death. Others were meant to thrive at the edge of streams, where they would survive the coursing waters all around their roots, but beyond that, their roots helped hold the earth herself in place. Held tight in their embrace, the earth would not lose herself to the rushing waters.

The moral of this story is that what is revealed to each of us is for us. Our truths are not weakened by the validity of other truths. But neither is it guaranteed that what helps strengthen one will help all others. It might help someone who was created exactly the same way (how often does that occur?), but it could harm others — one man's ceiling is another man's floor. This is why developing your own awareness using all your senses is so important.

Ironically for the Native Americans who first encountered Europeans, their openness to embrace other ways led to their befriending these immigrants. Indeed, it is no secret that it was only through the help and goodwill of Native American tribes that the colonists were able to survive those first years. Their generosity was rewarded with things like broken treaties, blankets covered with chicken pox, rape, and genocide, reaffirming the saying that "No good deed goes unpunished." Must this be so? Obviously not, but it does reflect the values of our current paradigm.

So it is that the ways of the inner human create continuity, healing, self-awareness, inner strength and resiliency, while developing the outer human focuses us on accumulation of material goods and power. As I said, this focus leads not to community, but to domination.

Developing our connection to ourselves and the divine takes courage and perseverance. We must often become intrepid explorers, discovering our own Mt. Everests, everglades, deserts and oases. And this, especially in situations where we have no formal guidance, can bring up fears.

When something triggers a warning inside us (that we may, out of habit, interpret as a fear), we need to pause in what we are doing and analyze the "flavors" and the nuances of what we are experiencing. How is it different or similar to other things we have experienced? Sometimes it is only through following this feeling to its conclusion that its true nature is revealed. For example, if I wake suddenly in the night, my first reaction is to listen quietly and see if there is an outside reason. If all is still, then I need to look within for the source of my anxiety. The resulting information then contributes to my developing understanding of myself and the world around me, seen and unseen.

We humans tend not to like or trust things or people we know nothing about. Not trusting something you don't know is smart; it has evolutionary advantages. You have no basis to trust it. Being smart means be conscious, be aware, but being afraid is not warranted. Fear does not let us function normally. Adrenalin kicks in. Did you ever read *Dune* by Frank Herbert? At the beginning of the book we are introduced to the Bene Gesserit (a powerful, elite order of women that is both spiritual and political) and to a litany they use to teach novices how to guard against fear.

Herbert refers to fear as "the mind killer," describing fear's ability to alter our thought process. "Fear is the little death that brings total obliteration," which implies that fear can do more than just interfere with our ability to think clearly. It also suggests that fear may lead us to experience the exact thing we are afraid of. The Bene Gesserit litany suggests allowing "fear to pass over and through me." I visualize myself becoming like smoke so that the emotion cannot find purchase in me. This is an actual technique used to access your power in the imaginal realm. From here we can begin to transform fear alchemically. Herbert then tells us that we should look inside ourselves and see the path that this fear has taken, and witness that it has transformed as we allowed it to pass through us. This is a way to reinforce our intention, all in the imaginal realm. And as you witness that the fear has passed, notice all the levels that you can be aware of: mental, emotional, physical and spiritual (third eye, intuition, heart and gut). They will all have impressions that can teach you about your vehicle, your instrument. Herbert also asks us to be aware of the fact that, after the fear (no matter how great), has passed through us, we still remain.

Teaching stories often describe somatically the experience of fear or other strong emotions as well as how to deal with them. Visualizing something washing over us sets our intention, as well as setting into motion the vibrational state we wish to move into. What we focus on grows. This is the power we have been given. Learn to harness it. Sitting with the sensory input that accompanies such a visualization will provide a wealth of information. This information gives us the ability to incorporate more of what we want in our lives, or alter it if it is something we want less of.

Sit with the sensation but don't become attached to the experiences; this is an essential Buddhist concept, yet it is also universal. What I am describing is a practice. You may not get immediate results and that should be perfectly OK. (Normally I don't like to "should" on myself or others ... but it is appropriate here.) Remember, it is up to you to make it OK.

We are taught (by TV and our mechanized world) to look for immediate results. I remember how I used to feel about my weight. I wanted to be thinner, but I wanted to be thinner NOW! Therefore I was willing to starve myself (not much foresight in that — and it is certainly not maintainable), but even with starvation and swimming two miles a day, the weight did not go away overnight.

So I struggled for decades with this cycle. Was it just youth? I do believe that there is something to the saying "ages and stages," even though there are exceptions. All I can say is that I am so thankful for the gift (now in my life) of patience, of being able to see patterns, and of being aware of my own process that I can trust. If you want to get to this place too, just keep putting one foot in front of the other. Employ any or all of the techniques in this book, and you will make progress! Most of us do not start out where we wish to be. It's a journey. Remember anything that you can feel, you can heighten or lessen in your life by intending to do so. Find the technique that works for you. Experiment. You might be surprised by the places where you can find examples or teachings.

For example, I learned many things from the hundreds of science fiction books I read as a teenager and young adult. Some of my favorite authors were Andrea Norton, Anne McCaffrey, Marion Zimmer Bradley,

Piers Anthony and Rodger Zelazny. I share them with you because these authors have created worlds where energy and human ability to work with it are manifest. Immersing ourselves in these worlds gives us new ways to experience things. Remember Maxwell Maltz found that neurologically our bodies cannot tell the difference between something we imagine vividly and something that is actually happening. We know our emotions are tied into our neurons (it's hard to be happy when you are terribly tense, isn't it?). And we also know that how we feel and what we visualize can be manifested as conditions within our bodies.

So, today, because of our teachings (or lack thereof), we have a proclivity to deny and/or be disturbed by natural phenomena, as well as our own gifts. We are subsequently turned away from ever finding peace with ourselves because these abilities are a part of us, as much as our fingerprints are.

In an attempt to handle this dichotomy, we do our best to ignore as much of the information coming in as we can. We all are successful to varying degrees, but even if we are totally successful in denying the import of this information, even if we are able to completely deaden our awareness of our bodies' reaction to it, *the information does not go away.* Nor does the source of the information go away or our bodies' awareness of it. This is important to wrap our brains around, because as we discussed in "Can We See Vibrational Frequency," things we don't see (or acknowledge) can kill us. For instance, if you were in denial of temperature, you could leave your house every day with the same amount of clothing on. You could do it, but most of us would suffer from doing so. Some temperatures could even kill us.

On another level, can you imagine the amount of personal resources it takes to continuously block out certain information? It can be exhausting, and if you have multiple things that you are denying it takes even more energy. Not only that, but most of us experience fear, or at least a disturbance in the "force," from ignoring these things.

Only for a relatively short period of time in human history have these built-in survival skills been labeled taboo. Prior to that, anyone with these skill sets fully functioning stood a greater chance of surviving than those without. A group of hunters with even one "sensitive" among them stood a greater chance of finding prey or not becoming dinner themselves. *There has to be a part of us that is terrified that we are not utilizing the information coming in from all eight senses.* For example, if we were to take a family of squirrels away from experiencing the changing seasons and feed them regularly for generations, they would still develop and exhibit neurosis and anxiety every fall if they could not search for and "squirrel away" nuts.

In zoos they have found that the cellular need to forage is so strong in many animals that the inability to do so, no matter how comprehensive the rest of the care provided, produces serious stress problems. Behaviors that allowed our ancestors to survive are hardwired into our genetic information (epigenetics). We cause disturbances in our mental/emotional makeup when we disconnect ourselves from honoring these directives. Eventually these disturbances make their way into our bodies.

Because we cannot identify the source of this anxiety, it becomes "free floating" and we, as rational beings, try to associate it with things that are occurring around us that we *do* accept. That gives us false information. In other words, it contributes to our sense of confusion, unease (dis-ease), being out of control, disconnected, etc. Such things don't lead to happy, well-adjusted people and therefore create a "hungry" population — hungry for external solutions, because we are not left any choices for dealing with these feelings. We are convinced by our paradigms, our cultures, our corporations, our media and our religions that the solution lies outside of us. It's the perfect conundrum, because seeking outside ourselves will never ease our hungers or our maladies. Such external remedies may bring a reprieve for a time from our symptoms but do not cure them.

As a young blond girl traveling in the Far East, I didn't go anywhere without tuning into my sixth sense. It saved my life on several occasions. One day, while wandering away from camp in the Himalayas, I came to a small path that led to a pond. I love sitting by water and tuning into the energies of all the wildlife, as well as the water itself. I took out my journal and wrote for about twenty minutes in sheer bliss. Suddenly my skin prickled. I heard a twig snap and I looked up in time to watch six or seven men materialize around me. I assessed the energy in a nanosecond and knew beyond a doubt that I had seconds to take advantage of their surprise and move out of there. I stood up and pushed past them, like a boat cutting through waves, holding strength around me like a cloak. I did not run ... I felt everything energetically. It was crystal clear to me exactly where things could have gone had I not stepped out of there.

It was like I was in a canoe and "saw" two separate paths downstream. The currents were trying to carry me on the course that lay straight ahead, but a smaller opening branched off to the left. It was hard to steer the boat (and the energy) in that direction. My boat was moving quickly, as was the timeline, but I knew I had to change the energy that was beginning to build and I had only seconds to do it. I would not be their victim. If I had stayed there, I have no doubt what would have happened.

It's really hard to respond to things like that if you don't know how to read the energy coming at you. I suppose it was my traumatic childhood that caused me to need to find ways to protect myself. And this is where hindsight can reveal to us the gifts that we are able to receive from hardship. My "normal" life had to be uncomfortable enough to cause me to search out alternative ways to function, and so it did.

How *can* you get to a place where you open up and trust your intuition? You do it by adopting and playing with states of experiential learning, not burdened by expectations or beliefs. What an amazing world we would live in if our scientists, our doctors, our educators, our parents and our neighbors learned this way. This type of thinking is what is required to form a holistic, unbiased, un-prejudiced, understanding of anything. Practice makes perfect. We have a long way to go to get there, but we can.

Until recently there were no scientific means to measure minute energy transmissions from people and objects, making it virtually impossible for the awareness of these things to be scientifically validated. For people who are aware of energy's relevance in our everyday life, the struggle today is much like Galileo's as he tried to present his evidence that the earth orbited the sun. Too many people have too much invested in the old way of thinking for things to change quickly.

It's very exciting for me that scientific equipment has reached the point where it *is* sensitive enough to measure many things it could not previously. Recent discoveries have led science to reexamine avenues it had dismissed, such as the studies in quantum physics revealing how the observer affects the observed. That is, our thoughts and emotional states can affect the smallest components that make up all matter in our world, subatomic particles.

We can now validate that our ancestors *knew* certain things that they could not possibly have known other than via discernment or intuition. This understanding was possible because they were aware of energy and open to intuited information.

Doesn't it make sense for this old information to be re-examined now and for its merits to be explored as practices in our daily lives? We need to re-member ourselves — honor the complex, amazingly sensitive creatures that we are and stop turning away from the totality of what we can do and what we can be aware of.

73. The Heart

"There are, in fact, two modes of cognition available to all human beings — the brain-based linear and the heart-based holistic."[239] That is from an outstanding book that is not only beautifully written, but filled with amazing insights into the natural world. It is *The Secret Teachings of Plants: The Intelligence of the Heart in the Direct Perception of Nature*, in which Stephen Harold Buhner shares information that he gleaned from studying with indigenous peoples.

In my Native American studies, I was taught that the heart is the best place to make decisions from. Located between the gut and the brain, the heart is like a wise mediator. Knowledge becomes wisdom when it journeys to the heart. More than this, according to ancient and indigenous peoples *the heart is an organ of perception.* Just as with our intuition and discernment, we need to develop both the heart's ability to gather information and our ability to interpret it accurately. It takes practice.

This is exactly the opposite of what we are taught in the USA. We are led to believe that our heart is a fickle, unreliable thing (in regard to emotions). We don't make decisions based in our hearts, we make them based on thoughts and wants in our heads. If our head makes a decision that is unwise and our heart gets hurt, somehow it becomes our heart's fault.

We are encouraged to live in our heads. We are taught at worst to fear, or at best to ignore, our other forms of intuition, discernment, and awareness. This is so sad because if we remain only in our heads, we are being set up to fail.

My head (because I am such a thinker) can vacillate endlessly between facts and conclusions; not so my heart (nor other forms of awareness, although they take more time to learn than the heart's messages). When I still the chatter coming from my head and drop into my heart, the answers

---

[239] Stephen Harold Buhner, *The Secret Teachings of Plants.* Rochester, Vt.: Bear & Company, 2004.

here are steady. They do not bounce or vacillate, but they do not have the attention-grabbing quality of thoughts. It takes practice to become familiar with the heart's forms of communication.

I have heard some people claim to hate their hearts, or proclaim that they will "never trust my heart again." If only they realized that all the decisions that they made that "led them astray" originated in their heads.

Look at it this way. Emotions reside in the body; sexual passion, for example, no more resides in the heart than hate does. It's fairly easy to identify where sexual passion resides, isn't it? Remember the feeling and then identify where it is generated. Now think of something that you have hated. Identify where this sensation is located. Hate is a thought. It does not reside in the body. Anger however does. Anger is generated in the liver according to the ancient teachings of acupuncture (and the five element theory) and we will get into that in a moment. Emotions are generated in many parts of your physical body. The Hindus and other East Asians have mapped out the locations of certain centers in the body that are linked with emotions. For example, in the five-element theory in Chinese medicine, the lungs are associated with grief and the liver with anger. Have you known people who just radiate anger when they have had a lot to drink? Alcohol stresses your liver, and the liver produces or holds anger.

Would it surprise you to know that according to traditional Chinese medicine, "The heart is the seat of consciousness."[240] According to an article put out by the National Library of Medicine, "Western medicine characterizes emotional disorders using 'neural' language while East Asian medicine uses 'somatic' language"[241] These findings supported a connection between the following emotions and organs:

> anger with the liver, happiness with the heart, thoughtfulness with the heart and spleen, sadness with the heart and lungs, fear with the kidneys and the heart, surprise with the heart and the gallbladder, and anxiety with the heart and the lungs.[242]

Since the heart is involved somatically with all of these processes, doesn't it make sense to learn to tune into your heart?

---

[240]Arizona School of Acupuncture and Medicine, *Five Elements: The Basics.* ASAOM, https://www.asaom.edu/five-elements.

[241]"Understanding Mind-Body Interaction from the Perspective of East Asian Medicine," National Center for Biotechnology Information, U.S. National Library of Medicine, https://www.ncbi.nlm.nih.gov/pmc/articles/PMC5585554/.

[242]Ibid.

Emotionally-based decisions are not coming from your heart; instead they are the brain's interpretations of your body's emotional reactions to stimuli.

Learning to center yourself in your heart takes conscious intention and practice, like many of the practices we have discussed in this book. This is why elders who have done their "heart work" (homework) are such treasures for the community they reside in. Wisdom takes decades of constant vigilance to attain.

I recently had a choice. I met someone who came from a background so radically different from mine that what he had done to survive scared me. Initially, I listened to the fear in my head and I ran (cutting off all contact with this person) for almost six months. But my heart would not leave the situation be; I kept thinking about him in such a fond way. It was eerie. I finally could stand it no longer and started communicating with him. I am so glad I did. Not only did I discover that he had been trying to push me away with an exaggerated, fabricated story, but he has become one of my most treasured friends. In order to be present for this relationship, I had to learn not just to drop into my heart, but to stay there for extended periods of time.

From my heart, I never questioned his purity or trustworthiness. But from my head, I felt fear that was generated by the thoughts that were being entertained. How I process information in my head, with its awareness of different possibilities and its differing opinions on each of those, can leave me spinning. If I drop into my heart, all I receive is the vibration, the feelings both coming from this man and being generated by him within me. If I had stayed closed because of the information from my head, I never would have let this person in. That would have been such a loss!

If you are unclear about what heart energy specifically might be or feel like, try this practice. The next time you are driving in your car and someone is tailgating you, focus on what you feel. You might feel anger or annoyance, or you might be aware of a sense of pressure; the feeling might originate just below your heart, in your solar plexus area. The Hindus established long ago that the solar plexus is the seat of the will. So if someone is trying to assert his will over yours, such as by trying to make you drive faster than you are comfortable with, you can feel it in this area. Different people react to this kind of infringement differently; some people automatically acquiesce, others push back, some get angry or feel anxiety. Whatever your initial reaction is, I want you to try something different. Take a deep breath and "see" in your mind (or if you can feel energy in your body, "feel" through your heart) and send a beam of "heart energy" to the person that is tailgating.

If you can't feel energy, do not worry. Trust me — this doesn't mean that the energy is not there, or that you cannot work with it or move it. You can! Simply imagine that there is energy from your heart that grows every time you inhale. As you exhale, see, feel, or imagine that it travels backwards to the other person in the vehicle behind you. Breathe slowly; this should feel quite relaxing. Try this for three to five breaths and notice what happens. Nine times out of ten the person traveling on your bumper will almost immediately drop back to a comfortable distance.

This is a great introduction to working with the wisdom and power of your heart. It never ceases to amaze me how powerful this exercise is and how far-reaching the effect of where we chose to come from every moment of each day. Imagine if we all used heart energy to resolve conflicts instead of trying to dominate each other ....

As you repeat this practice, become familiar with what working with your heart feels like. Remember that each time we do something, we create what I like to envision as groves in our brains that correspond to these actions, making it easier to access a particular state of mind. Imagine pouring water on the floor. It will spread out evenly in all directions (if the surface is level). This even spread dissipates the energy of both the pour and the outward spreading of the water. Now imagine pouring water on a surface that has channels cut or worn into it. The water travels in a much more focused way when it is channeled. It is also much easier for the water to run in an accustomed channel than it is for it to start traveling in a newly forming one. But with repetition, the new channel can become deeper than the old, causing it to be the water's first choice.

It may surprise you to learn that when working with energy you are not confined to the present moment. Experiment with sending your heart energy ahead of you (in time) to an upcoming meeting, or sending it behind you to a past meeting that did not go well. In the latter, see and/or feel this energy soothing the ruffled edges of people or situations. In the former, see or feel the energy playing out in a calm way that is beneficial to all. As your awareness of what being in this heart space feels like develops, you can also experiment with making decisions from here. Once you are aware of the sensations you receive when you are in your heart, you can try seeking the answer to a question. Sit quietly in a pleasant place, but if you are not in a pleasant space physically, imagine yourself sitting in one. Shift your awareness to you heart, and/or on any of the sensations you have come to associate with this center. When you feel yourself in this energy ask your question out loud or in your mind. See if you can "feel" or "hear" the answer. It may become clear to you suddenly, or you may have to sit quietly in this sensory place for a while.

I have the practice (when I am not in a hurry to get to an appointment) of taking a few minutes to tune into my heart when I am getting into my truck. I will sit there, with my eyes either open or closed, and allow myself to feel through my heart center. I do this to see if I can feel a direction (or location) that I am being drawn to. I love writing in cafes, so on special days that I could dedicate to writing, I would do this to see where I was being guided to be that day.

I will also use this method it to see if I can confirm that where I am planning to go is in alignment with where I need to be. I have had some absolutely magical results due to this practice, and I bet you will too!

Only you can develop a relationship with this organ of perception that resides in your chest. It is an inner world, a way of being that we very much need to cultivate in our outer life.

74. Auras and Energy Fields

Have you ever seen a light around people, animals or objects? I don't usually, but I have occasionally. Yet I work in people's energy fields all the time. I can't see the fields, but I can *feel* them. I can feel their parameters, as well as being aware to varying degrees of stuff that is stuck in there.

Often, when I am doing a Reiki session with someone, I find it more powerful (in terms of the results) if I work *only* in their energy field. I will still touch someone, because a very powerful healing occurs from being touched by another who is there for you completely but does not require anything from you. It can be quite humbling. We rarely if ever experience that once we reach a certain age, and, actually, we are lucky if we truly experience that as children.

When I start a session, I will run my hands above the person's body from head to toe. My hands will find the appropriate placement for each individual, usually between four to sixteen inches above the physical body. From here I begin to get an awareness of what this client is dealing with. I have noticed a particular sensation in the palms of my hands when I encounter an area that has blocked energy. The feeling is very similar to the tickle you can feel in the palm of your hands when you make a balloon animal and you twist the balloon against itself. I can feel that tingly vibration in my hands when I hold them above the person's body in their energy field when there is a block. I can also tell if the client has some deep emotional pain or trauma locked up in specific areas.

People hold pain in different places within their bodies and auric fields. When I feel pain or blockages, I first become aware of the emotion, through my own instrument, which is very similar to how I would experience my own emotions, my own feelings. For example, I will become aware of a deep sadness by experiencing it. Because I can feel it, I also have a sense of what it is connected to. Nine times out of ten, when I share what I am picking up with my clients, they confirm it. Occasionally they don't, at which point I have to assume that what I picked up was *mine* in some way.

The other possibility could be that the person I'm working on is in complete denial about some trauma and has no conscious idea of any unresolved emotions lurking in the energy fields or the body. It can be very confusing to a new practitioner, and it takes lots of practice to begin to tell the difference.

I had a striking example of this very early in my Reiki career. I was participating as a Reiki provider at a healing fair in Connecticut, where many healing practitioners offered mini sessions to participants. This allowed the facilitators to practice as well as to pick up new clients. The participants got to try new modalities at a low price.

It was my first time doing anything like this. One of my first clients was a woman who was a little older than myself. I did not do the energy scan that I mentioned above because we had so little time to actually give Reiki (about fifteen minutes compared to my normal hour and a half). So it was awkward trying to pace myself and figure out how to miniaturize the session. I started working on her head, moved to her heart and then her solar plexus, all without incident. When I placed my hands above her womb, I almost dropped to my knees, I was so overpowered by sadness.

It's hard to tell where strong emotions are coming from when the part of me that reads energy is tied into the pathways that I experience my own feelings with. It truly takes practice working with sensing energy to develop clear communication between these senses and the conscious mind.

It's easier for me to describe this experience to women because women are familiar with waking up one morning and finding that, overnight, your whole life (which had be OK to great the day before) suddenly sucks. You feel depressed. Joy feels like it's so far away that you can't even imagine ever feeling it again. It is intense. For the first decade or so of having my menses, I was ruled by these wildly divergent feelings, which would strike without warning. It was easy to feel victimized by these surging emotions. Yet the fact that I was totally immersed in intense feelings of angst did not make sense because I went to bed feeling just fine about everything. Overnight my world would turn dark. The shift in my hormones and the ensuing emotions were so all-encompassing that, if I did not hold up the mirror of how I had felt the day before, I would believe my life now totally sucked! (Talk about an education in different timelines and "reality"!)

As I got older, I was able to identify almost instantaneously that this massive fluctuation of emotions was not actually tied to the happenings in my life. Instead, I let the experience of sudden mood shifts be the signal to check and see where I was in my cycle. If it was anywhere near my time, I just breathed into the areas that had tightened, and visualized letting these tensions go. I also sought out herbs like chaste tree berry, and later as I got closer to end of my menses, black cohosh. These herbs help a great deal.

Now for you men, I don't know how to describe the experience of suddenly finding that your perceptions of life have shifted radically. It feels as if what you are experiencing is connected to actual events in your life, but it is not. It is only your perception that has changed.

This is why it is so important to practice identifying these sensations; it is the only way you will be able to tell the difference between something that is generated within versus outside you.

If you are naturally empathic, then perhaps you have had some experiences with feeling things that are not generated from within you. Suffice it to say that on the surface such feelings can seem exactly like your own, because you are receiving the vibration something else is emitting and you are translating it through your emotional band within your own instrument. There are nuances that allow you to be able to discern this with time ... but I cannot describe them to you. Your instrument is different — you were created with your own sensitivities and your own medicines. You must discover them on your own, through practice. Our job as energy workers, empaths and healers is to tune into our instrument and learn to read what is coming into us versus what we are generating.

Getting back to that session with a client, I was almost sobbing with the intensity of the emotions I was feeling when I placed my hands above this woman's womb. I had not yet learned to ask clients before the session if they wanted me to share anything I picked up, so I was very hesitant to mention this. But an opportunity presented itself in the course of our saying goodbye. When I told her what I had felt, she looked at me blankly and said, "No, that wasn't coming from me."

That took me aback ... so that was *mine*? I couldn't believe it; it did not feel accurate, but I had to accept her dismissal. The whole thing not only shook me (I had never had such a strong reaction to working on anyone prior to this), but it left me feeling very unsure of myself.

My last client that day was a beautiful young lady who was a massage therapist also offering her services at the fair. After I worked on her, we swapped tales about our experiences at the fair. As we were talking, she said "I'm so glad you worked on my mom." Curious, I asked her who her mom was. When she told me, I realized it was the woman I just told you about! I described my odd experience of being overwhelmed with grief working on her mother's lower abdomen, and that her mom had said she wasn't experiencing any grief or trauma in that area. The young lady looked at me solemnly and said, "My mom had an abortion."

Wow! I felt so much relief because I had accurately read the emotions as originating within her. Being told "no" had made me doubt everything I had pieced together. It is difficult to learn to read energy if you share your interpretations with a client who is so dissociated from his or her own "stuff" that he or she does not hold a conscious awareness of the experience and so will not be able to identify with what you "see" when you share it. It was disorienting to have the client not identify with what I picked up while working on her. Trying to own the feelings, to accept them as originating within myself, was not really possible, but her denial was forcing me to attempt to do just that. Realizing that I had been correct helped me greatly in learning to differentiate between intuited or empathically felt things, as opposed to how something that originates within me feels. It also gave me more confidence to do so. It is only through conscious examination of these experiences that we learn anything.

Looking at the Aura

The aura is understood in many spiritual practices to be a part of the energy field that surrounds a living being. These fields, to people who can see them, look like layers. Each layer is associated with different levels of physical existence. Some go into the body, although it's easier to see the ones outside. Those who can see these energy fields all say the same thing, that disease originates in these planes outside the physical body.

From a shamanic perspective these *things* (whether they are actual objects or denser energies) that get stuck in our energy fields would be called intrusions. If we do not address these intrusions, they move through the energy layers, coming closer to the body and eventually becoming lodged in it. Here they can interrupt the normal flow of energy, causing physical symptoms.

Intrusions either come from outside us, or they originate inside us but mutate over time. Often the latter type of intrusions formed inside us for a specific purpose. They can be invited or created in response to a singular traumatic experience or an ongoing one. Whenever a being finds itself in a situation where it cannot protect itself, there is a strong chance that an archetypal hero will be contacted or brought into being to help the person without power survive. Being powerless is an intolerable state for a being with free will. And finding ourselves being harmed while we are powerless to stop it is worse. It puts us in an unusual state of mind, where reality operates differently.

In such a state, the solutions we create or discover (if we survive our ordeal) can be seen as teachers or medicines which get magnetized into our energy fields, either consciously or unconsciously. The ones that get invited in or created internally can start off as boons to us. However, over the years, as we grow and become better able to care for ourselves, these aids can turn into dead weights that hinder us (just like outgrown clothing that begins to restrict our movements or cut off circulation). We can witness a demonstration of this process in many older cultures.

More on Medicine

Some Native Americans would study the strengths and habits of the creatures they shared the earth with. By studying animals or other aspects of nature (the four directions, the elements, etc.) they were able to determine their strengths or "medicine." Each medicine was recognizable by its qualities in humans as well; for instance, elementally speaking a person might have a fiery temperament, leading with his or her passion, while another might be an ice queen, cool, calm, and collected. Remember there are no judgments here; neither trait is better or worse than the other. There are simply times and places where each is more beneficial. Remember also that what we are aiming for is balance, to feel better about our relationships and develop skills to help us achieve that goal!

Here is an example of animal medicine in a human: let's say you were a child living with an alcoholic parent. When your dad was drinking, he might be belligerent. You would undoubtedly benefit from not attracting attention when he was drunk. Holding your tongue in these situations might save you from getting beaten. Learning to play dead (like opossum) could actually save your life. So without consciously reaching for it, you might invite in opossum medicine. You would form a relationship with this totem, even if you were unaware that you were doing so. And for a portion of your life it would benefit you. Opossum medicine allows you to shut down all physical signs or reactions to the outside world. It's a dissociative medicine, very helpful when having to deal with a more powerful opponent. But once you were old enough to leave, not being able to stand up for yourself, not having a voice, would no longer serve you. Using that medicine would encourage people to walk over you because you would be unable to state your boundaries. Depending on how long opossum medicine had been at play in your life, you might not even be aware of your own needs. They would just be experienced as uncomfortable places in your thoughts or body.

Transforming Outdated Survival Modes

To transform an outdated survival mechanism or adopted medicine, you need to sit down and start a conversation with this aspect. A good place to begin is thanking it for all its help. You are offering your recognition of how it did benefit you at one point. Wait for any kind of sensed response. If there is one, react to it. When the internal dialoging stops, you can ask this medicine to change its role in your life. Sometimes there is a natural transformation that is obvious, like someone who adopted eagle medicine to get away from his or her problems. This person might be said to always "have his head in the clouds." Be creative when dealing with old medicines that have outgrown their usefulness. Asking the eagle (or eagle medicine) to spend more time in the trees could help. Or perhaps eagle medicine has completely served its purpose and now it is time for another medicine to take its place.

Consciously adopting a different medicine and letting eagle know, let's say, that wolf or mouse is walking with you now and therefore you will not be needing its services as much would be another way of beginning to shift energies within you.

Again, thank the former medicine for its help. Perhaps in the future, you might want to call on this medicine when you need creative solutions to issues in your life (e.g., ones that would benefit from the perspective of height in an eagle's flight).

In the realm of intrusions, some become almost like sub-personalities and can take on a life of their own within us. It's difficult to explain, but once we outgrow the need for those things that once served or even saved us, they can become cranky or resentful and can start causing problems for us. They are our allies, but if we preempt them often enough, so that they can't do their job, they become frustrated. They need a job and they want the job they were "contracted" to do.

When either the client or I identifies an intrusion, or energy block, located somewhere in the client's body or energy field, I ask the client to describe it to me. I ask the client to see if it has a color, a texture, or a density to it. Then I ask him or her to feel it. Does it have a temperature? Does it have a feeling associated with it? Often these intrusions are dark and malignant feeling, like a completely foreign entity. Once we have examined this together, I ask the client if he or she wants to change its color, its size or its temperature. I have the client dialogue with the intrusion (if it is comfortable to do so).

For example, I have the client ask "Why are you here?" I often need to explain to clients that you don't just listen with your ears, you allow yourself to observe without judgment images, color changes, sensations, temperature changes, etc. Don't discount anything when you are new to this type of work.

Even if initially the client wanted nothing but to be rid of this intrusion, we discovered, nine times out of ten, after dialoguing with it, that the client often has formed a deep connection with this aspect and now wishes it to stay. If he or she had been experiencing some physical symptoms, these usually fade or completely disappear. It is powerful work.

Auras in Different Cultures

You may think that the concept of auras came into being in the New Age, but visualizing an energy or light surrounding the human body goes back thousands of years.

We can find references to this phenomenon in the Bible, Islam, Dzogchen Buddhism, Taoism, Vajrayana, Yoga, Sufism, the martial arts and Hermeticism. The names for this phenomenon are beautiful descriptions of how auras appear: "body of light," "light body," "rainbow body," "diamond body," "body of bliss," "most sacred body," "true and genuine body" and "immortal body." It sounds like all these cultures placed a lot of value on something that we in the West ignore! There is an Iranian word *farr* found in religious texts that refers to the aura or "glory" which is similar in the Kabalistic Tree of Life.

The *Bhagavad Gita*, an important part of Hindu tradition in both literature and philosophy, teaches that the subtle body is one of a series of psycho-spiritual layers of living beings. The subtle body is composed of mind, intelligence, and ego. It is said to control the gross or physical body. It is believed by some teachers that spiritual practice gradually transforms this aura into a spiritual halo.

In Hinduism and the tantric tradition, the subtle body consists of seven colors, the same as the light spectrum. Both Hindu and Buddhist texts liken the colors of the aura to those of the chakras, which are the also the colors of the visible light spectrum.

Jainism, an ancient religion from India, instructs its followers on how to live a good life that will carry its practitioners past the need to reincarnate. A part of Jainism is the concept of Lesya. "Lesya is a psychic color varying according to the karma of the soul. There are six colors: black, dark blue, gray, rose, yellow and white."[243] These colors of the aura represent different states of mental and emotional dispositions, with the most desirable being at the end of that spectrum. In both the Kabbalah and Western Neoplatonism, the aura is referred to as an "astral body," which is connected to the planetary heavens, and like Lesya reflects certain mental states or abilities. These in turn correspond not just to colors, but to shapes, sounds and smells, just like chakras and the five elements in Chinese medicine. In Western tradition it is common to depict saints and the Virgin Mary with a halo. That holo may either reflect an open crown chakra or be a part of one's aura. Nicola Tesla was the first person to develop a way to photograph these emanations in 1891.[244]

In advanced martial arts, we can also find teachings regarding the energy or light surrounding the body. For instance in his book the *Essence of Ninjutsu*, Dr. Masaaki Hatsumi (Bunjukan Grandmaster) describes the importance of discovering within oneself a world of nothingness. He taught that from this place of nothingness, one is able not only to develop the sixth sense that is so important to martial artists, but enlightenment as well.[245] He is not alone in his insistence that to succeed in martial arts, one must master the ability to see auras and read an opponent's energy. In the early 1980s Grandmaster Glenn Morris released his scientific system that students were able to use to awaken their Kundalini. In this training students learn specific physical skills that immediately show if the students are accurately reading their opponents' energy. It's a simple test: if you read the opponent energies correctly, you are able to avoid a strike; if not, you get hit.

> Grandmaster Glenn Morris included perception of the aura in his advanced martial artists training. Meditation is an important part of Hoshin, as the student must learn to become aware of the personal self, but also of the integrated whole of existence and the realization that all things are connected.[246]

He taught a simple exercise that produced big results, in which his students learned: "Sensing intention, Seeing and feeling energy, Seeing and feeling

---

[243] *Leshya, aka:Lesya; 15 Definition(s)*, Wisdom Library updated November, 20, 2019, https://www.wisdomlib.org/definition/leshya (accessed December, 11, 2019).

[244] "What is an Aura? Defining Aural Meaning," December, 14, 2018 https://www.auraphoto.com › fundamentals › whatis.

[245] Masaaki Hatsumi, *Essence of Ninjutsu* , Chicago: Contemporary Books, 1988, ch. 6.

[246] Ibid.

the aura, Chakra diagnosis, and Moving energy around the body, just to name a few."[247] He points out that even the most skillful blow from a martial artist will have added impact if he or she is adjusting the strikes with information gained by reading his or her opponent's aura.

Morris describes the layers of energy surrounding our bodies, saying that they start at varying distances from the body. This is consistent with what has been said about the aura and energy fields for centuries. He goes on to say that some of these layers can be seen merging into or existing within the body. He describes the ones that are farthest from the body as easiest to see and as being both lighter and at the same time denser than air. These outer layers can range from a half to quarter of an inch thick. Surrounding this he describes a yard-thick egg-shaped layer reflecting hormonal states that he linked to the emotional body. He says there are other barely perceptible layers farther out, corresponding to the mental body and beyond.

In Chinese tradition these layers correlate to the etheric body. The etheric body is made up of chi (energy or lifeforce) and forms a structure of meridians throughout the body. These meridians pass through all the major organs, glands, nerves, chakras, and other energy centers. This system suffuses the physical body with the etheric energy, supporting and sustaining it.

The concept of the aura or energetic body became the basis for energy medicine. Energy medicine does more than remove energy blockages (disease) from a person's body. It can also transmute, shift, neutralize, or remove conditions in one's energy field before these reach the body.

Dr. Edward Bach wrote about this in the early 1900s in his first book *Heal Thyself*. He is the father of Bach Flower Remedies, which are truly powerful remedies for emotional imbalances of all kinds.

> Five hundred years before Christ some physicians of ancient India, working under the influence of the Lord Buddha, advanced the art of healing to so perfect a state that they were able to abolish surgery, although the surgery of their time was as efficient, or more so, than that of the present day. Such men as Hippocrates with his mighty ideals of healing, Paracelsus with his certainty of the divinity in man, and Hahnemann who realized that disease originated in a plane above the physical – all these knew much of the

---

[247] Robert Morgan, "Hoshin Roshi Ryu," *Fight Times*, April 20, 2015, https://magazine.fighttimes.com/hoshin-roshi-ryu/.

real nature and remedy of suffering. What untold misery would have been spared during the last twenty or twenty-five centuries had the teaching of these great masters of their art been followed, but, as in other things, materialism has appealed too strongly to the Western world, and for so long a time, that the voices of the practical obstructers have risen above the advice of those who knew the truth.[248]

The concept that "disease originates in a plane above the physical body" would correspond to the layers around the body that masters of energy work can perceive. There are too many supporting pieces of information from across time that share this viewpoint for us to ignore it. Yet we do! Why? Our current paradigm is why, and it does not support our highest good!

Akashic Records?

Linda Gadbois talks about her studies of the Esoteric Sciences. In them the Akashic field is seen as existing within the astral plane. It is filled with archetypal ideas (perhaps similar to the imaginal realm?) of everything that has been and is yet to be. She says that these archetypal ideas serve as:

> ... a generic prototype for creating in the physical realm and are accessed and absorbed into the mind through sympathetic resonance. Within this same astral plane are also stored "thought-forms" produced by humans as emotional memories that exist as a holographic template that's "recorded" on the Ether (the Akashic book of Life), and not only forms the memory of our soul and body, but also populates the Astral plane of what we call "the Collective Unconscious," or mass consciousness with virtual memories. Our DNA as a crystalline transmitter and receiver draws in (resonates with) the thought-forms of others (group mind) as well as ideas from the higher dimension of the mental plane of Universal archetypes, where both come as the holographic information that ultimately serves to program our DNA.[249]

I was taught that the Akashic records exist in a plane or dimension that humans can access. Here records of everything that has ever

---

[248] Edward Bach, *Heal Thyself*, Bach Center, Mount Vernon Ltd 1931.
[249] Linda Gadbois, *DNA-the phantom effect, quantum hologram and the etheric body*, https://medcraveonline.com/MOJPB/dna-the-phantom-effect-quantum-hologram-and-the-etheric-body.html.

happened, or will happen, are stored. Some people can access this information on their own. I have also heard that one can access this through working with a tabular quartz crystal. Oddly, I have always been strongly attracted to "tabbies," as we call them. I sometimes wonder if the place I "see" when I go into my mind in a certain way is this plane. From here it seems as though I see everything I have ever learned spread out above me like constellations in a night sky. The name for this book came from that experience, because, when I learn something new, it's almost as if I can watch that piece of information floating up to find its place in those constellations. As it settles in its place, any "dots" that pertain to it glow, and I see the connections between these dots or stars.

75. Going Wild

It amazes me that so many falsehoods have been created around the efficacy of natural healing modalities that they are now seen as folk tales at best (which grants them a small standing) or supernatural at worst! Supernatural, by the way, is defined as "departing from what is usual or normal especially so as to appear to transcend the laws of nature."[250] How ironic! Natural remedies cannot be above nature, can they? They are taken directly from nature after all. However, some of the remedies the pharmaceutical companies produce absolutely fit that description!

When did natural things become un-natural? This is a question we all need to examine, because through that doorway, we will not just find higher quality lives and relationships, but the world will become a much healthier, safer, cleaner and more natural place.

Contrast Western culture with others that have not woven these parts of life out of their world view. (That gets harder with each passing year as "progress" spreads deeper into the pockets of humanity that still live in harmony with the earth and their inner natures.) Not being raised in cultures that connect us to our natural abilities or the wisdom contained therein, we do not have a deep comfort level with them. As our culture became more advanced technologically and the discoveries we were making seemed to set us apart from nature, we began to dismiss any information coming from older, less technologically advanced civilizations, as though the wisdom these older cultures had amassed for thousands of years was valueless.

That is arrogant, don't you think? I suppose for a time (a few centuries) it actually seemed to be true. A perfect example of this would be my favorite scene from *Raiders of the Lost Ark* when Indiana Jones is faced with an impressive sword-wielding opponent who is blocking his way. Indiana

---

[250]"Supernatural" https://www.merriam-webster.com/dictionary/supernatural, (accessed 22 December 2019).

says something like "Oh heck," pulls out his gun and shoots the guy from ten feet away.

In a game of dominance shooting a gun, a relatively easy skill to learn compared to martial arts or developing inner wisdom, offers a quick and easy win. A bullet trumps a sword, a train or car trumps a horse, and we thought for a while that a pharmaceutical product trumped a natural one and that food from a grocery store was better than food grown on a small farm. Now we have come face to face with the long-term effects of these lifestyle choices. How are we doing? How is the earth (the source of all our food) doing?

When European settlers first came to this country, they depended on help from the natives. Instead of dominating the land, these natives taught the settlers how to practice a form of permaculture (prior to that term being coined). They utilized natural farming techniques like the Three Sisters (beans, corn and squash), whose growth habits feed and support each other. Beans fix nitrogen in the soil, feeding the other two plants. The corn becomes stakes for the beans while the squash's basal foliage shades the roots of the other two, as well as keeping weeds down. These natives also taught the settlers how to put a piece of fish at the bottom of a hole when seed is planted, to provide extra nutrients for the plants. This is a natural way to fertilize the plants that has zero negative effect on the environment or our bodies. How is it that advanced methods of farming pollute both?

I think part of the reason that European settlers believed that Native Americans had been here for a relatively short time was how pristine the environment was. They could not fathom a civilization that could live in harmony with the land rather than dominating it.

In actuality Native Americans have been on this continent for at least ten thousand years. Their philosophy of staying in "right relationship" to *all other beings* was the reason that this continent was pristine after so many centuries of humans living here. There is much to be said for going wild . . . .

Just look at the Americas that the white settlers found, the proverbial "land of milk and honey." The natural resources seemed endless, there was virtually no disease, and existence was relatively easy for the people living here. But it wasn't really *just* the land, was it?

It was not a magical land that could continue to pour out riches and an ease of healthful living endlessly. No, not without proper stewardship. Long ago Europe was lush and rich as well. What was different between these two continents? The people that inhabited them and their philosophies, that's what. The Native Americans were the *real treasure* here. Their stewardship practices are what created the Garden of Eden on this continent, just the way ours is destroying it. Ironically, here in the States, our ancestors (European settlers) almost wiped out their ancestors (the first Americans) ... and with that stroke of greed, the true "gold" of this continent was all but lost.

Yet we are in luck. There are still First Nation peoples who are willing to teach the ways that created a beautiful, healthy thriving continent. Any land would have flourished under their stewardship.

How has the land has fared under our care? With our superiority complex and all our souped-up chemicals, fertilizers, and mass farming techniques? I would say not well ... we have changed that beautiful delicate balance, haven't we?

76. Hair

It should be obvious by now that we haven't evolved randomly. We often ignore some interesting physical developments; for instance, why does the hair on our heads grow longer and faster than any other hair on our bodies? As mentioned earlier, the Bible makes a big deal about women's hair.

There is a fascinating book called *The Descent of Woman*[251] by Elaine Morgan that discusses the possible advantages of our unique hair in the realm of primates (for one thing) from an evolutionary standpoint. She examines many attributes that we have that other primates don't: subcutaneous fat, nostrils, a pronounced brow line, the ability to cry saline tears, the shape of our buttocks, and our development of breasts as well as the long hair on our heads. She also takes into account the fact that the first tools *homo sapiens* used were rounded rocks or pebbles. Her research is based on finding answers that make sense from an evolutionary standpoint, which is very similar to how I like to decipher things.

She starts out by bashing Darwin's theory of evolution. She points out that in the Pliocene period, as the jungles of Africa were dwindling, the only primates that would have had the strength to retain access to the declining resources and real estate of the jungle canopies would be the Great Apes. Evolutionists do not believe that we are descendants of the Great Apes. Rather our evolutionary forbears are supposed to be much smaller, more like chimps. These smaller primates would not have stood a chance competing for food and resources against apes. Look at the difference between tooth and body size, as well as weight.

Darwin's theory that our ancestors started throwing stones to protect themselves from predators is a little shaky. Even modern-day chimps can't throw well. It doesn't make a lot of sense that these ancestors of ours started throwing rocks to protect themselves. And protect themselves they needed to do. Robert W. Sussman and Donna Hart say:

---

[251] Elaine Morgan, *The Descent of Woman*, Souvenir Press, London 1972.

The idea of "Man the Hunter" is the generally accepted paradigm of human evolution. It developed from a basic Judeo-Christian ideology of man being inherently evil, aggressive and a natural killer ... In fact, when you really examine the fossil and living non-human primate evidence, that is just not the case. *Australopithecus afarensis* was probably quite strong, like a small ape ... Adults ranged from around 3 feet to 5 feet tall and weighed 60–100 pounds. They were basically smallish bipedal primates. Their teeth were relatively small, very much like modern humans, and they were fruit and nut eaters. These early humans simply couldn't eat meat. If they couldn't eat meat, why would they hunt? It was not possible for early humans to consume a large amount of meat until fire was controlled and cooking was possible.[252]

Sussman points out that the first tools didn't appear until two million years ago. There isn't good evidence of humans using fire until 800,000 years ago.

In fact, some archaeologists and paleontologists don't think we had a modern, systematic method of hunting until as recently as 60,000 years ago. *Australopithecus afarensis* was an edge species. Primates that are edge species, even today, are mainly prey species, not predators. Approximately six to ten percent of early humans were preyed upon, according to evidence such as teeth marks on bones, talon marks on skulls and holes in a fossil cranium into which saber-tooth cat fangs fit.[253]

Now picture our proposed ancestral primate, running for its life on an open savannah. Spying a rock while traveling (on all fours) at 20 miles an hour, it stops and picks up the rock (costing this creature tens of seconds), then straightens up and takes time to carefully aim the rock at a charging saber tooth cat.

I don't think that would end well, at least not for our primate; the big cat, however, just landed supper for herself and the kids. In Darwin's theory of rock-throwing primates, which primates do you think would be the first to be picked off in the open savannah? Imagine a pack of monkeys running full out with a pack of predators on their proverbial tails; who would move the slowest? The old, the pregnant, the mothers carrying their

---

[252] Robert W. Sussman and Donna Hart, *Man the Hunted: Primates, Predators, and Human Evolution*, Avalon Publishing, March 2005.

[253] Neil Schoenherr, "Early Humans Were Prey, not Killers: 'Man the Hunter' theory debunked in new book," February 25, 2005 https://source.wustl.edu/2005/02/early-humans-were-prey-not-killers/ (accessed June 6, 2017).

babies, the sick and the young, that's who. Soon you would have a very limited gene pool, if any at all.

However, if some lucky members of this tribe of smaller primates, running in terror from a pride of predators, happen to run into the ocean in blind terror — and, as time ticks by, discover that they are not pursued and consequently, are the only ones who survived the attack — this would be a huge epiphany. And if just one of those monkeys happened to be a leader, then, as we witnessed in "The Hundredth Monkey," this survival technique would catch on quickly.

Imagine a group of chimp-like monkeys huddling miserably in the shallows, perhaps chest or neck deep in water, clinging together as they watch the other members of their clan being eaten. Those chimpanzees would probably be in shock, not really understanding why they were spared. But finding themselves safe from these predators is something that they could feel, even if they didn't understand it.

This theory also provides a better explanation as to why we first started throwing rocks. I will expound on that shortly.

I recalled Elaine Morgan's theory, detailed in *The Descent of Woman*, when I was in Thailand in 1983, when I found myself in a dangerous situation. I was staying on a small island called Ko Samui, learning how to connect to the energies there. I had rented a small bungalow on the beach about fifteen feet from the edge of the Gulf of Thailand.

As far as I was concerned, it was paradise. I had no stove or fire pit to cook meals, so I would walk to different places spread out along the shoreline that offered food to tourists staying there. I often found others who were heading back to Palm Beach, where my bungalow was. But sometimes I made the journey by myself. One night as I was making my solitary way home by moonlight, I suddenly found myself ambushed by a pack of wild dogs. Thank God I was between them and the ocean when they came upon me. They materialized from the jungle's edge and formed a semicircle around me, cutting off any escape. I had not heard of this happening to other travelers, so I was completely taken by surprise. I analyzed the situation in nanoseconds, and in my mind was that passage from *The Descent of Woman*. Without taking my eyes off them I backed into the ocean. Obviously this was not something they were expecting. I was not sure if any of them could swim or if they would follow me. I went in about waist deep. As seconds turned into minutes, it seemed as though I had saved myself. And so we stood, eighteen pairs of golden eyes seeing into my soul, weighing my character ... or perhaps trying to decide what sauce I would be best served with.

Even with the moonlight the water was very dark. There were sharks and killer whales that I had seen in the daylight swimming in these waters. I was not happy about being out there alone. Movement in the dark, especially in combination with movement against your skin, is very intense. Was it just the water brushing against me?

I can't say how long this went on, but it was long enough for me to realize I was going to have to do something to change the energy. I couldn't come out of the water with the dogs waiting there, and I had no desire to swim the mile or so to my bungalow in the dark.

As the stalemate continued, I accepted that the dogs did not appear to be losing interest. I did not have many options. There was no one to call out to for help (and this was long before cell phones). I decided to try something that might seem foolish, but I honestly could not come up with any other ideas.

As I stood waist deep in the moonlit sparkling water, I calmed my breathing and reached for energy. I began filling myself with as much energy as I could. At the same time, I focused on every ounce of rage I had ever felt. I mixed these two together, and started making my way closer to shore as I did this, so that I would be able to move more easily. What I was doing was similar to a technique I had developed to deter human predators when I was trekking in Nepal and northern Thailand. There I had imagined myself to be a giant thousand-pound sabretooth tiger stalking through the streets. You can read about this in my memoir, to be released soon, called *Winging It.* I pulled that familiar form around me as I drew and mixed these energies. When I was full, I did not shut my connection to this energy but rather stayed open to draw in more energy as I released my mixture. Once I was in water only a foot deep, I raised my arms above my head and began screaming as loud as I could. As I screamed, I ran out of the water and rushed the dogs. I aimed for what seemed to be the lead dogs and slammed them with my rage.

Call me crazy. I certainly was not confident it would work. But I read the energy of the situation and followed my instinct. It worked! The dogs melted back into the jungle, just like that. I was shaking from adrenalin as I made my way home. I clung to the water's edge, just in case, but the dogs did not reappear.

I imagine that our ancestors had similar experiences with predators. The ones that survived may well have had to stay in those shallows all night and all the following day. Who knows? At some point they made the connection that the water was protecting them. They might well have started hanging around the water's edge (just as I had). I imagine that they began looking for food here. There probably would have been seaweeds, which are very nutritious, floating on the surface of the water. There would also have been plenty of shellfish at the water's edge. These are hard to access with one's teeth and nails. So some ingenuity would be needed to extract them. And guess what was readily at hand? Round pebbles and rocks worn smooth by the water.

Just as the Japanese macaque monkeys learned to wash sweet potatoes before eating them, these primates could have learned to crack open the shellfish with the stones. Keep in mind that the earliest tools found with human-like creatures were made from water-rounded rocks!

The drought lasted long enough (twelve million years) for our now semi-aquatic ancestors to change physically. If you look at some of the differences between humans and other primates, Ms. Morgan's theory makes sense. Hair on the body is good for keeping you warm in winter and protecting you, but it would not be good for semi-aquatic primates, because it would keep them wet longer and would cause drag when swimming. So as a quick adaptation, dropping the fur on the body to a minimum would help land creatures function better in water. How many other primates are hairless? Absolutely none, and remember there had to be a reason for that.

An extra layer of fat would be helpful for keeping one warm, especially without fur. Think about which other mammals have subcutaneous fat layers. Only whales, dolphins, and manatees — but not a single primate (except us) has a layer of fat just below the skin. Interestingly, there are theories that these three-air breathing aquatic species started out on land. If you look at the bones in dolphins' flippers, the bones resemble those of human hands.[254]

The only other mammals that developed fatty breasts are manatees, so that their young could feed more easily in the water. No other primates have similar fatty protrusions as breasts.

Hairless man is the only primate with downward-opening nostrils. All the other primates' nostrils are just holes that open on the front of their faces. It is hard to imagine why growing a piece of cartilage in front of those holes and covering it with skin to form downward-facing nostrils

---

[254] "All About Dolphins," *Scholastic*, http://teacher.scholastic.com/dolphin/about2.htm.

412

would be a useful adaptation on land. It would, however, be useful if the primate does a lot of diving, in which case the nostrils would help keep water from getting forced into the nasal cavities. The nose, pointy with a sharp ridge, would be more efficient at parting the water, as opposed to a broad flat nose.

A raised or pronounced brow ridge would help shield eyes from the glare of sunlight on water, an adaptation that the primates who dwell exclusively on land did not need (and therefore they never developed), but humans did.

Our development of a bulbous gluteus is also unique among primates. This muscle mass would need to be formed by specific exercise that other primates did not participate in. It would not be needed for walking or running. If these activities caused muscles to grow that way, then all primates would have nice butts like ours. But they don't. Neither do dogs or cats for that matter, and they can run much faster than we, but their butts are as flat as the other primates. It's obvious that all of these land-dwelling creatures do not require so much muscle there. However, those bulbous butt muscles certainly could develop from swimming and or treading water for long periods of time.

Pelicans cry pure saline tears after they scoop up and swallow a fish from the ocean. Doing so allows them to maintain the salt level in their bodies. We cry saline tears too, an adaptation that may have occurred to help us with our salt levels as well during an extended ocean stay.

Darwin's theory of humans evolving stone-throwing skills on the open plains does not explain any of the adaptations I just mentioned. However, take his theory and place our ancestors in the water — now that picture begins to make sense. Imagine our troupe of chimpanzees running into the water to escape a pride of saber-toothed cats. As my experience with the wild dogs suggests, a hungry predator will wait for its prey to come out of its "hole." Think about it, chimps standing waist deep in water for hours, day after day, would have had the time to pick up rocks and learn to aim and throw them in relative safety. So the fact that river rocks were the tool of choice for early man would be appropriate for beings that lived in or near water.

Even babies' survival would be improved with the troop in the water, if for no other reason than because mom was safer there. Since a pregnant or nursing mother is encumbered her child, she would not be the fastest runner during these periods of her life. And the loss of fertile females would be an eventual death sentence to any group.

Why do we have hair on top of our heads? Can you think of how this adaption would help our primates on the open plains? I can't. However, hair that grew long from the top of the head could be a great aid to a young babe if its mother spent a lot of time in the water. Human infants also are born making fists, and their grip is *strong*. An infant that grabs hold of your hair (and they always do that, don't they?) has quite a tenacious grip (almost as if their lives depended on it).

Have you ever noticed a man or woman with long hair in the water? Hair spreads out around them like a nimbus, floating on or very near the surface. It would make a perfect tether for a floating infant to grab hold of.

We unthinkingly accept that our heads are the only place on our bodies where we have hair. An important distinction here is that hair continuously grows, while fur has a predetermined length. Humans possess both hair and fur (even though we mis-label the keratin that grows from the follicles on our arms, legs, and torsos as "hair").

As we discussed, long hair on our heads would be advantageous for survival, but could there be other reasons? (We left the water a long time ago, and evolution has not seen fit to change that aspect of our bodies.)

In many cultures, hair traditionally was believed to imbue power. Why would that be? We have already established how the innate electromagnetic reception and transmission capabilities of our instruments, our bodies, have been hidden from us in this era. Could long hair be important in our ability to receive energy?

I have been aware of energy as long as I can remember. I also stopped allowing my hair to be cut when I was around six years old. Many children are deeply disturbed by the thought of getting their hair cut, even to the extent of kicking, screaming or running away. Doesn't that strike you as odd behavior? Hair has no nerve endings, so physically the children are not experiencing pain from having their hair cut. Given that, what would cause such a strong reaction? Could they be in touch with a facet of possessing long hair that we forgot?

There is a very interesting story about a study conducted by the US Army after employing legendary Navaho trackers. These trackers were enlisted because their skills were amazing, even uncanny. Once they enlisted, they had to cut their hair, as is army code, and can you guess what occurred? According to this article, their abilities diminished greatly. There is some controversy here, but let's just ask, if this did happen, what might be the cause?

The mammalian body has evolved over millions of years. Survival skills of human and animal at times seem almost supernatural. Science is constantly coming up with more discoveries about the amazing abilities of man and animal to survive. Each part of the body has highly sensitive work to perform for the survival and well-being of the body as a whole. The body has a reason for every part of itself. Hair is an extension of the nervous system, it can be correctly seen as exteriorized nerves, a type of highly evolved 'feelers' or 'antennae' that transmit vast amounts of important information to the Brainstem, the Limbic system, and the Neocortex. [255]

This theory is controversial. However, it warrants experimenting with.

When our hairs stand up on the back of our necks when we're in danger or feel threatened (known as goose bumps, or horripilation), is that a reflex of something we detect with our other senses, an unconscious perception affecting the hair? Or is it our hair affecting us, sending us a warning?[256]

There are many other tales involving hair from ancient cultures around the world. Play with them and with your hair, and see what you come up with. Here is one way you can experiment with transforming your life through working with your hair, based in Native American tradition:

When combing our hair each day, we are re-minded to keep our thoughts pure. The hair that falls out and gathers in our brushes and combs is gathered up and kept in a special place or pouch, for the 28 days of the Moon/month. This hair is a recollection, a record of our past thoughts and deeds. At the time of the Full Moon, the time of illumination and completeness, the Hearts of the Families, the Women, gather in ceremony and offer the thoughts of their families, their bundled Hair, to the Spirits of Fire, Earth and Air.

When our offerings of Hair are placed in fire, our thoughts are uplifted, sent through the smoke, moved by the power of the Moon, and prayerfully given to our Father, the Creator God or if

[255] "The Truth About Hair – Covered Up Since The Vietnam War," *Apparently Apparel News Watch*, Sept. 29, 2011 https://www.apparentlyapparel.com/news/the-truth-about-hair-covered-up-since-the-vietnam-war (accessed Dec. 5, 2014).

[256] Liz Leafloor, "Legendary Locks: Can Hair Act as a Sixth Sense, Protecting us from Danger?" December 6, 2015, Ancient Origins, https://www.ancient-origins.net/human-origins-folklore/legendary-locks-can-hair-act-sixth-sense-protecting-us-danger-004844 (accessed March 18, 2020).

buried, returned to Our Mother, the Earth and She relays our intent, through the Moon, to Our Father. In this way the Creator reads your families' thoughts and sends His Spirits/Angels to guide you on the Sacred Path, correcting your Mind, Heart and Soul, strengthening the Body of Oneness, till the next Full Moon. Holding Sacred thoughts, choosing to walk a path of light, One that is pleasing to the Creator God, strengthens the individual Family, and the Greater Family of Universal Oneness, that every One is a part of.

Your hair teaches you that your thoughts are to flow in all directions but are to be informally directed. Yellow, Red, Black and White the four colors of hair symbolizing the major directions of Earth, and the direction of those constant in the flow of thought/Spirit. Also, the four directions in between, Gold, Orange, Brown, Blue/Grey, Hair indicating those continual in thought/Spirit, flowing throughout the Universe. Your hair is just one way of indicating to others another conviction you carry throughout your lifetime. When the color of your hair changes, naturally, that means you have been Elevated, by God. You have more responsibility in and for Life.[257]

Being naturally grey, I really like those last two sentences. Elevated by God! It's interesting how many dots can be connected to a single facet of human existence.

I stopped coloring my hair a few years ago for several reasons. One was that I knew that dyes were not good for me. I recognized that my hair was healthier and softer when it wasn't color treated. I also felt strongly that I wanted to be a role model for other women in finding acceptance in aging gracefully. I was curious if the removal of coloring agents and the stripping process they entail would leave my hair feeling more powerful energetically.

I had recognized an innate power in my hair when I was a teenager. I experimented with focusing on a particular young man while I braided my hair …. It had definite results. Beyond a doubt it increased that young man's interest in me, almost instantaneously! I don't know what prompted me to do that, any more than I did when I ran my hands down the horse's

---

[257] Paula Lightning Woman Johnson. "Elders talk about the significance of long hair in Native American Cultures," *White Wolf Pack,* http://www.whitewolf-pack.com/2013/08/ elders-talk-about-significance-of-long.html (accessed July 2016).

legs and ended up healing him. I had been so isolated by my mother's constant moving and by the fact that she was not a social creature that I spent close to two decades sitting alone in nature or my room. This isolation caused me to be more aware of my inner promptings.

Interestingly, it did not take me long to realize that a relationship gained this way did not hold my interest for long, as well as that there was a part of me that felt distinctly uncomfortable with the process. I believe that along with my heightened awareness of energy came an elevated code of morals as well. Both of these seemed like an innate part of my makeup.

77. Gratitude

Gratitude is a powerful force. As I was working on finalizing this manuscript, I received an email from the website of Eckart Teachings with this very synchronistic quote: "It is through gratitude for the present moment that the spiritual dimension of life opens up for us."

By focusing on things that we are grateful for, we draw to us more things to be grateful for (remember what we focus on grows). We also feel better in the present moment because, as explained in the chapter "Intention and Manifesting," we are focusing our intention on growing the somatic experience of a positive feeling.

Gratitude lists are a great way to raise your awareness and thereby manifest more things to be grateful for. To do this, sit with a piece of paper and write down the things you are grateful for in your life right now. Keep this paper where you will read it at least once a day. Notice how you feel when you read this list.

Remember, what we focus on becomes excited in an energetic way, increasing its energy, growing, and creating a stronger magnetic force in our life.

You can also keep a journal by your bed, and every evening write down three things you are grateful for that day. Do this even if it is a struggle at first. Trust me; you can change that pattern — fake it until you make it. Give it three weeks and see what happens.

Credits

The author wishes to express her thanks to:

Rob Bockholdt, an amazing graphic artist from Germany. He is so talented and such a great communicator that he was a pleasure to work with. Thank you for such a beautiful cover!

Donna Coane and Alice Joe Porter of the Haudenosaunee Iroquois Confederacy for information about the Hiawatha belt and permission to use the image.

Dr. Martin Martinez-Ripoll, Research Professor Emeritus, Department of Crystallography & Structural Biology at the Spanish National Research Council for permission to use four images in Ch. 12.

Vladimir Savchik of ahuman.org for permission to reproduce the drawing of the human gut (Figure 2, page 8).

Ethan Vorly of alchemyrealm.com for permission to use the quotation about plants' healing properties (page 264).

Key to Cover Illustration

Front cover, from top left:

Scarlet Macaw parrot – Ch. 8.

Serpent/Snake – Ch. 66.

Apple – Ch. 68.

Opossum – Ch. 56 and 73.

DNA strand – Ch. 11.

Butterfly – Ch. 18.

Carbon molecule, lump of coal and faceted diamond – Chs. 12 and 43.

Bird of Paradise flower and plant, not mentioned directly but see Ch. 55 "Healing Plants."

Little girl pointing to reflection of the big dipper – a representation of the author, who was born with the big dipper on her left arm in freckles.

Quartz crystal cluster – Ch. 12.

Female Macaque monkey washing a sweet potato – Ch. 15 and 76.

Orchid – Ch. 46.

Wheel – Chs. 28 and 29.

White mouse – Ch. 4.

Lit sage wand in abalone shell – Ch. 35.

Couple, strong and native, moving together along the path that is before them, perhaps Adam and Eve?

Caduceus – Ch. 68.

Black cat – Ch. 66.

DNA strand – Ch. 74.

Owl – Ch. 56.

About the Author

LIA RUSS was born high in the Rocky Mountains of Colorado in a town so small that only three other children were born there that year. Perhaps because of the sparseness of human population and the vastness of the natural world, Lia learned to open her senses to connect with the energies of everything around her. However, she became uncomfortable when, at age ten, she moved to Westchester County, New York, where she immediately felt removed from its huge human population. She has devoted her life to understanding the things that she saw and felt around her that no one else seemed aware of.

Lia loves nature, animals, solving mysteries, writing, creating art and dancing. She has traveled extensively in the United States and Asia and currently lives in upstate New York with her boyfriend, two dogs, two cats, two parrots and many plants. Lia collects strays, crystals, and dots.

NOTES

Made in the USA
Las Vegas, NV
10 January 2024

84200613R00246